SEVEN SEAS ENTERTAINMENT

MAGICAL GI

story and art by **KENTARO SATO**

VOLUME 10

10-19

TRANSLATION
Wesley Bridges

ADAPTATION
Janet Houck

LETTERING AND RETOUCH
Meaghan Tucker

COVER DESIGN
Nicky Lim

PROOFREADER
B. Lana Guggenheim

EDITOR
Jenn Grunigen

PRODUCTION MANAGER
Lissa Pattillo

MANAGING EDITOR
Julie Davis

EDITOR-IN-CHIEF
Adam Arnold

PUBLISHER
Jason DeAngelis

MAHO SYOJYO SITE Volume 10
© Kentaro Sato 2018
Originally published in Japan in 2018 by Akita Publishing Co., Ltd..
English translation rights arranged with Akita Publishing Co., Ltd. through
TOHAN CORPORATION, Tokyo.

Seven Seas press and purchase enquiries can be sent to Marketing Manager
Lianne Sentar at press@gomanga.com. Information regarding the distribution
and purchase of digital editions is available from Digital Manager CK Russell
at digital@gomanga.com.

Seven Seas and the Seven Seas logo are trademarks of
Seven Seas Entertainment. All rights reserved.

ISBN: 978-1-64275-700-2

Printed in Canada

First Printing: September 2019

10 9 8 7 6 5 4 3 2 1

FOLLOW US ONLINE: www.sevenseasentertainment.com

READING DIRECTIONS

This book reads from ***right to left***, Japanese style.
If this is your first time reading manga, you start
reading from the top right panel on each page and
take it from there. If you get lost, just follow the
numbered diagram here. It may seem backwards at
first, but you'll get the hang of it! Have fun!!

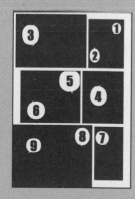

Loading . . . Please Wait

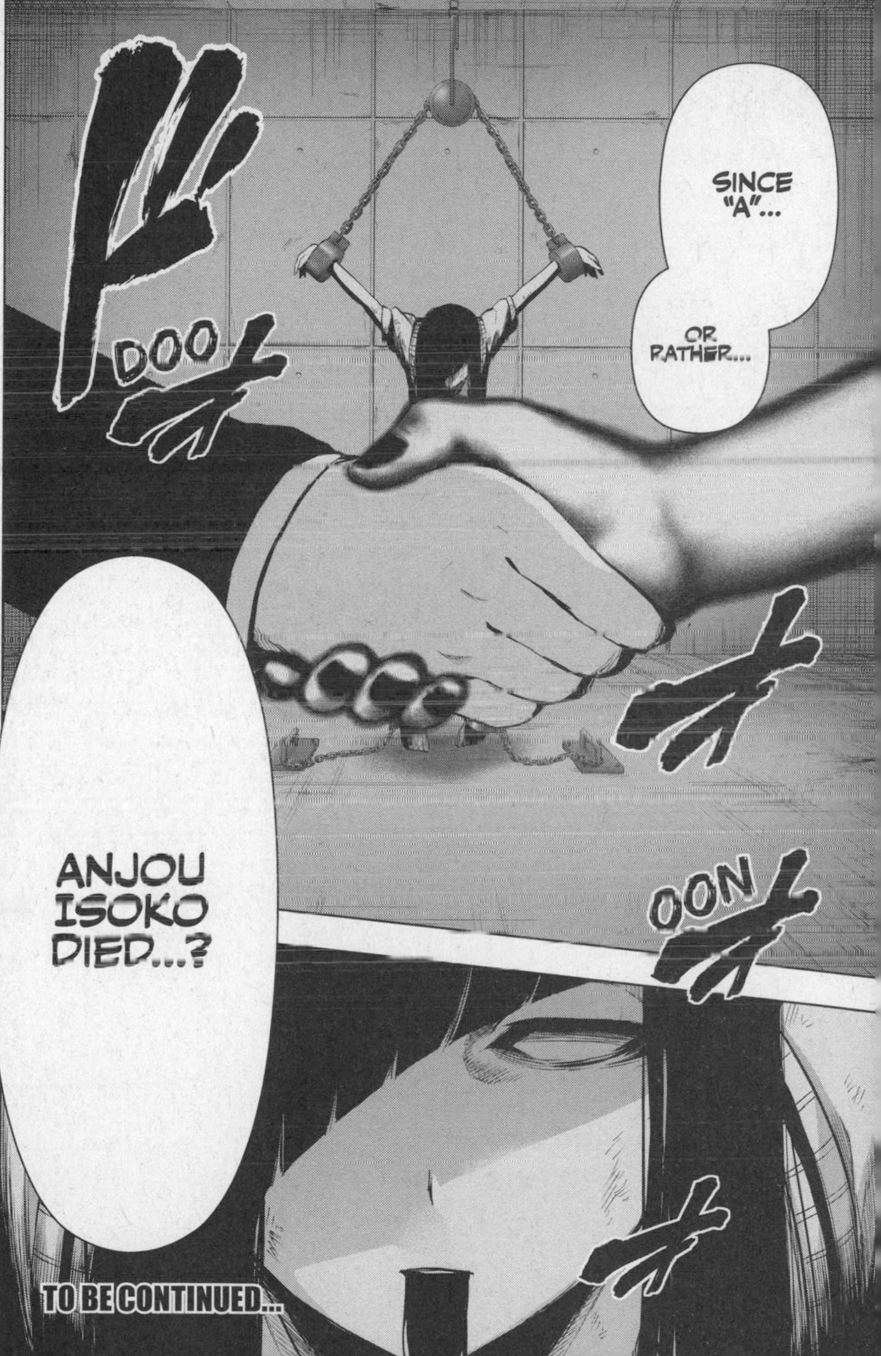
SINCE "A"...
OR RATHER...
DOO
ANJOU ISOKO DIED...?
OON
TO BE CONTINUED...

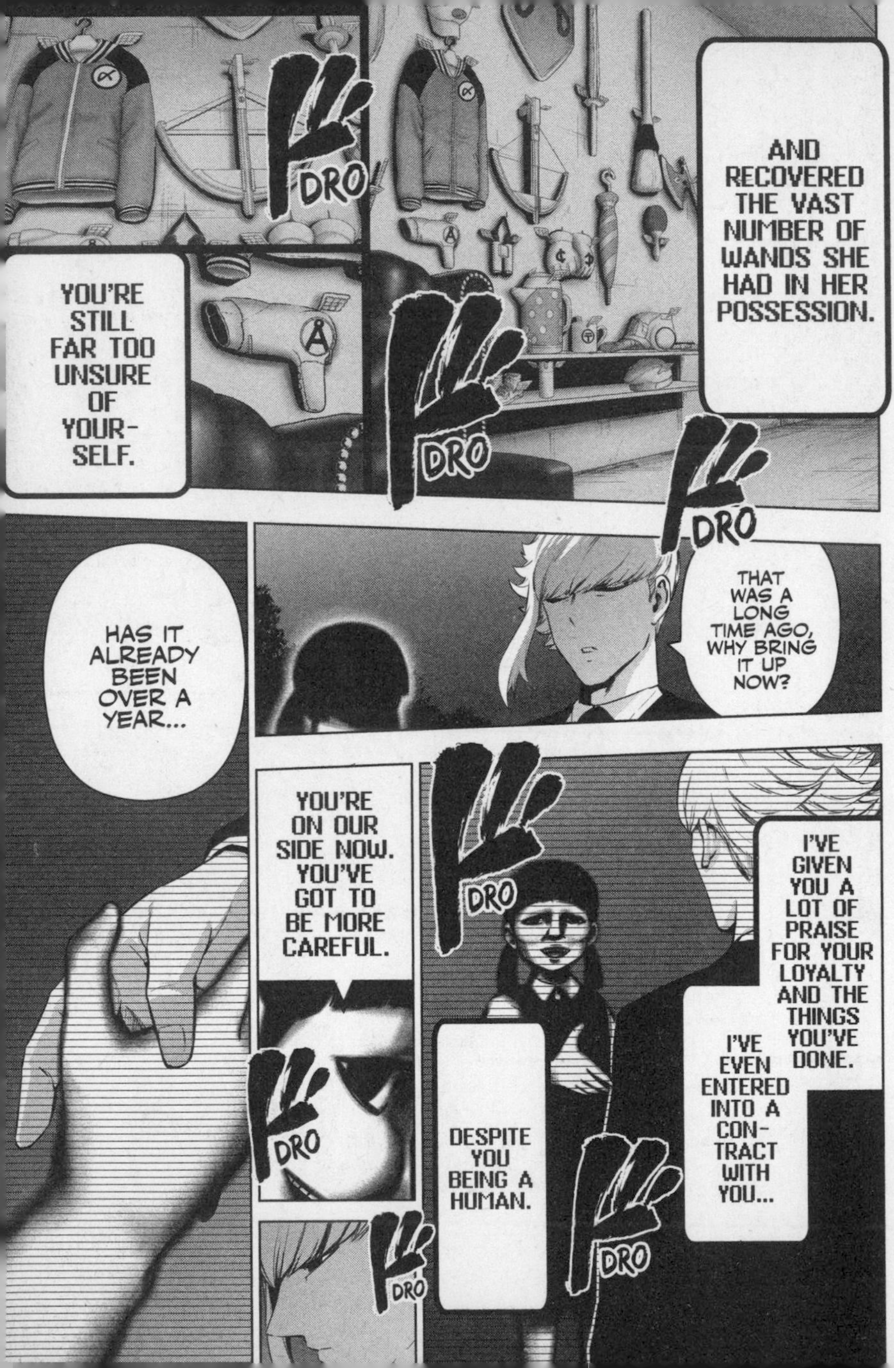
AND RECOVERED THE VAST NUMBER OF WANDS SHE HAD IN HER POSSESSION.
DRO
DRO
DRO
YOU'RE STILL FAR TOO UNSURE OF YOUR-SELF.
DRO
THAT WAS A LONG TIME AGO, WHY BRING IT UP NOW?
HAS IT ALREADY BEEN OVER A YEAR...
I'VE GIVEN YOU A LOT OF PRAISE FOR YOUR LOYALTY AND THE THINGS YOU'VE DONE.
I'VE EVEN ENTERED INTO A CON-TRACT WITH YOU...
DESPITE YOU BEING A HUMAN.
DRO
DRO
YOU'RE ON OUR SIDE NOW. YOU'VE GOT TO BE MORE CAREFUL.
DRO
DRO

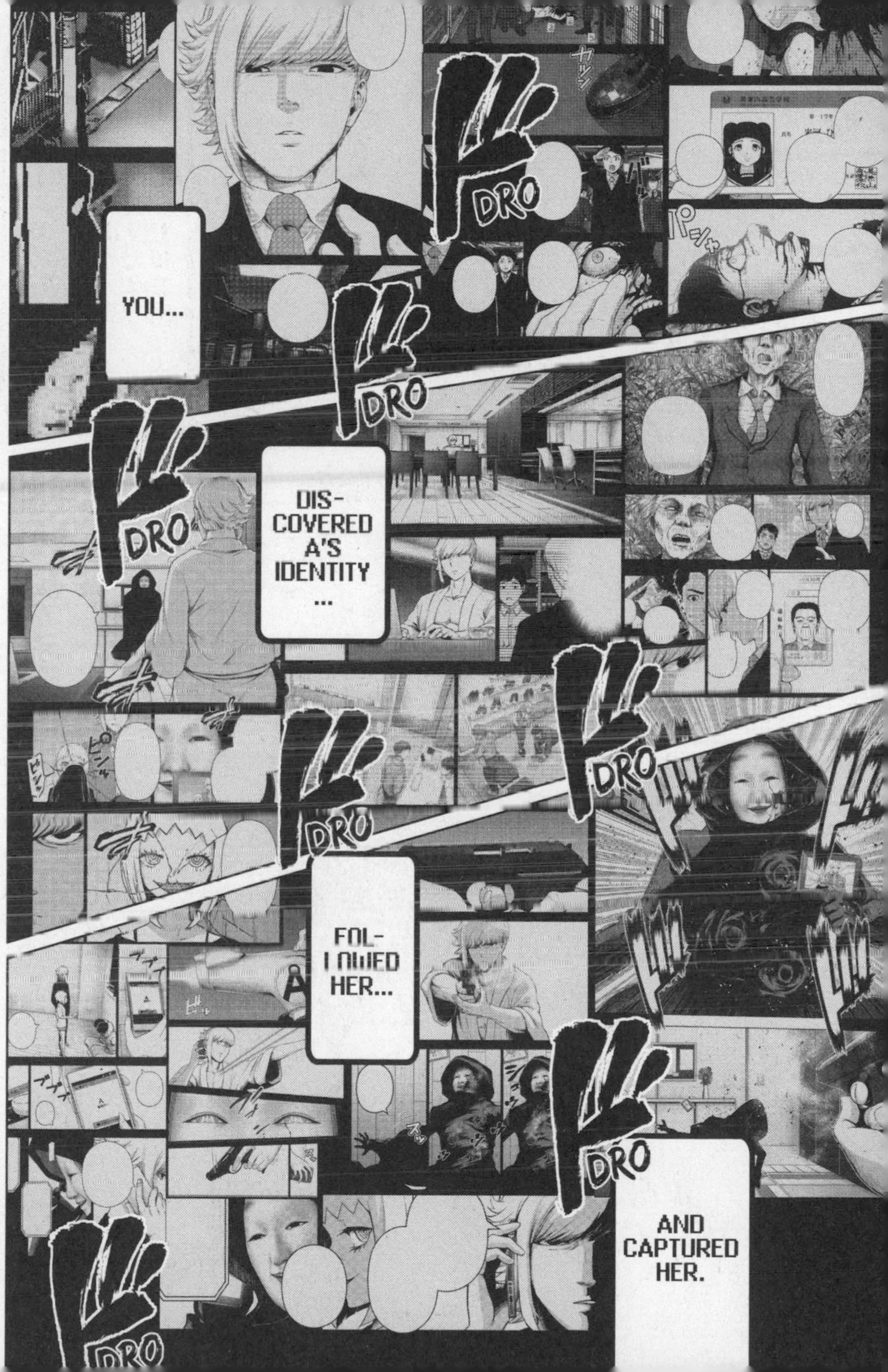
DRO
YOU...
DRO
DRO
DIS-COVERED A'S IDENTITY ...
DRO
DRO
DRO
FOL-LOWED HER...
DRO
AND CAPTURED HER.
DRO

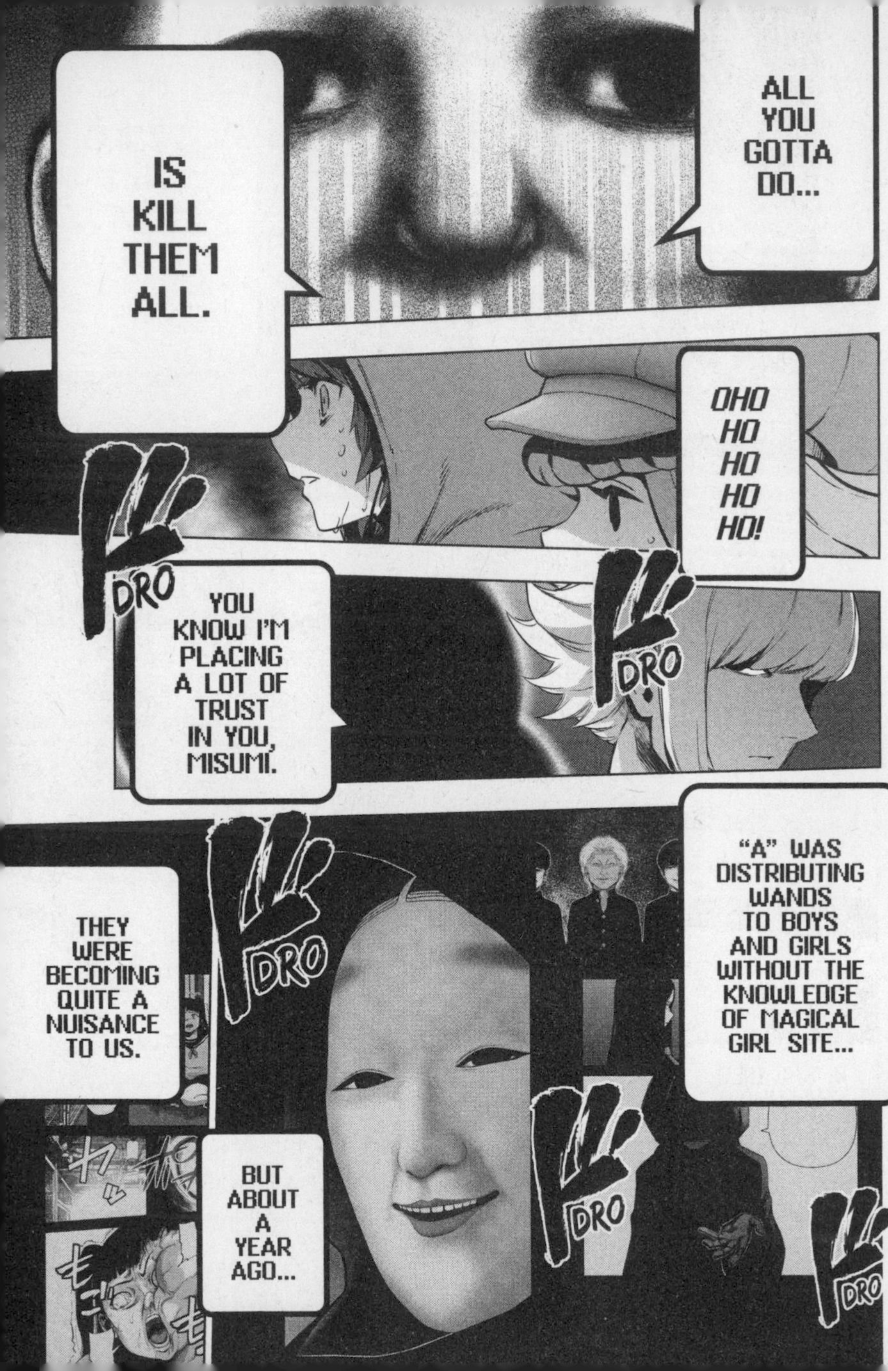
ALL YOU GOTTA DO...
IS KILL THEM ALL.
OHO HO HO HO HO!
DRO
DRO
YOU KNOW I'M PLACING A LOT OF TRUST IN YOU, MISUMI.
"A" WAS DISTRIBUTING WANDS TO BOYS AND GIRLS WITHOUT THE KNOWLEDGE OF MAGICAL GIRL SITE...
DRO
THEY WERE BECOMING QUITE A NUISANCE TO US.
DRO
DRO
BUT ABOUT A YEAR AGO...

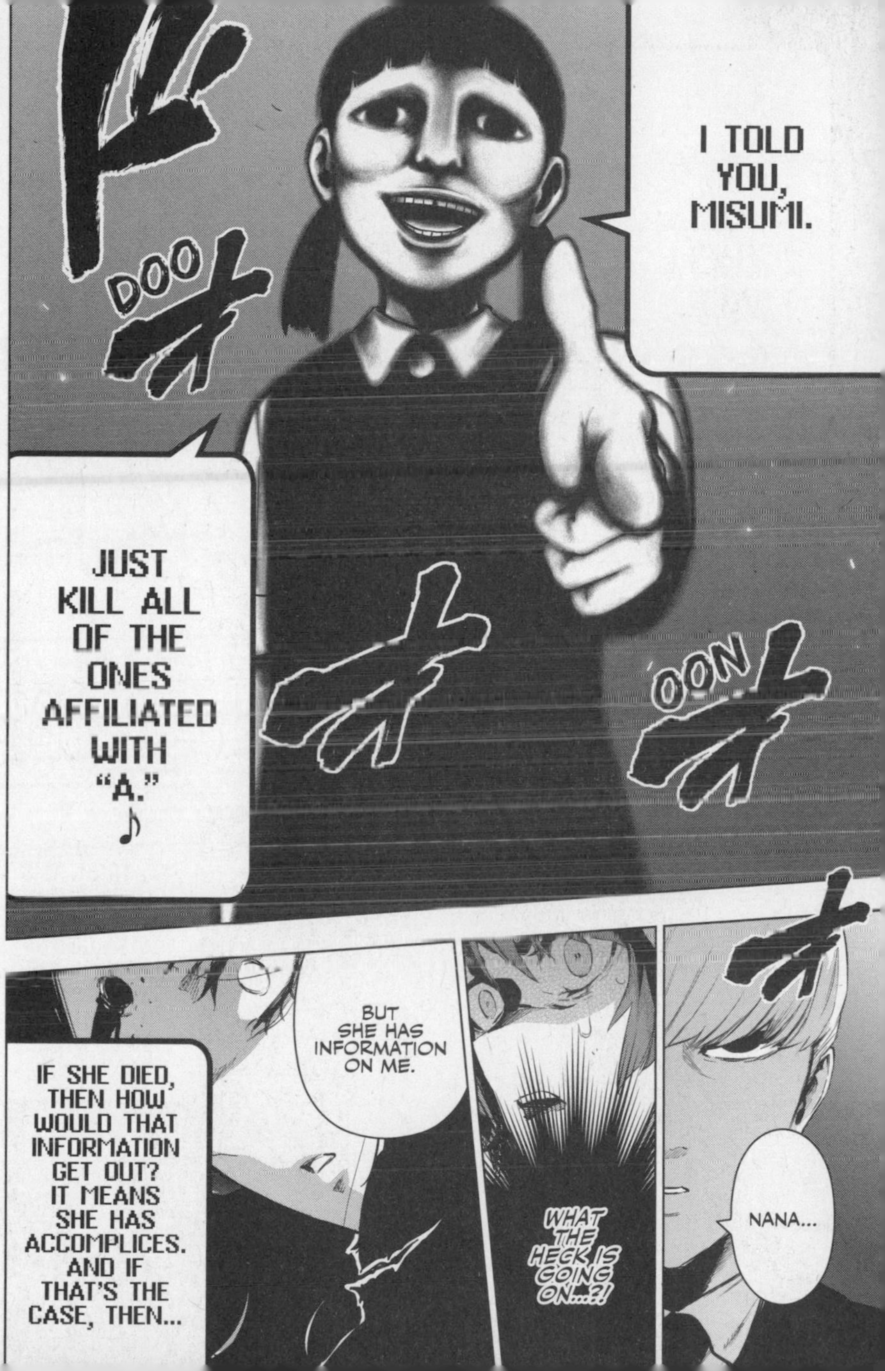
I TOLD YOU, MISUMI.
DOO
JUST KILL ALL OF THE ONES AFFILIATED WITH "A." ♪
OON
NANA...
WHAT THE HECK IS GOING ON...?!
BUT SHE HAS INFORMATION ON ME.
IF SHE DIED, THEN HOW WOULD THAT INFORMATION GET OUT? IT MEANS SHE HAS ACCOMPLICES. AND IF THAT'S THE CASE, THEN...

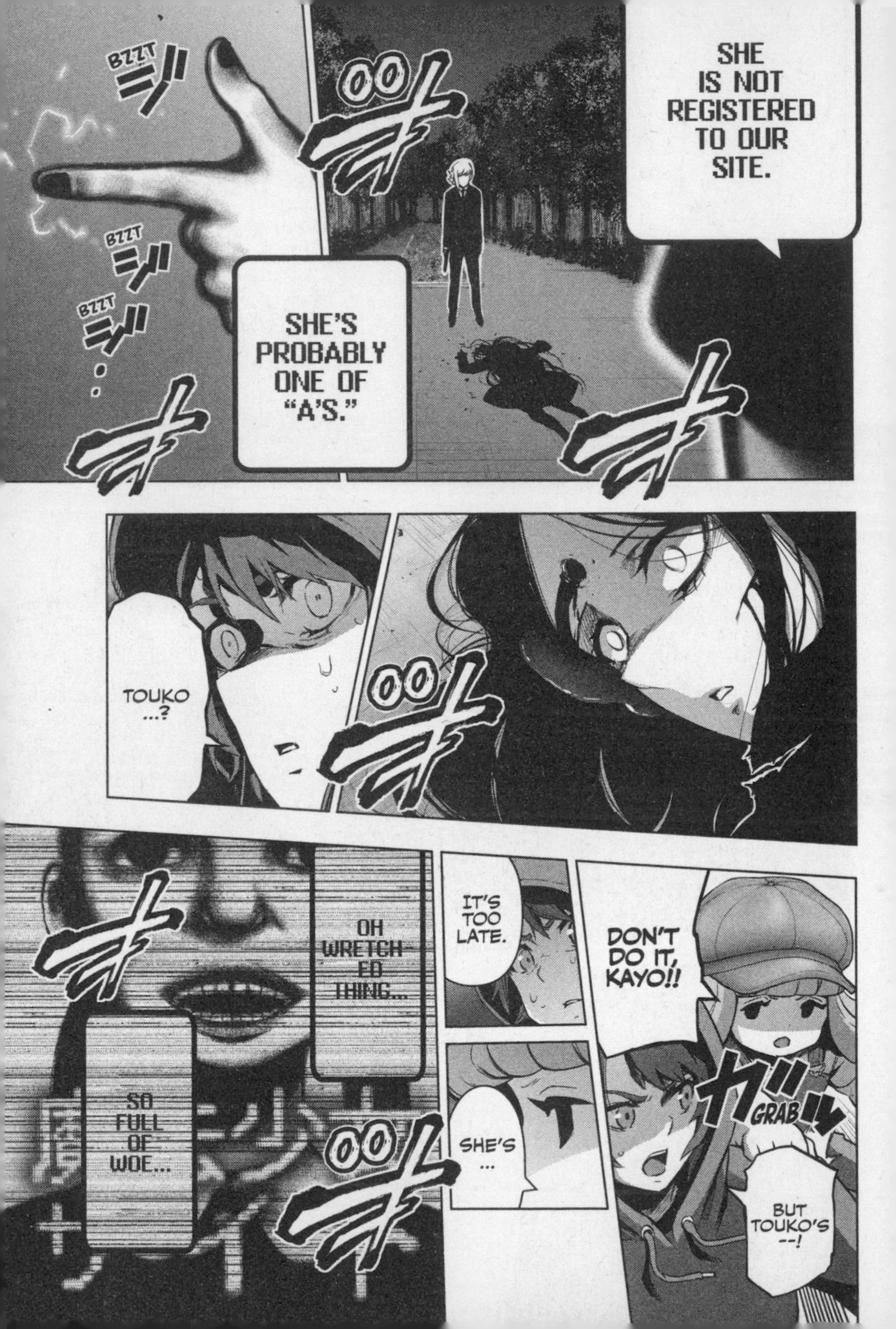
SHE IS NOT REGISTERED TO OUR SITE.
SHE'S PROBABLY ONE OF "A'S."
OO
BZZT
BZZT
BZZT
OO
TOUKO ...?
DON'T DO IT, KAYO!!
GRAB
BUT TOUKO'S --!
IT'S TOO LATE.
SHE'S ...
OO
OH WRETCHED THING...
SO FULL OF WOE...

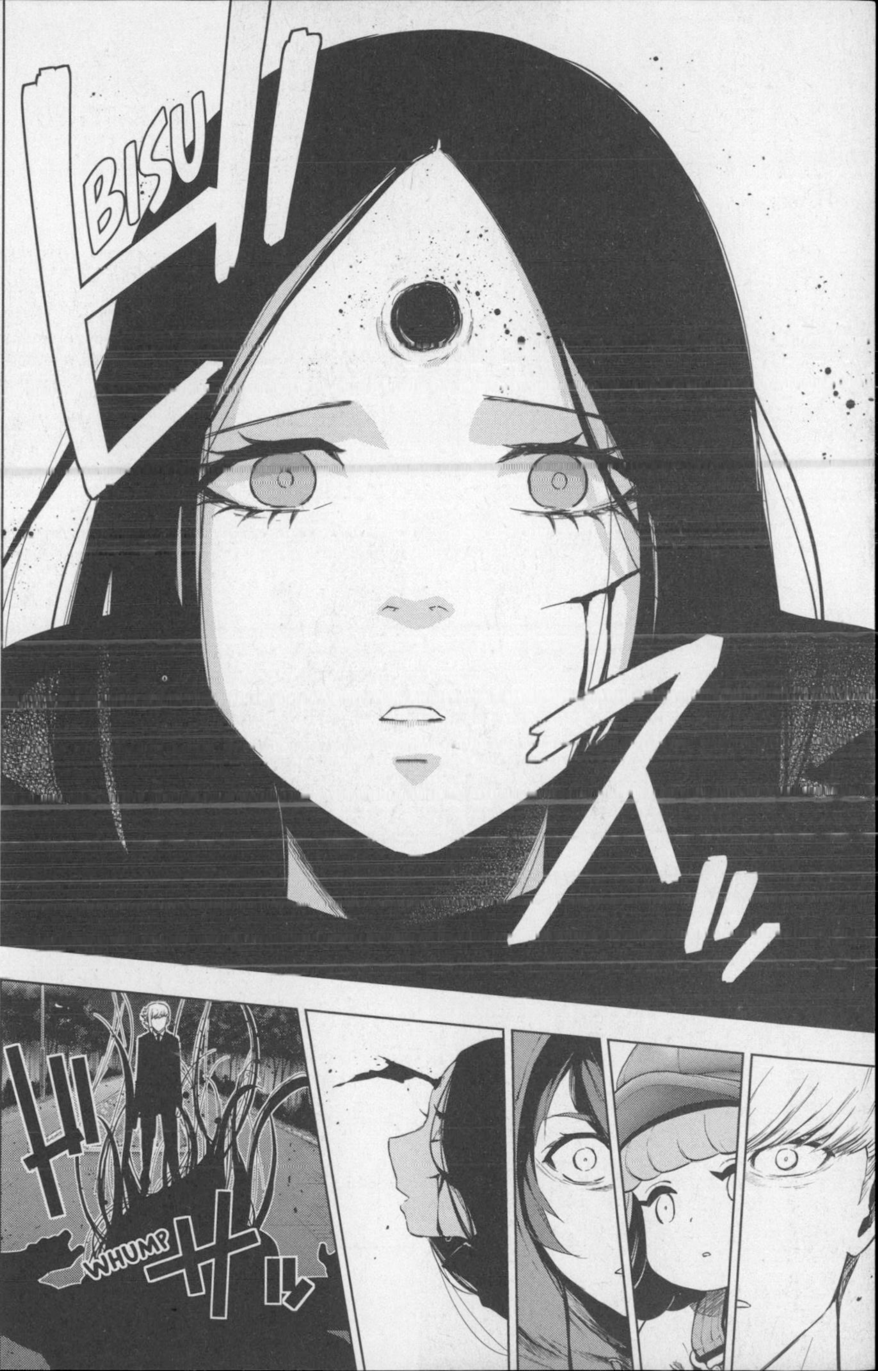
BISU
WHUMP

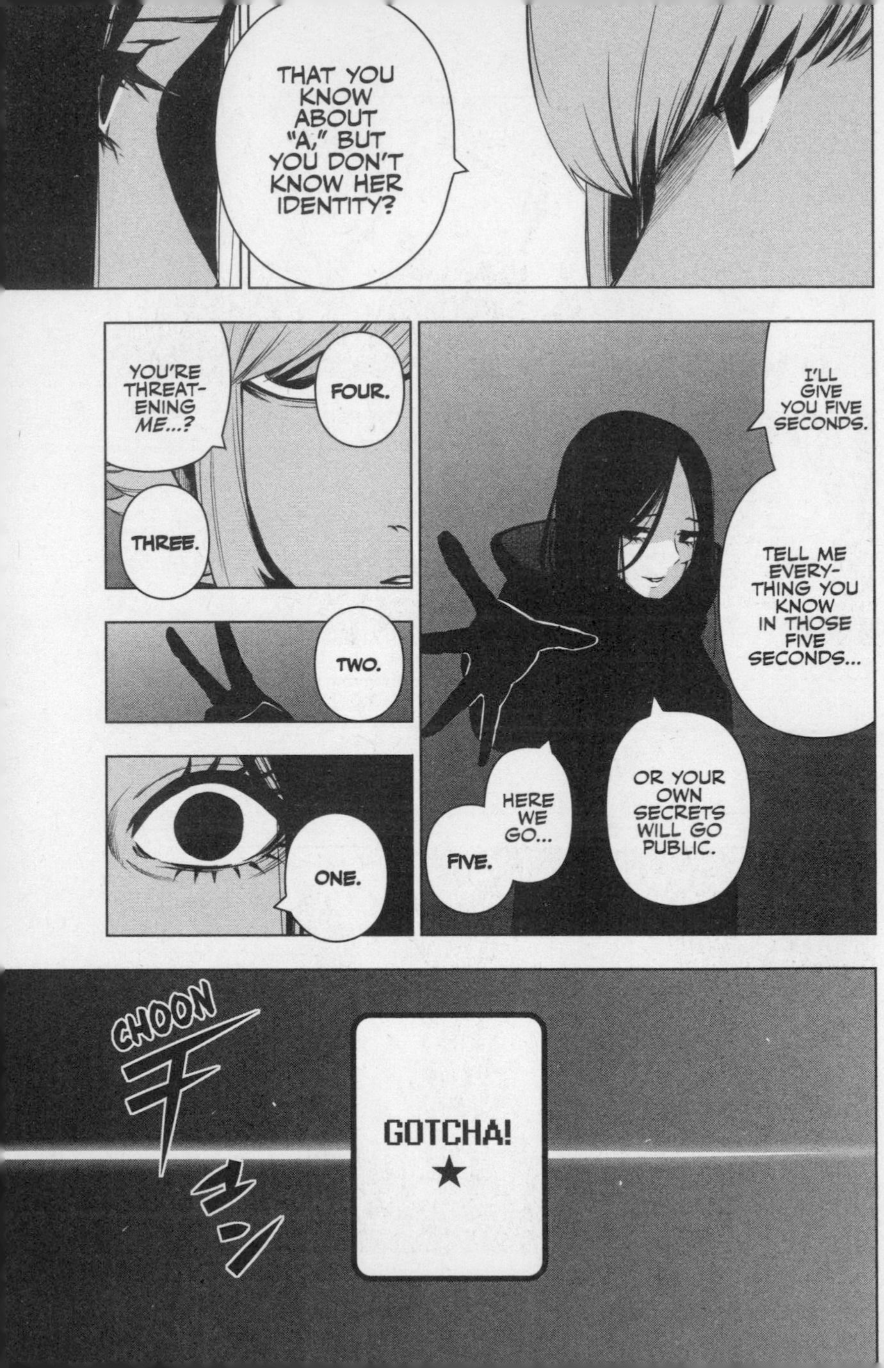
THAT YOU KNOW ABOUT "A," BUT YOU DON'T KNOW HER IDENTITY?
I'LL GIVE YOU FIVE SECONDS.
TELL ME EVERYTHING YOU KNOW IN THOSE FIVE SECONDS...
OR YOUR OWN SECRETS WILL GO PUBLIC.
HERE WE GO...
FIVE.
FOUR.
YOU'RE THREATENING *ME*...?
THREE.
TWO.
ONE.
GOTCHA!
★
CHOON

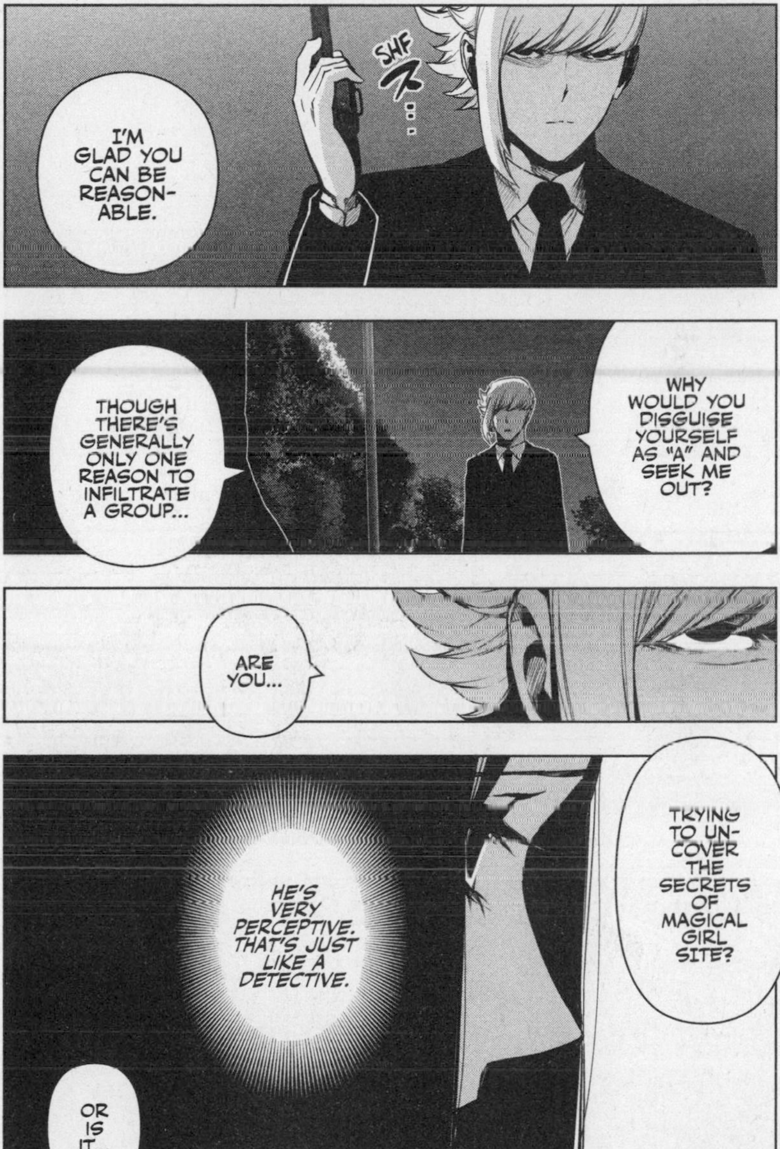
SHF
I'M GLAD YOU CAN BE REASON-ABLE.
WHY WOULD YOU DISGUISE YOURSELF AS "A" AND SEEK ME OUT?
THOUGH THERE'S GENERALLY ONLY ONE REASON TO INFILTRATE A GROUP...
ARE YOU...
TRYING TO UN-COVER THE SECRETS OF MAGICAL GIRL SITE?
HE'S VERY PERCEPTIVE. THAT'S JUST LIKE A DETECTIVE.
OR IS IT...

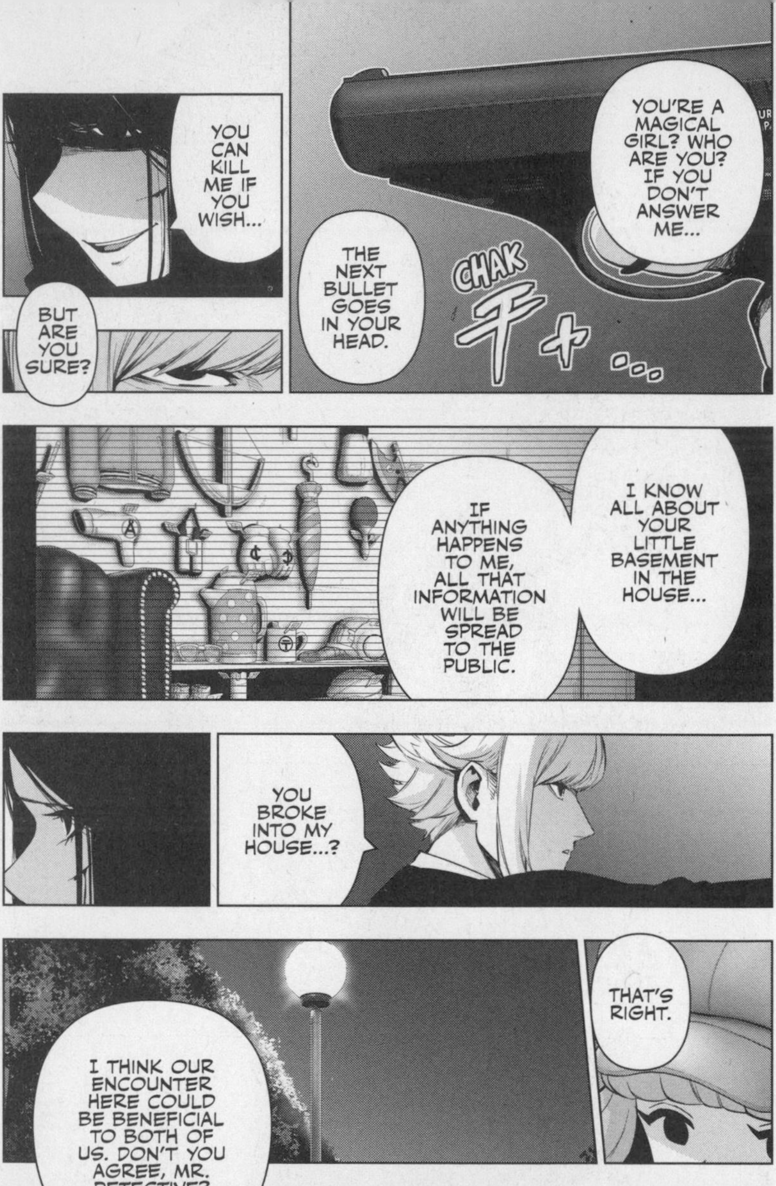
YOU'RE A MAGICAL GIRL? WHO ARE YOU? IF YOU DON'T ANSWER ME...
CHAK
チャ...
THE NEXT BULLET GOES IN YOUR HEAD.
YOU CAN KILL ME IF YOU WISH...
BUT ARE YOU SURE?
I KNOW ALL ABOUT YOUR LITTLE BASEMENT IN THE HOUSE...
IF ANYTHING HAPPENS TO ME, ALL THAT INFORMATION WILL BE SPREAD TO THE PUBLIC.
YOU BROKE INTO MY HOUSE...?
THAT'S RIGHT.
I THINK OUR ENCOUNTER HERE COULD BE BENEFICIAL TO BOTH OF US. DON'T YOU AGREE, MR. DETECTIVE?

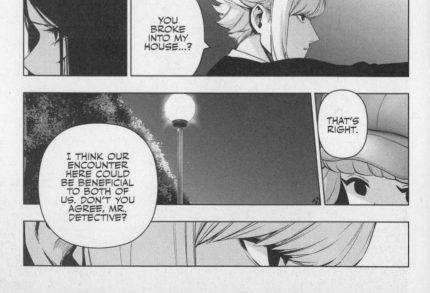

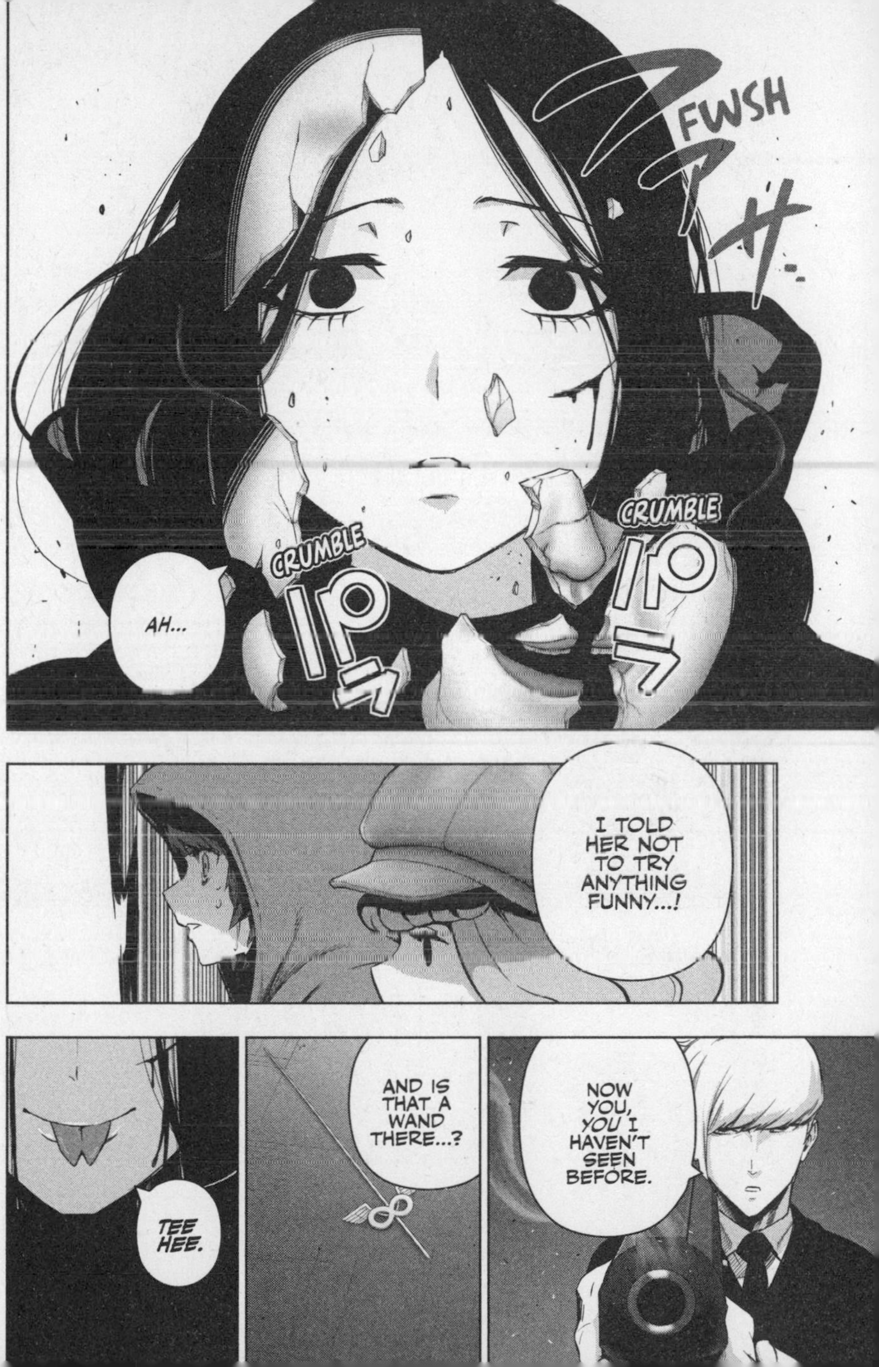
FWSH
CRUMBLE
CRUMBLE
AH...
I TOLD HER NOT TO TRY ANYTHING FUNNY...!
NOW YOU, *YOU* I HAVEN'T SEEN BEFORE.
AND IS THAT A WAND THERE...?
TEE HEE.

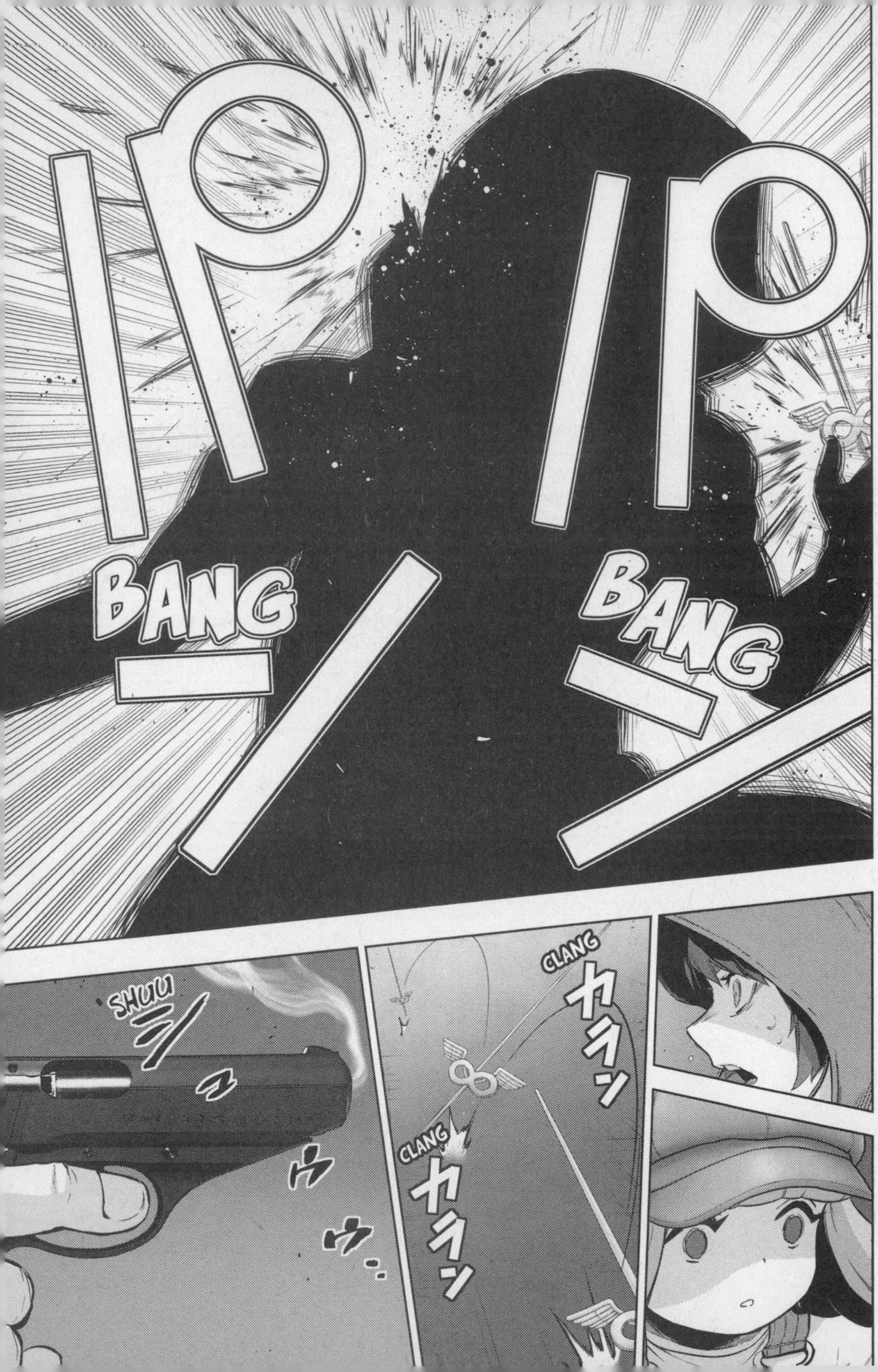
BANG
BANG
CLANG
カラン
CLANG
カラン
SHUU

THAT "A" WAS JUST A DOUBLE, A FAKE.
I'M THE REAL "A."
I AM NOT DEAD, BECAUSE I CANNOT DIE.
SUU
I SEE...

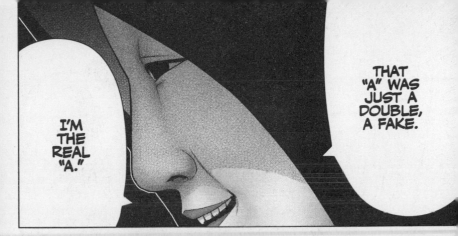

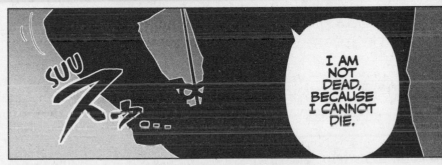

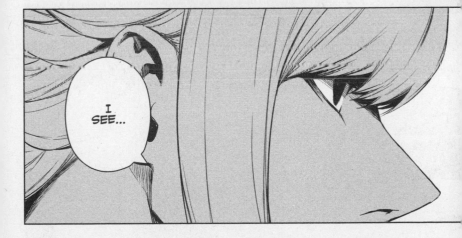

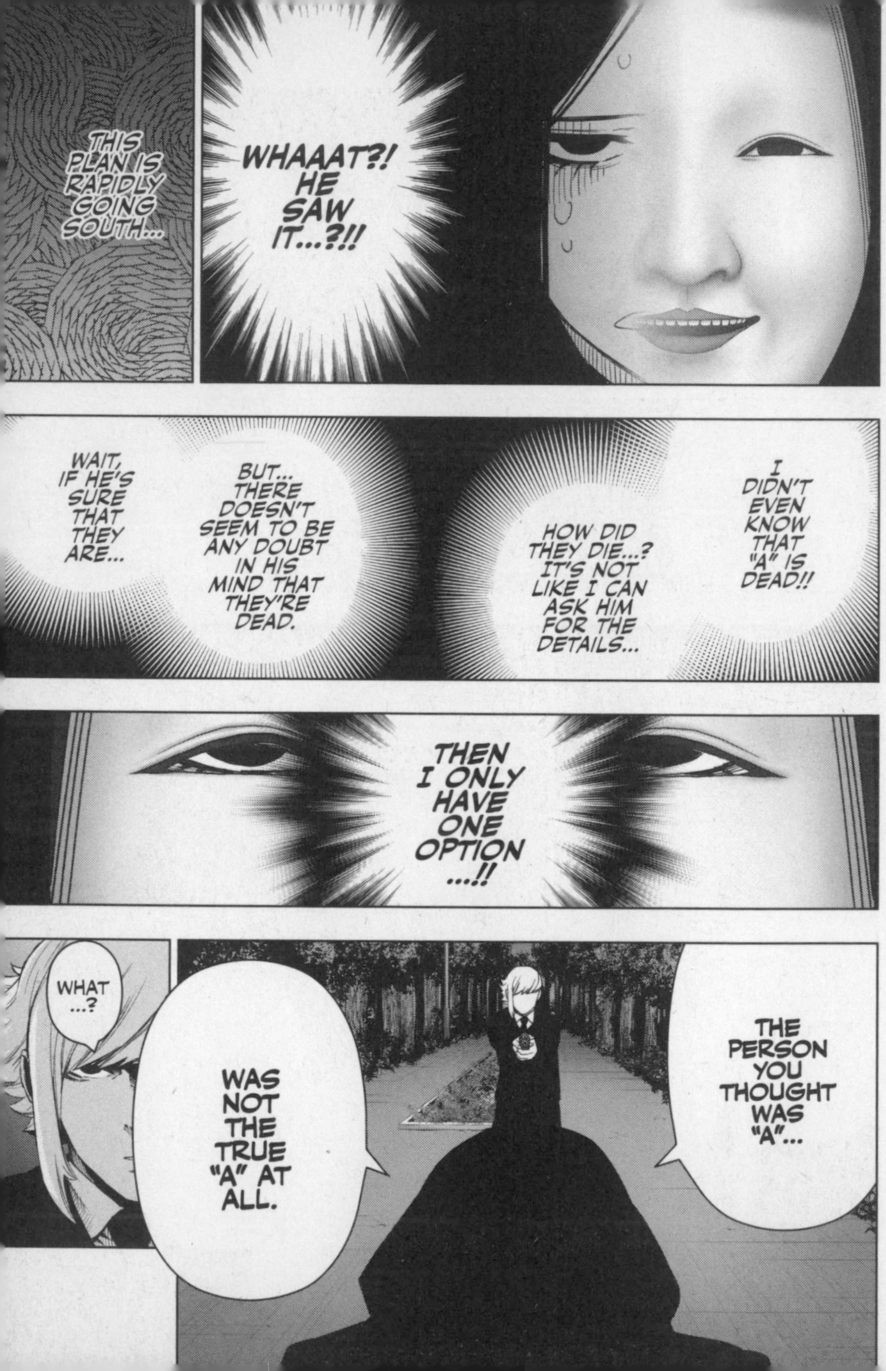
WHAAAT?! HE SAW IT...?!!
THIS PLAN IS RAPIDLY GOING SOUTH...
I DIDN'T EVEN KNOW THAT "A" IS DEAD!!
HOW DID THEY DIE...? IT'S NOT LIKE I CAN ASK HIM FOR THE DETAILS...
BUT... THERE DOESN'T SEEM TO BE ANY DOUBT IN HIS MIND THAT THEY'RE DEAD.
WAIT, IF HE'S SURE THAT THEY ARE...
THEN I ONLY HAVE ONE OPTION ...!!
THE PERSON YOU THOUGHT WAS "A"...
WAS NOT THE TRUE "A" AT ALL.
WHAT ...?

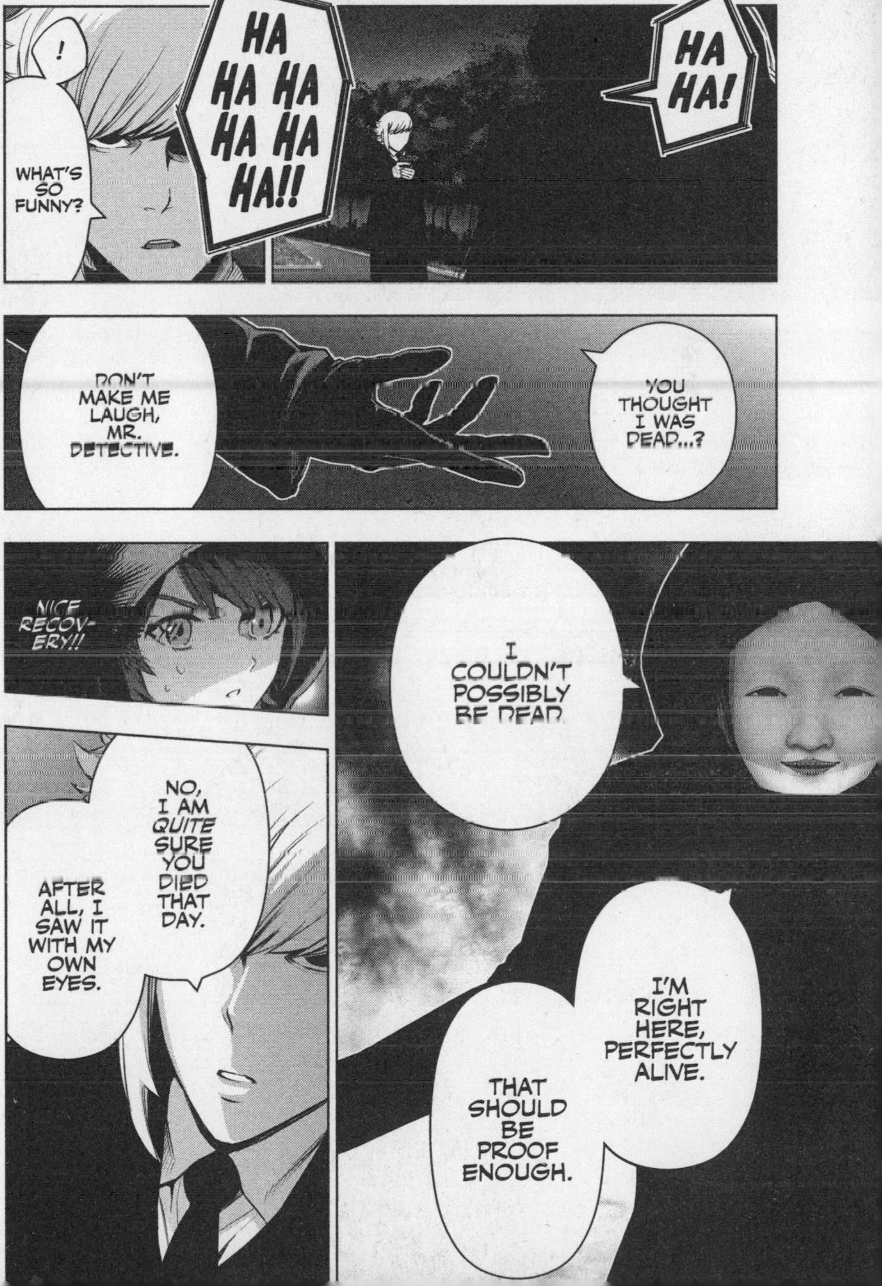
HA HA!
HA HA HA HA HA HA!!
!
WHAT'S SO FUNNY?
YOU THOUGHT I WAS DEAD...?
DON'T MAKE ME LAUGH, MR. DETECTIVE.
I COULDN'T POSSIBLY BE DEAD.
I'M RIGHT HERE, PERFECTLY ALIVE.
THAT SHOULD BE PROOF ENOUGH.
NICE RECOVERY!!
NO, I AM QUITE SURE YOU DIED THAT DAY.
AFTER ALL, I SAW IT WITH MY OWN EYES.

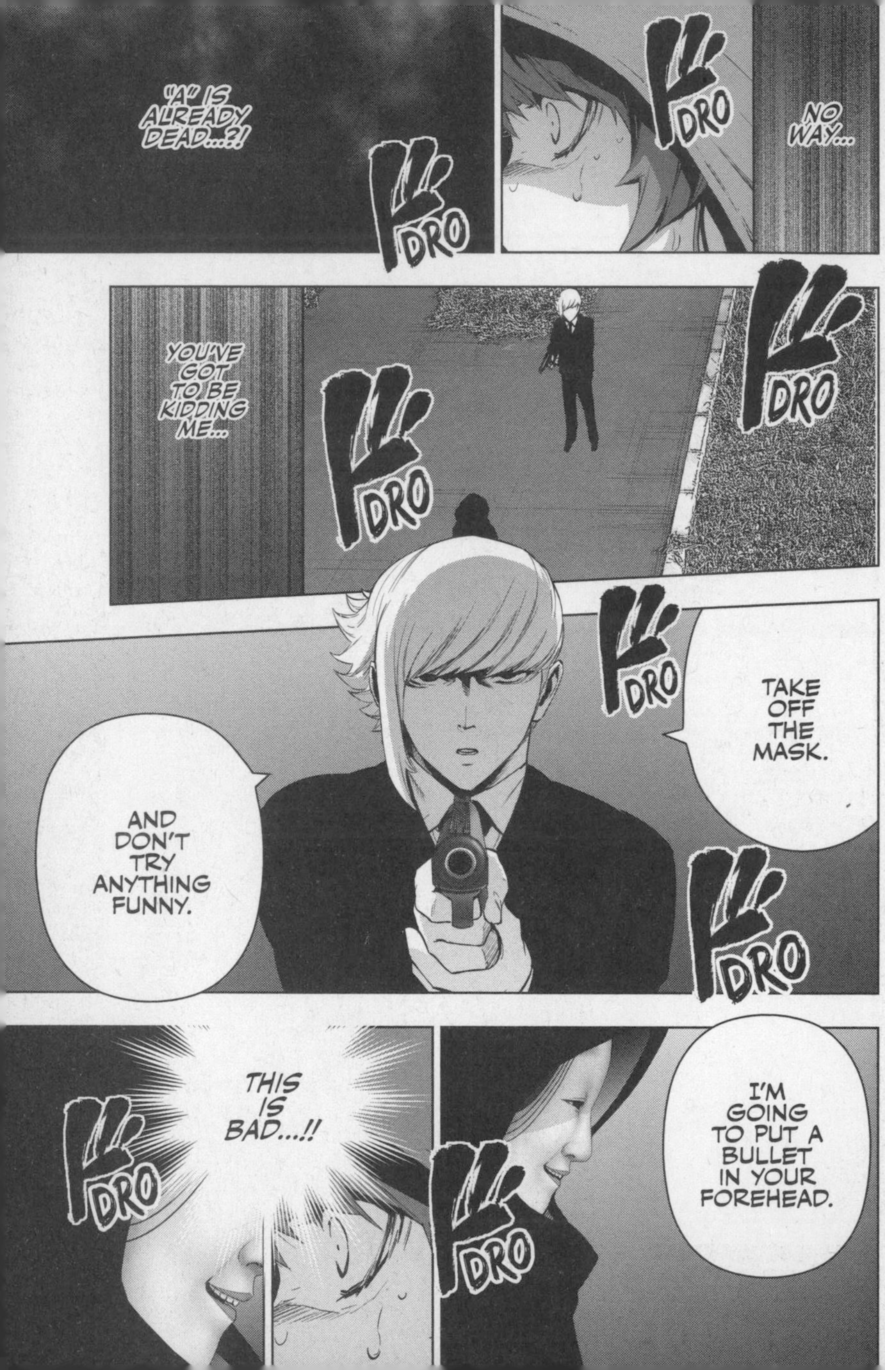

DRO
NO WAY...
"A" IS ALREADY DEAD...?!
DRO
DRO
YOU'VE GOT TO BE KIDDING ME...
DRO
DRO
TAKE OFF THE MASK.
AND DON'T TRY ANYTHING FUNNY.
DRO
I'M GOING TO PUT A BULLET IN YOUR FOREHEAD.
DRO
THIS IS BAD...!!
DRO

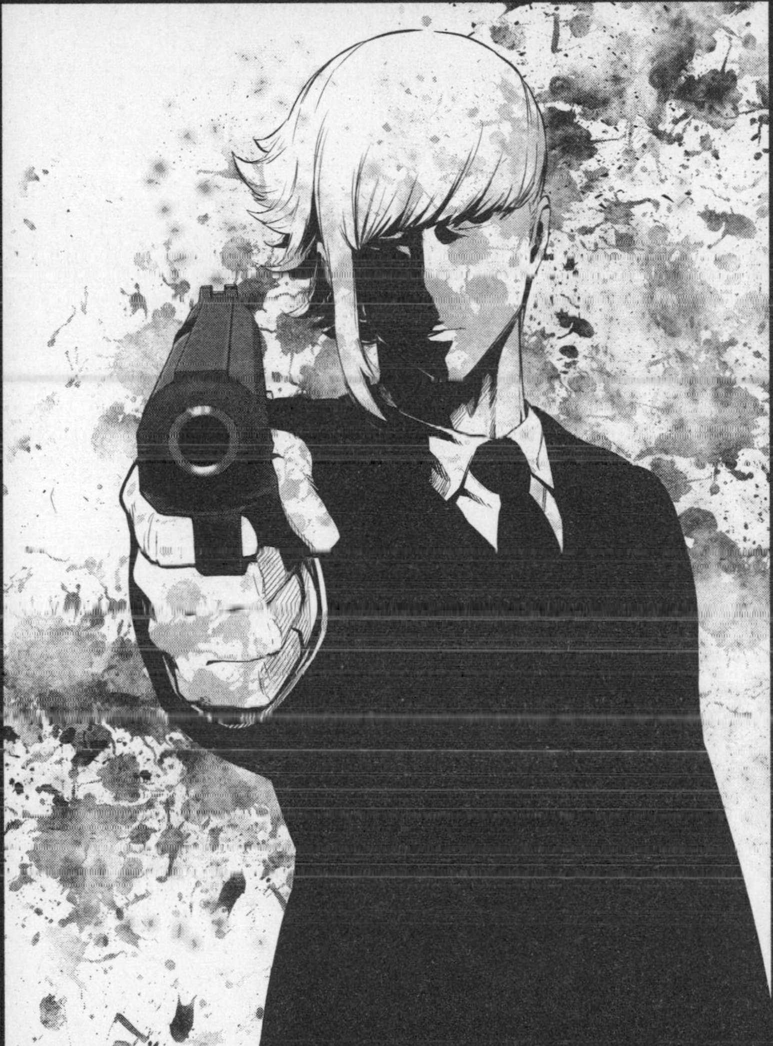

ENTER.75 CONTRACT

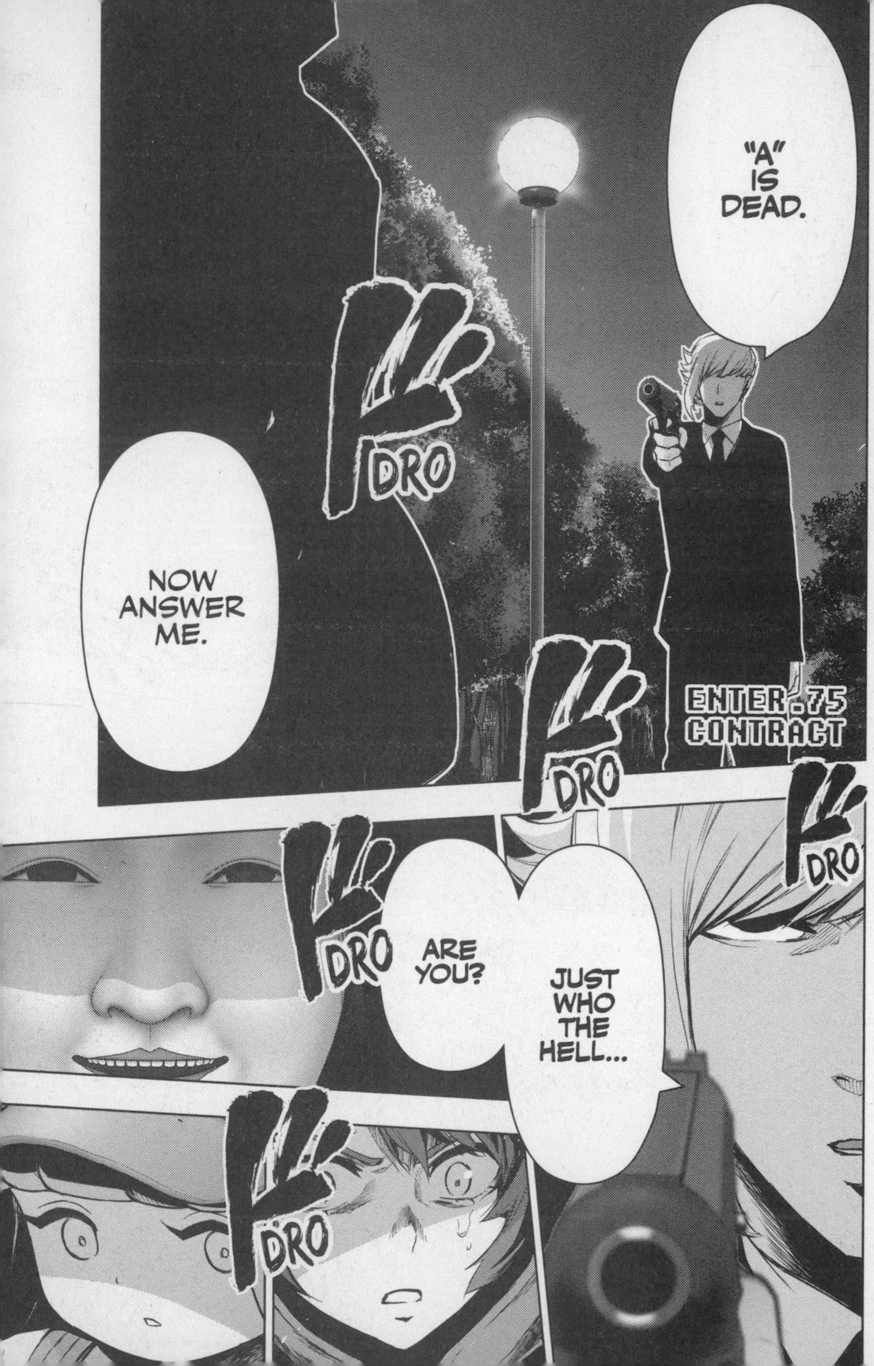
"A" IS DEAD.
DRO
ENTER.75 CONTRACT
NOW ANSWER ME.
DRO
DRO
JUST WHO THE HELL...
ARE YOU?
DRO
DRO

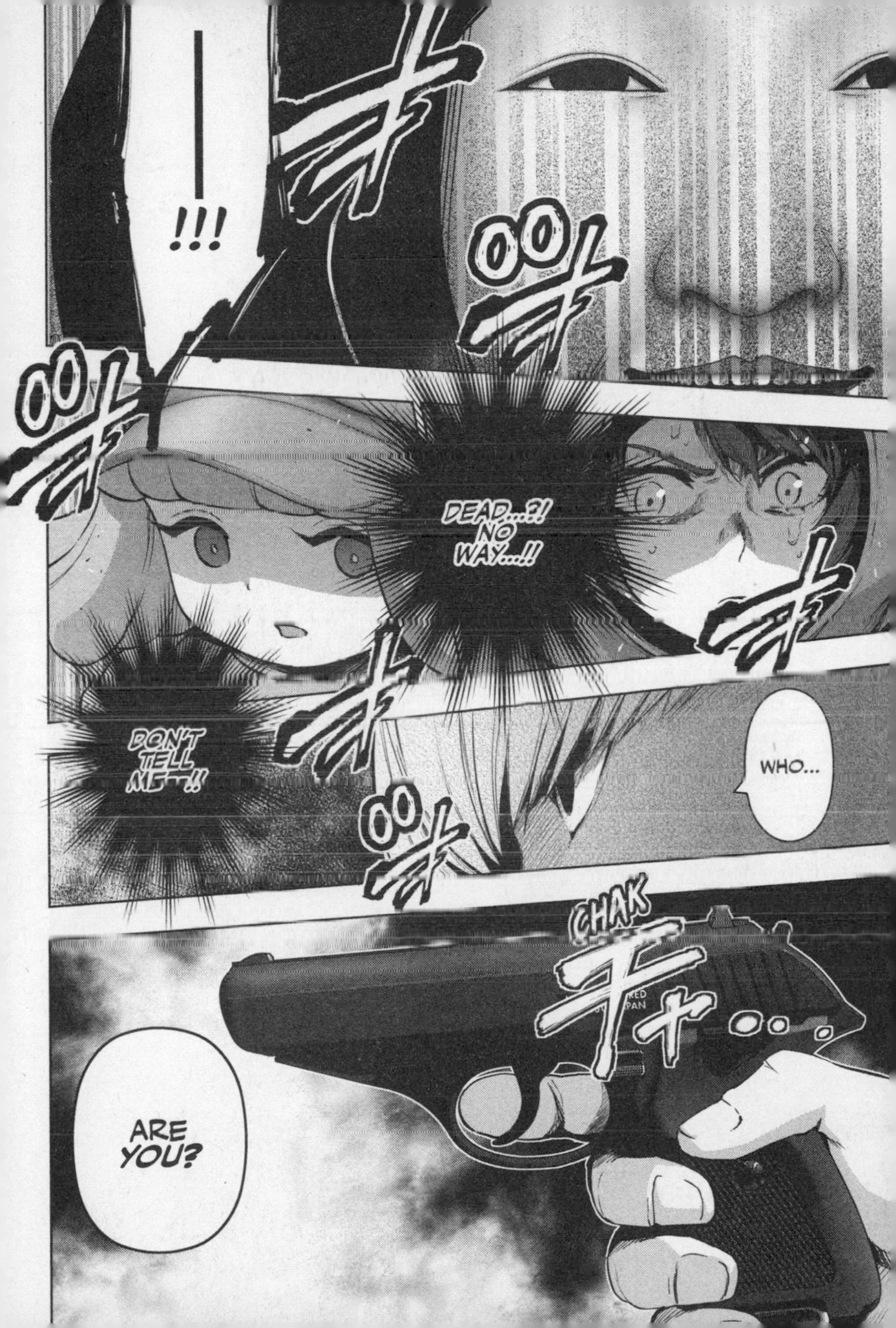
!!!
DEAD...?! NO WAY...!!
DON'T TELL ME...!!
WHO...
CHAK
ARE YOU?

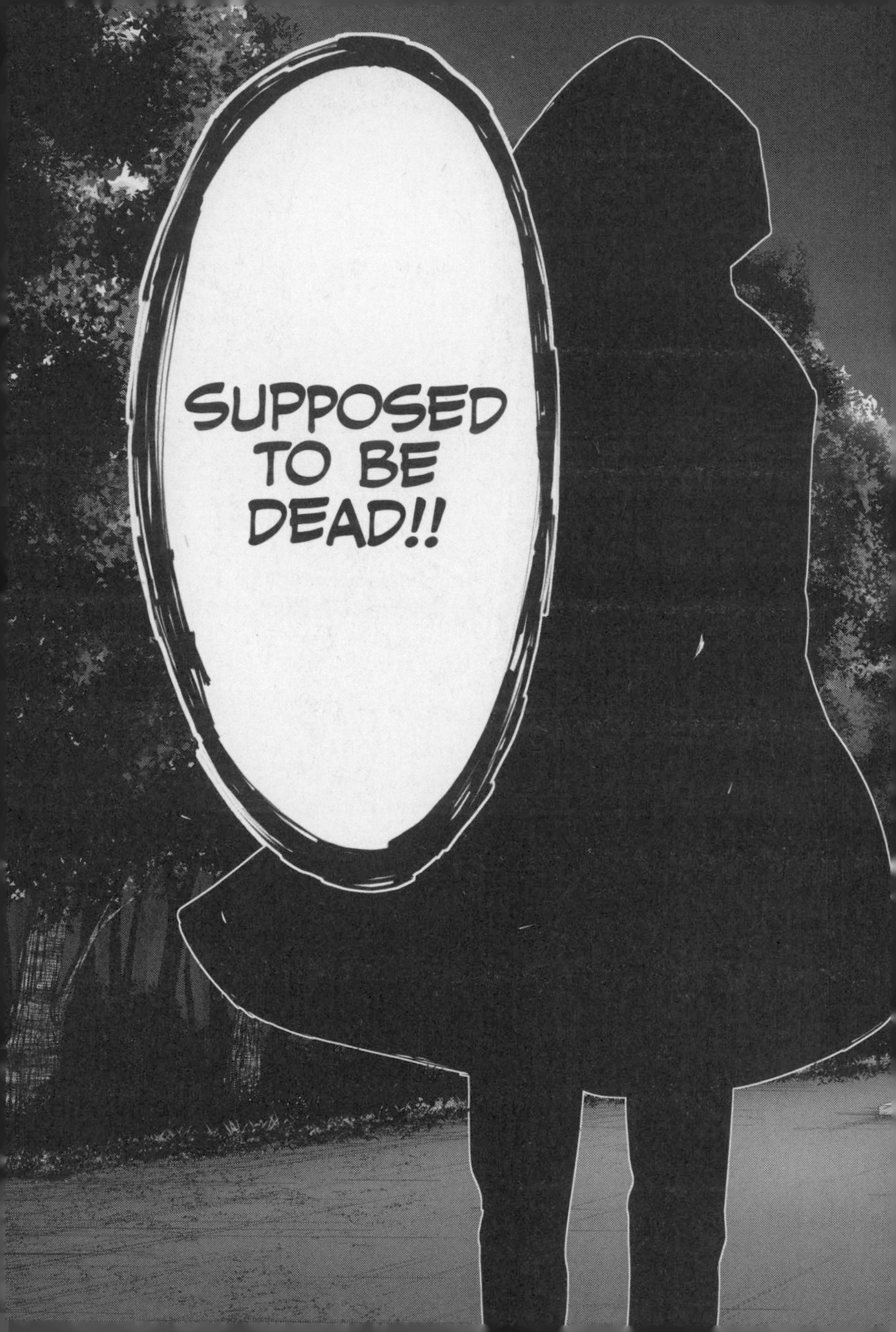
SUPPOSED TO BE DEAD!!

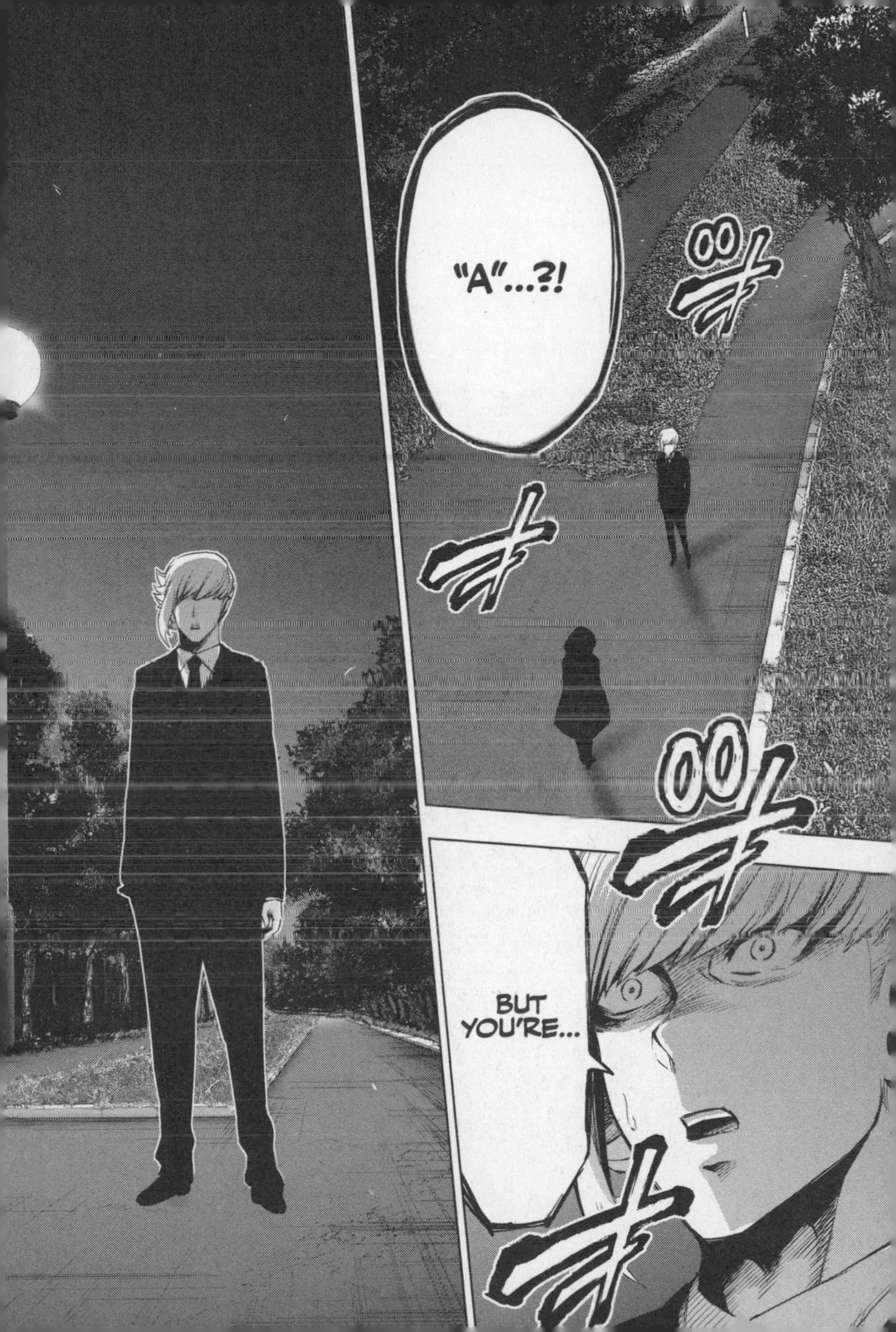
"A"...?!
BUT YOU'RE...

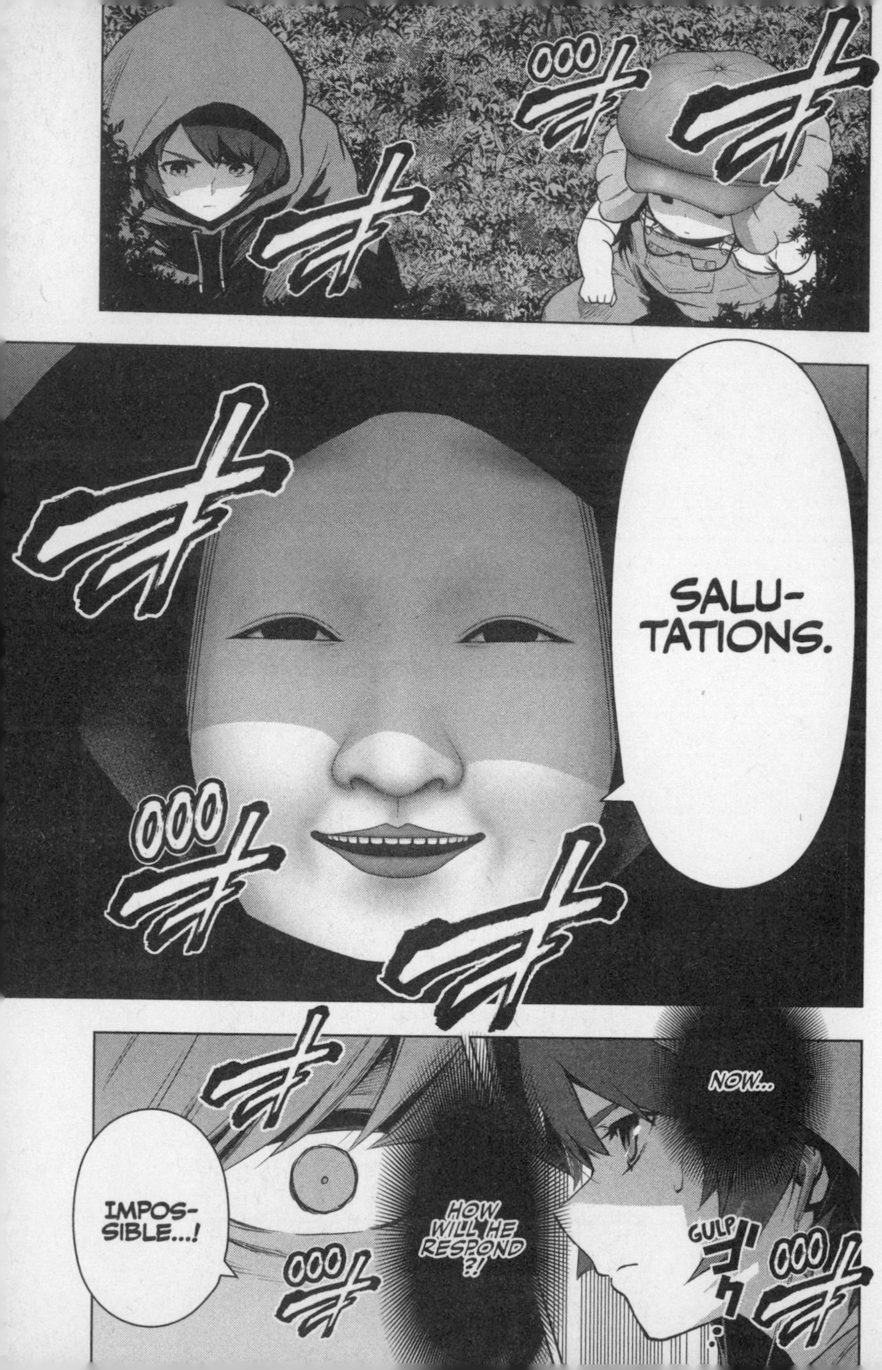
OOO
SALUTATIONS.
OOO
NOW...
GULP
OOO
HOW WILL HE RESPOND?!
IMPOSSIBLE...!
OOO

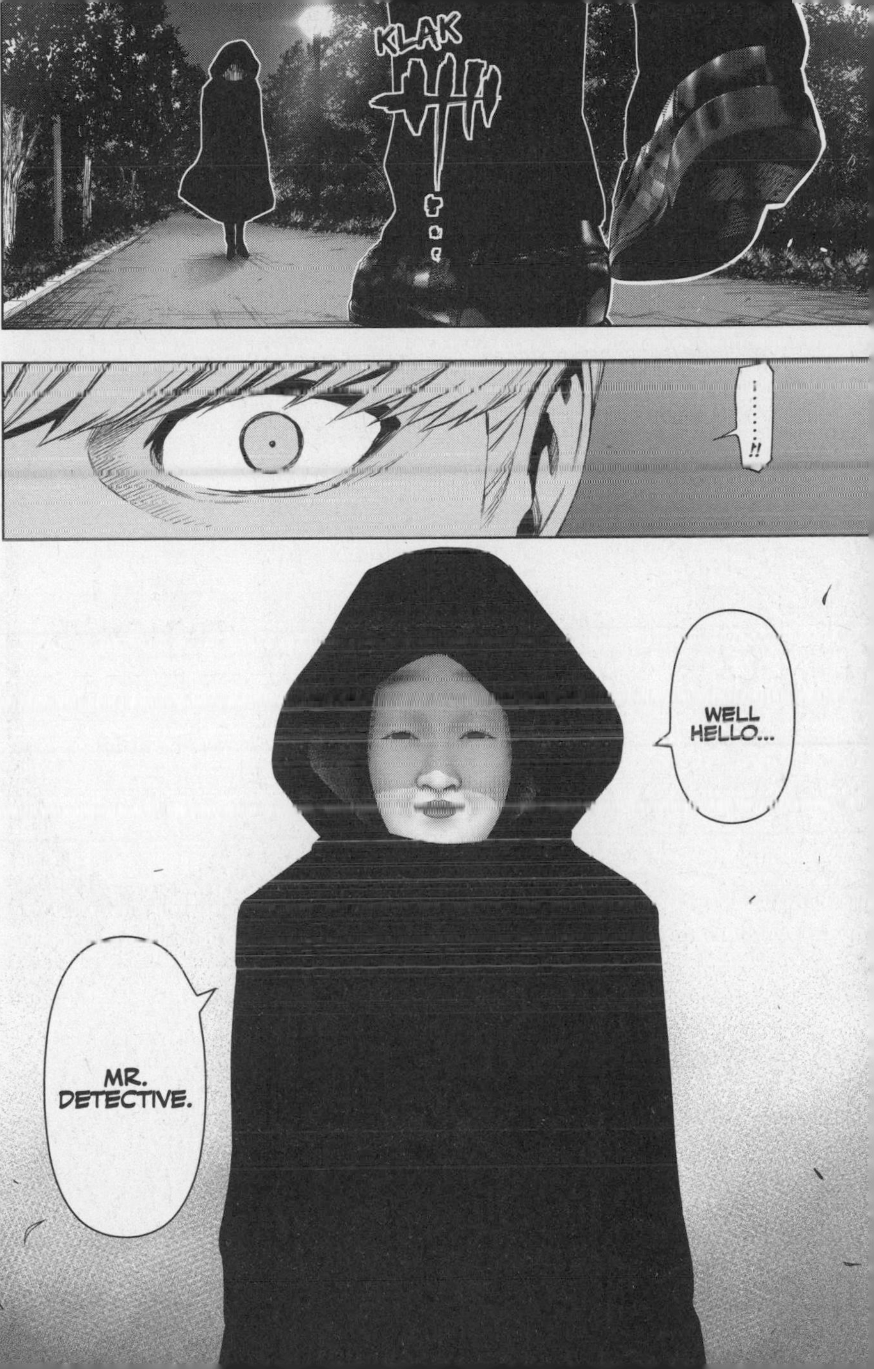
KLAK
......!!
WELL HELLO...
MR. DETECTIVE.

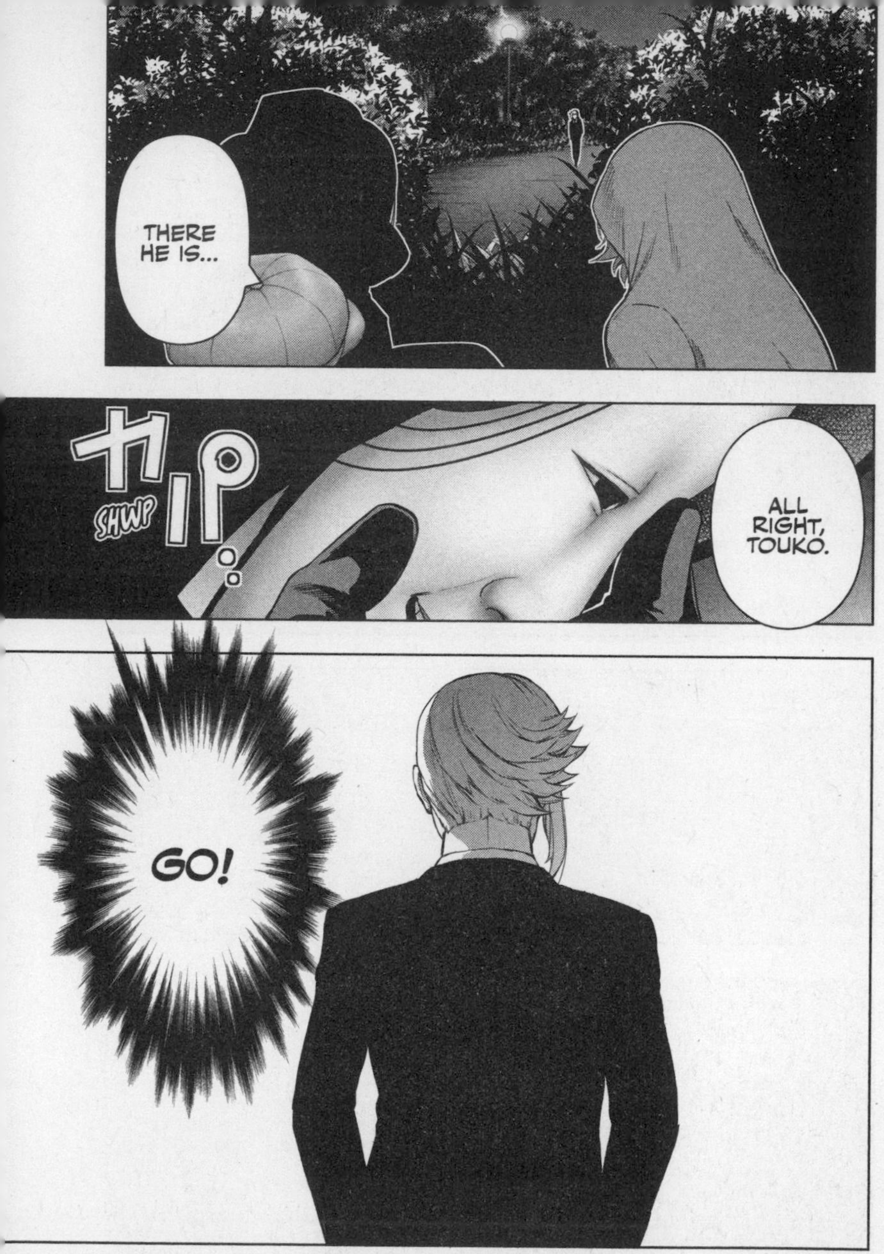
THERE HE IS...
ALL RIGHT, TOUKO.
SHWP
GO!

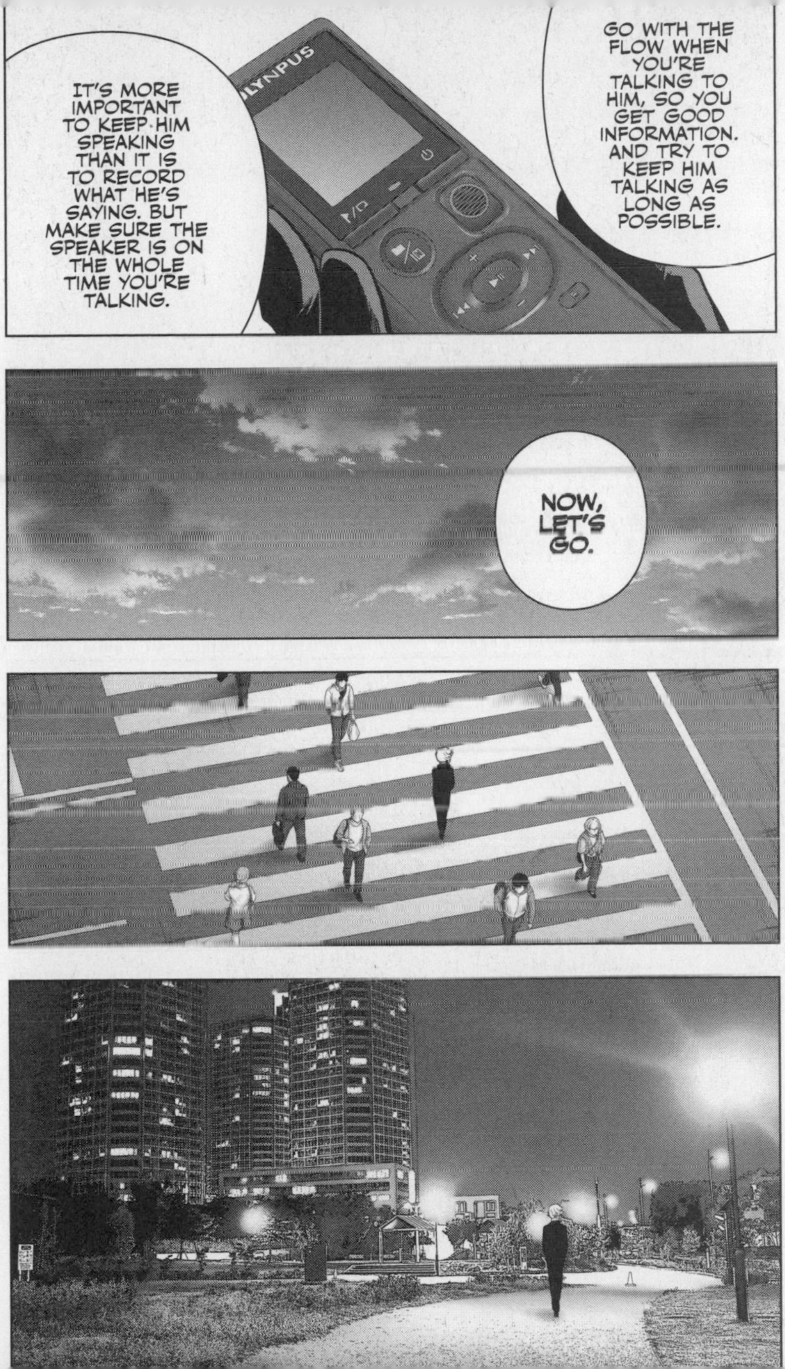
GO WITH THE FLOW WHEN YOU'RE TALKING TO HIM, SO YOU GET GOOD INFORMATION. AND TRY TO KEEP HIM TALKING AS LONG AS POSSIBLE.
IT'S MORE IMPORTANT TO KEEP HIM SPEAKING THAN IT IS TO RECORD WHAT HE'S SAYING. BUT MAKE SURE THE SPEAKER IS ON THE WHOLE TIME YOU'RE TALKING.
NOW, LET'S GO.

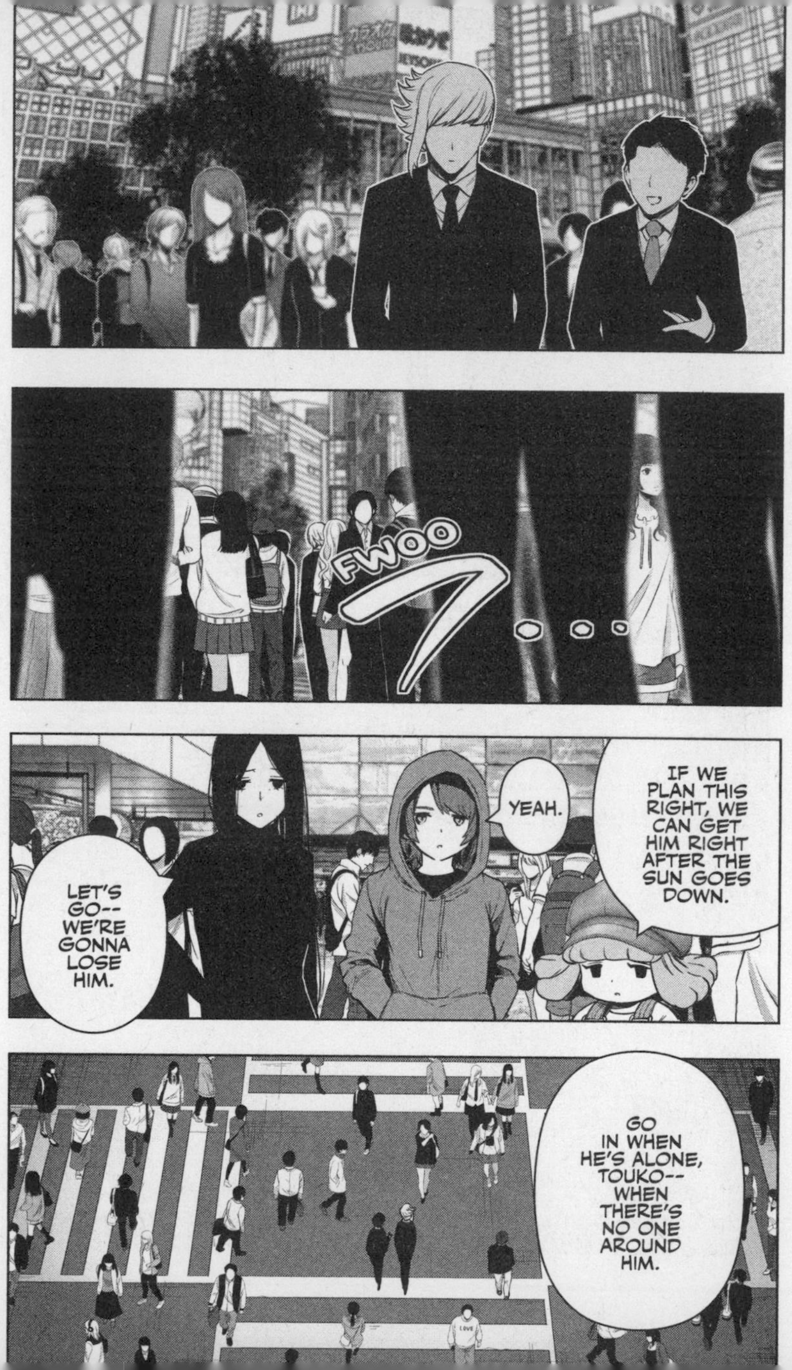
FWOO...
IF WE PLAN THIS RIGHT, WE CAN GET HIM RIGHT AFTER THE SUN GOES DOWN.
YEAH.
LET'S GO-- WE'RE GONNA LOSE HIM.
GO IN WHEN HE'S ALONE, TOUKO-- WHEN THERE'S NO ONE AROUND HIM.
LOVE

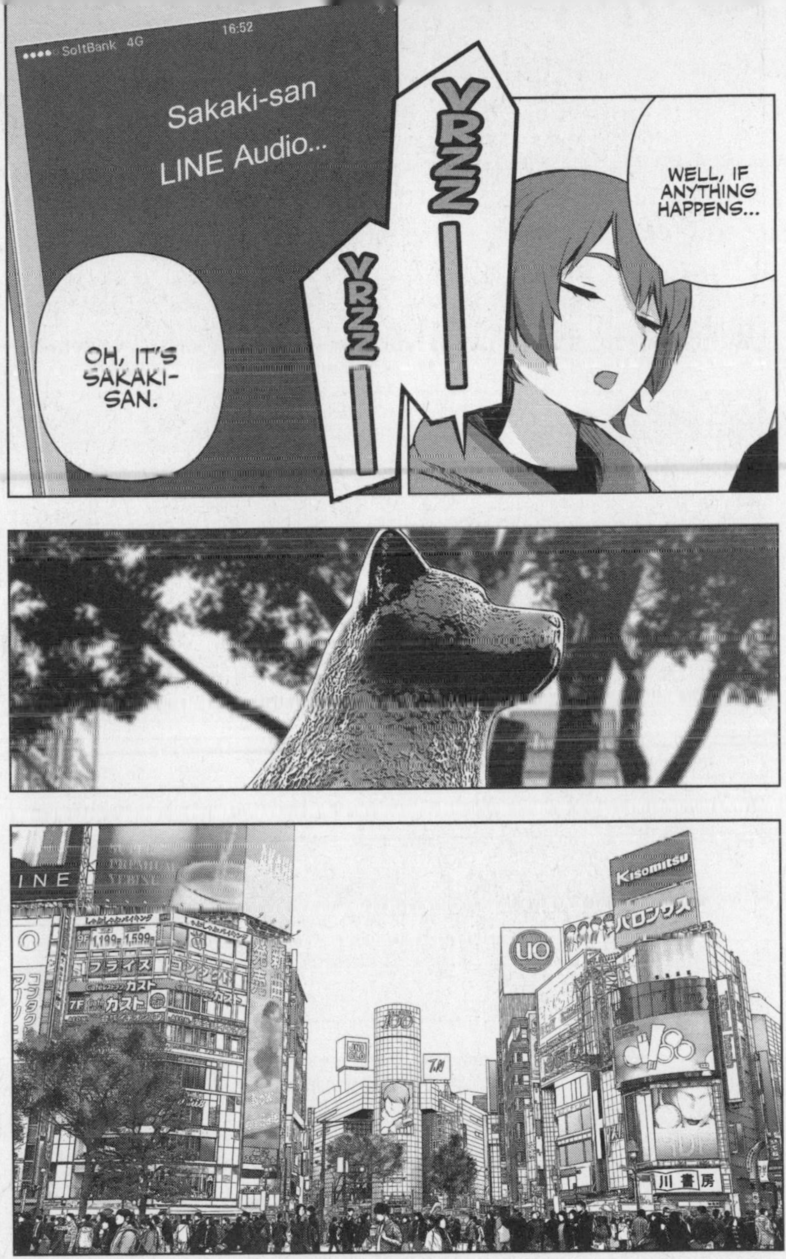
WELL, IF ANYTHING HAPPENS...
VRZZ
VRZZ
SoftBank 4G
16:52
Sakaki-san
LINE Audio...
OH, IT'S SAKAKI-SAN.
Kisomitsu

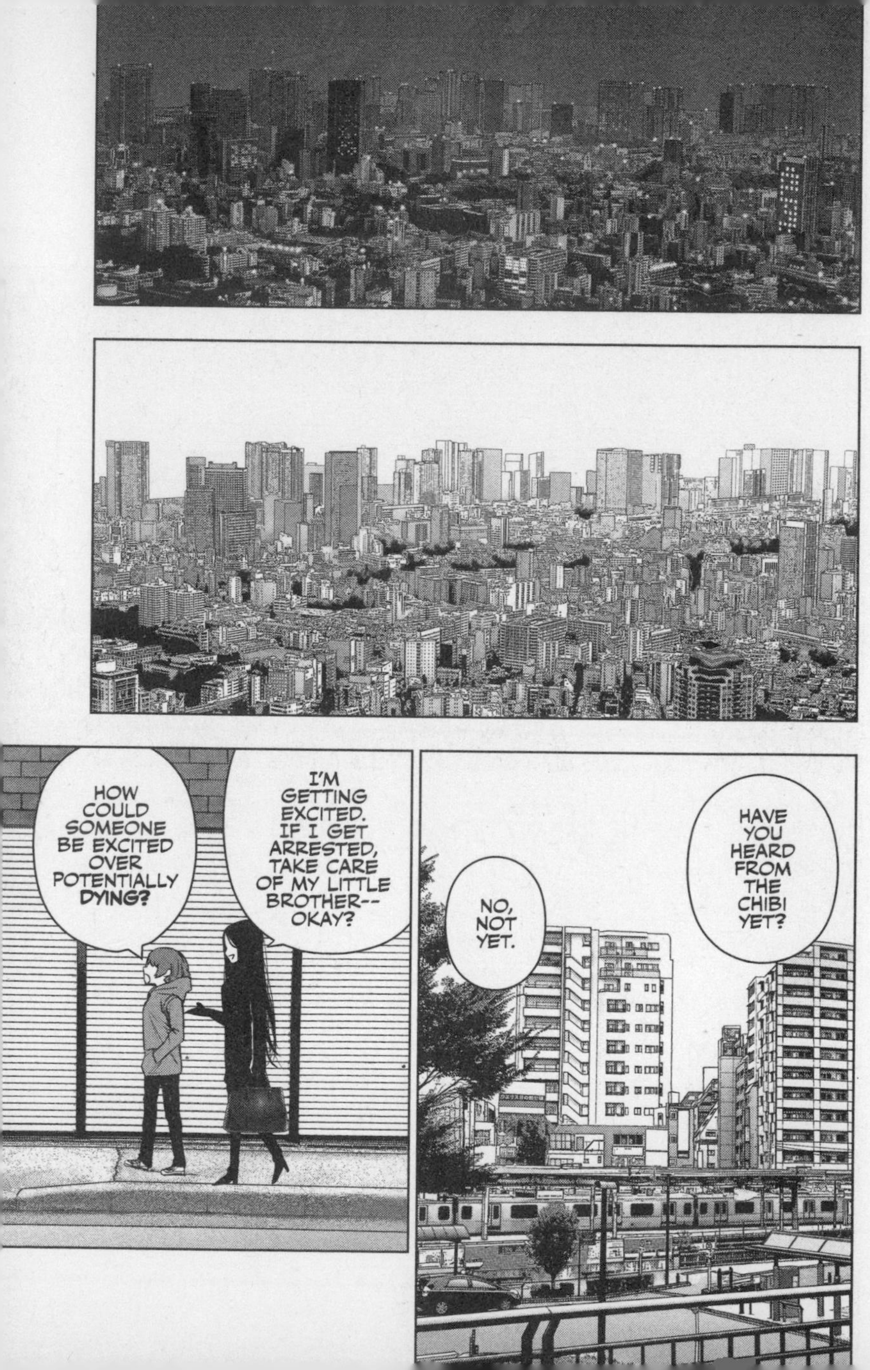
HAVE YOU HEARD FROM THE CHIBI YET?
NO, NOT YET.
I'M GETTING EXCITED. IF I GET ARRESTED, TAKE CARE OF MY LITTLE BROTHER--OKAY?
HOW COULD SOMEONE BE EXCITED OVER POTENTIALLY DYING?

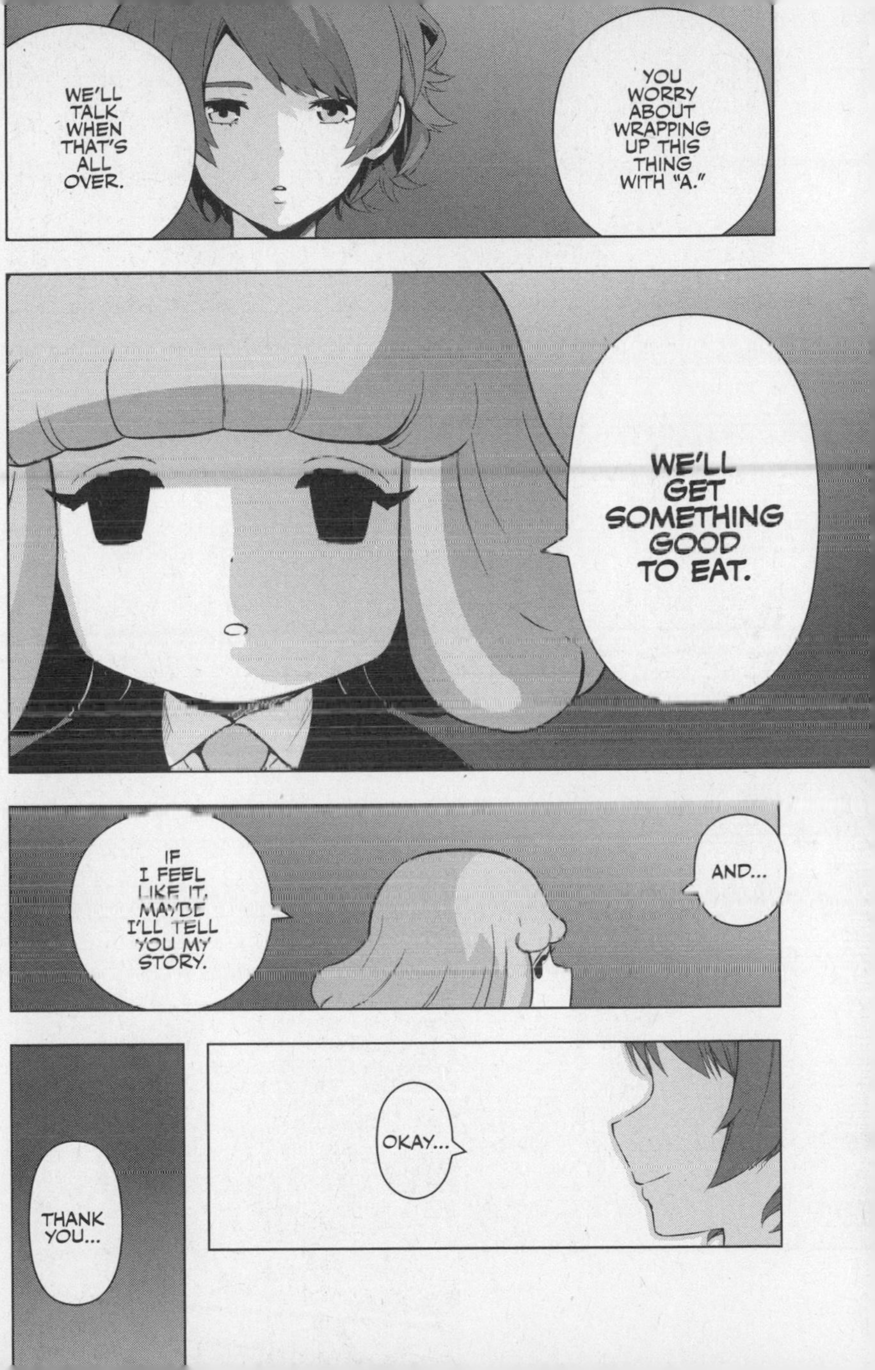
YOU WORRY ABOUT WRAPPING UP THIS THING WITH "A."
WE'LL TALK WHEN THAT'S ALL OVER.
WE'LL GET SOMETHING GOOD TO EAT.
AND...
IF I FEEL LIKE IT, MAYBE I'LL TELL YOU MY STORY.
OKAY...
THANK YOU...

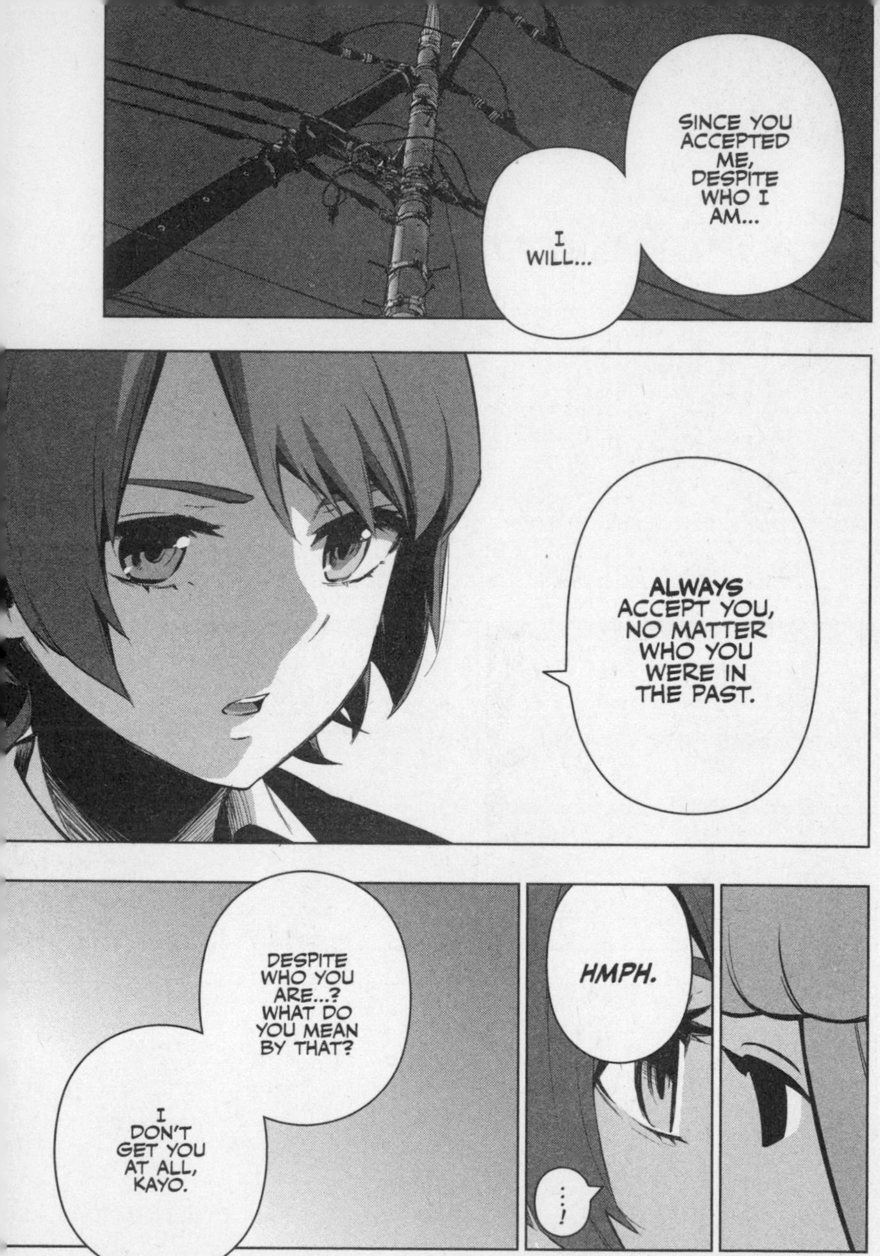
SINCE YOU ACCEPTED ME, DESPITE WHO I AM...
I WILL...
ALWAYS ACCEPT YOU, NO MATTER WHO YOU WERE IN THE PAST.
HMPH.
...!
DESPITE WHO YOU ARE...? WHAT DO YOU MEAN BY THAT?
I DON'T GET YOU AT ALL, KAYO.

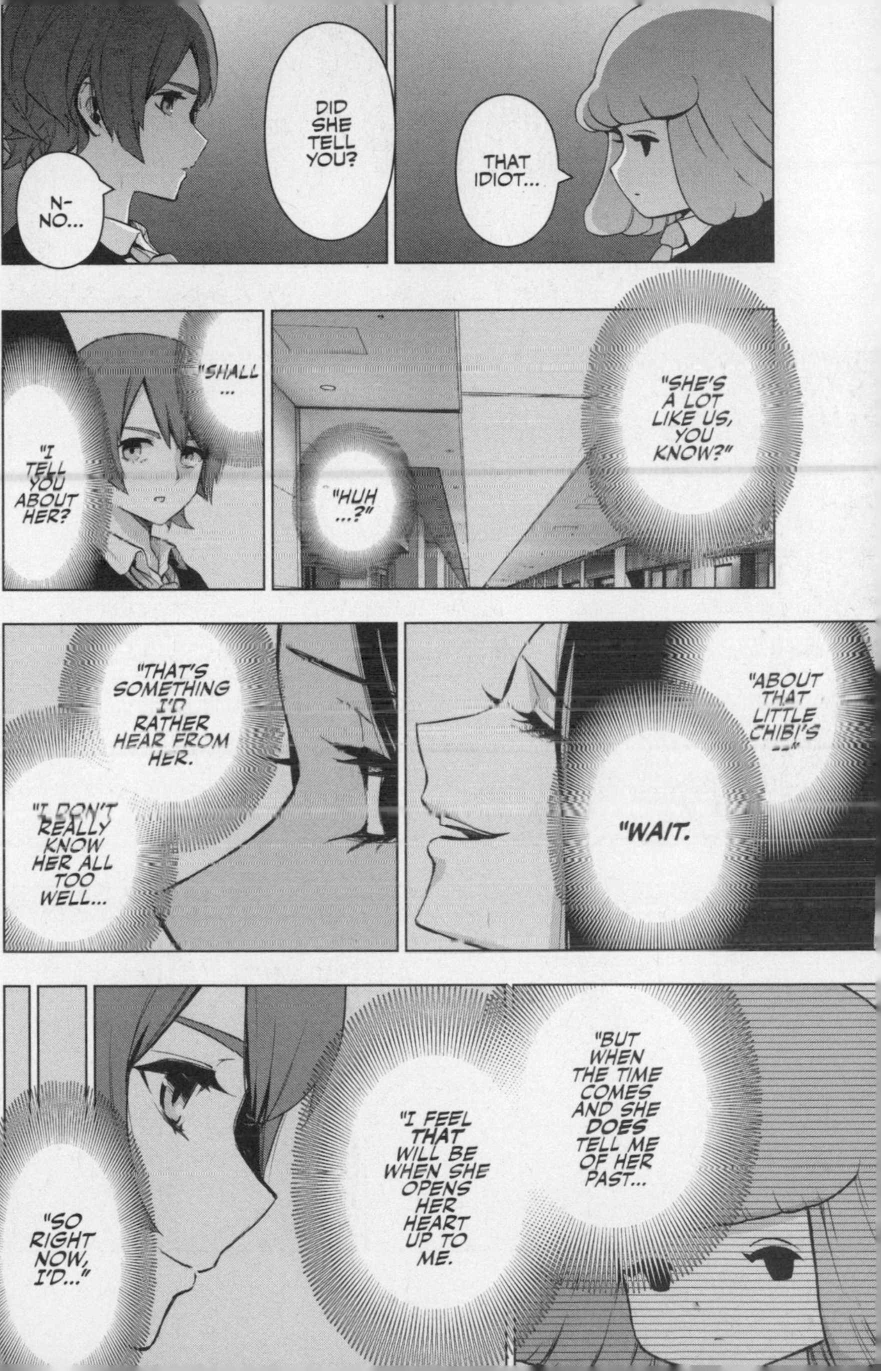
THAT IDIOT...
DID SHE TELL YOU?
N-NO...
"SHE'S A LOT LIKE US, YOU KNOW?"
"HUH...?"
"SHALL...
"I TELL YOU ABOUT HER?
"ABOUT THAT LITTLE CHIBI'S--"
"WAIT.
"THAT'S SOMETHING I'D RATHER HEAR FROM HER.
"I DON'T REALLY KNOW HER ALL TOO WELL...
"BUT WHEN THE TIME COMES AND SHE DOES TELL ME OF HER PAST...
"I FEEL THAT WILL BE WHEN SHE OPENS HER HEART UP TO ME.
"SO RIGHT NOW, I'D..."

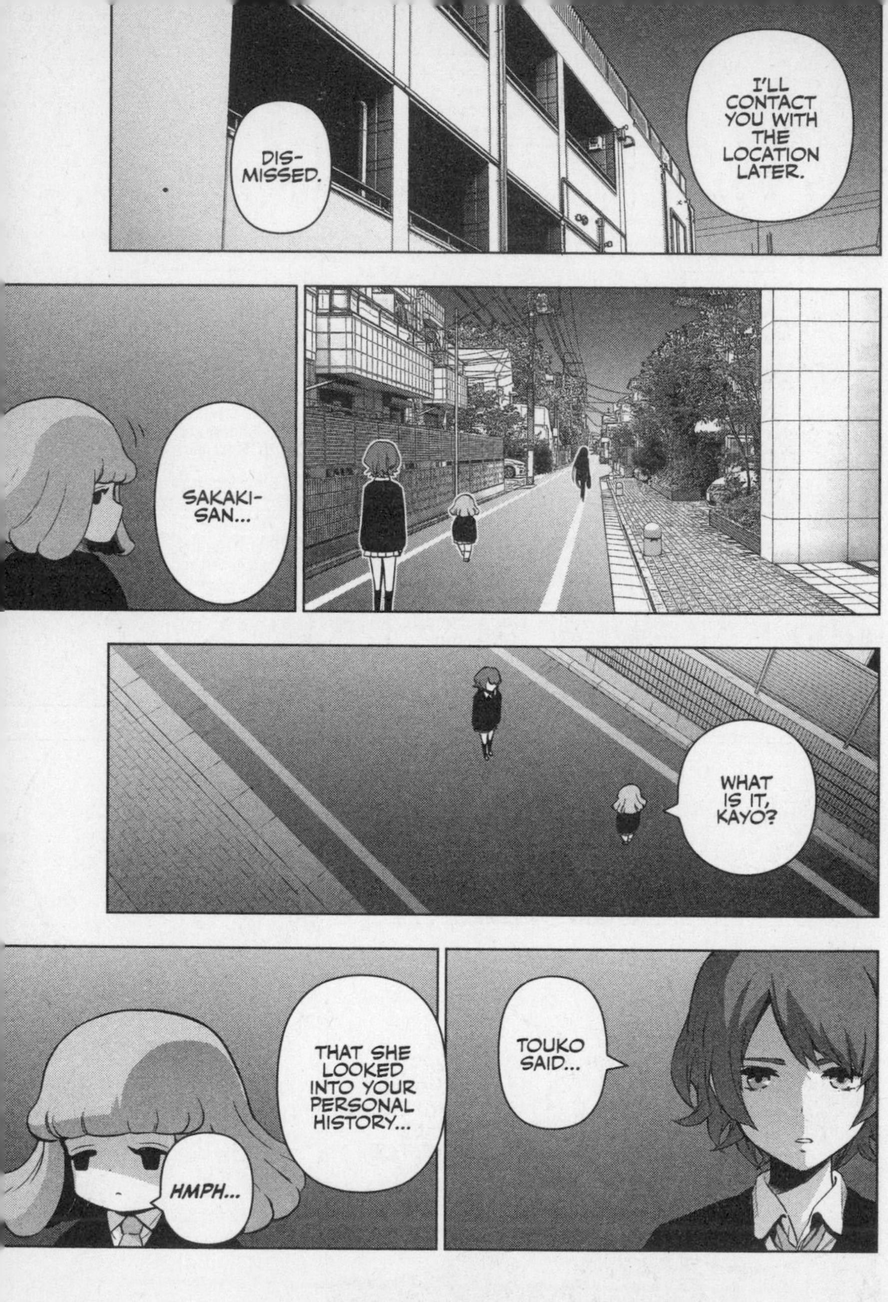
I'LL CONTACT YOU WITH THE LOCATION LATER.
DIS-MISSED.
SAKAKI-SAN...
WHAT IS IT, KAYO?
TOUKO SAID...
THAT SHE LOOKED INTO YOUR PERSONAL HISTORY...
HMPH...

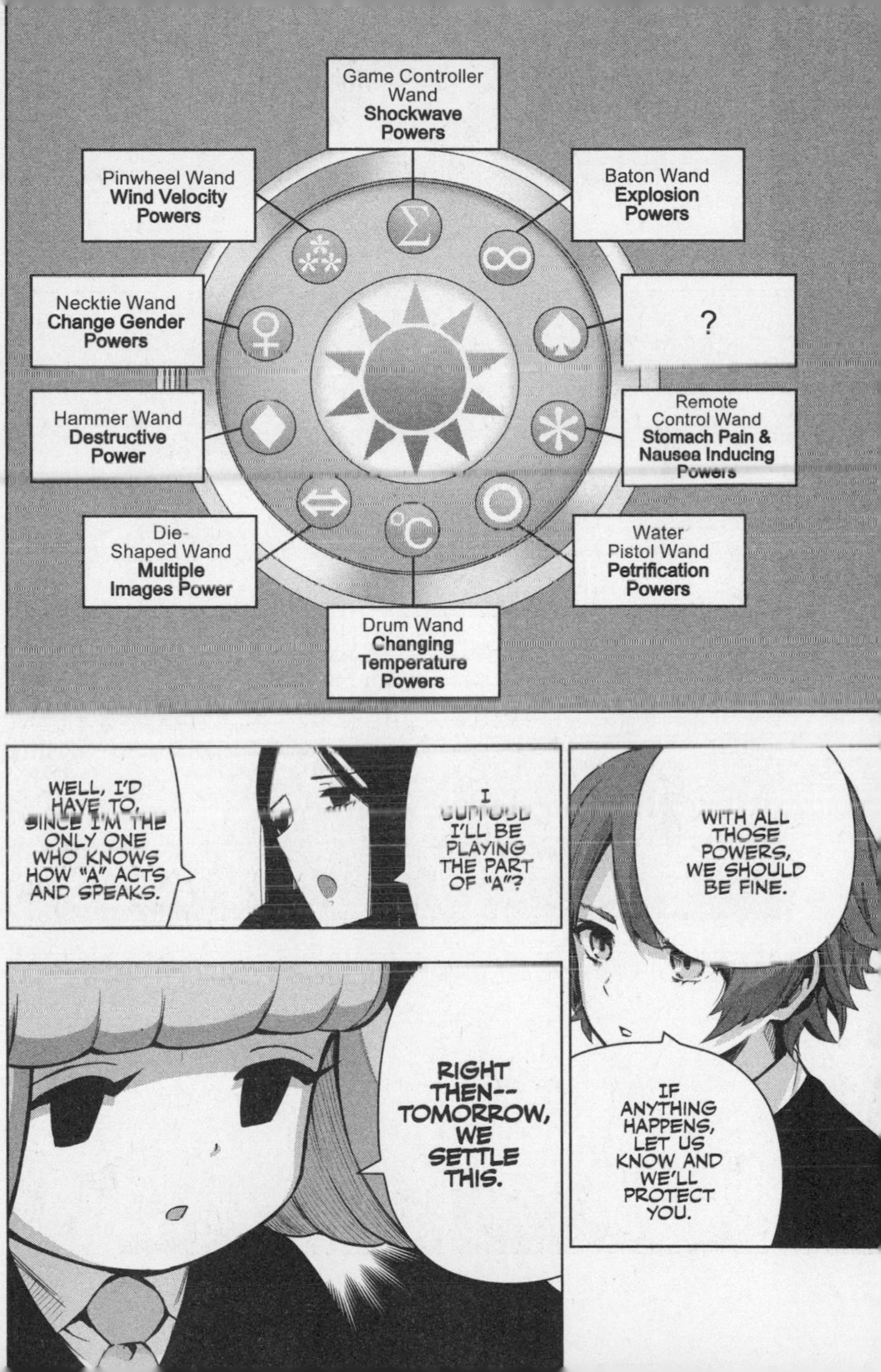

Game Controller Wand **Shockwave Powers**
Baton Wand **Explosion Powers**
?
Remote Control Wand **Stomach Pain & Nausea Inducing Powers**
Water Pistol Wand **Petrification Powers**
Drum Wand **Changing Temperature Powers**
Die-Shaped Wand **Multiple Images Power**
Hammer Wand **Destructive Power**
Necktie Wand **Change Gender Powers**
Pinwheel Wand **Wind Velocity Powers**
WITH ALL THOSE POWERS, WE SHOULD BE FINE.
IF ANYTHING HAPPENS, LET US KNOW AND WE'LL PROTECT YOU.
I SUPPOSE I'LL BE PLAYING THE PART OF "A"?
WELL, I'D HAVE TO, SINCE I'M THE ONLY ONE WHO KNOWS HOW "A" ACTS AND SPEAKS.
RIGHT THEN-- TOMORROW, WE SETTLE THIS.

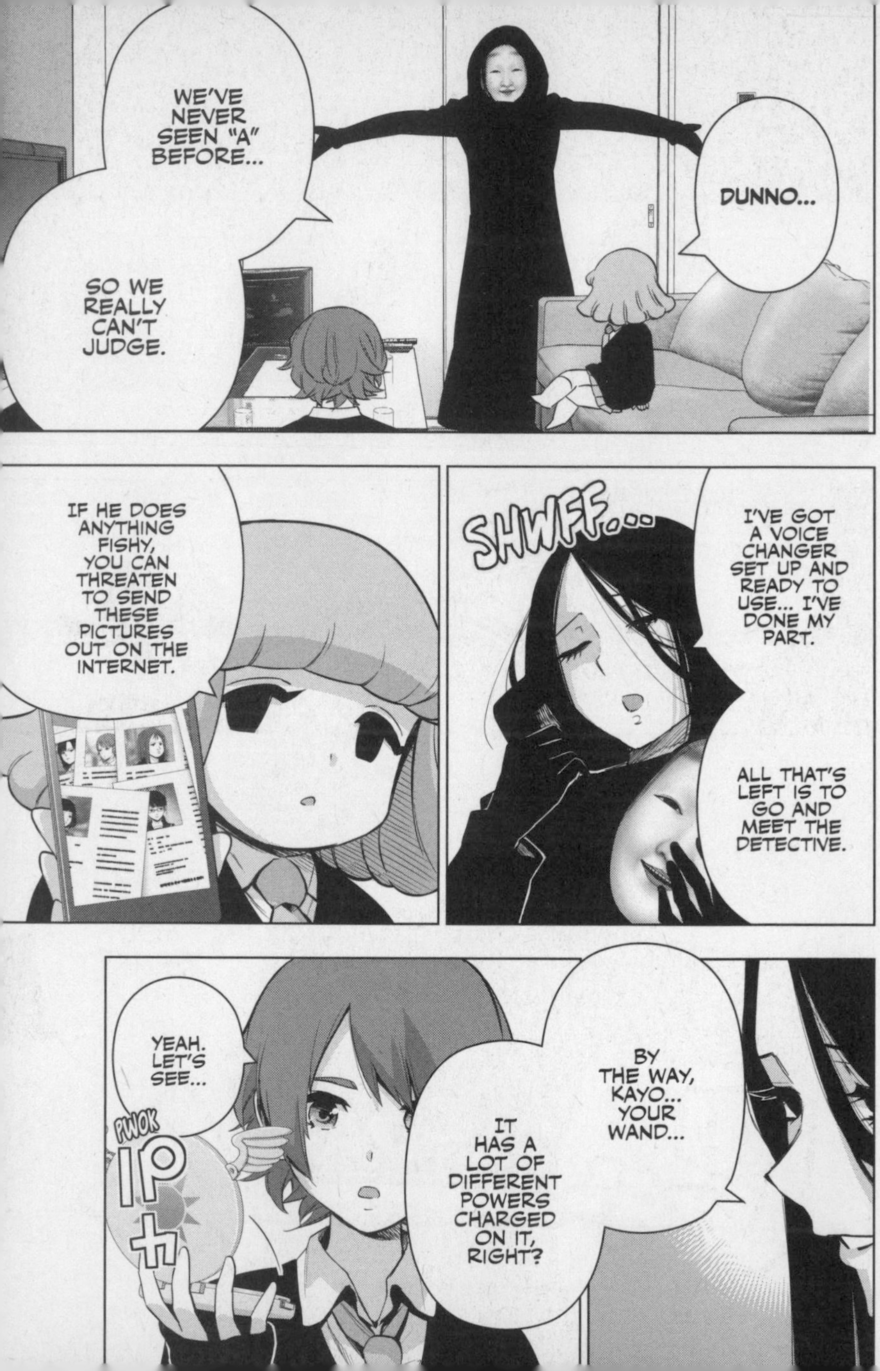
DUNNO...
WE'VE NEVER SEEN "A" BEFORE...
SO WE REALLY CAN'T JUDGE.
SHWFF...
I'VE GOT A VOICE CHANGER SET UP AND READY TO USE... I'VE DONE MY PART.
ALL THAT'S LEFT IS TO GO AND MEET THE DETECTIVE.
IF HE DOES ANYTHING FISHY, YOU CAN THREATEN TO SEND THESE PICTURES OUT ON THE INTERNET.
BY THE WAY, KAYO... YOUR WAND...
IT HAS A LOT OF DIFFERENT POWERS CHARGED ON IT, RIGHT?
YEAH. LET'S SEE...
PWOK

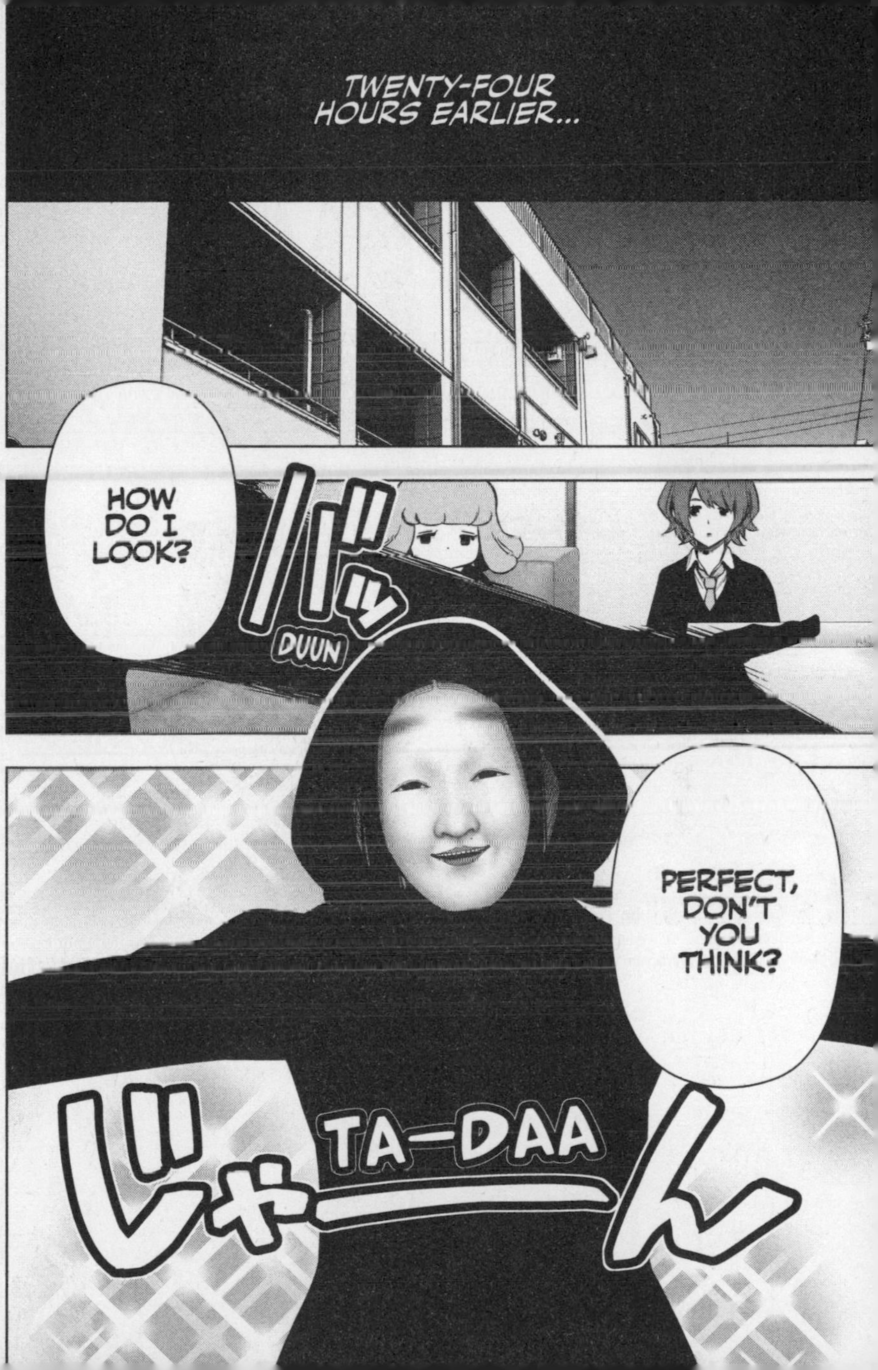
TWENTY-FOUR HOURS EARLIER...
HOW DO I LOOK?
バッ
DUUN
PERFECT, DON'T YOU THINK?
じゃーん
TA-DAA

ENTER.74 MISSION: "A"

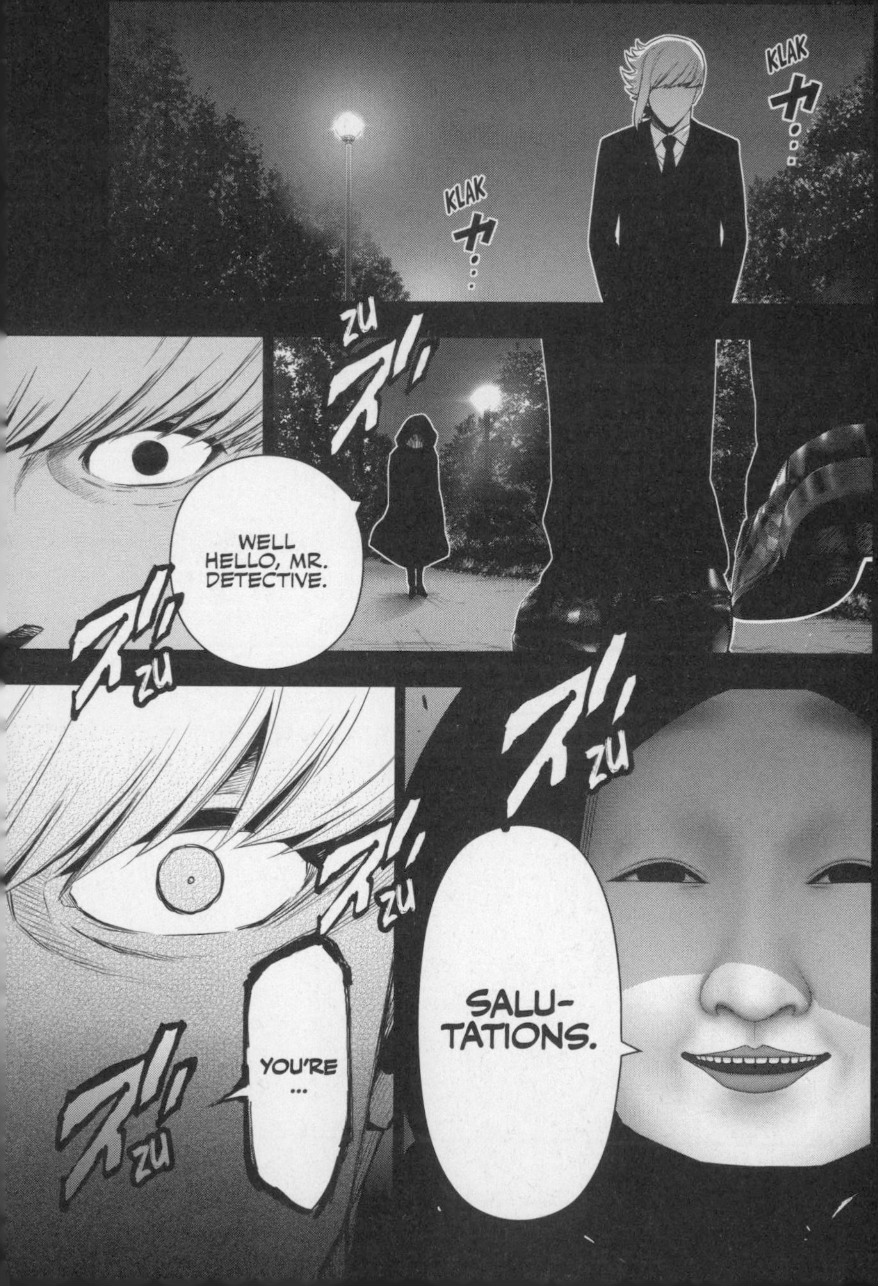
KLAK
KLAK
ZU
WELL HELLO, MR. DETECTIVE.
ZU
ZU
SALU-TATIONS.
ZU
YOU'RE ...
ZU

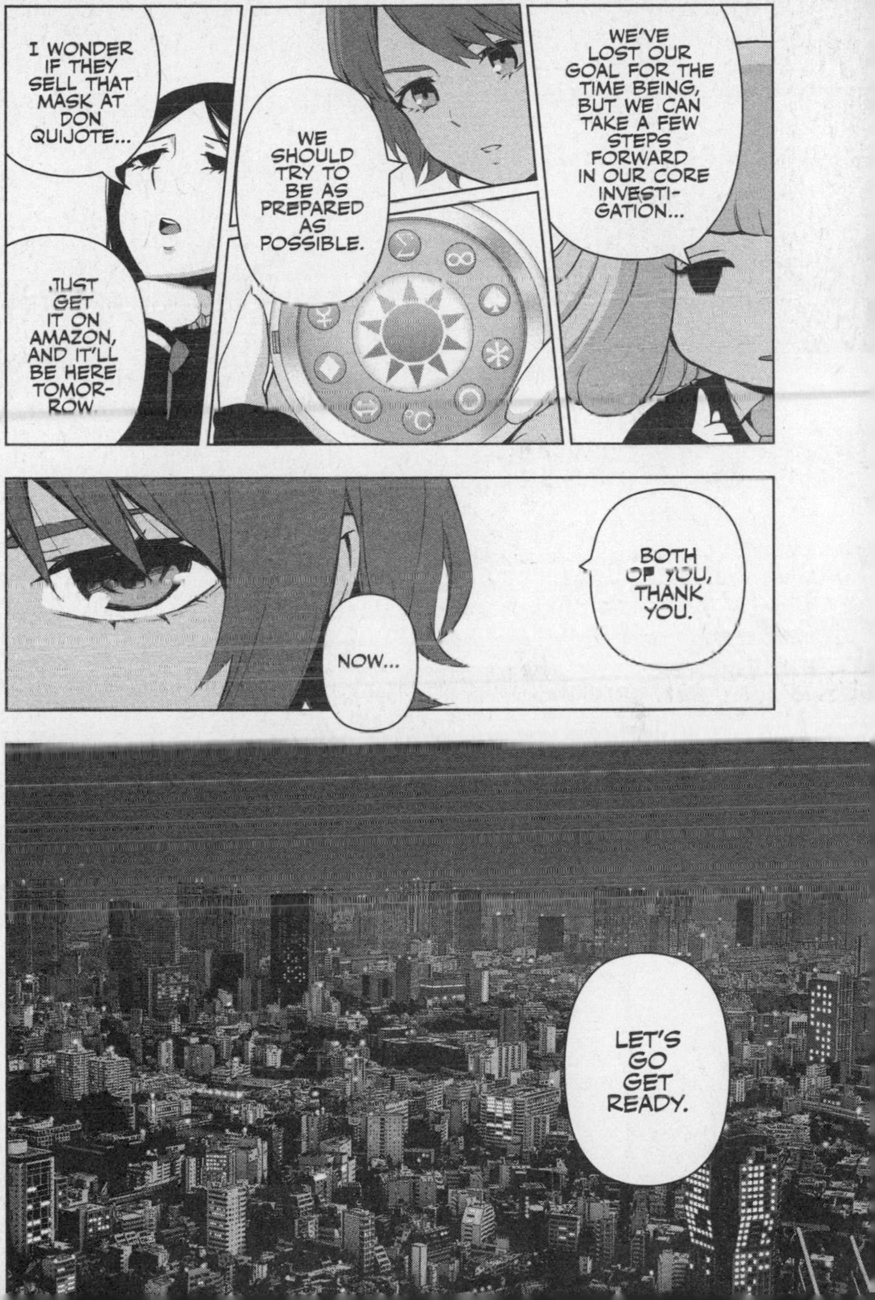
WE'VE LOST OUR GOAL FOR THE TIME BEING, BUT WE CAN TAKE A FEW STEPS FORWARD IN OUR CORE INVESTI-GATION...
WE SHOULD TRY TO BE AS PREPARED AS POSSIBLE.
I WONDER IF THEY SELL THAT MASK AT DON QUIJOTE...
JUST GET IT ON AMAZON, AND IT'LL BE HERE TOMORROW.
BOTH OF YOU, THANK YOU.
NOW...
LET'S GO GET READY.

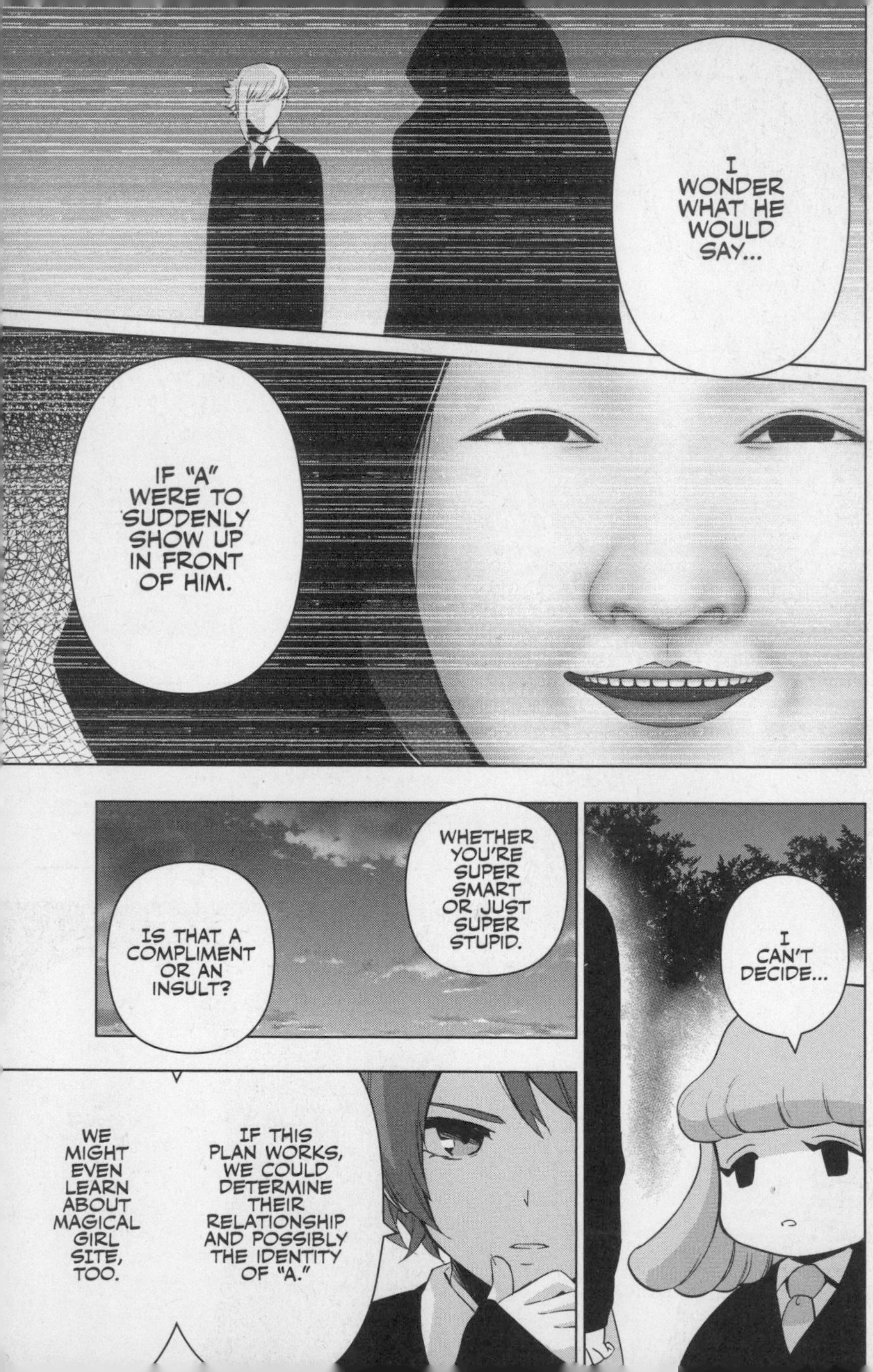
I WONDER WHAT HE WOULD SAY...
IF "A" WERE TO SUDDENLY SHOW UP IN FRONT OF HIM.
I CAN'T DECIDE...
WHETHER YOU'RE SUPER SMART OR JUST SUPER STUPID.
IS THAT A COMPLIMENT OR AN INSULT?
IF THIS PLAN WORKS, WE COULD DETERMINE THEIR RELATIONSHIP AND POSSIBLY THE IDENTITY OF "A."
WE MIGHT EVEN LEARN ABOUT MAGICAL GIRL SITE, TOO.

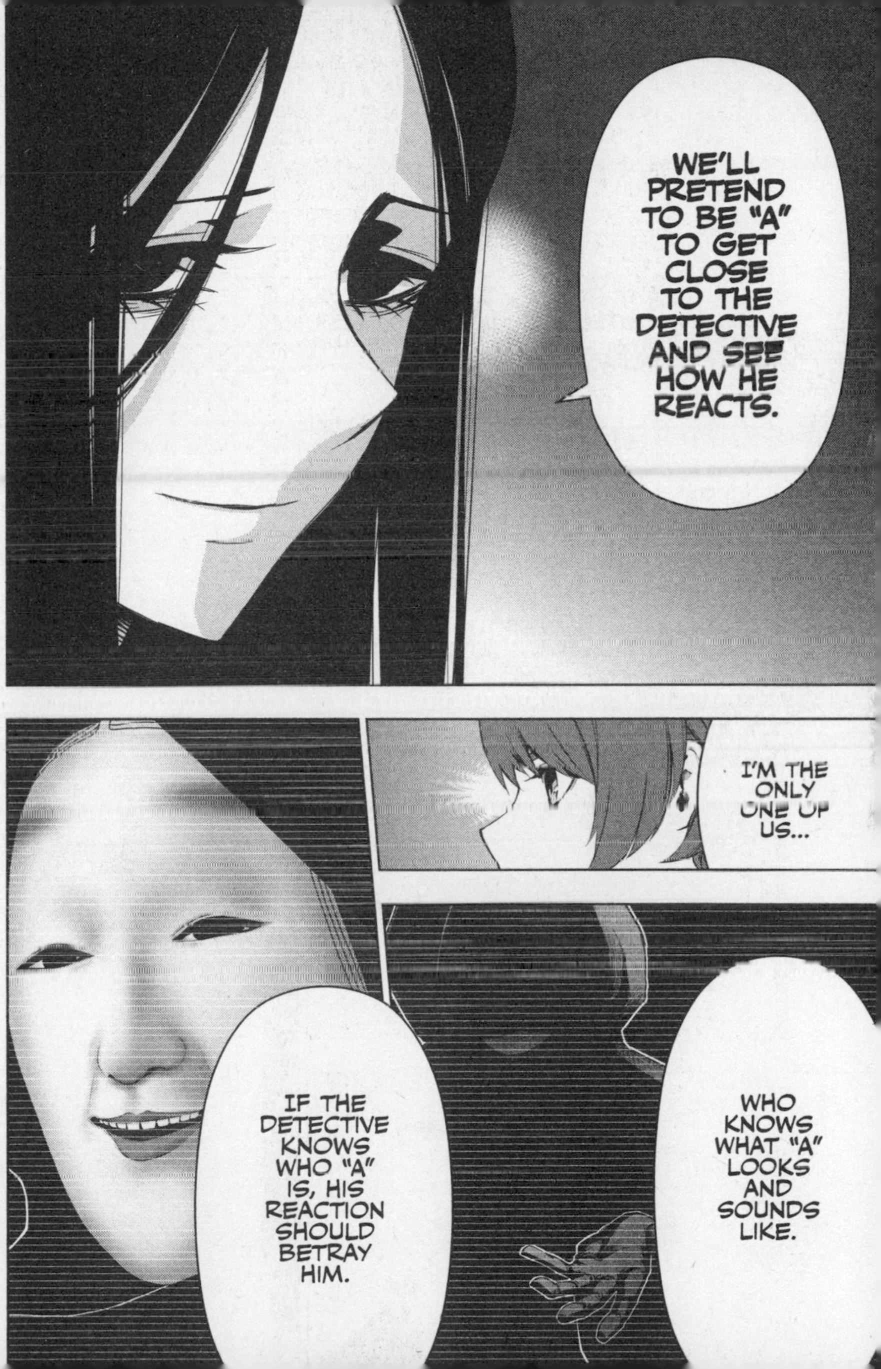
WE'LL PRETEND TO BE "A" TO GET CLOSE TO THE DETECTIVE AND SEE HOW HE REACTS.
I'M THE ONLY ONE OF US...
WHO KNOWS WHAT "A" LOOKS AND SOUNDS LIKE.
IF THE DETECTIVE KNOWS WHO "A" IS, HIS REACTION SHOULD BETRAY HIM.

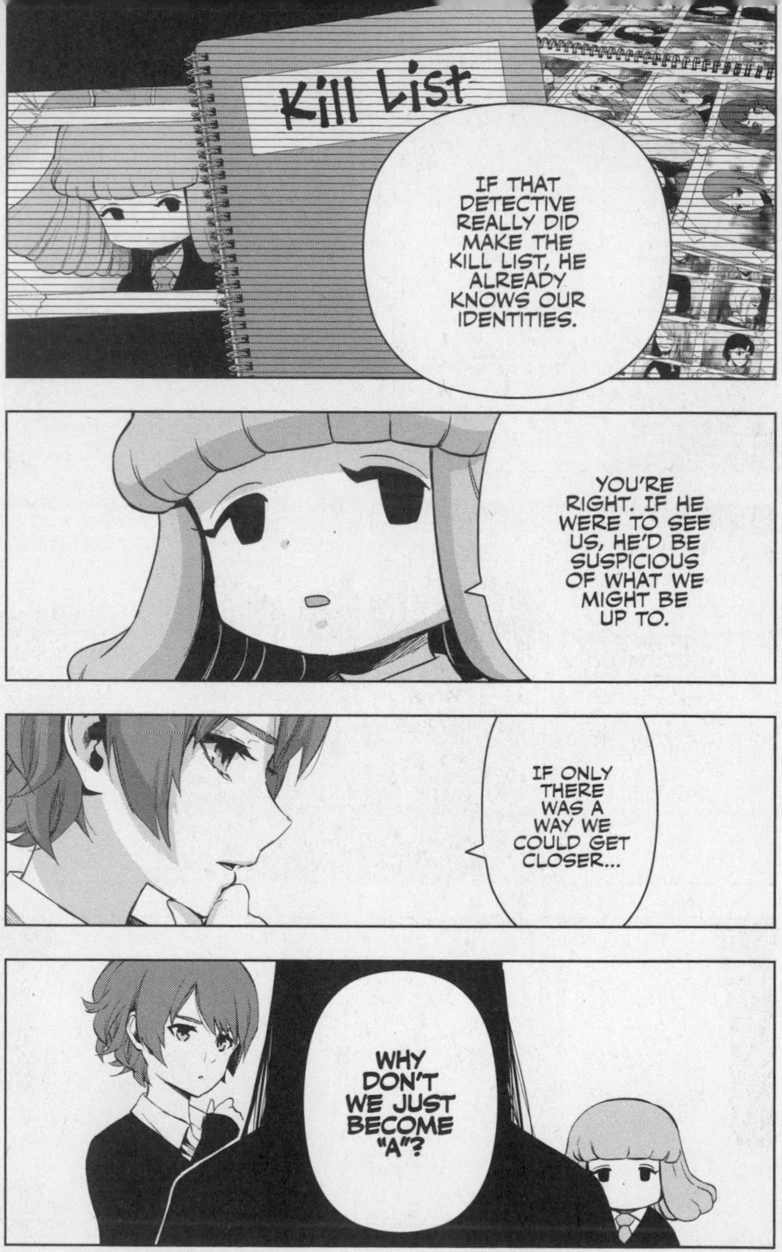
Kill List
IF THAT DETECTIVE REALLY DID MAKE THE KILL LIST, HE ALREADY KNOWS OUR IDENTITIES.
YOU'RE RIGHT. IF HE WERE TO SEE US, HE'D BE SUSPICIOUS OF WHAT WE MIGHT BE UP TO.
IF ONLY THERE WAS A WAY WE COULD GET CLOSER...
WHY DON'T WE JUST BECOME "A"?

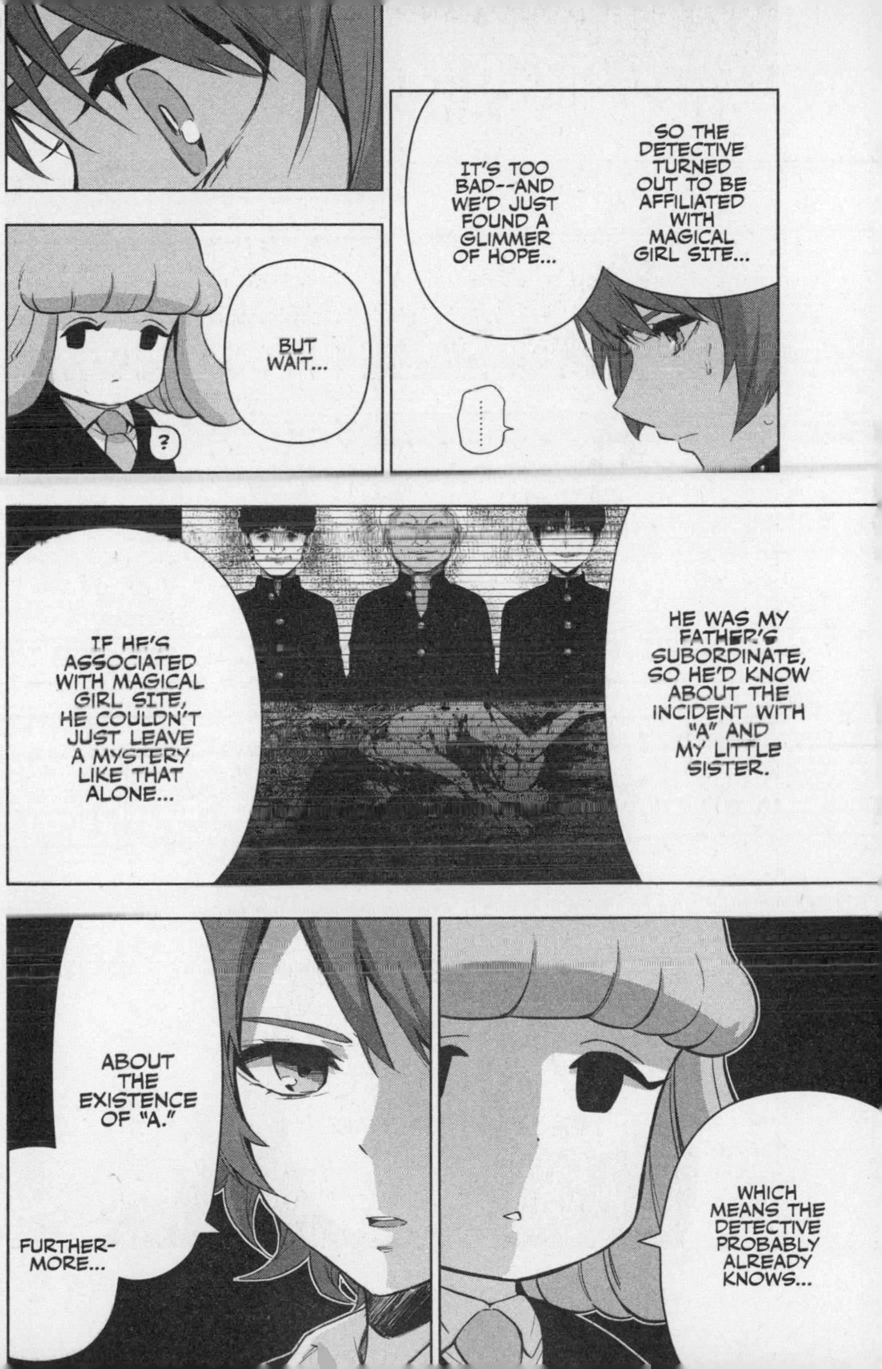
SO THE DETECTIVE TURNED OUT TO BE AFFILIATED WITH MAGICAL GIRL SITE...
IT'S TOO BAD--AND WE'D JUST FOUND A GLIMMER OF HOPE...
......
BUT WAIT...
?
HE WAS MY FATHER'S SUBORDINATE, SO HE'D KNOW ABOUT THE INCIDENT WITH "A" AND MY LITTLE SISTER.
IF HE'S ASSOCIATED WITH MAGICAL GIRL SITE, HE COULDN'T JUST LEAVE A MYSTERY LIKE THAT ALONE...
WHICH MEANS THE DETECTIVE PROBABLY ALREADY KNOWS...
ABOUT THE EXISTENCE OF "A."
FURTHER-MORE...

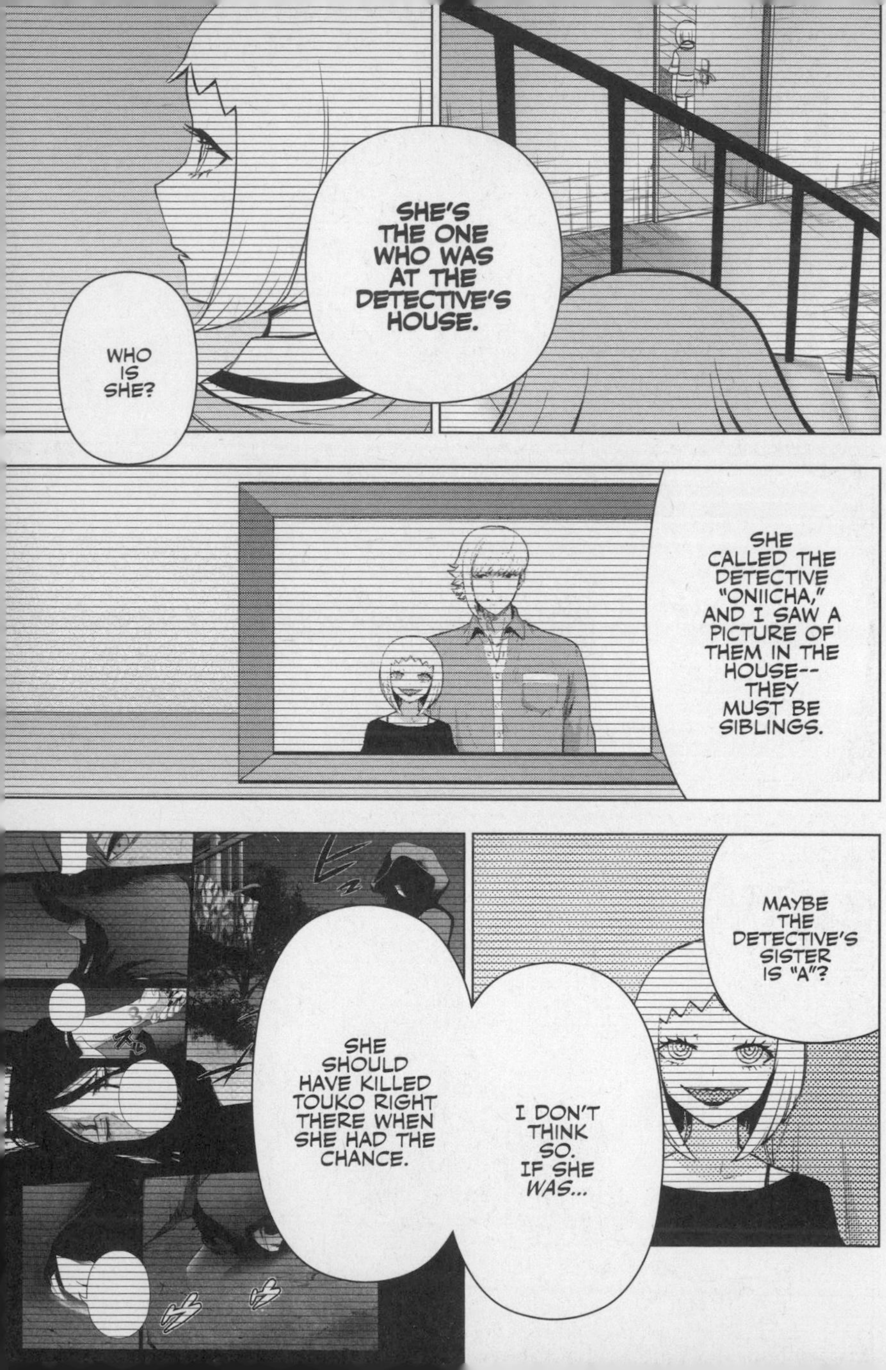
SHE'S THE ONE WHO WAS AT THE DETECTIVE'S HOUSE.
WHO IS SHE?
SHE CALLED THE DETECTIVE "ONIICHA," AND I SAW A PICTURE OF THEM IN THE HOUSE-- THEY MUST BE SIBLINGS.
MAYBE THE DETECTIVE'S SISTER IS "A"?
I DON'T THINK SO. IF SHE *WAS*...
SHE SHOULD HAVE KILLED TOUKO RIGHT THERE WHEN SHE HAD THE CHANCE.

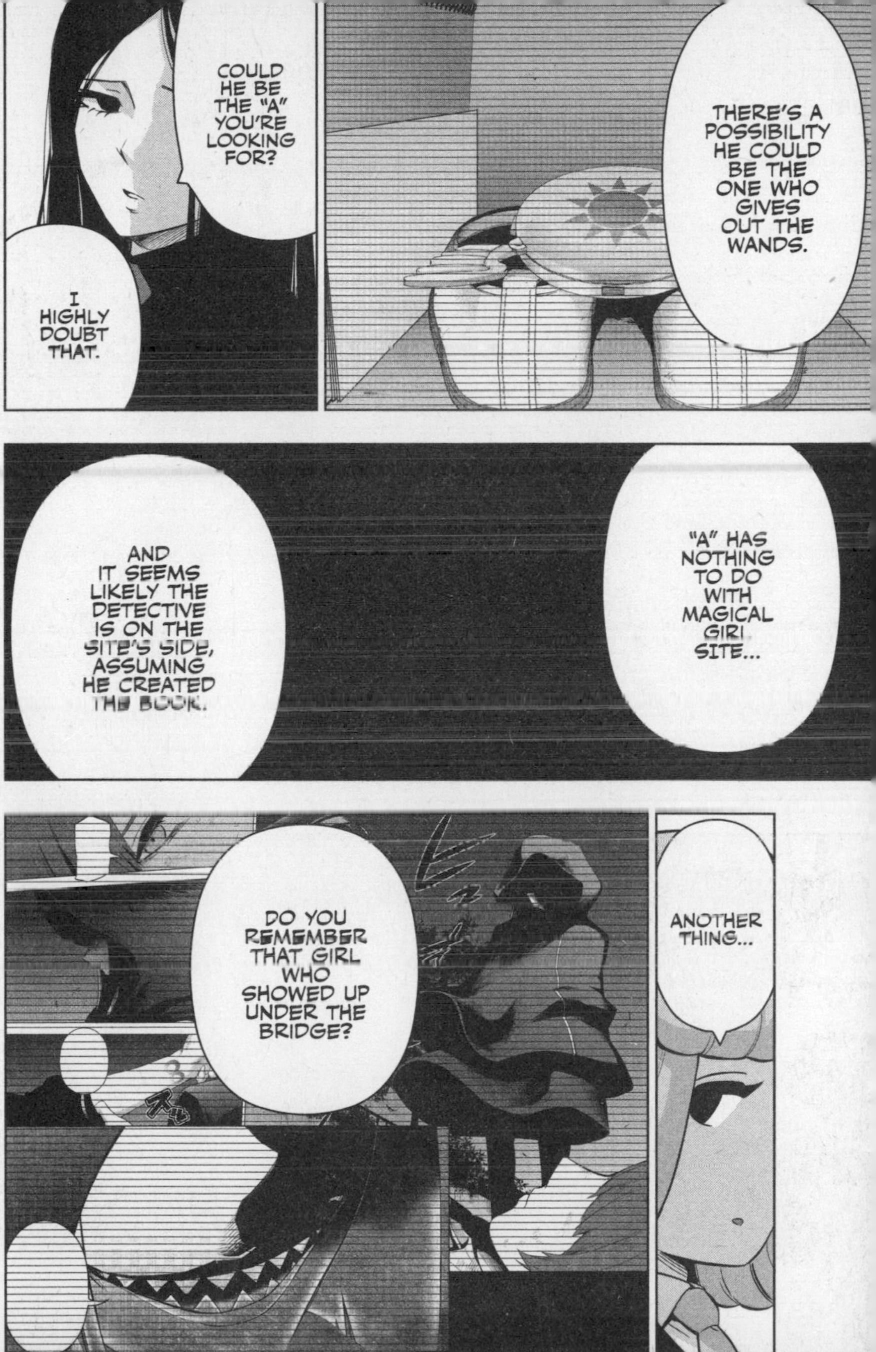
THERE'S A POSSIBILITY HE COULD BE THE ONE WHO GIVES OUT THE WANDS.
COULD HE BE THE "A" YOU'RE LOOKING FOR?
I HIGHLY DOUBT THAT.
"A" HAS NOTHING TO DO WITH MAGICAL GIRL SITE...
AND IT SEEMS LIKELY THE DETECTIVE IS ON THE SITE'S SIDE, ASSUMING HE CREATED THE BOOK.
ANOTHER THING...
DO YOU REMEMBER THAT GIRL WHO SHOWED UP UNDER THE BRIDGE?

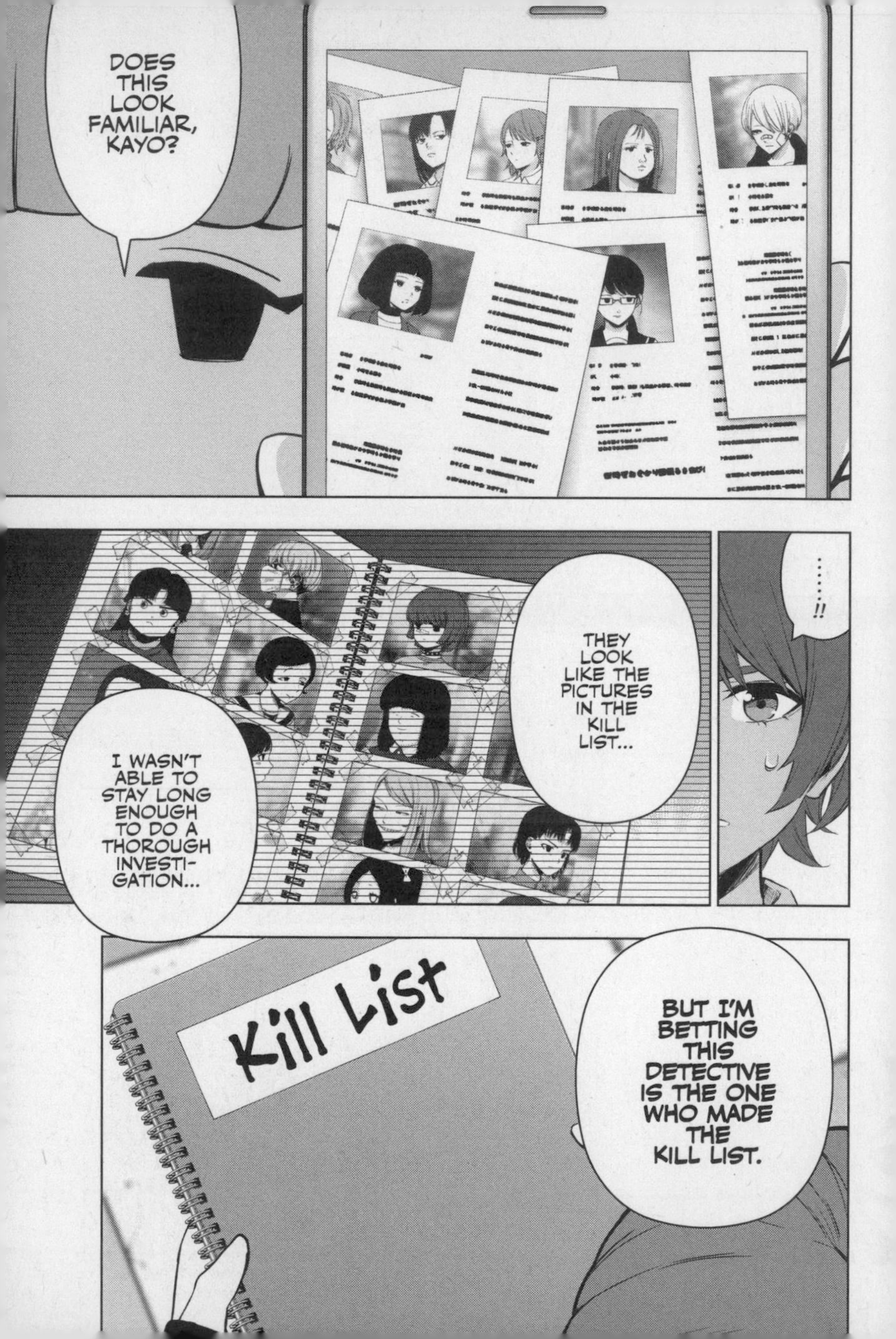
DOES THIS LOOK FAMILIAR, KAYO?
......!!
THEY LOOK LIKE THE PICTURES IN THE KILL LIST...
I WASN'T ABLE TO STAY LONG ENOUGH TO DO A THOROUGH INVESTIGATION...
BUT I'M BETTING THIS DETECTIVE IS THE ONE WHO MADE THE KILL LIST.
Kill List

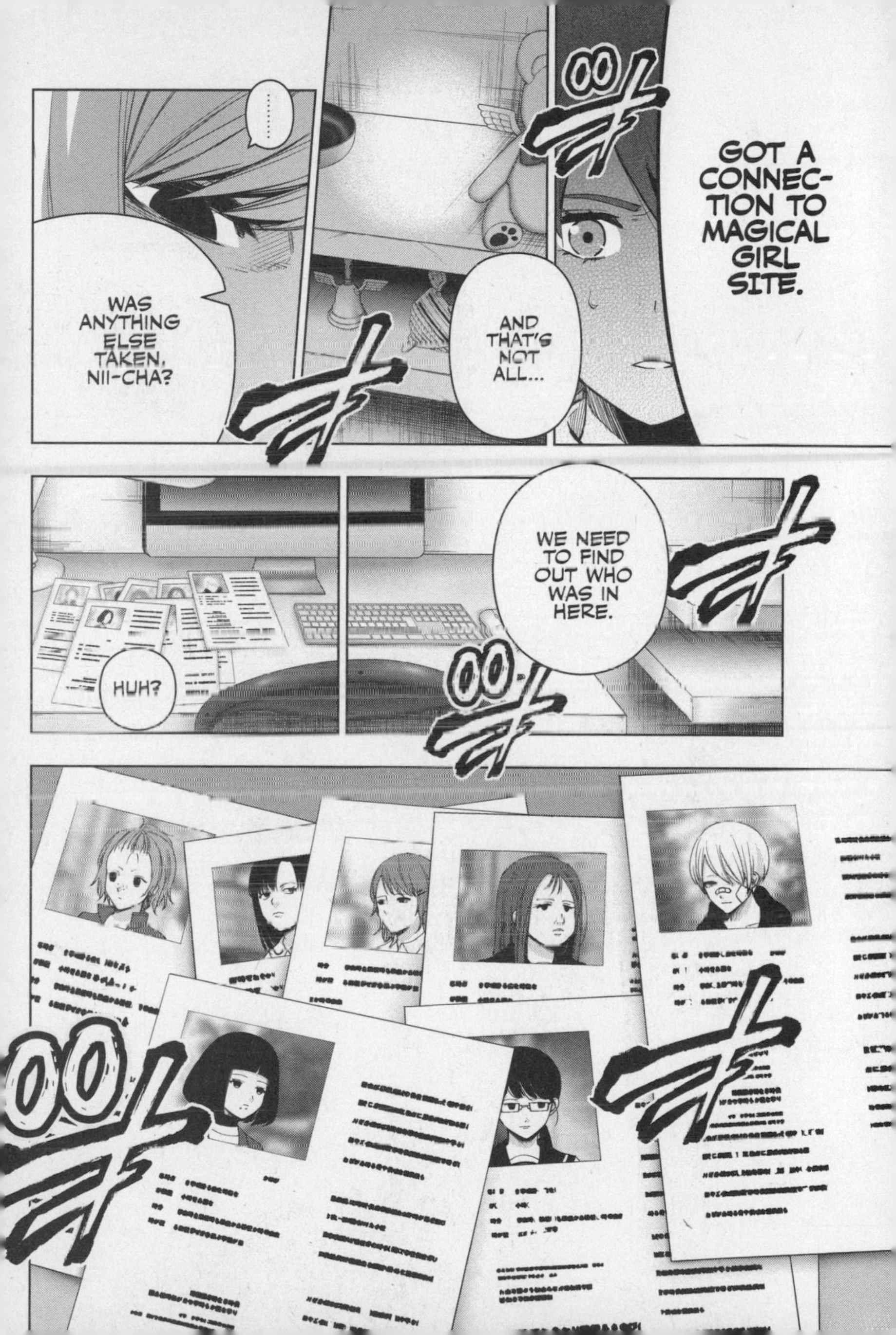
GOT A CONNECTION TO MAGICAL GIRL SITE.
AND THAT'S NOT ALL...
......
WAS ANYTHING ELSE TAKEN, NII-CHA?
WE NEED TO FIND OUT WHO WAS IN HERE.
HUH?

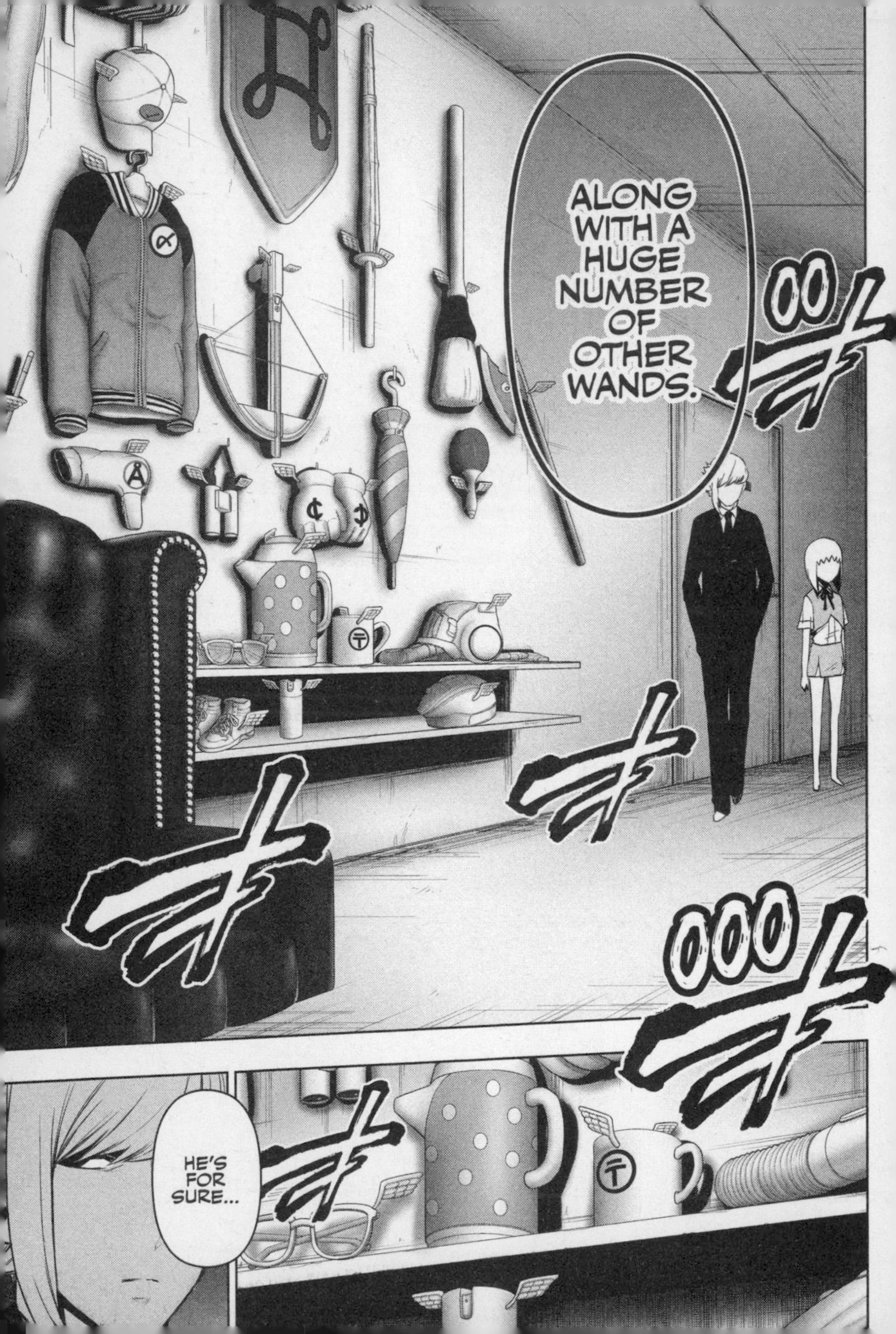
ALONG WITH A HUGE NUMBER OF OTHER WANDS.
OO
OOO
HE'S FOR SURE...

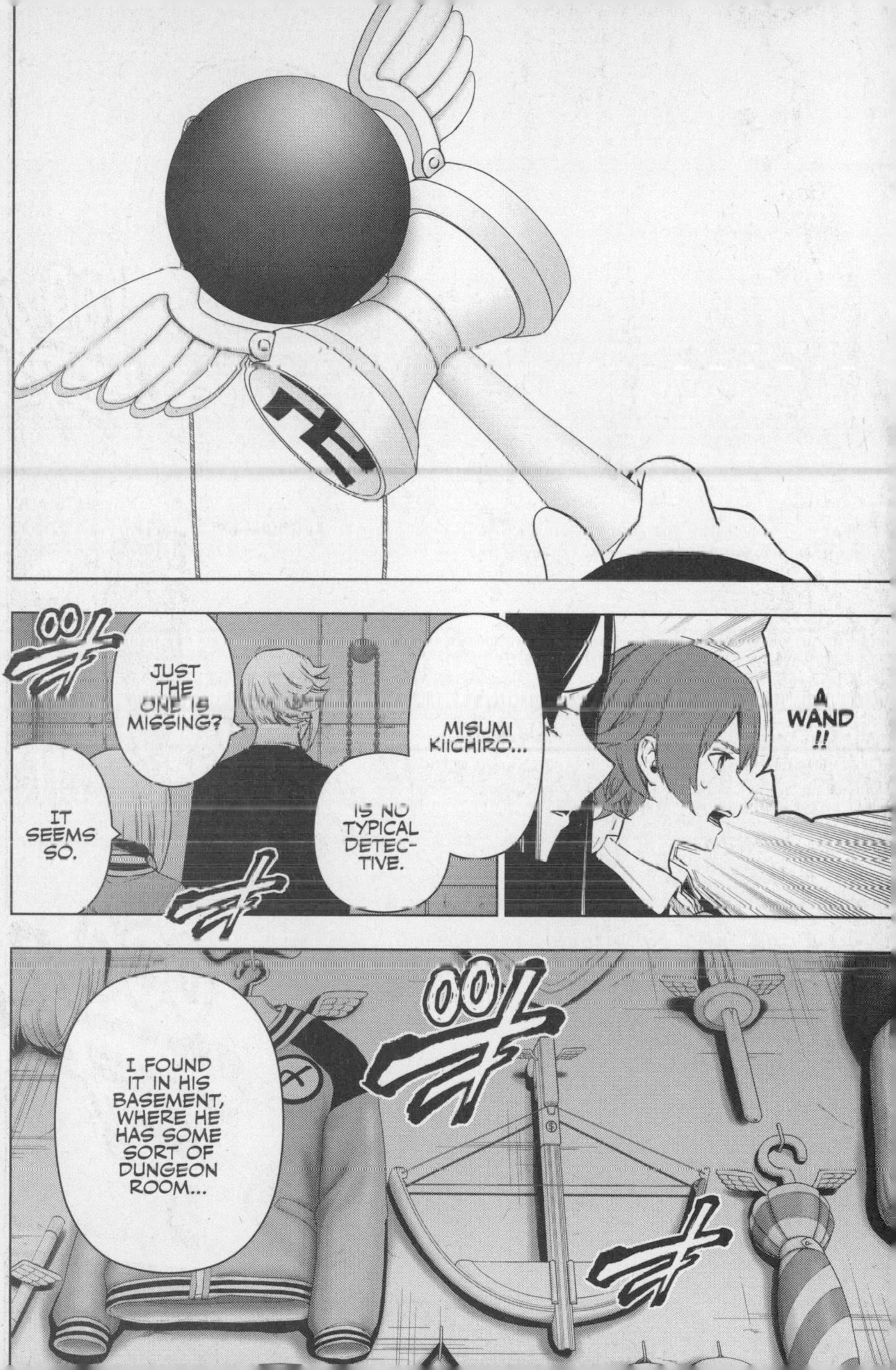
A WAND !!
MISUMI KIICHIRO...
IS NO TYPICAL DETECTIVE.
JUST THE ONE IS MISSING?
IT SEEMS SO.
I FOUND IT IN HIS BASEMENT, WHERE HE HAS SOME SORT OF DUNGEON ROOM...

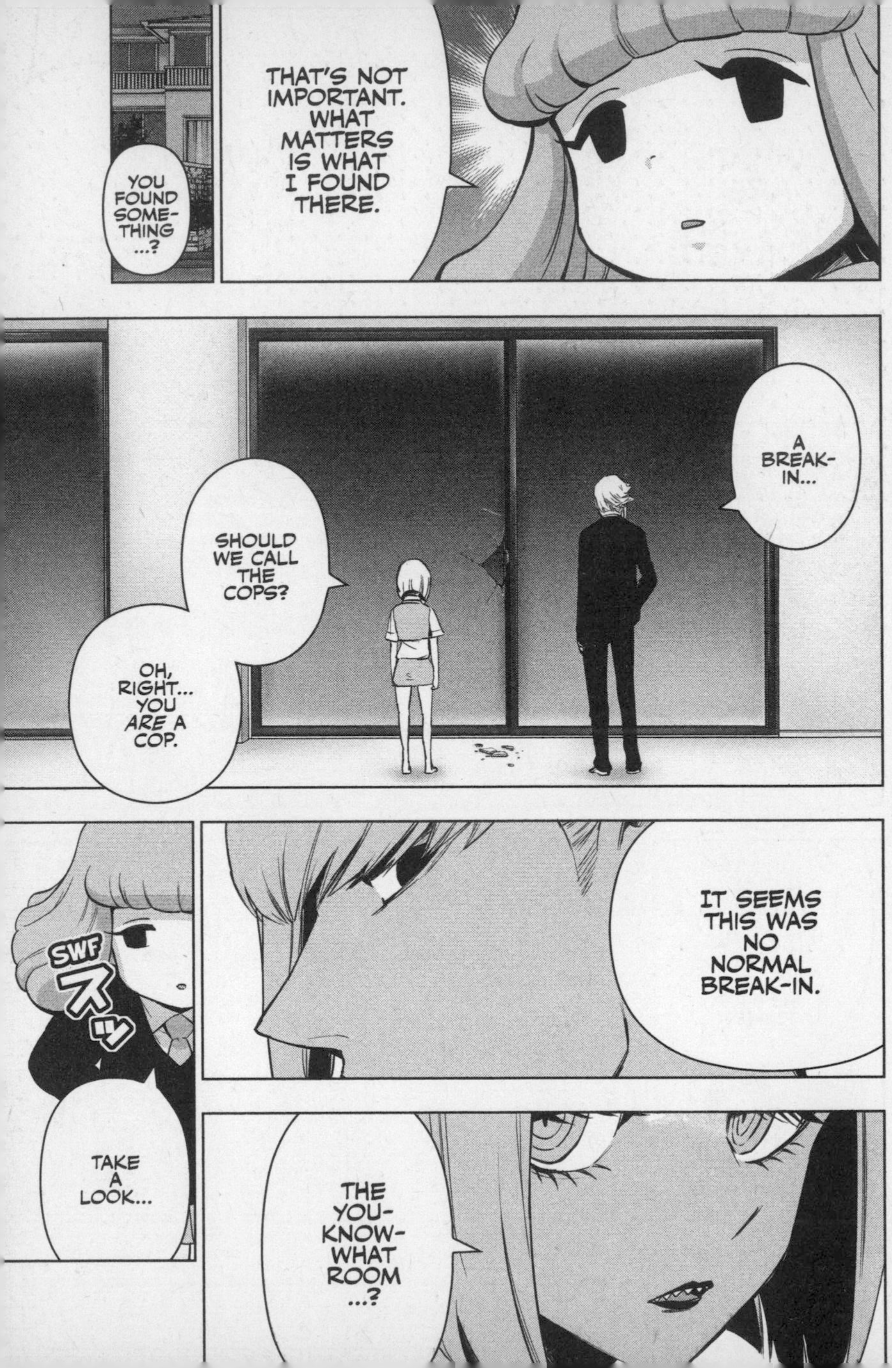
THAT'S NOT IMPORTANT. WHAT MATTERS IS WHAT I FOUND THERE.
YOU FOUND SOME-THING ...?
A BREAK-IN...
SHOULD WE CALL THE COPS?
OH, RIGHT... YOU *ARE* A COP.
IT SEEMS THIS WAS NO NORMAL BREAK-IN.
THE YOU-KNOW-WHAT ROOM ...?
SWF スッ
TAKE A LOOK...

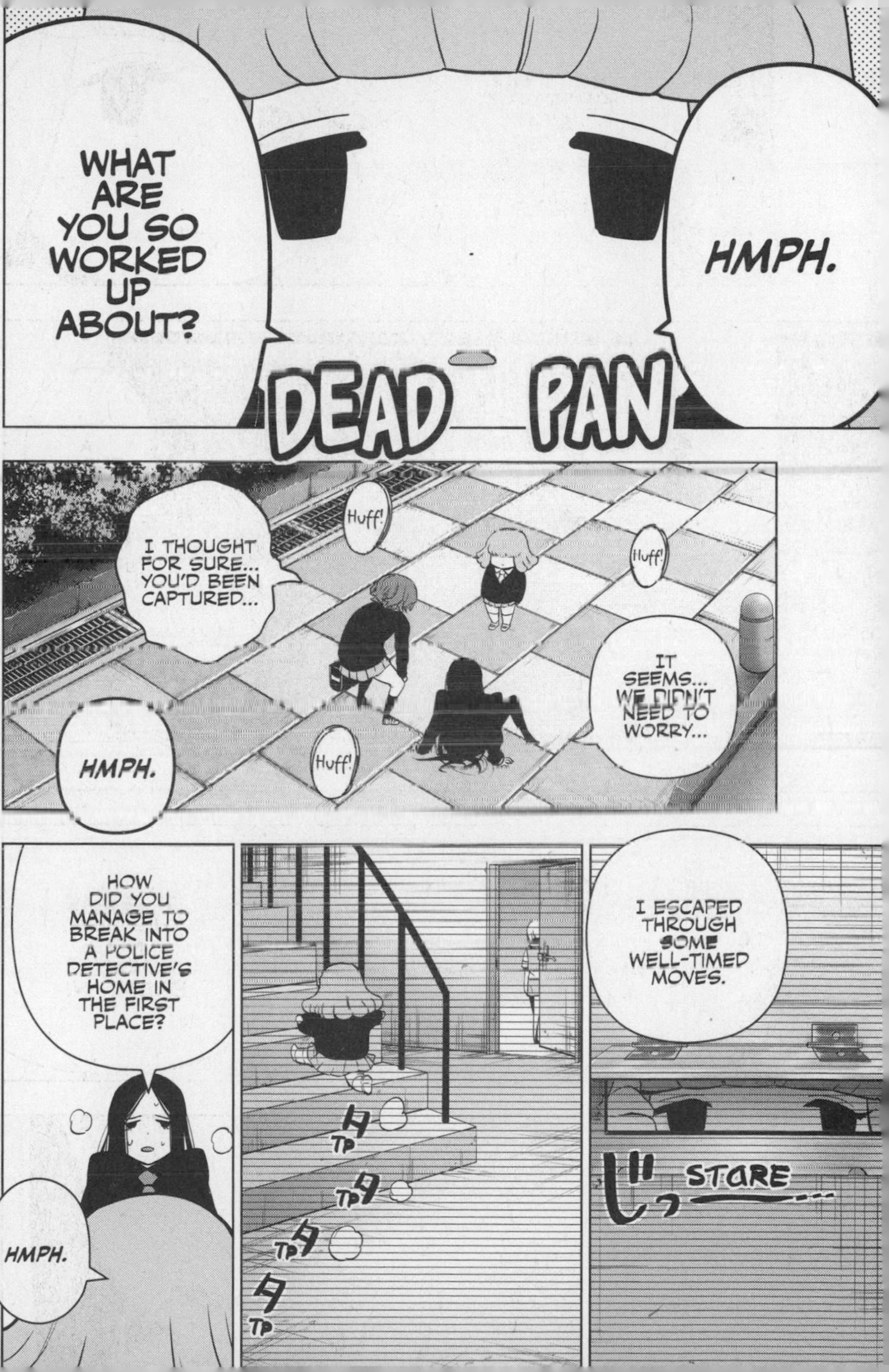
HMPH.
WHAT ARE YOU SO WORKED UP ABOUT?
DEAD PAN
Huff!
Huff!
I THOUGHT FOR SURE... YOU'D BEEN CAPTURED...
IT SEEMS... WE DIDN'T NEED TO WORRY...
HMPH.
Huff!
I ESCAPED THROUGH SOME WELL-TIMED MOVES.
じっ STARE
タ TP
タ TP
タ TP
タ TP
HOW DID YOU MANAGE TO BREAK INTO A POLICE DETECTIVE'S HOME IN THE FIRST PLACE?
HMPH.

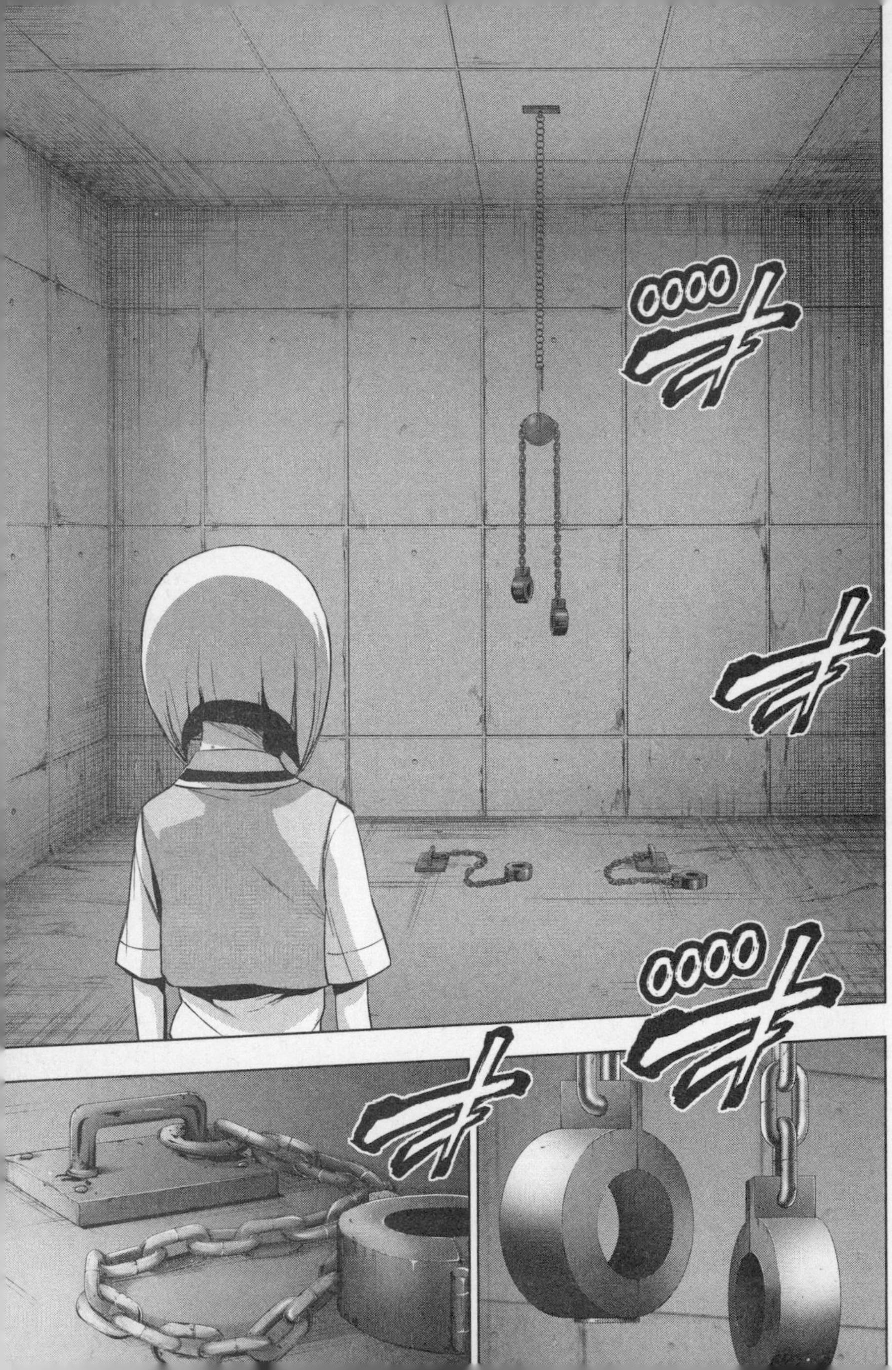

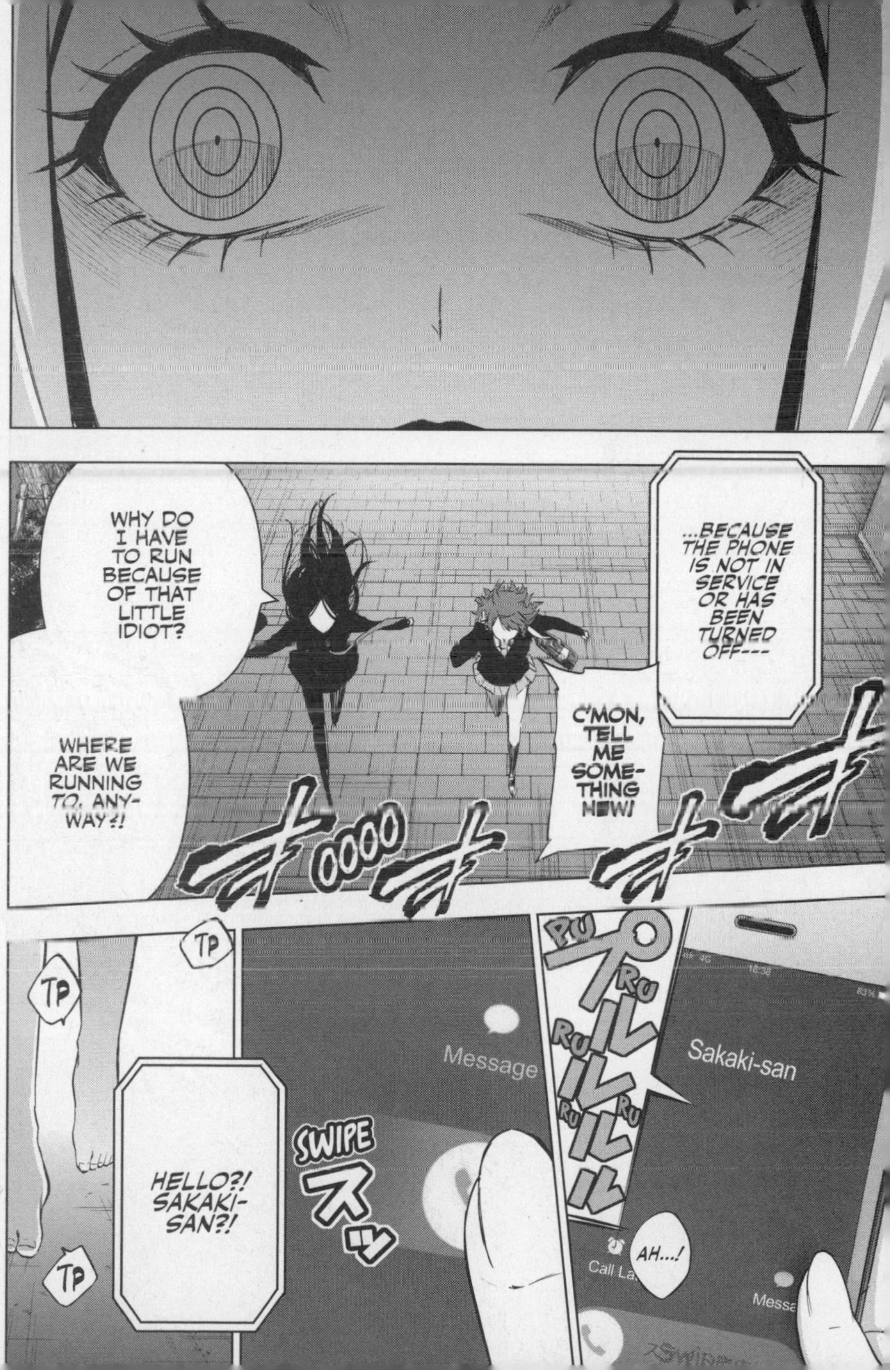
...BECAUSE THE PHONE IS NOT IN SERVICE OR HAS BEEN TURNED OFF---
C'MON, TELL ME SOME-THING NEW!
WHY DO I HAVE TO RUN BECAUSE OF THAT LITTLE IDIOT?
WHERE ARE WE RUNNING TO, ANY-WAY?!
OOOO
PU RU RU RU RU
Sakaki-san
Message
AH...!
SWIPE
HELLO?! SAKAKI-SAN?!
Tp
Tp
Tp

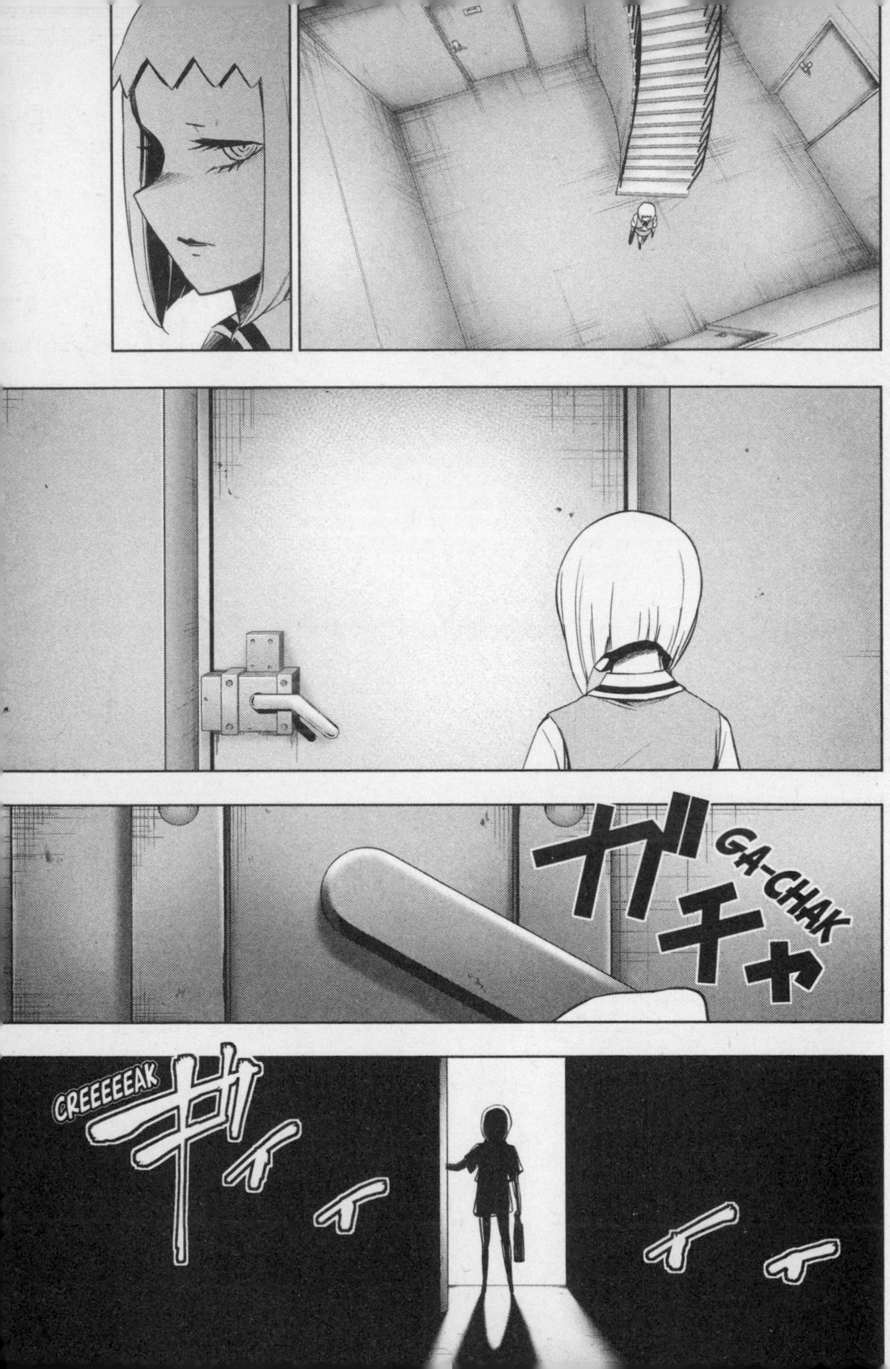
ガチャ
GA-CHAK
ギイイイイ
CREEEEEAK

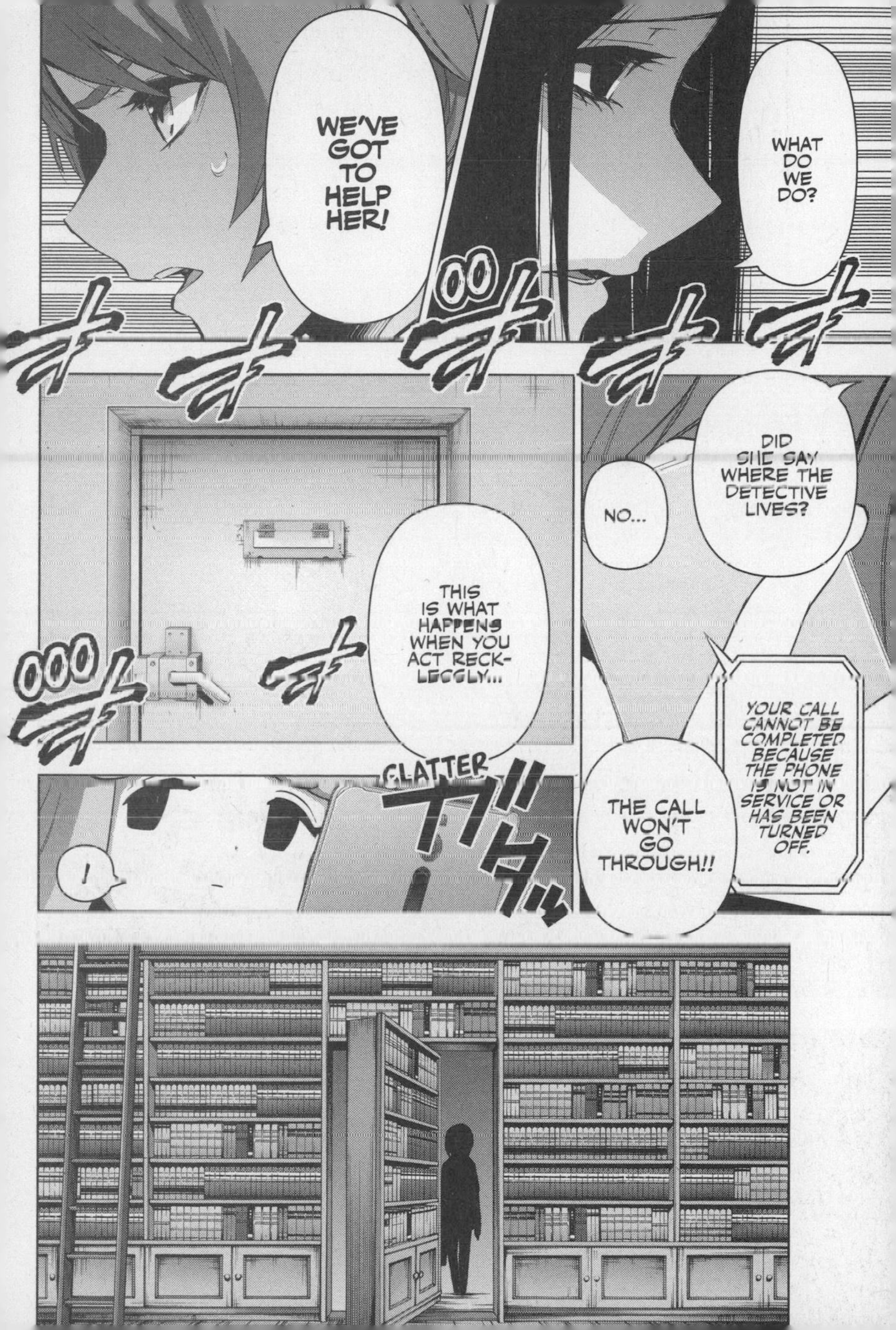
WHAT DO WE DO?
WE'VE GOT TO HELP HER!
DID SHE SAY WHERE THE DETECTIVE LIVES?
NO...
YOUR CALL CANNOT BE COMPLETED BECAUSE THE PHONE IS NOT IN SERVICE OR HAS BEEN TURNED OFF.
THE CALL WON'T GO THROUGH!!
THIS IS WHAT HAPPENS WHEN YOU ACT RECK-LESSLY...
CLATTER
!

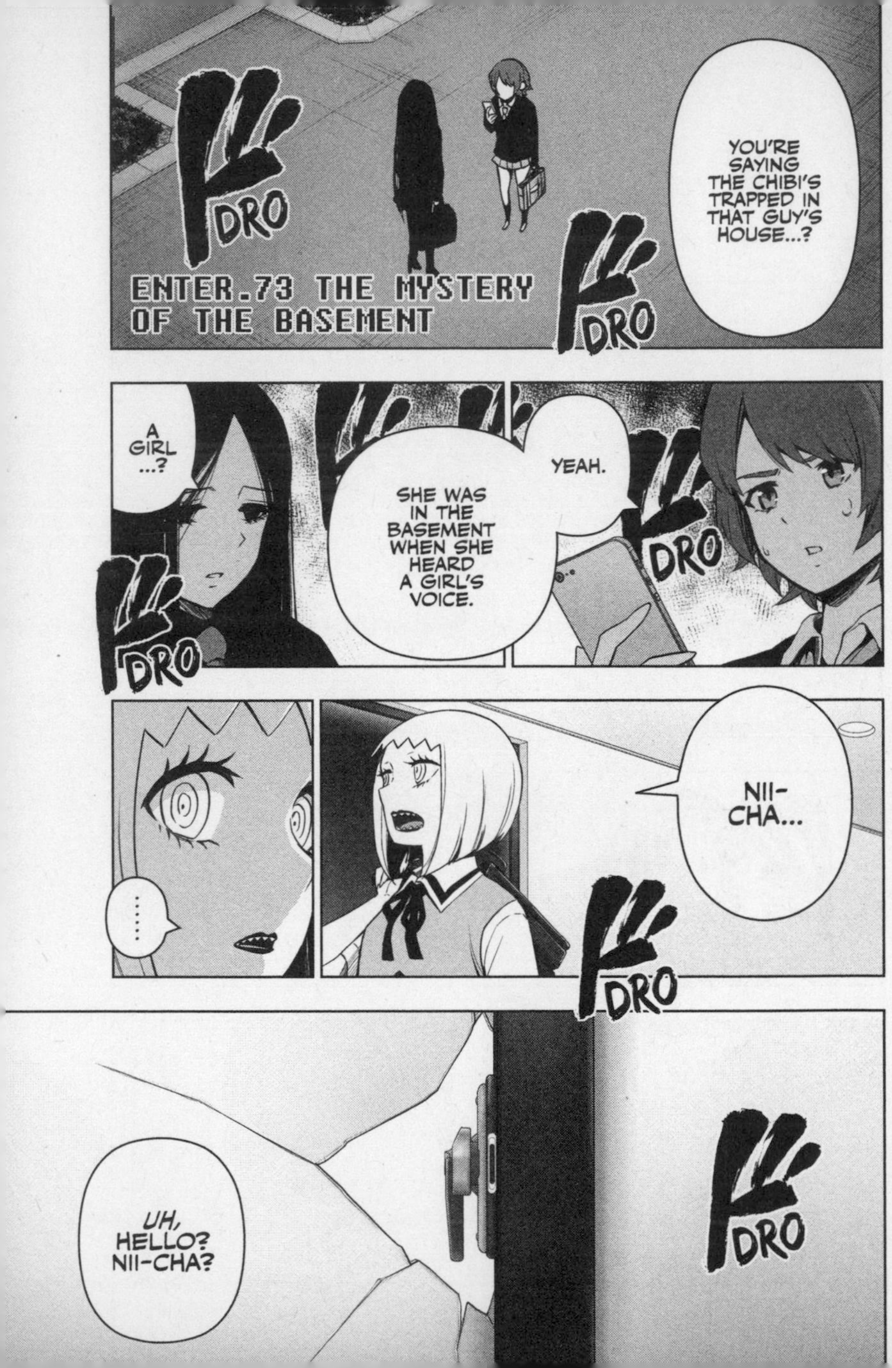
YOU'RE SAYING THE CHIBI'S TRAPPED IN THAT GUY'S HOUSE...?
DRO
DRO
ENTER.73 THE MYSTERY OF THE BASEMENT
YEAH.
SHE WAS IN THE BASEMENT WHEN SHE HEARD A GIRL'S VOICE.
DRO
A GIRL ...?
DRO
NII-CHA...
DRO
......
DRO
UH, HELLO? NII-CHA?

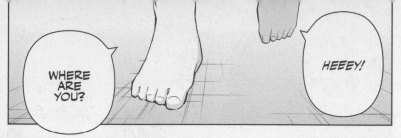

WHERE ARE YOU?

HEEEY!

I KNOW YOU'RE HOME!

ONIICHA...

DRO

NOT GOOD...

NO SERVICE

DRO

DRO

DRO

SAKAKI-SAN IS...

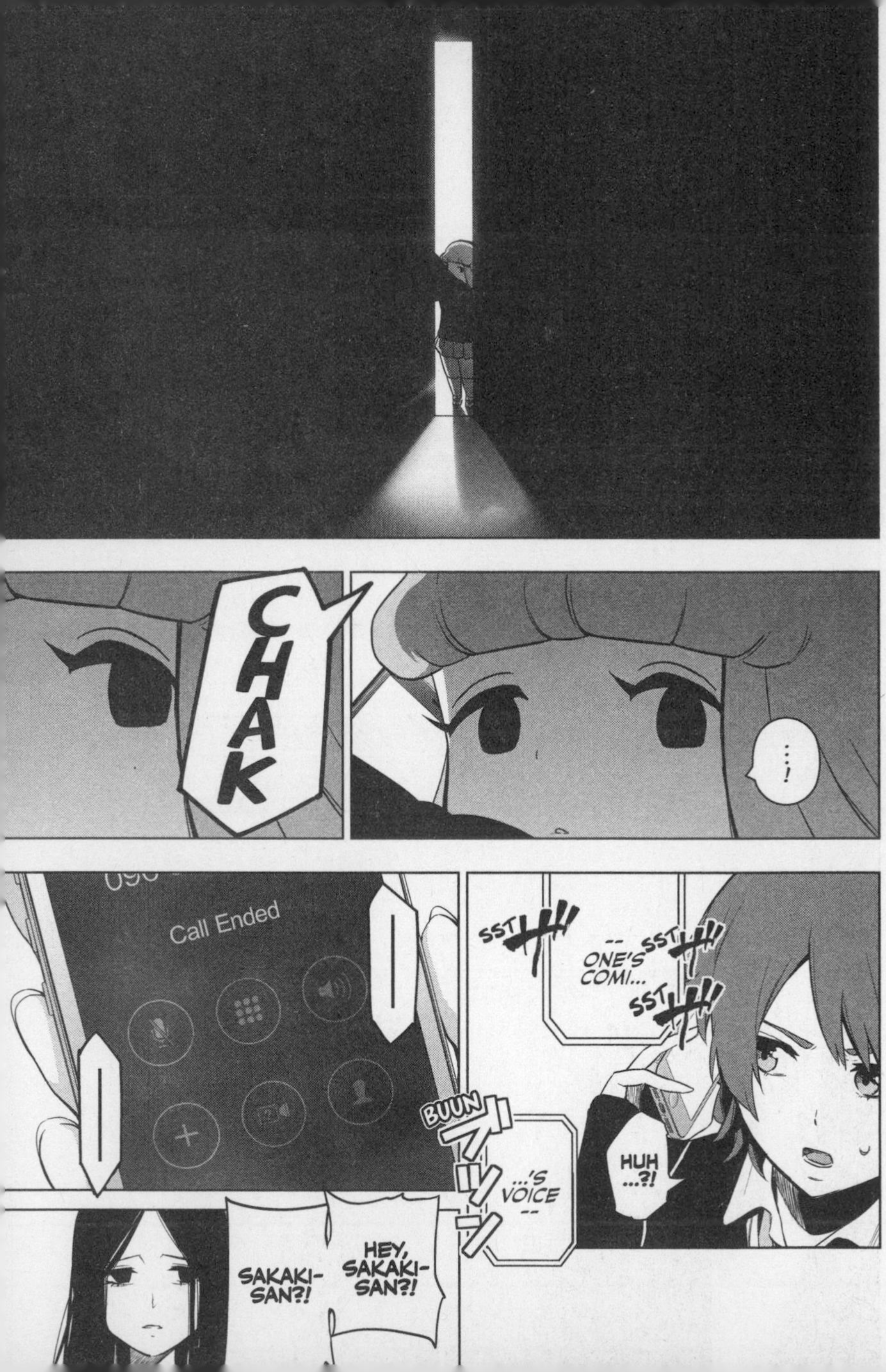

...!
CHAK
SST
-- ONE'S COMI...
SST
SST
HUH ...?!
...'S VOICE --
BUUN
Call Ended
HEY, SAKAKI-SAN?!
SAKAKI-SAN?!

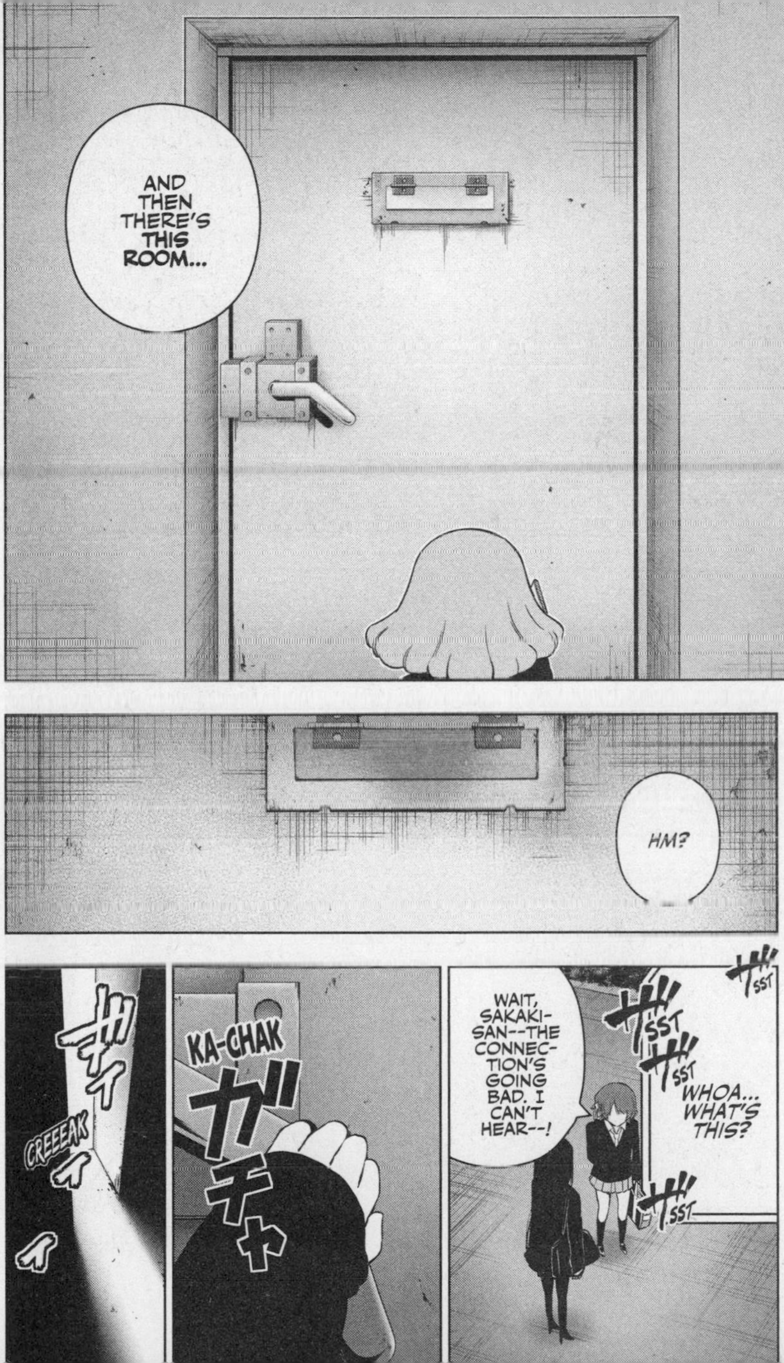
AND THEN THERE'S THIS ROOM...
HM?
ザッ SST
WAIT, SAKAKI-SAN--THE CONNECTION'S GOING BAD. I CAN'T HEAR--!
ザッ SST
ザッ SST
WHOA... WHAT'S THIS?
ザッ SST
KA-CHAK
ガチャ
ギィイイ
CREEEEAK

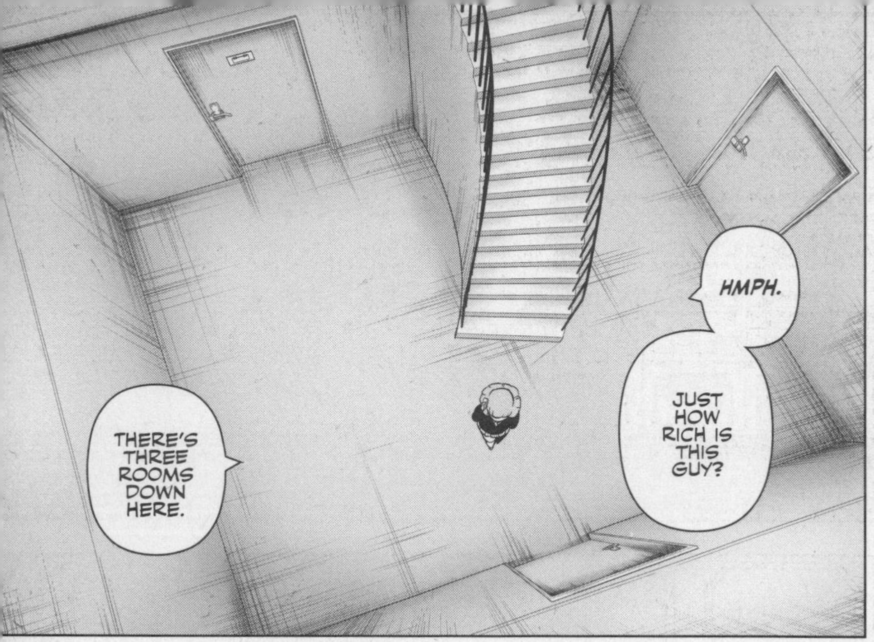
HMPH.
JUST HOW RICH IS THIS GUY?
THERE'S THREE ROOMS DOWN HERE.
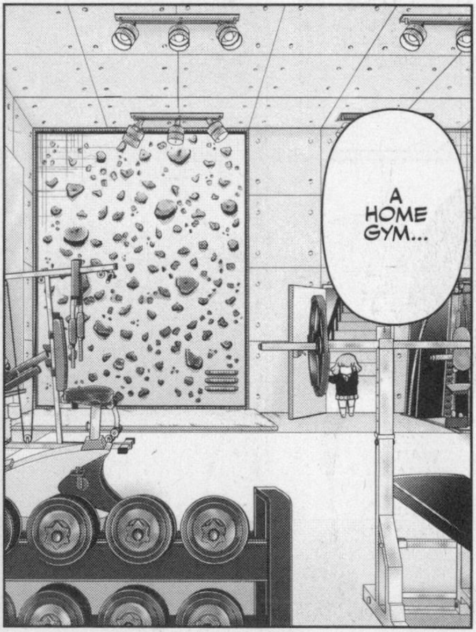
A HOME GYM...
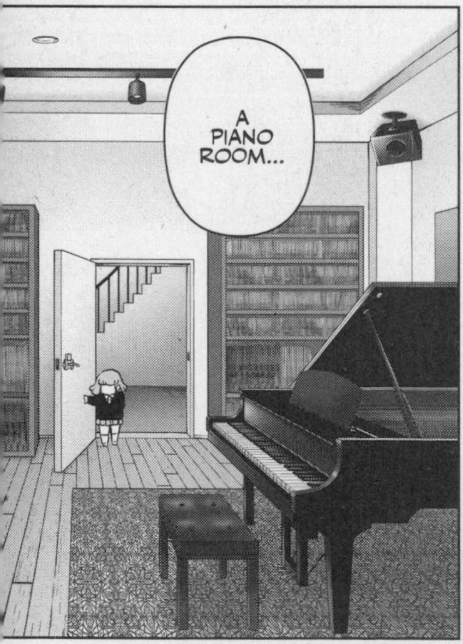
A PIANO ROOM...

A HIDDEN DOOR.

IT LEADS TO A BASE-MENT...

HEY, WAIT... SAKAKI-SAN, WHAT ARE YOU DOING?

PEER

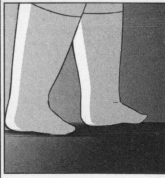

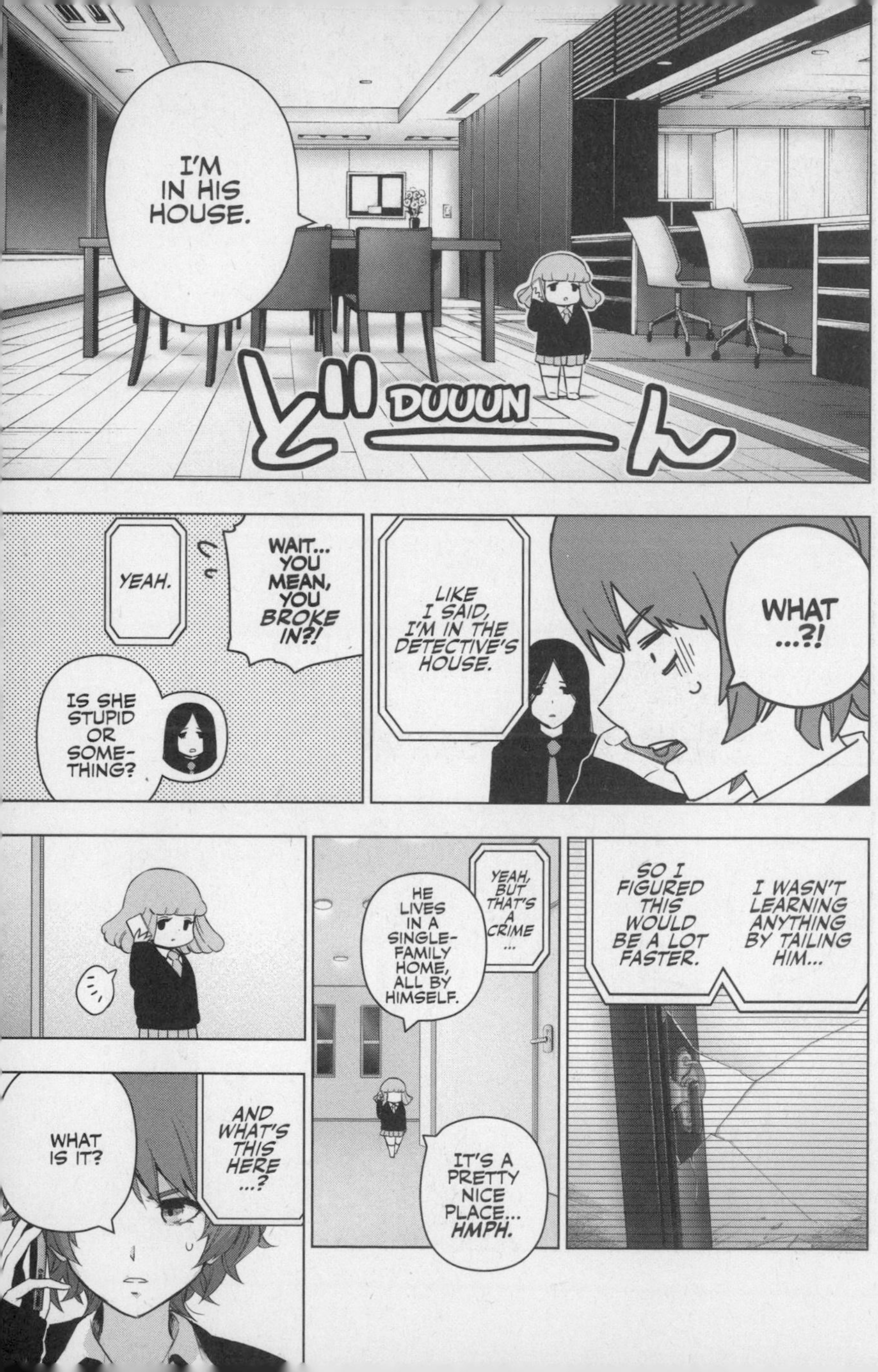
I'M IN HIS HOUSE.
DUUUN
WHAT ...?!
LIKE I SAID, I'M IN THE DETECTIVE'S HOUSE.
WAIT... YOU MEAN, YOU BROKE IN?!
YEAH.
IS SHE STUPID OR SOME-THING?
I WASN'T LEARNING ANYTHING BY TAILING HIM...
SO I FIGURED THIS WOULD BE A LOT FASTER.
YEAH, BUT THAT'S A CRIME ...
HE LIVES IN A SINGLE-FAMILY HOME, ALL BY HIMSELF.
IT'S A PRETTY NICE PLACE... HMPH.
AND WHAT'S THIS HERE ...?
WHAT IS IT?

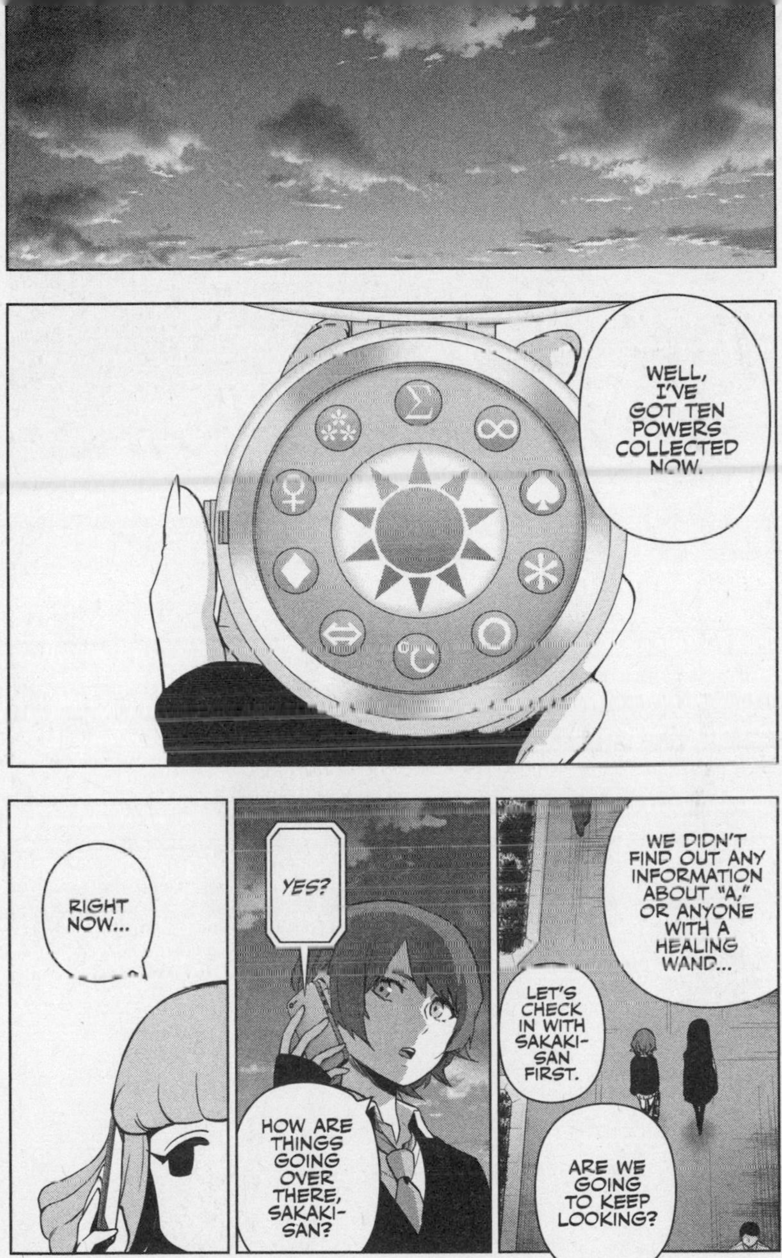
WELL, I'VE GOT TEN POWERS COLLECTED NOW.
WE DIDN'T FIND OUT ANY INFORMATION ABOUT "A," OR ANYONE WITH A HEALING WAND...
LET'S CHECK IN WITH SAKAKI-SAN FIRST.
ARE WE GOING TO KEEP LOOKING?
YES?
HOW ARE THINGS GOING OVER THERE, SAKAKI-SAN?
RIGHT NOW...

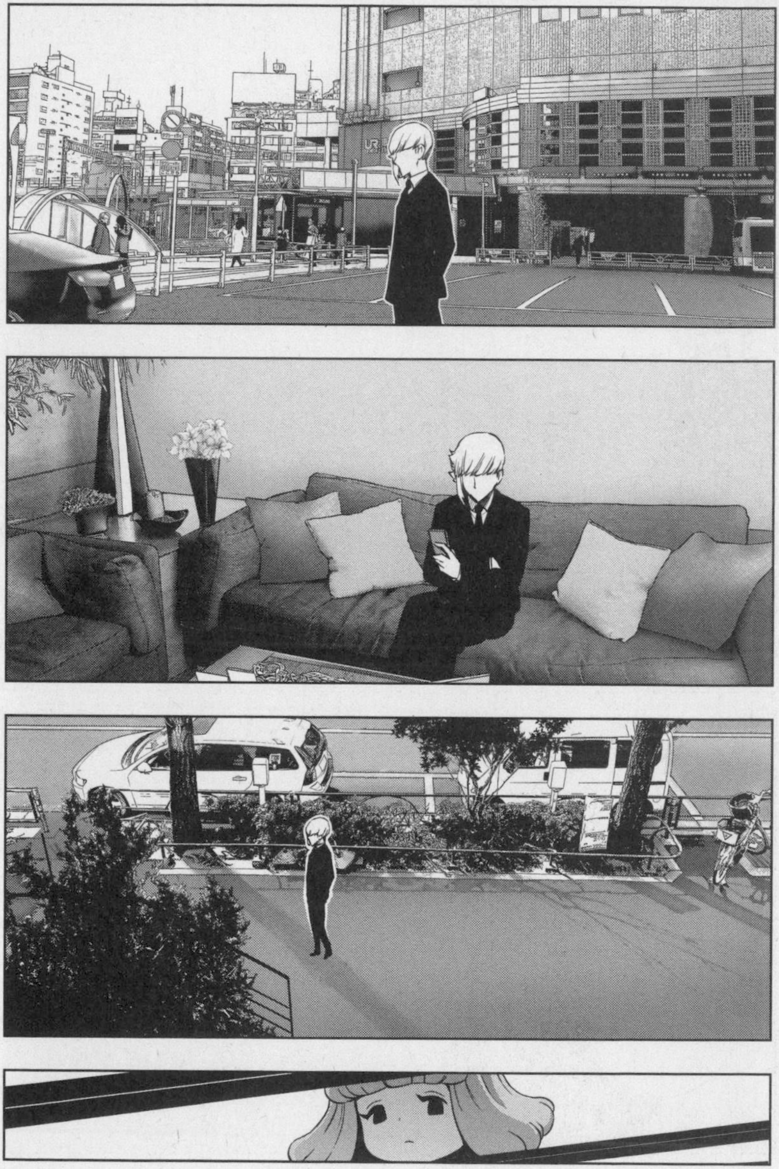

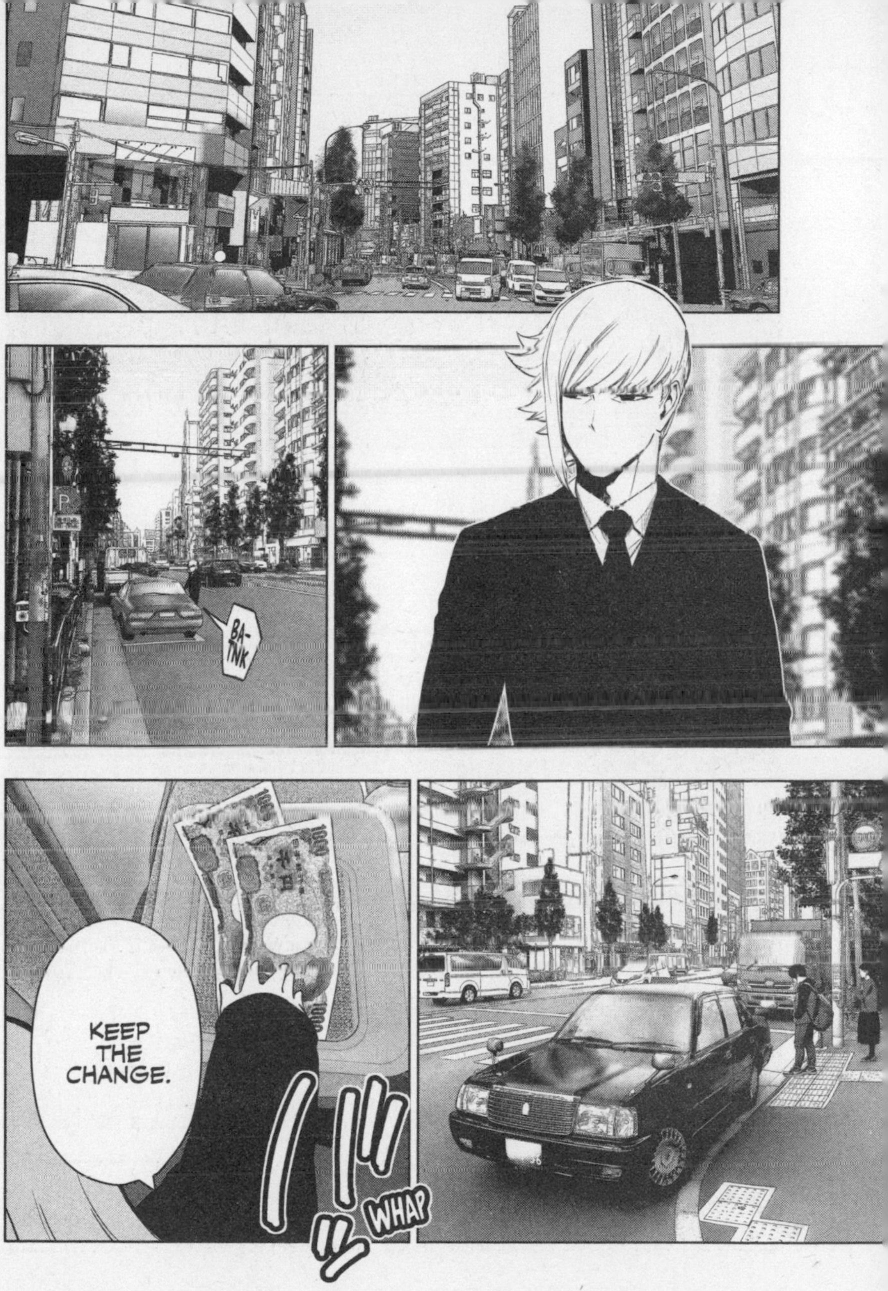
BA-TNK
KEEP THE CHANGE.
WHAP

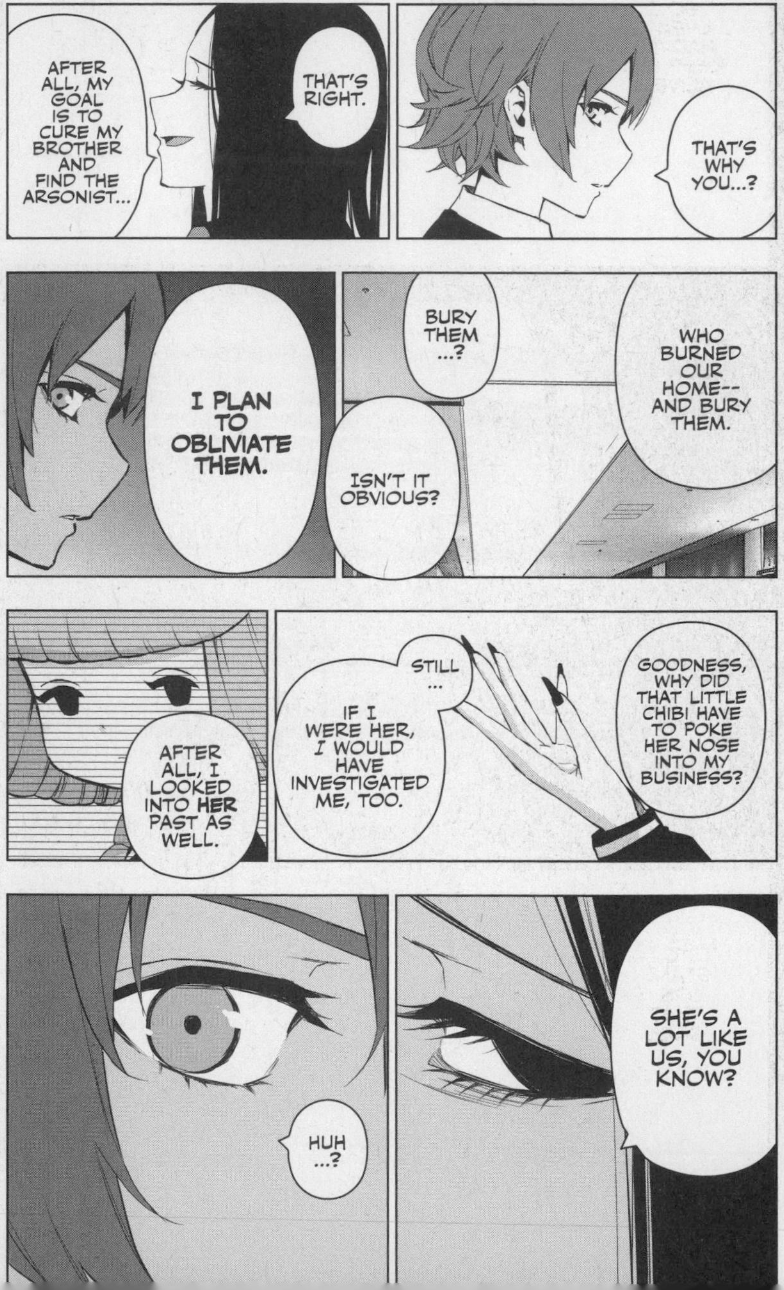
THAT'S WHY YOU...?
THAT'S RIGHT.
AFTER ALL, MY GOAL IS TO CURE MY BROTHER AND FIND THE ARSONIST...
WHO BURNED OUR HOME-- AND BURY THEM.
BURY THEM ...?
ISN'T IT OBVIOUS?
I PLAN TO OBLIVIATE THEM.
GOODNESS, WHY DID THAT LITTLE CHIBI HAVE TO POKE HER NOSE INTO MY BUSINESS?
STILL ...
IF I WERE HER, *I* WOULD HAVE INVESTIGATED ME, TOO.
AFTER ALL, I LOOKED INTO **HER** PAST AS WELL.
SHE'S A LOT LIKE US, YOU KNOW?
HUH ...?

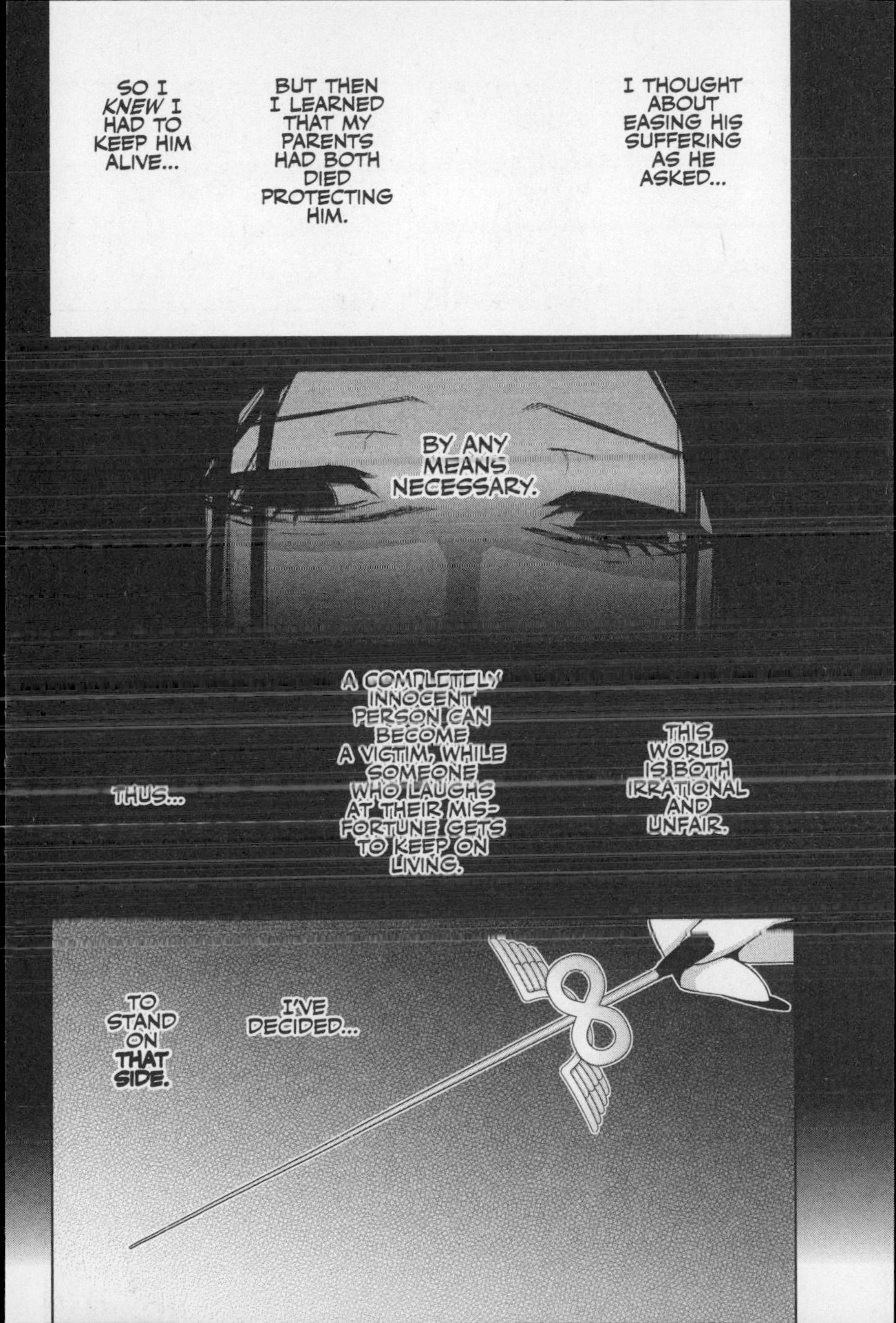
I THOUGHT ABOUT EASING HIS SUFFERING AS HE ASKED...
BUT THEN I LEARNED THAT MY PARENTS HAD BOTH DIED PROTECTING HIM.
SO I *KNEW* I HAD TO KEEP HIM ALIVE...
BY ANY MEANS NECESSARY.
THIS WORLD IS BOTH IRRATIONAL AND UNFAIR.
A COMPLETELY INNOCENT PERSON CAN BECOME A VICTIM, WHILE SOMEONE WHO LAUGHS AT THEIR MIS-FORTUNE GETS TO KEEP ON LIVING.
THUS...
I'VE DECIDED...
TO STAND ON **THAT** SIDE.

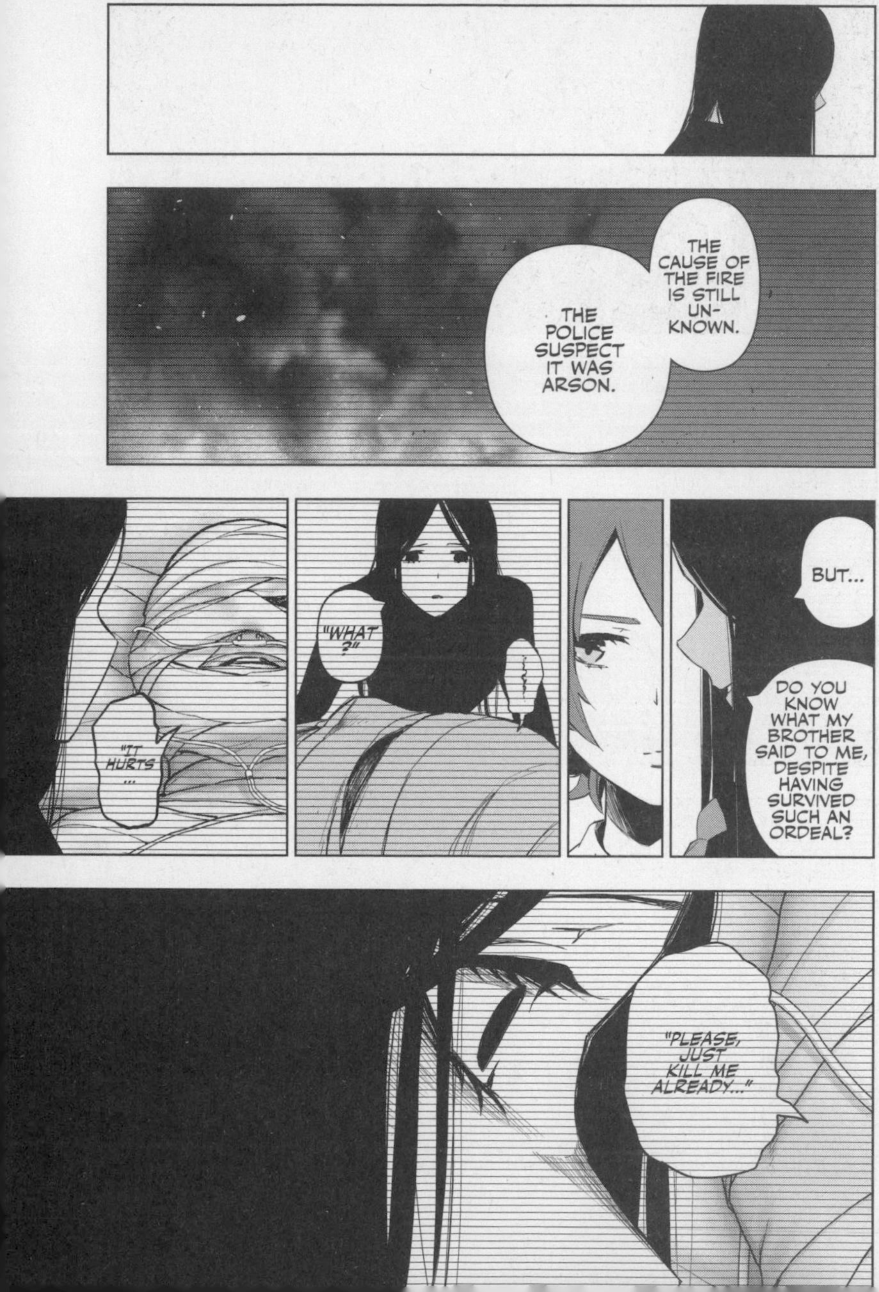
THE CAUSE OF THE FIRE IS STILL UN-KNOWN.
THE POLICE SUSPECT IT WAS ARSON.
BUT...
DO YOU KNOW WHAT MY BROTHER SAID TO ME, DESPITE HAVING SURVIVED SUCH AN ORDEAL?
"WHAT?"
"IT HURTS..."
"PLEASE, JUST KILL ME ALREADY..."

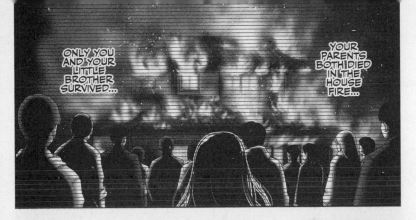

YOUR PARENTS BOTH DIED IN THE HOUSE FIRE...
ONLY YOU AND YOUR LITTLE BROTHER SURVIVED...
BUT HE WAS COVERED IN SEVERE BURNS.
NO MATTER HOW MUCH TIME PASSES, THE WOUNDS JUST DON'T SEEM TO HEAL...
TO THIS DAY, HE'S STILL IN THE ICU...

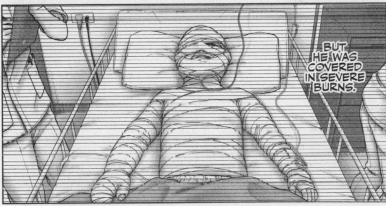

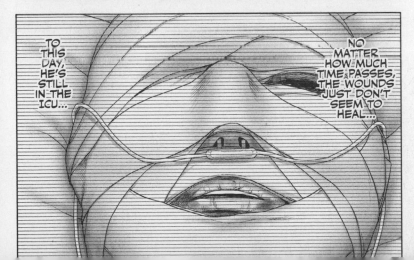

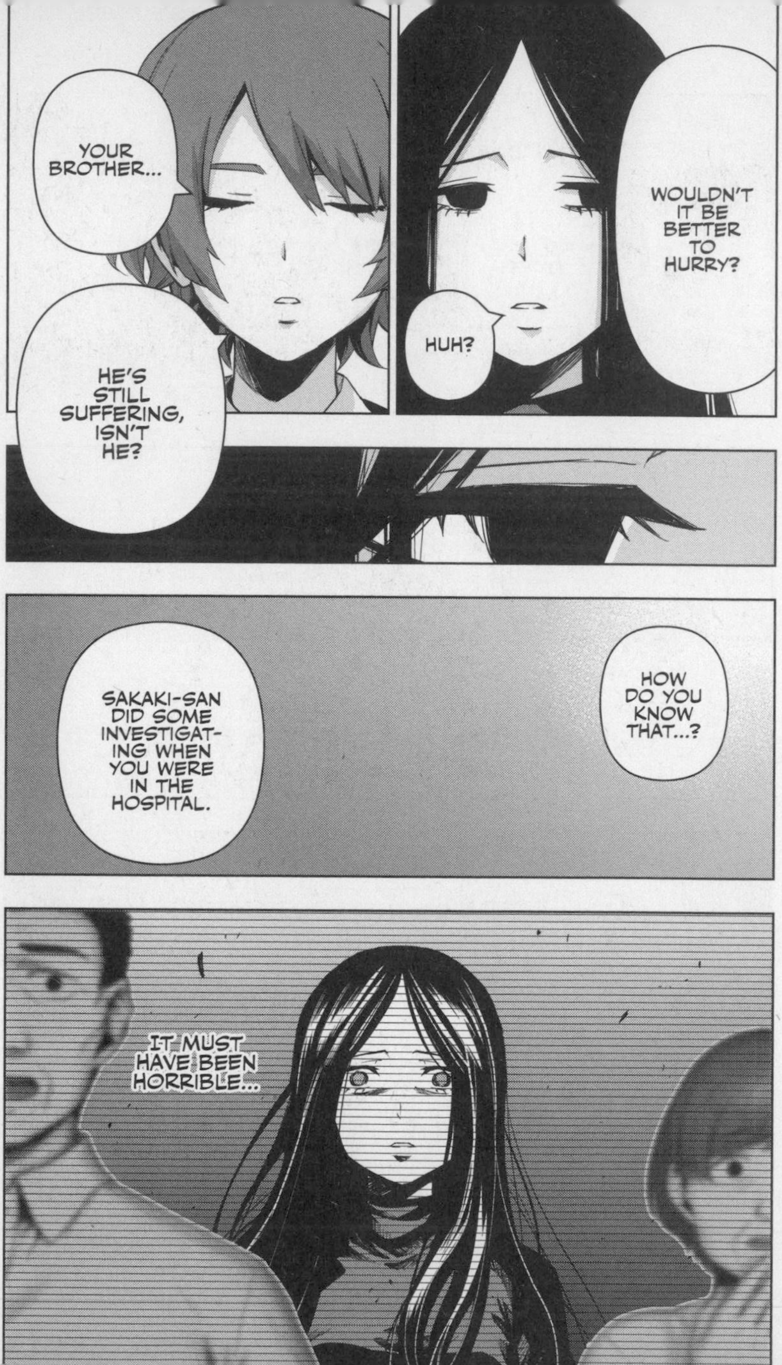
WOULDN'T IT BE BETTER TO HURRY?
HUH?
YOUR BROTHER...
HE'S STILL SUFFERING, ISN'T HE?
HOW DO YOU KNOW THAT...?
SAKAKI-SAN DID SOME INVESTIGAT-ING WHEN YOU WERE IN THE HOSPITAL.
IT MUST HAVE BEEN HORRIBLE...

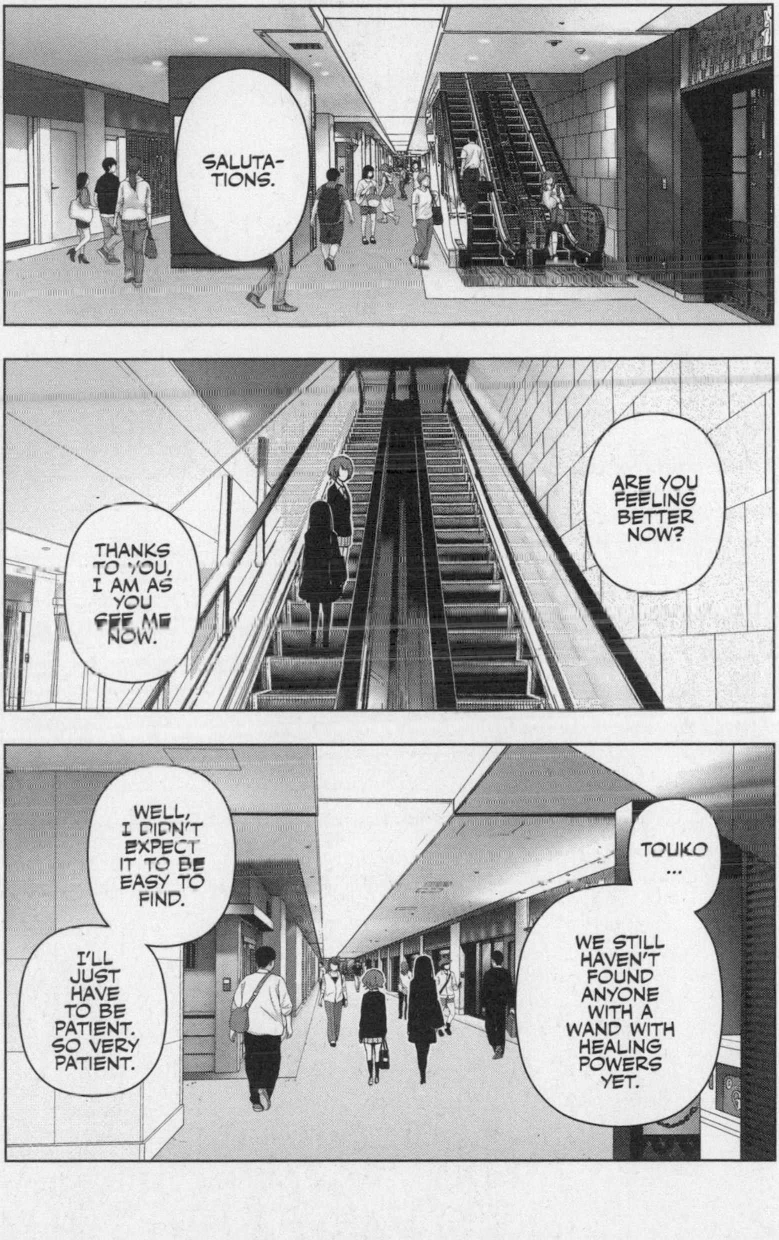
SALUTATIONS.
ARE YOU FEELING BETTER NOW?
THANKS TO YOU, I AM AS YOU SEE ME NOW.
TOUKO...
WE STILL HAVEN'T FOUND ANYONE WITH A WAND WITH HEALING POWERS YET.
WELL, I DIDN'T EXPECT IT TO BE EASY TO FIND.
I'LL JUST HAVE TO BE PATIENT. SO VERY PATIENT.

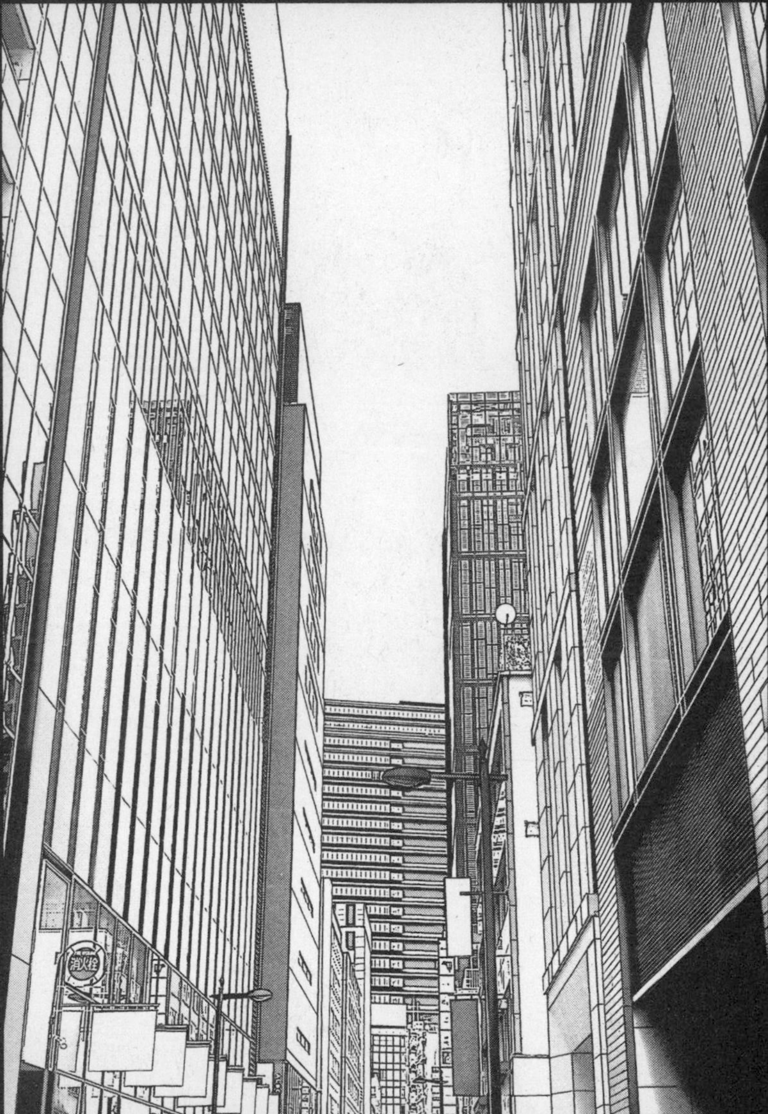
消火栓

ENTER.72 DETECTIVES AND INVESTIGATORS

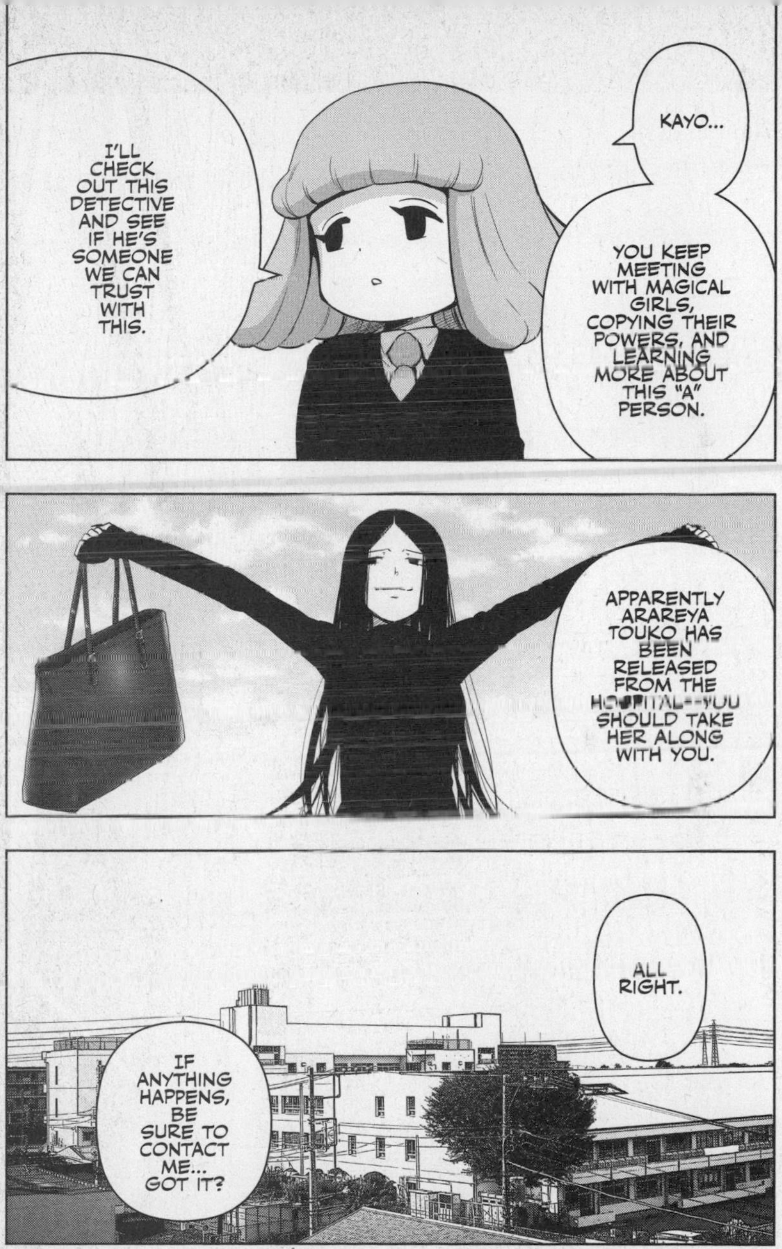
KAYO...
YOU KEEP MEETING WITH MAGICAL GIRLS, COPYING THEIR POWERS, AND LEARNING MORE ABOUT THIS "A" PERSON.
I'LL CHECK OUT THIS DETECTIVE AND SEE IF HE'S SOMEONE WE CAN TRUST WITH THIS.
APPARENTLY ARAREYA TOUKO HAS BEEN RELEASED FROM THE HOSPITAL--YOU SHOULD TAKE HER ALONG WITH YOU.
ALL RIGHT.
IF ANYTHING HAPPENS, BE SURE TO CONTACT ME... GOT IT?

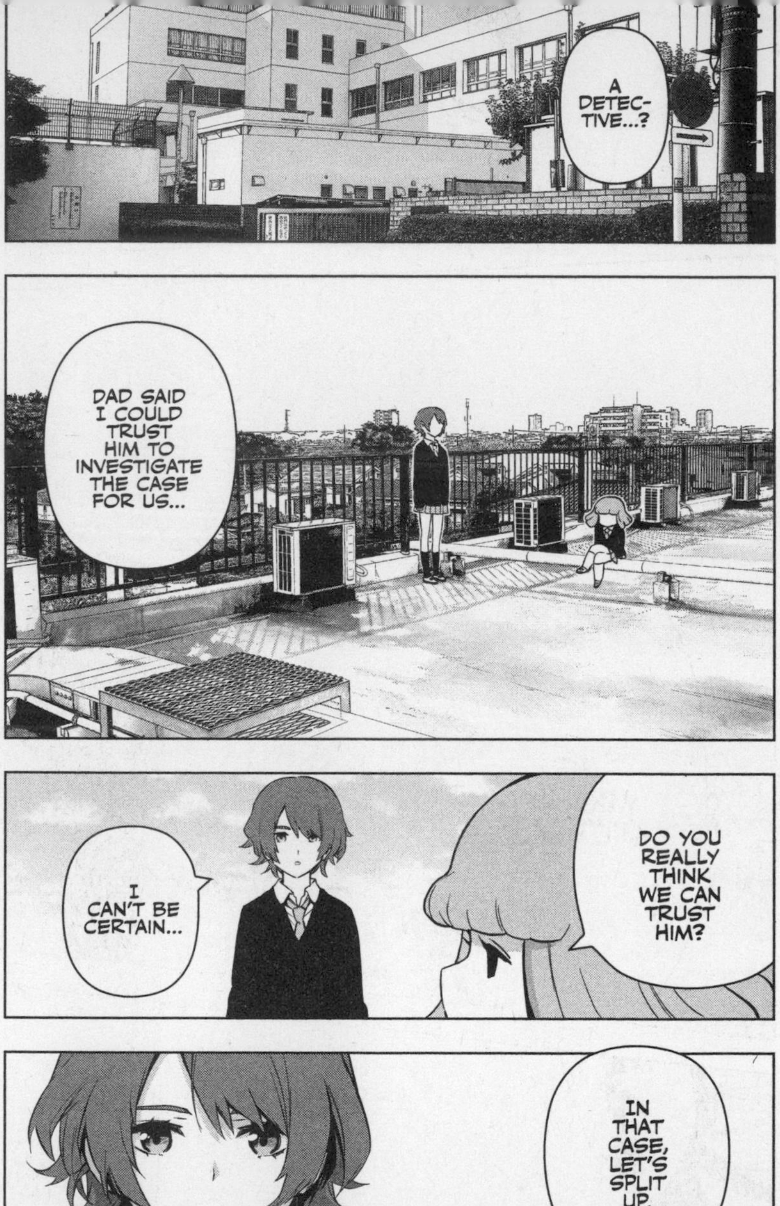
A DETECTIVE...?
DAD SAID I COULD TRUST HIM TO INVESTIGATE THE CASE FOR US...
DO YOU REALLY THINK WE CAN TRUST HIM?
I CAN'T BE CERTAIN...
IN THAT CASE, LET'S SPLIT UP.

ENTER.72 DETECTIVES AND INVESTIGATORS

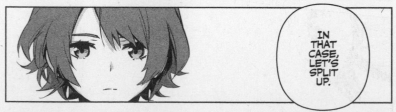

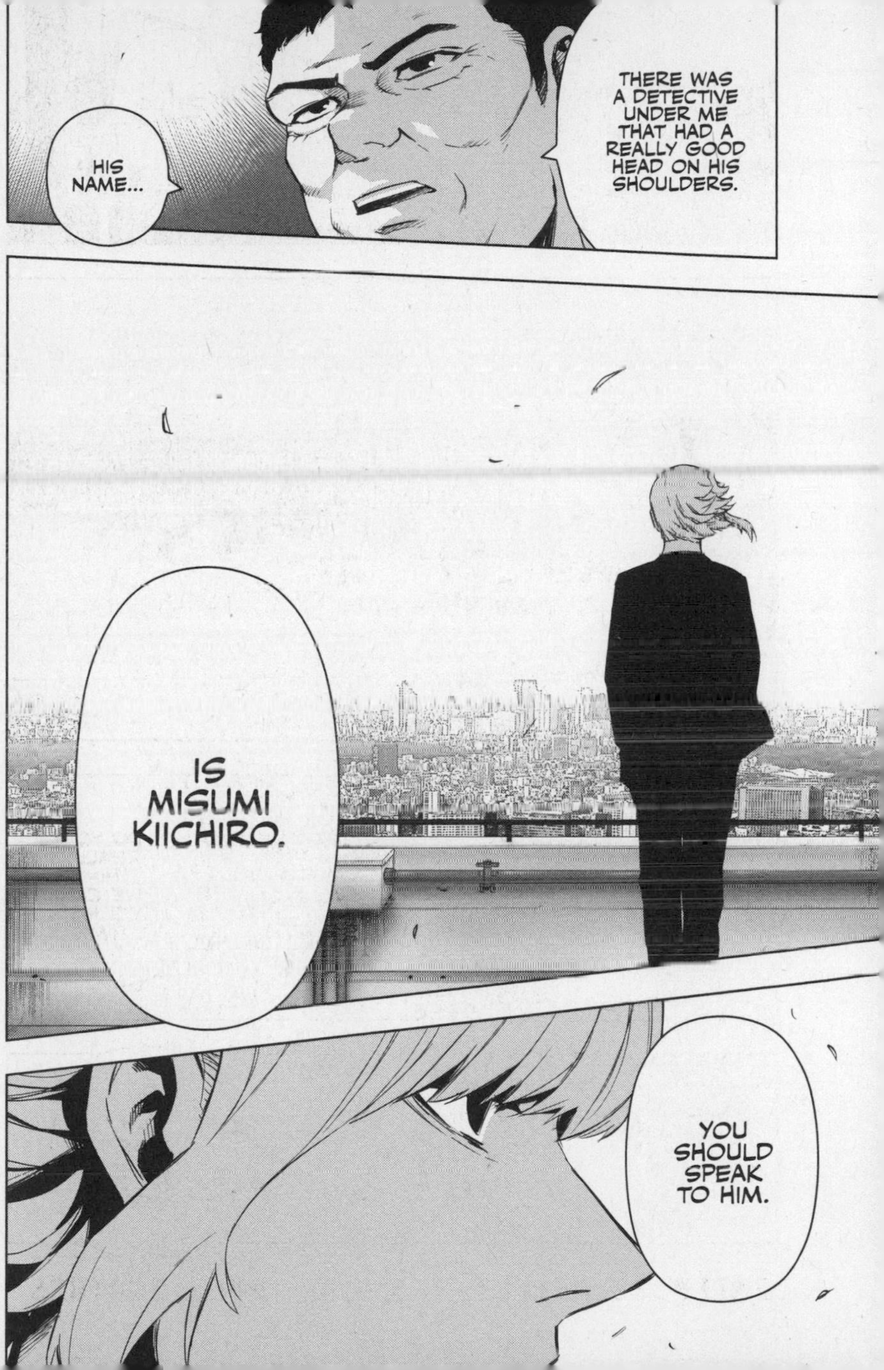
THERE WAS A DETECTIVE UNDER ME THAT HAD A REALLY GOOD HEAD ON HIS SHOULDERS.
HIS NAME...
IS MISUMI KIICHIRO.
YOU SHOULD SPEAK TO HIM.

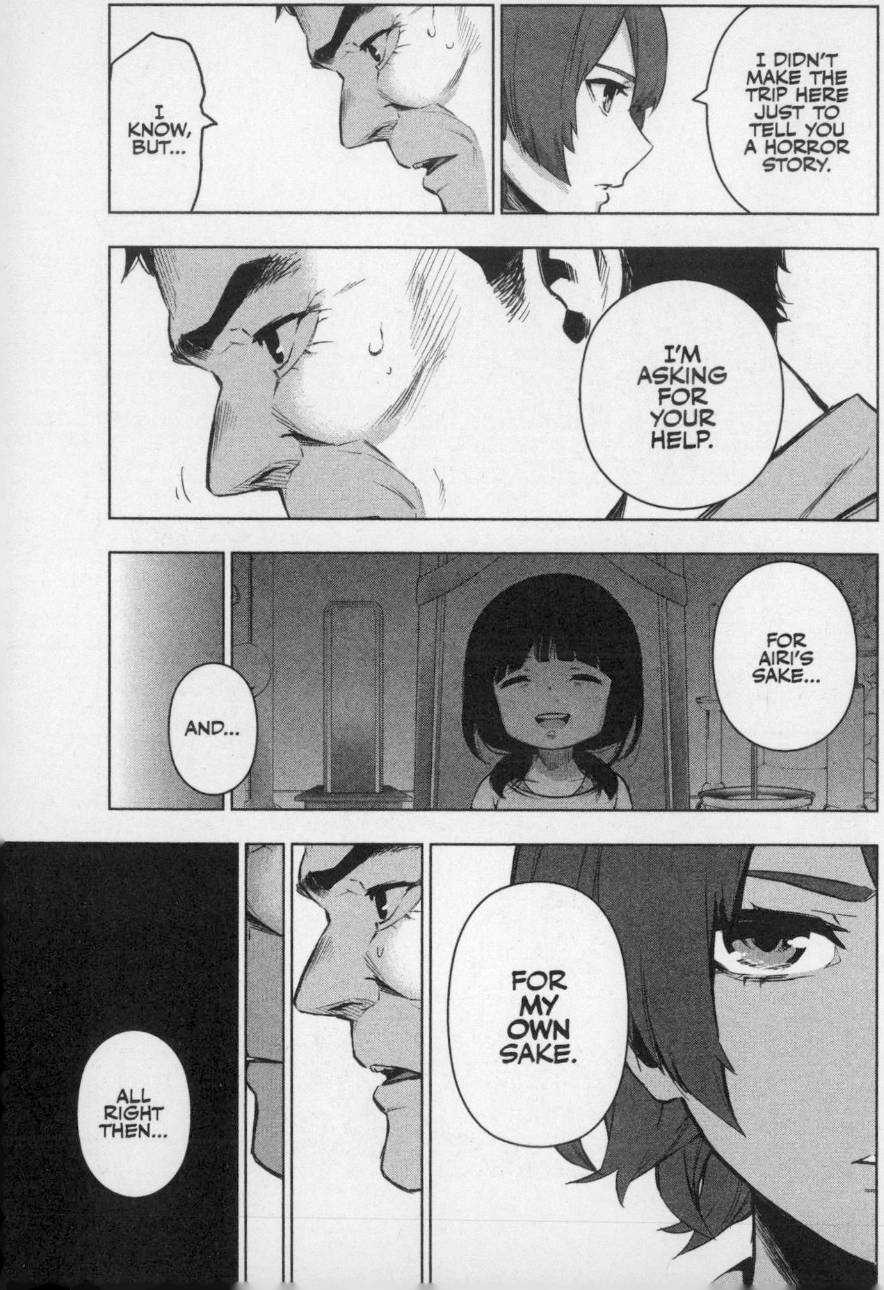
I DIDN'T MAKE THE TRIP HERE JUST TO TELL YOU A HORROR STORY.
I KNOW, BUT...
I'M ASKING FOR YOUR HELP.
FOR AIRI'S SAKE...
AND...
FOR MY OWN SAKE.
ALL RIGHT THEN...

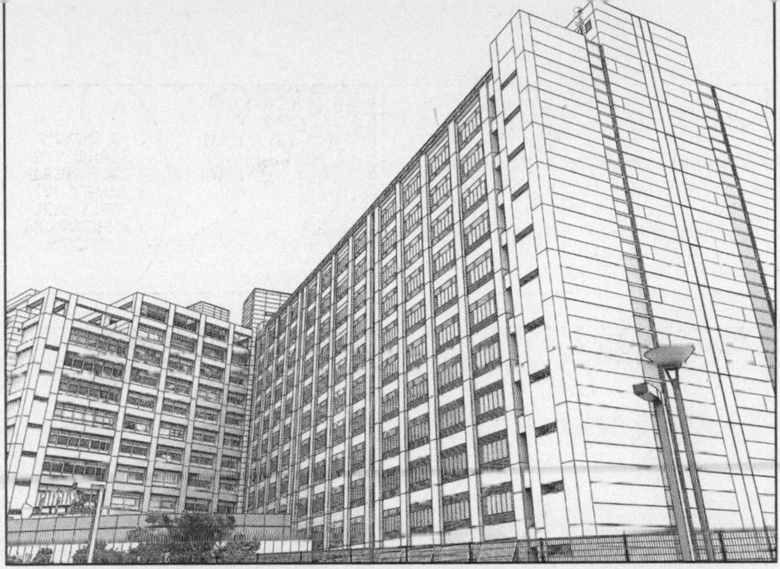

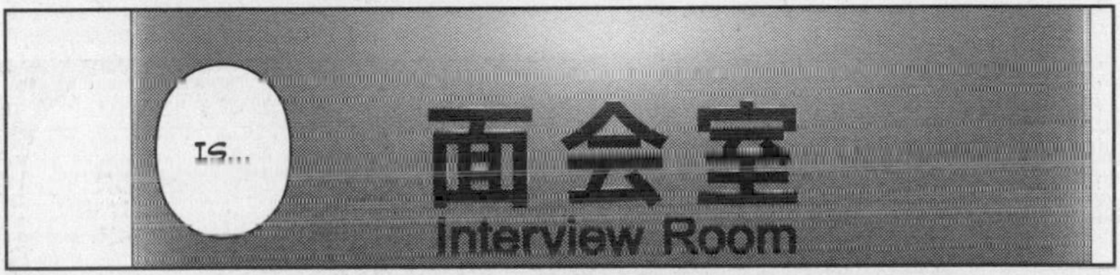
面会室
Interview Room
IS...

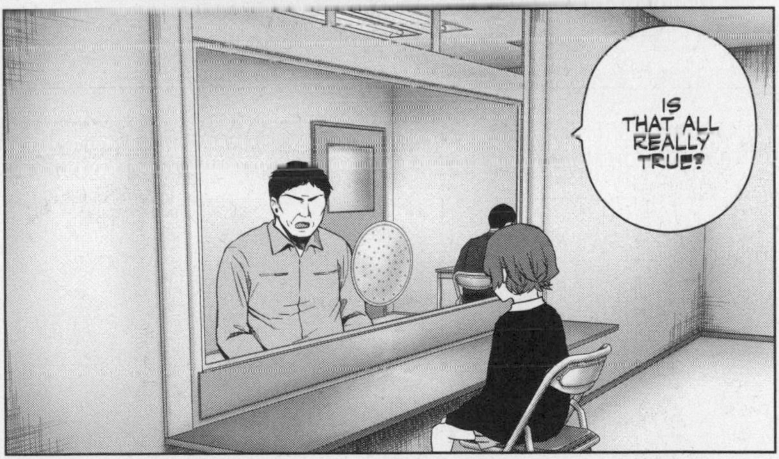
IS THAT ALL REALLY TRUE?

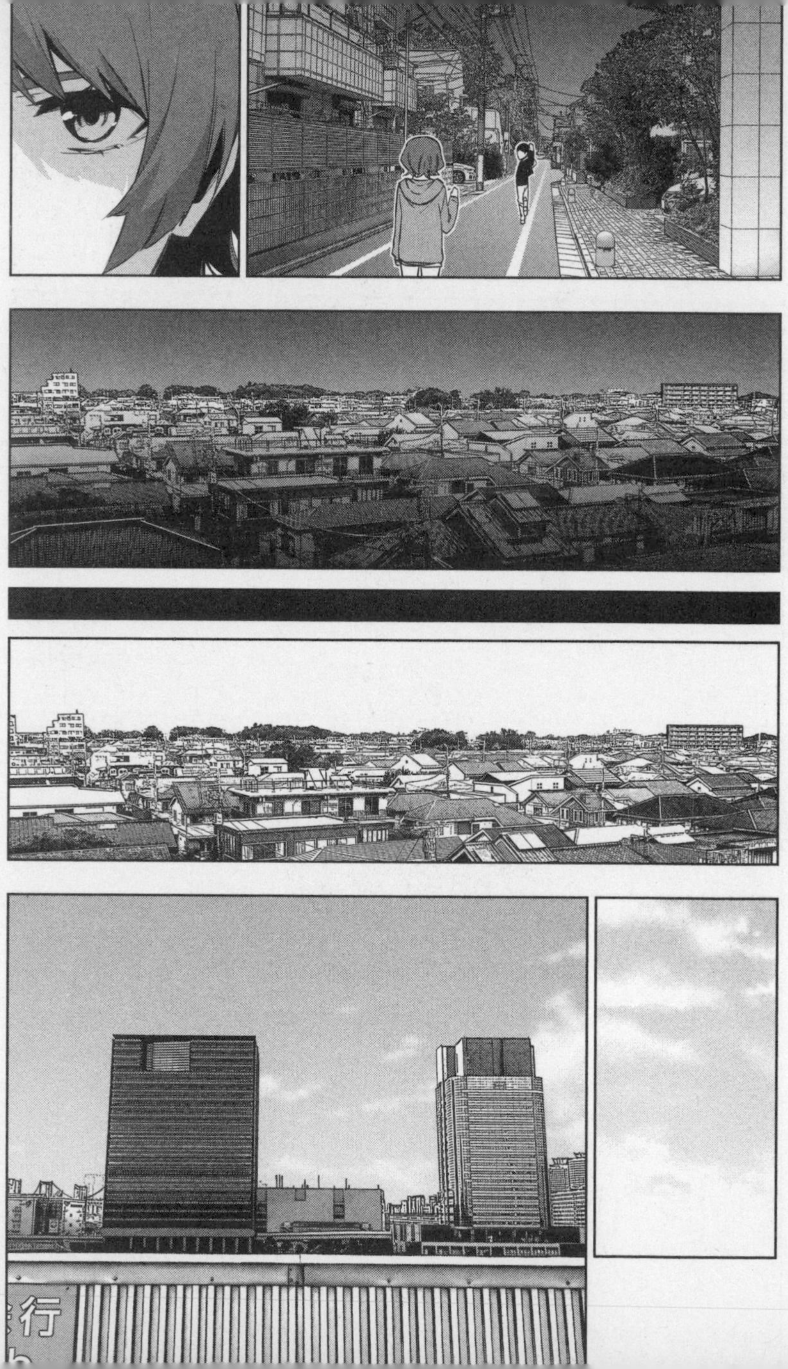

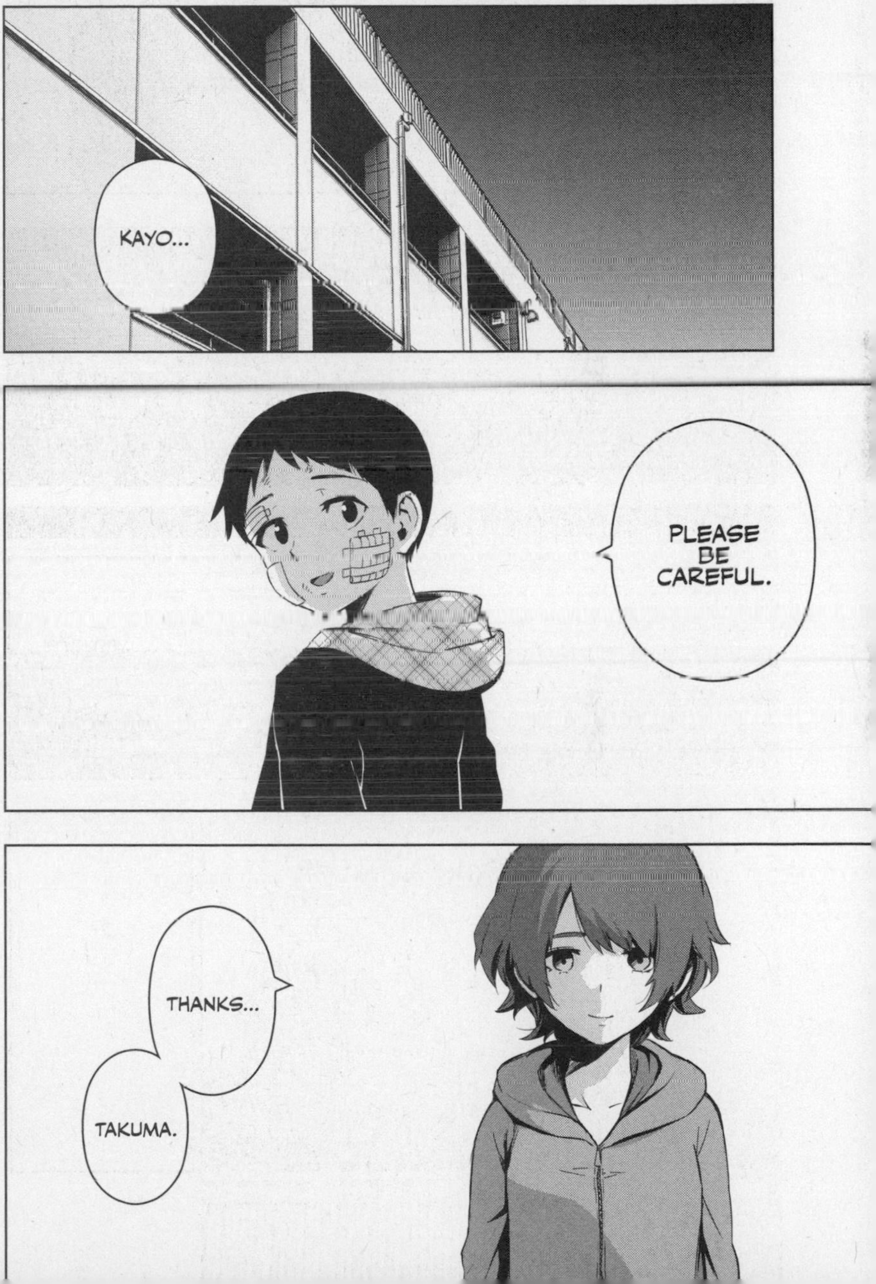

KAYO...
PLEASE BE CAREFUL.
THANKS...
TAKUMA.

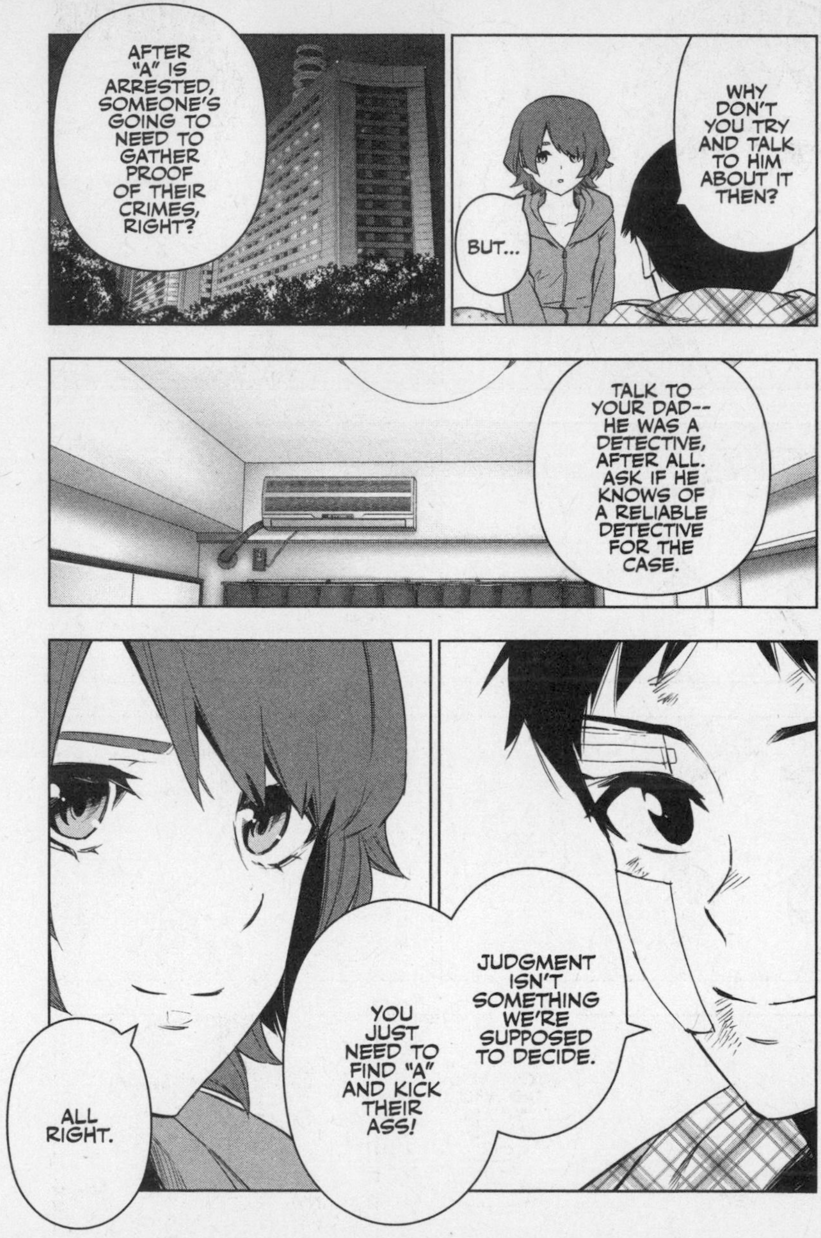
WHY DON'T YOU TRY AND TALK TO HIM ABOUT IT THEN?
BUT...
AFTER "A" IS ARRESTED, SOMEONE'S GOING TO NEED TO GATHER PROOF OF THEIR CRIMES, RIGHT?
TALK TO YOUR DAD-- HE WAS A DETECTIVE, AFTER ALL. ASK IF HE KNOWS OF A RELIABLE DETECTIVE FOR THE CASE.
JUDGMENT ISN'T SOMETHING WE'RE SUPPOSED TO DECIDE.
YOU JUST NEED TO FIND "A" AND KICK THEIR ASS!
ALL RIGHT.

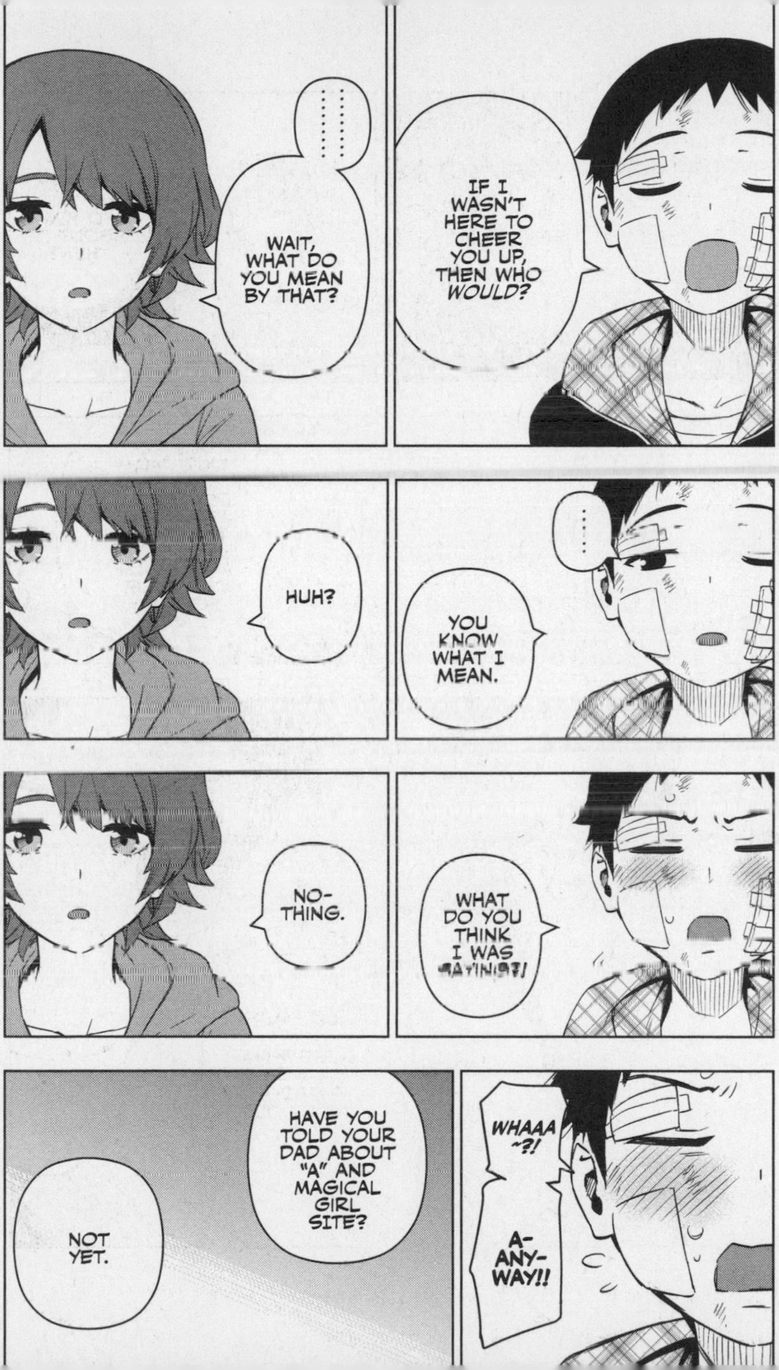
IF I WASN'T HERE TO CHEER YOU UP, THEN WHO *WOULD?*
......
WAIT, WHAT DO YOU MEAN BY THAT?
......
YOU KNOW WHAT I MEAN.
HUH?
WHAT DO YOU THINK I WAS SAYING?!
NO-THING.
WHAAA ~?!
A-ANY-WAY!!
HAVE YOU TOLD YOUR DAD ABOUT "A" AND MAGICAL GIRL SITE?
NOT YET.

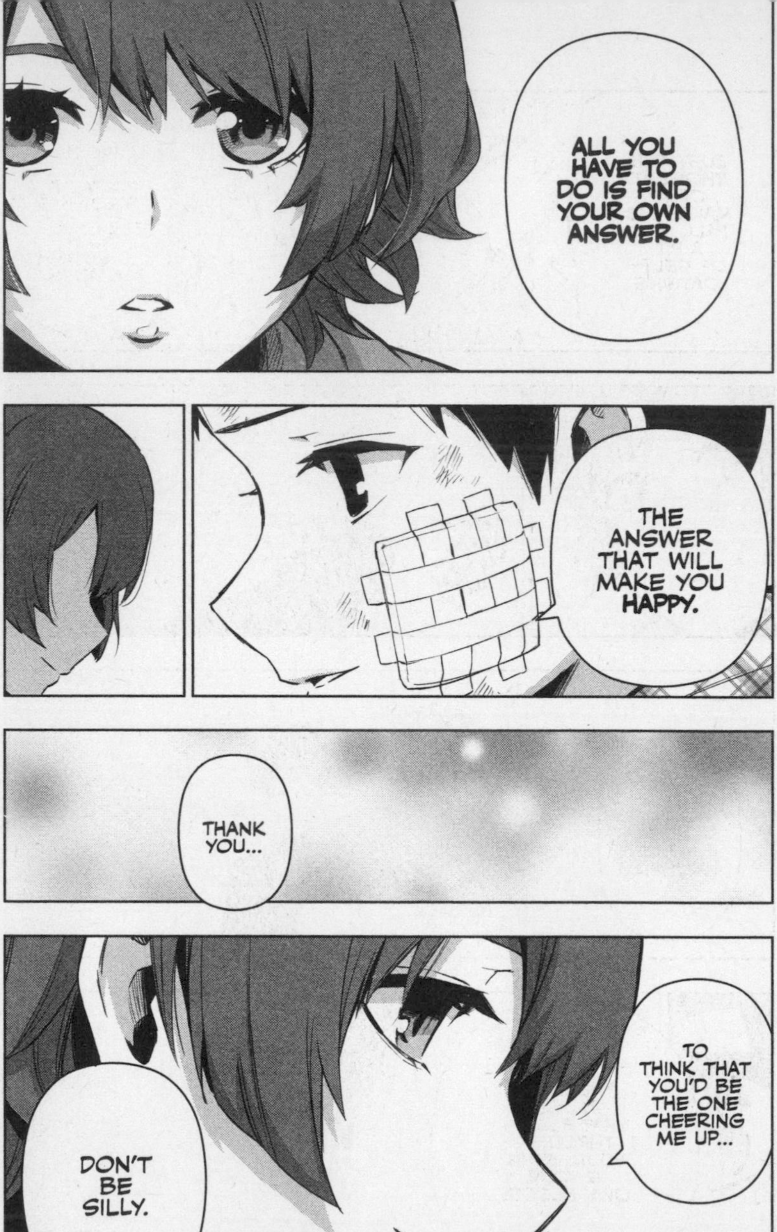
ALL YOU HAVE TO DO IS FIND YOUR OWN ANSWER.
THE ANSWER THAT WILL MAKE YOU HAPPY.
THANK YOU...
TO THINK THAT YOU'D BE THE ONE CHEERING ME UP...
DON'T BE SILLY.

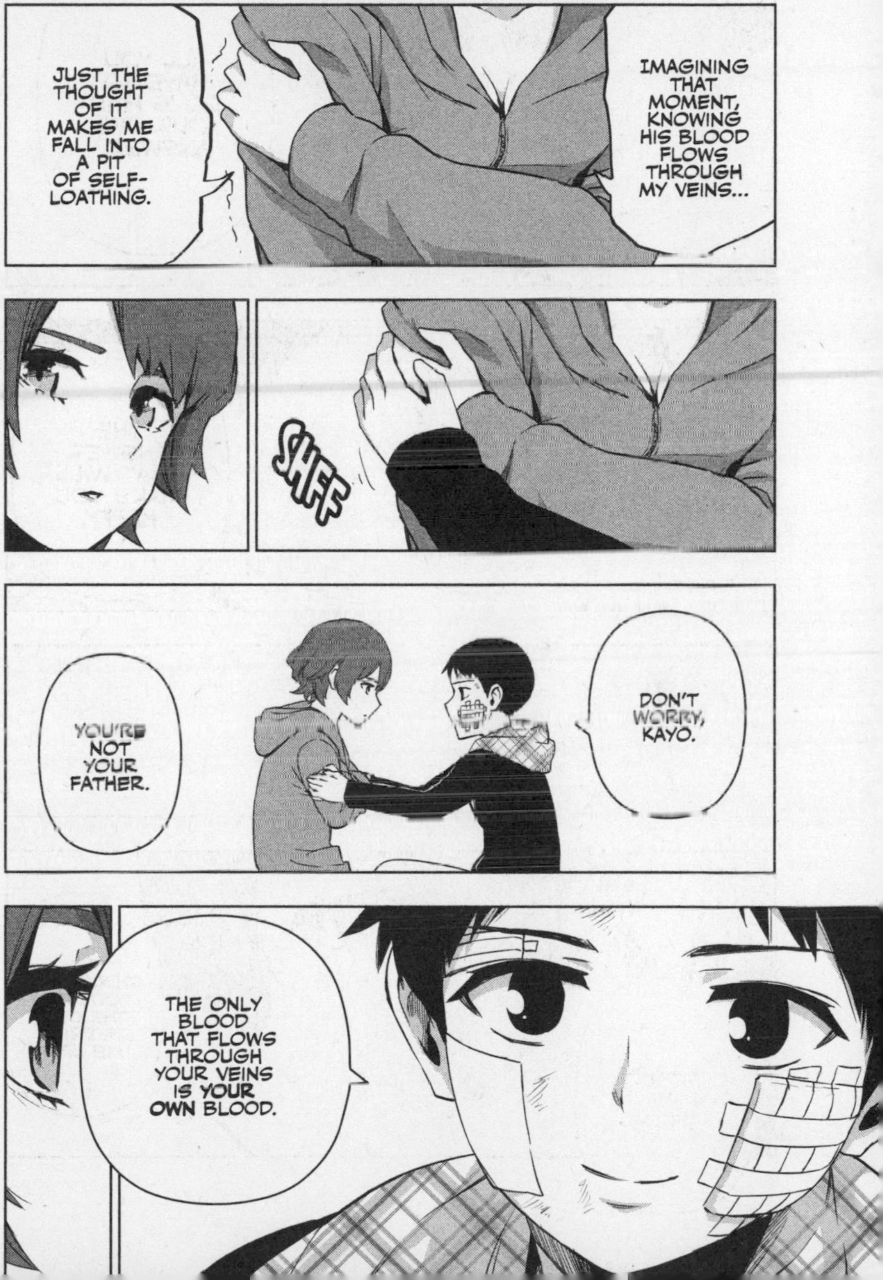
IMAGINING THAT MOMENT, KNOWING HIS BLOOD FLOWS THROUGH MY VEINS...
JUST THE THOUGHT OF IT MAKES ME FALL INTO A PIT OF SELF-LOATHING.
SHFF
DON'T WORRY, KAYO.
YOU'RE NOT YOUR FATHER.
THE ONLY BLOOD THAT FLOWS THROUGH YOUR VEINS IS YOUR OWN BLOOD.

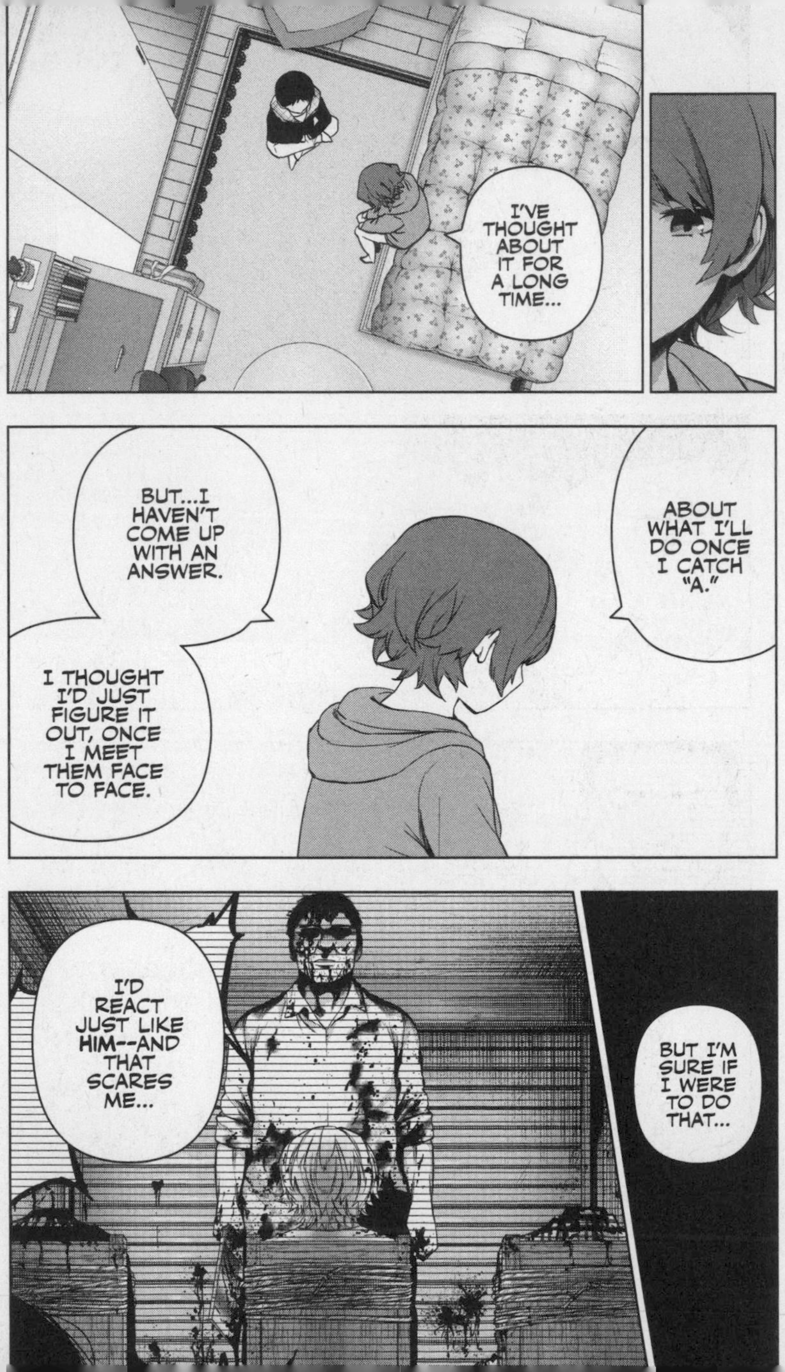
I'VE THOUGHT ABOUT IT FOR A LONG TIME...
ABOUT WHAT I'LL DO ONCE I CATCH "A."
BUT...I HAVEN'T COME UP WITH AN ANSWER.
I THOUGHT I'D JUST FIGURE IT OUT, ONCE I MEET THEM FACE TO FACE.
BUT I'M SURE IF I WERE TO DO THAT...
I'D REACT JUST LIKE HIM--AND THAT SCARES ME...

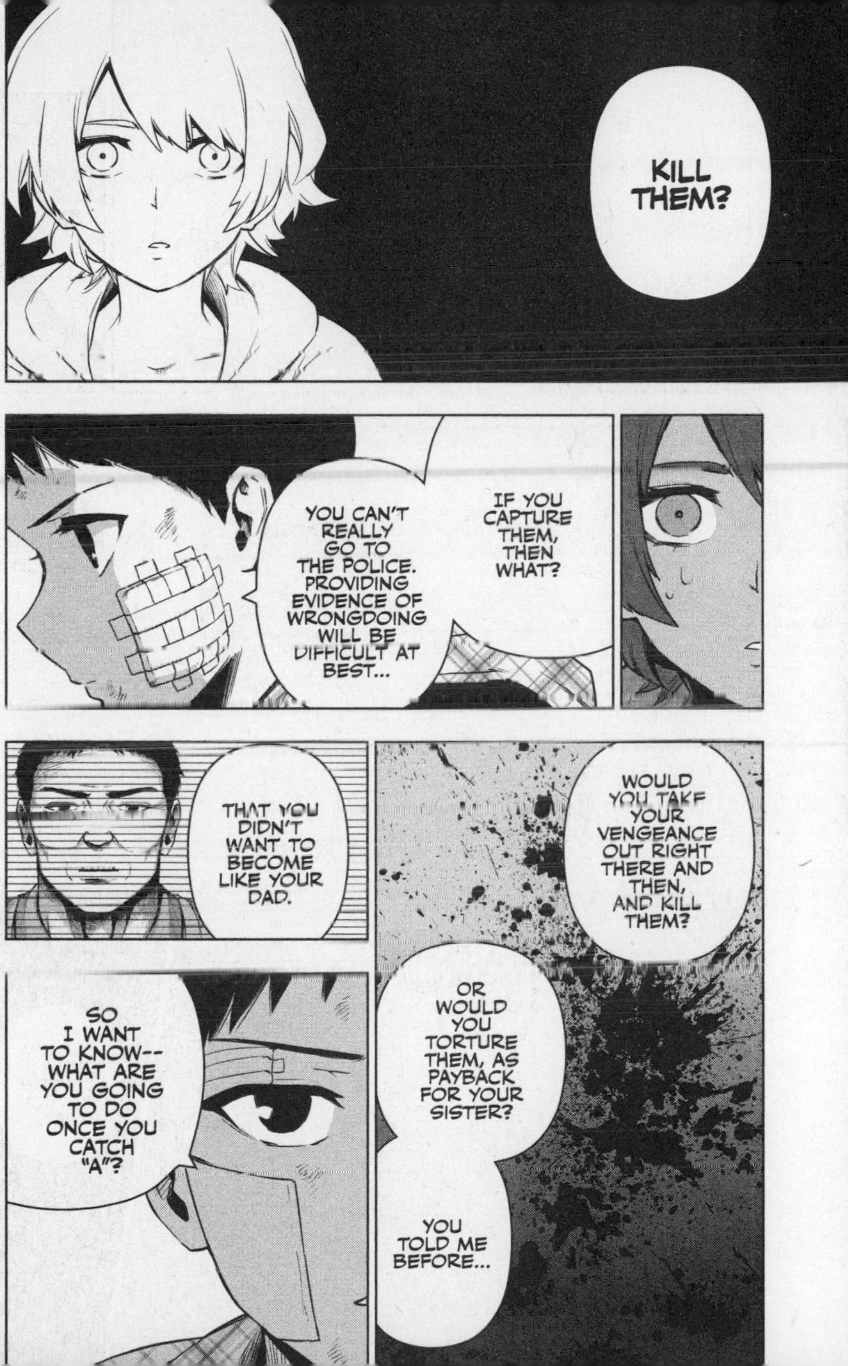
KILL THEM?
IF YOU CAPTURE THEM, THEN WHAT?
YOU CAN'T REALLY GO TO THE POLICE. PROVIDING EVIDENCE OF WRONGDOING WILL BE DIFFICULT AT BEST...
WOULD YOU TAKE YOUR VENGEANCE OUT RIGHT THERE AND THEN, AND KILL THEM?
OR WOULD YOU TORTURE THEM, AS PAYBACK FOR YOUR SISTER?
YOU TOLD ME BEFORE...
THAT YOU DIDN'T WANT TO BECOME LIKE YOUR DAD.
SO I WANT TO KNOW--WHAT ARE YOU GOING TO DO ONCE YOU CATCH "A"?

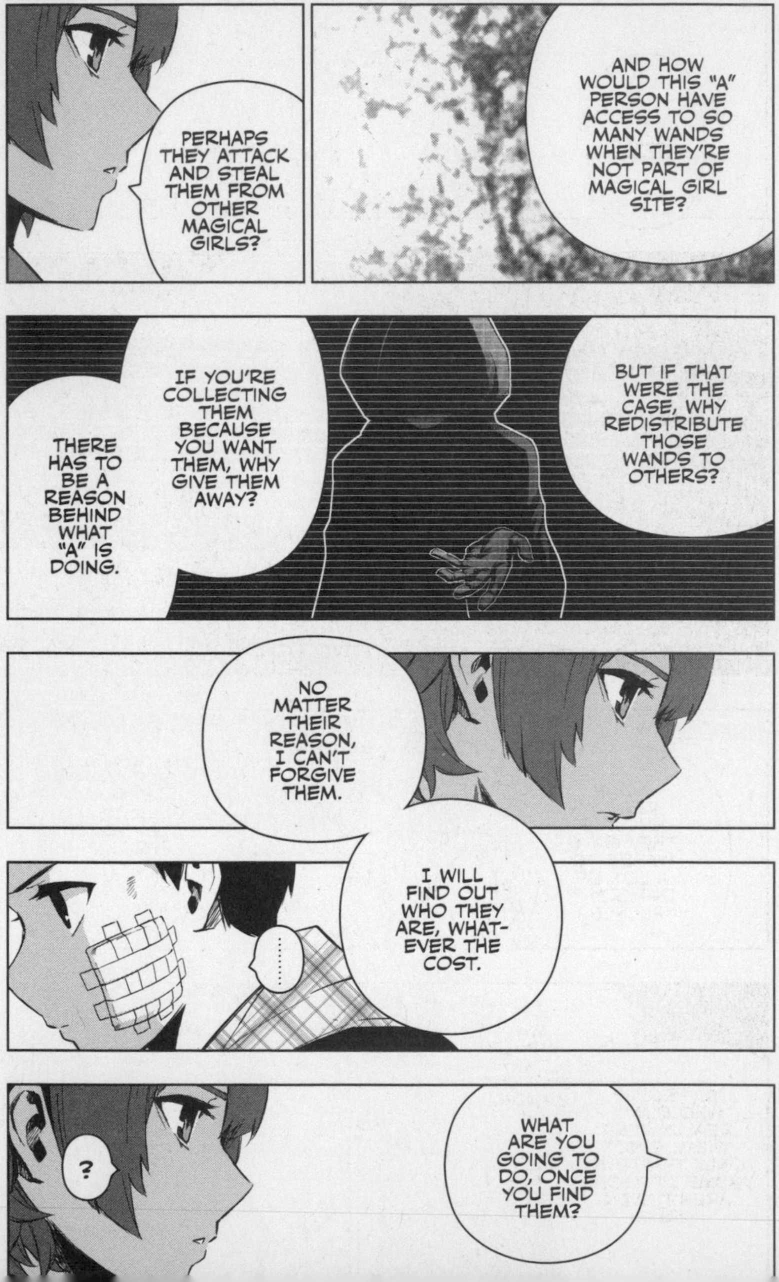
AND HOW WOULD THIS "A" PERSON HAVE ACCESS TO SO MANY WANDS WHEN THEY'RE NOT PART OF MAGICAL GIRL SITE?
PERHAPS THEY ATTACK AND STEAL THEM FROM OTHER MAGICAL GIRLS?
BUT IF THAT WERE THE CASE, WHY REDISTRIBUTE THOSE WANDS TO OTHERS?
IF YOU'RE COLLECTING THEM BECAUSE YOU WANT THEM, WHY GIVE THEM AWAY?
THERE HAS TO BE A REASON BEHIND WHAT "A" IS DOING.
NO MATTER THEIR REASON, I CAN'T FORGIVE THEM.
I WILL FIND OUT WHO THEY ARE, WHATEVER THE COST.
......
WHAT ARE YOU GOING TO DO, ONCE YOU FIND THEM?
?

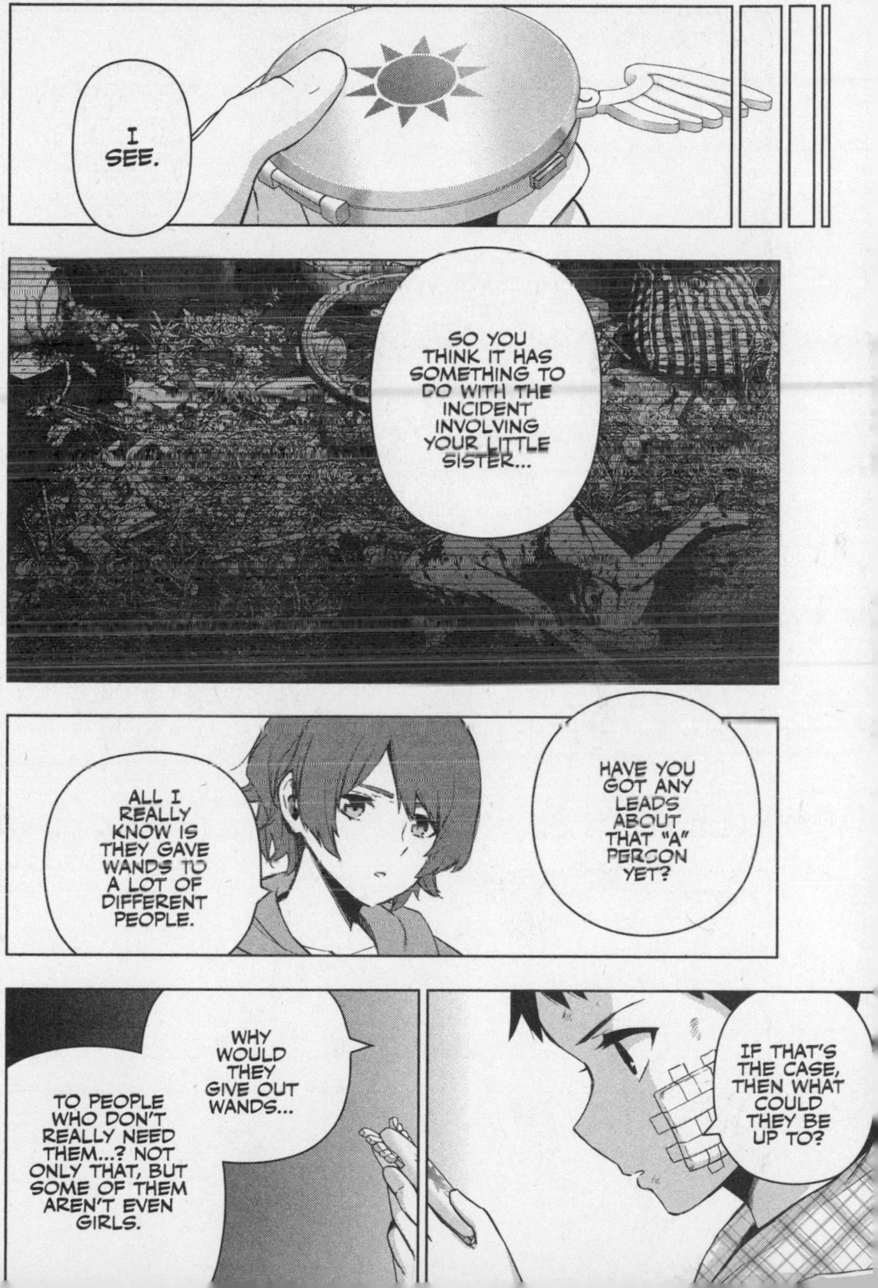
I SEE.
SO YOU THINK IT HAS SOMETHING TO DO WITH THE INCIDENT INVOLVING YOUR LITTLE SISTER...
HAVE YOU GOT ANY LEADS ABOUT THAT "A" PERSON YET?
ALL I REALLY KNOW IS THEY GAVE WANDS TO A LOT OF DIFFERENT PEOPLE.
IF THAT'S THE CASE, THEN WHAT COULD THEY BE UP TO?
WHY WOULD THEY GIVE OUT WANDS...
TO PEOPLE WHO DON'T REALLY NEED THEM...? NOT ONLY THAT, BUT SOME OF THEM AREN'T EVEN GIRLS.

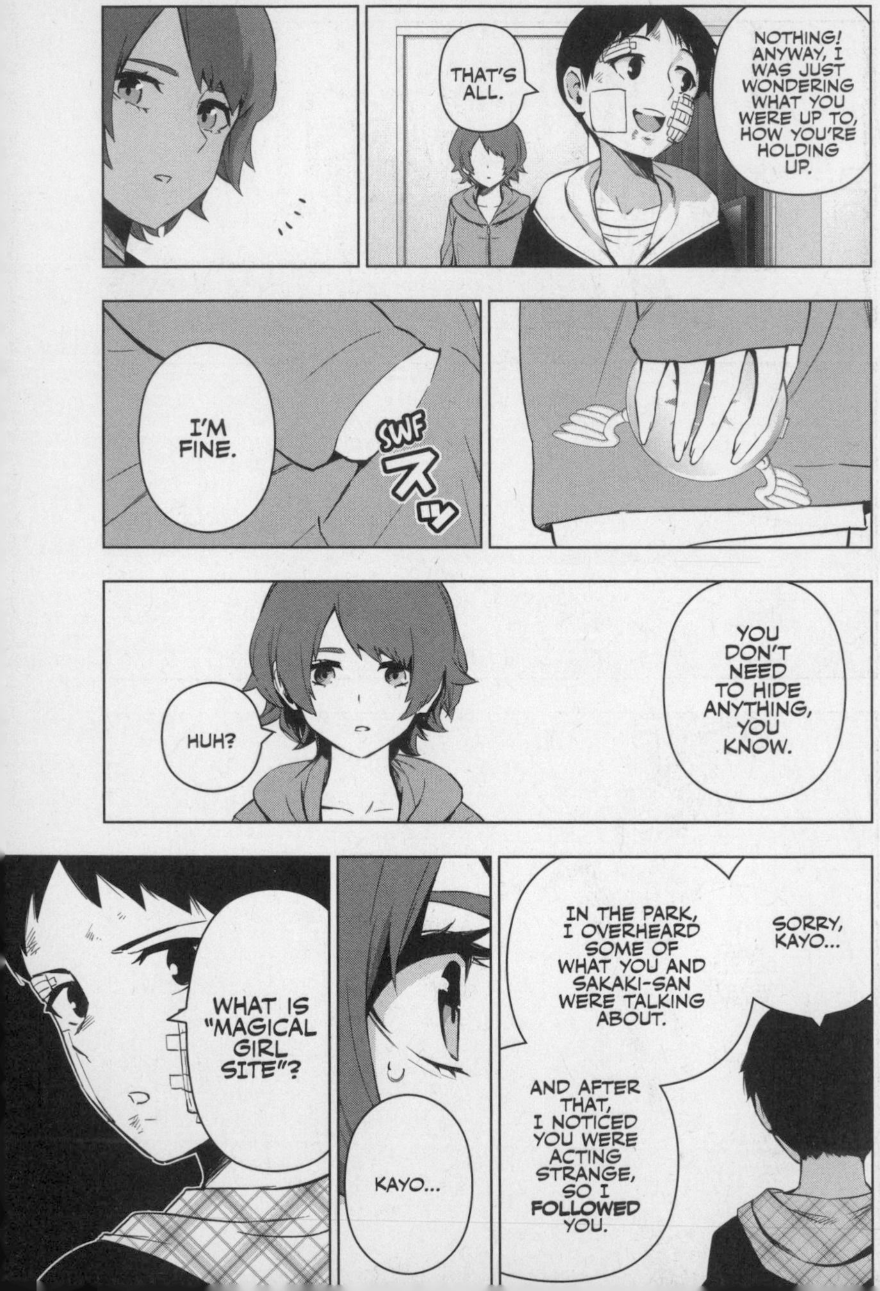
NOTHING! ANYWAY, I WAS JUST WONDERING WHAT YOU WERE UP TO, HOW YOU'RE HOLDING UP.
THAT'S ALL.
...
I'M FINE.
SWF
スッ
YOU DON'T NEED TO HIDE ANYTHING, YOU KNOW.
HUH?
SORRY, KAYO...
IN THE PARK, I OVERHEARD SOME OF WHAT YOU AND SAKAKI-SAN WERE TALKING ABOUT.
AND AFTER THAT, I NOTICED YOU WERE ACTING STRANGE, SO I **FOLLOWED** YOU.
KAYO...
WHAT IS "MAGICAL GIRL SITE"?

I'VE BEEN TO YOUR PLACE LOTS OF TIMES...
BUT THIS IS THE FIRST TIME I'VE BEEN IN YOUR ROOM.
IT'S GOT A NICE, GIRLY FEEL TO IT.
WHAT DO YOU MEAN BY THAT?

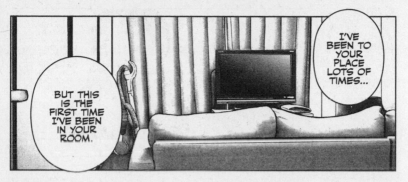

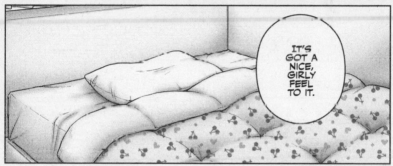

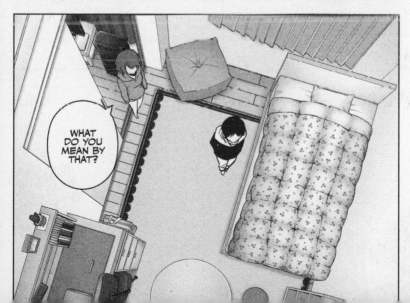

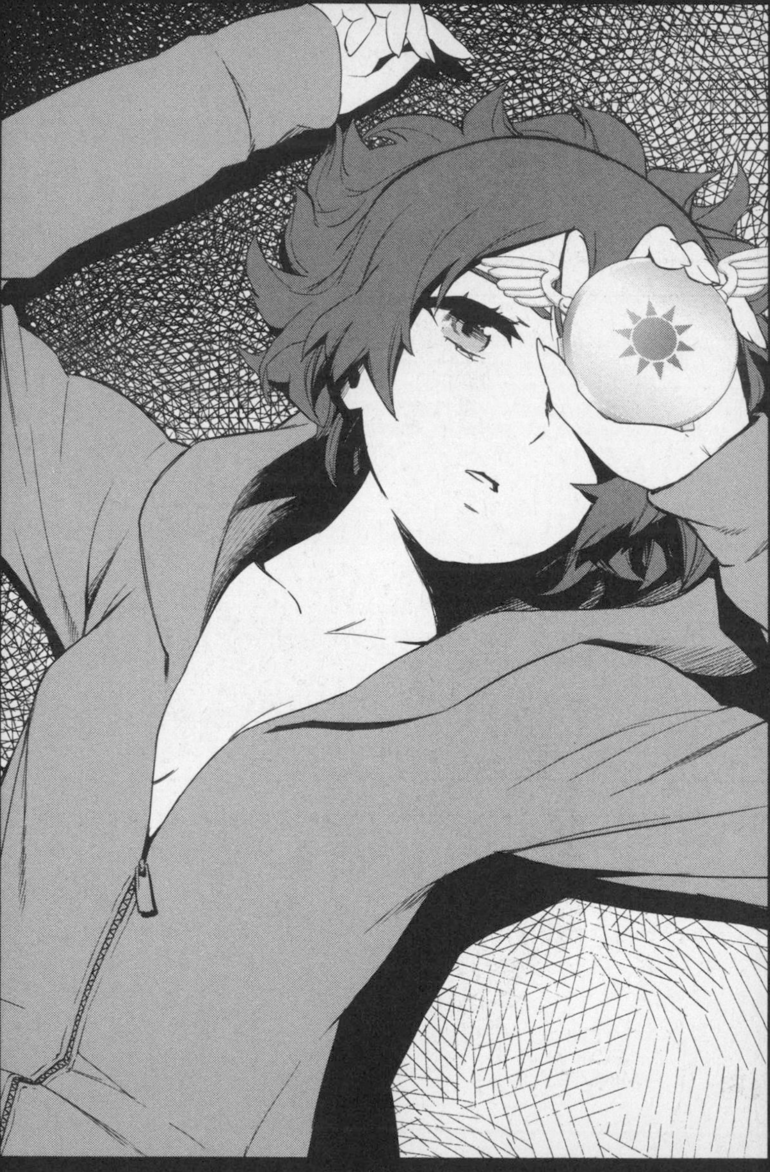

ENTER.71 ANSWER

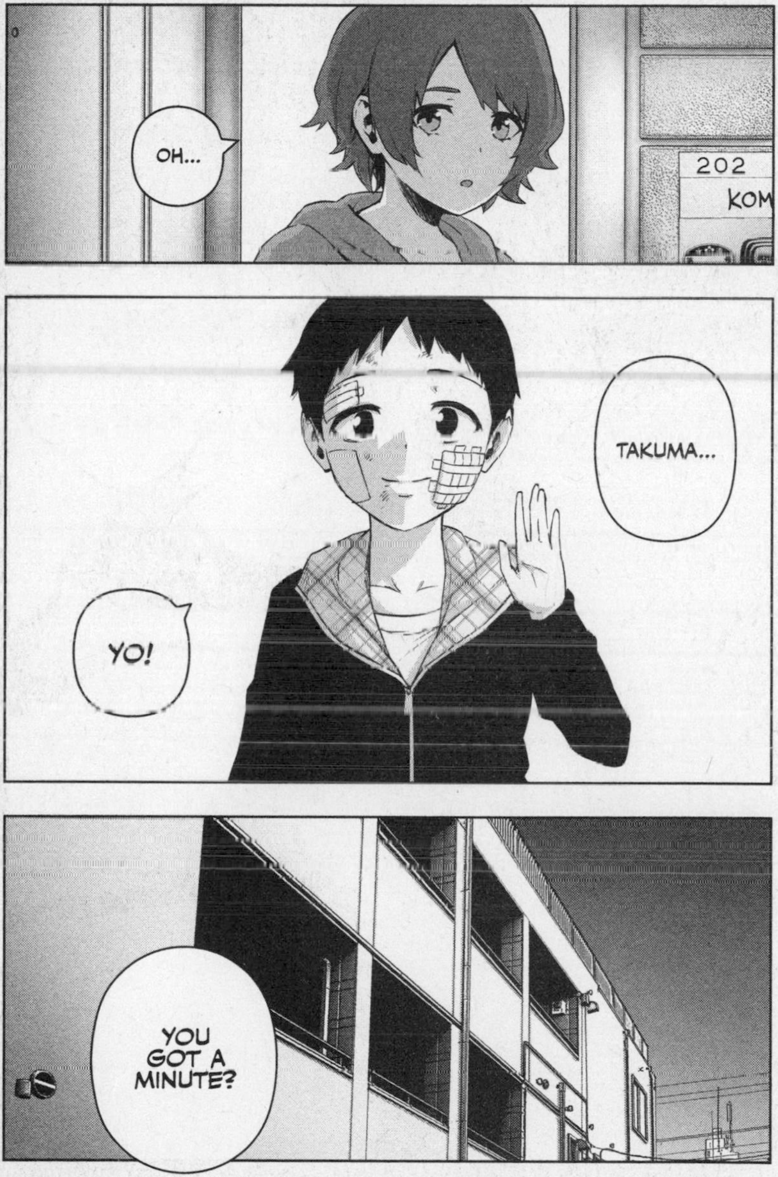
202
KOM
OH...
TAKUMA...
YO!
YOU GOT A MINUTE?

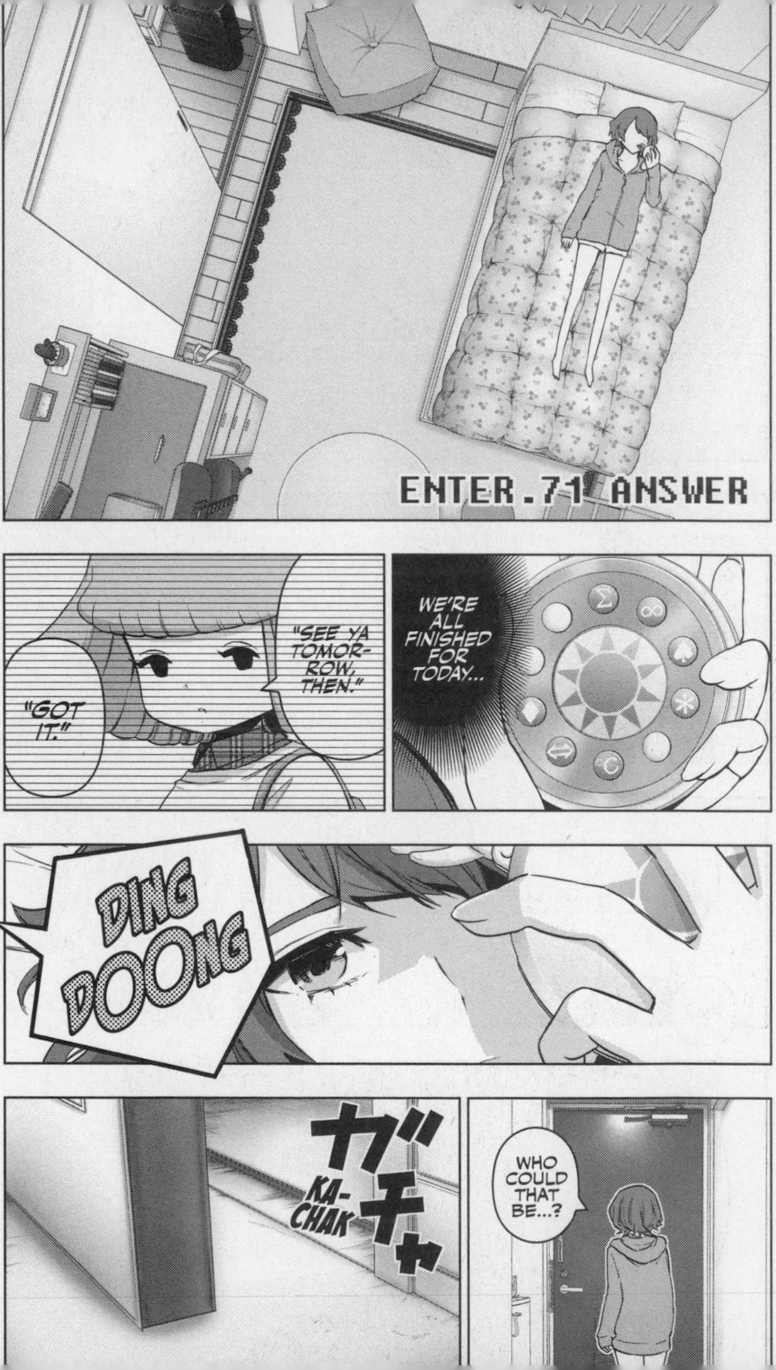
ENTER.71 ANSWER
WE'RE ALL FINISHED FOR TODAY...
"SEE YA TOMOR-ROW, THEN."
"GOT IT."
DING DOONG
WHO COULD THAT BE...?
KA-CHAK

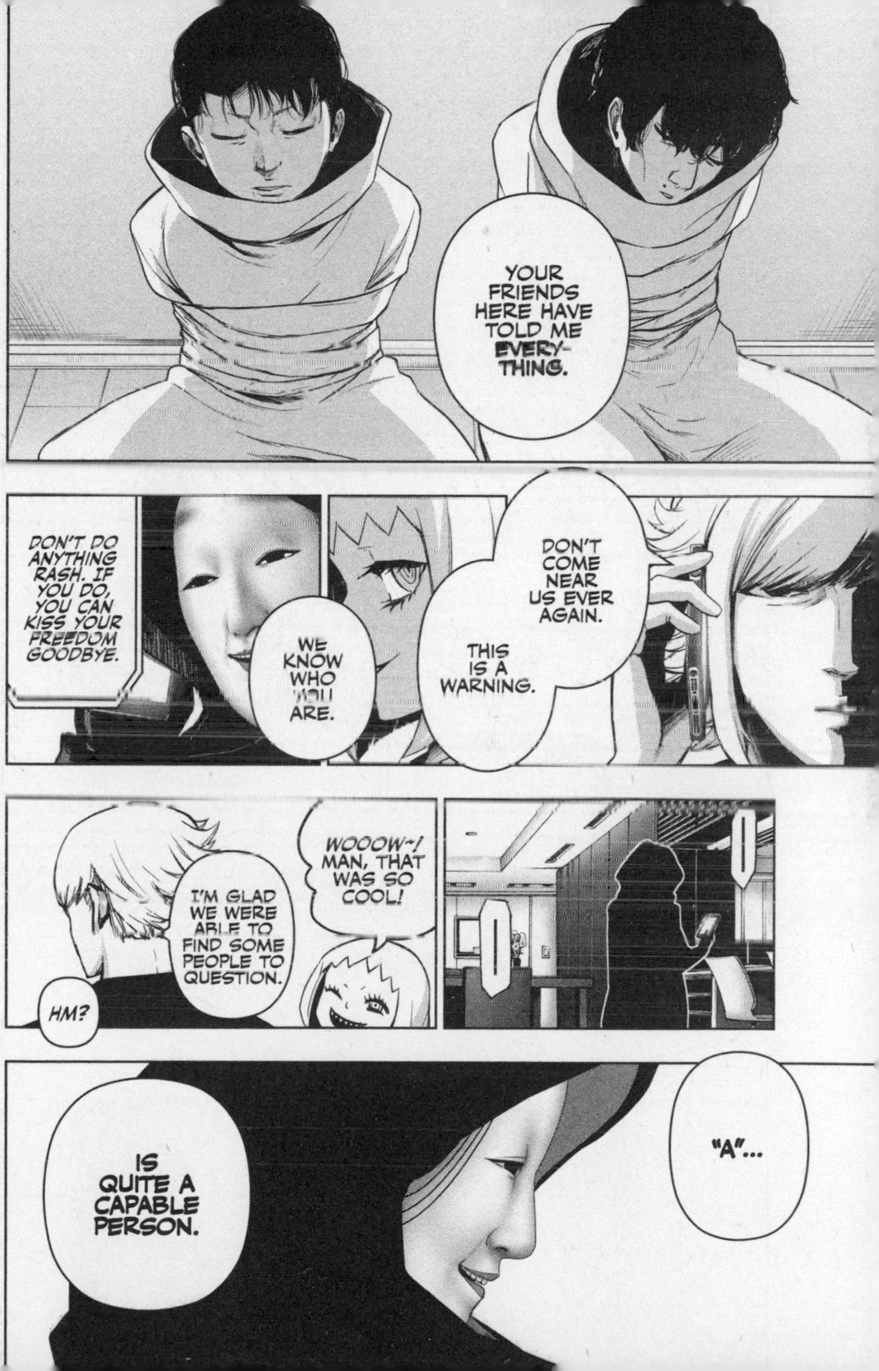
YOUR FRIENDS HERE HAVE TOLD ME EVERY-THING.
DON'T COME NEAR US EVER AGAIN.
THIS IS A WARNING.
WE KNOW WHO YOU ARE.
DON'T DO ANYTHING RASH. IF YOU DO, YOU CAN KISS YOUR FREEDOM GOODBYE.
WOOOW~! MAN, THAT WAS SO COOL!
I'M GLAD WE WERE ABLE TO FIND SOME PEOPLE TO QUESTION.
HM?
"A"...
IS QUITE A CAPABLE PERSON.

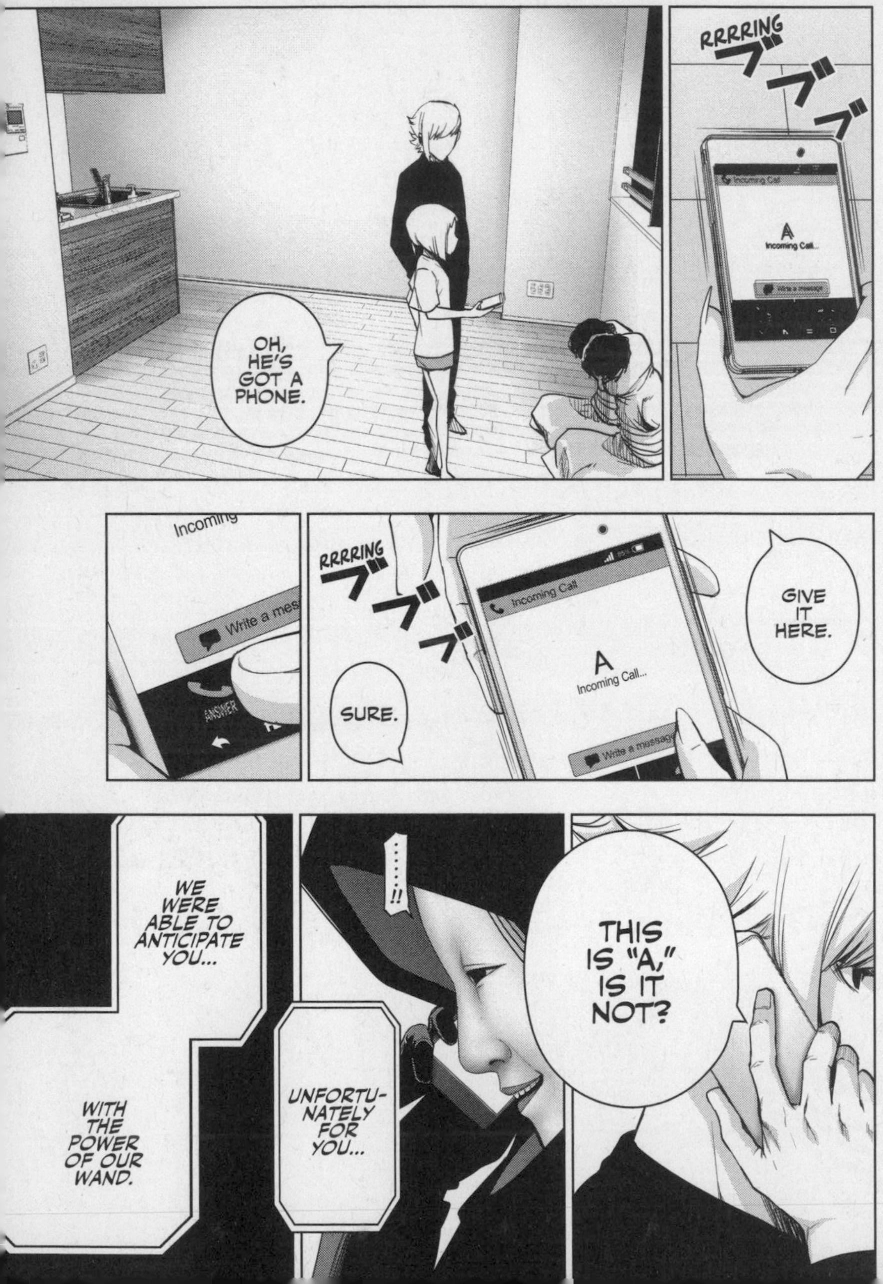
RRRRING
ブブブ
Incoming Call
A
Incoming Call...
Write a message
OH, HE'S GOT A PHONE.
GIVE IT HERE.
RRRRING
ブブブ
Incoming Call
A
Incoming Call...
Write a message
SURE.
Incoming
Write a mes
ANSWER
THIS IS "A," IS IT NOT?
......!!
UNFORTU-NATELY FOR YOU...
WE WERE ABLE TO ANTICIPATE YOU...
WITH THE POWER OF OUR WAND.

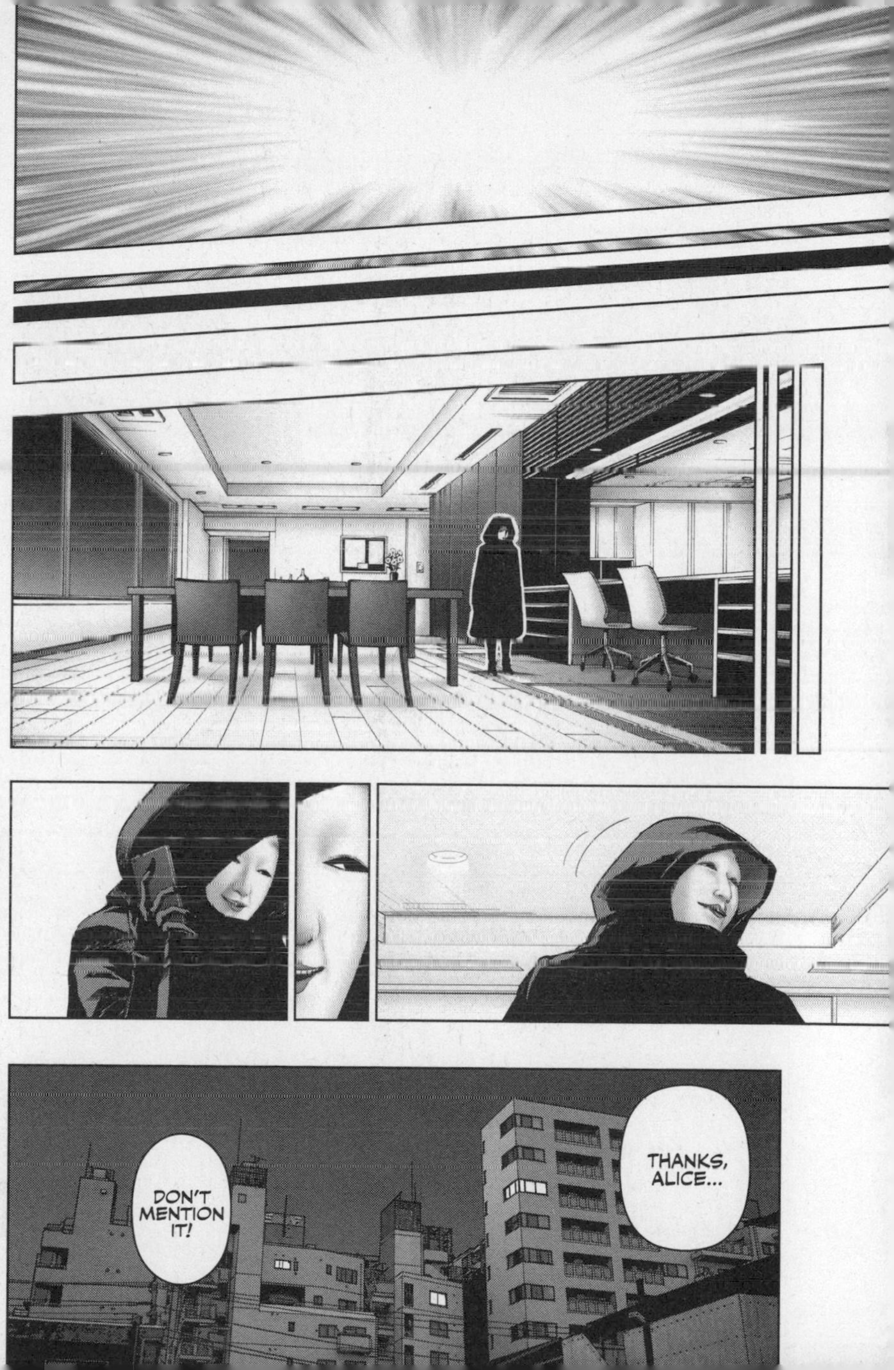
THANKS, ALICE...
DON'T MENTION IT!

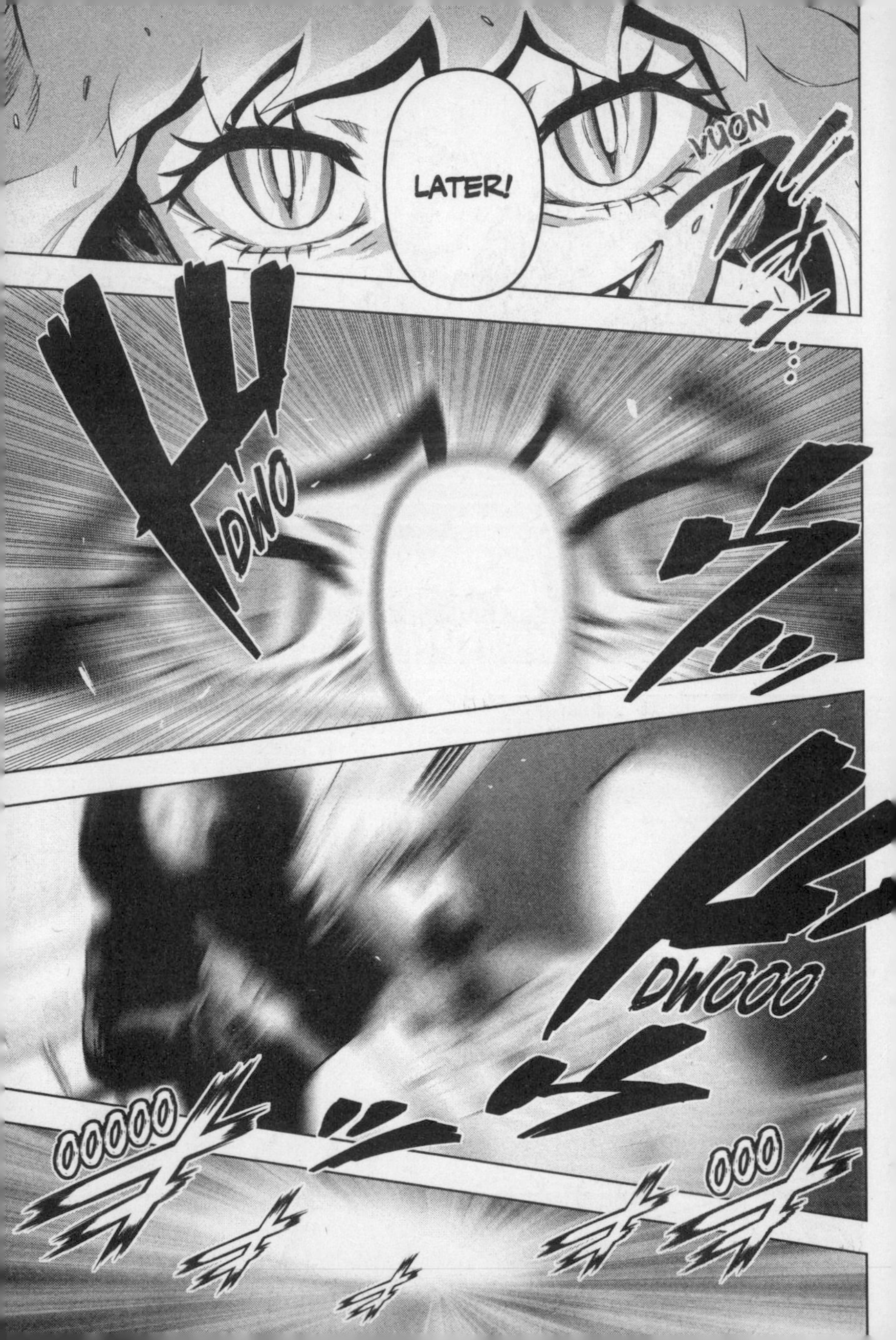
LATER!
VUON
DWO
DWOOO
OOO
OOOOO

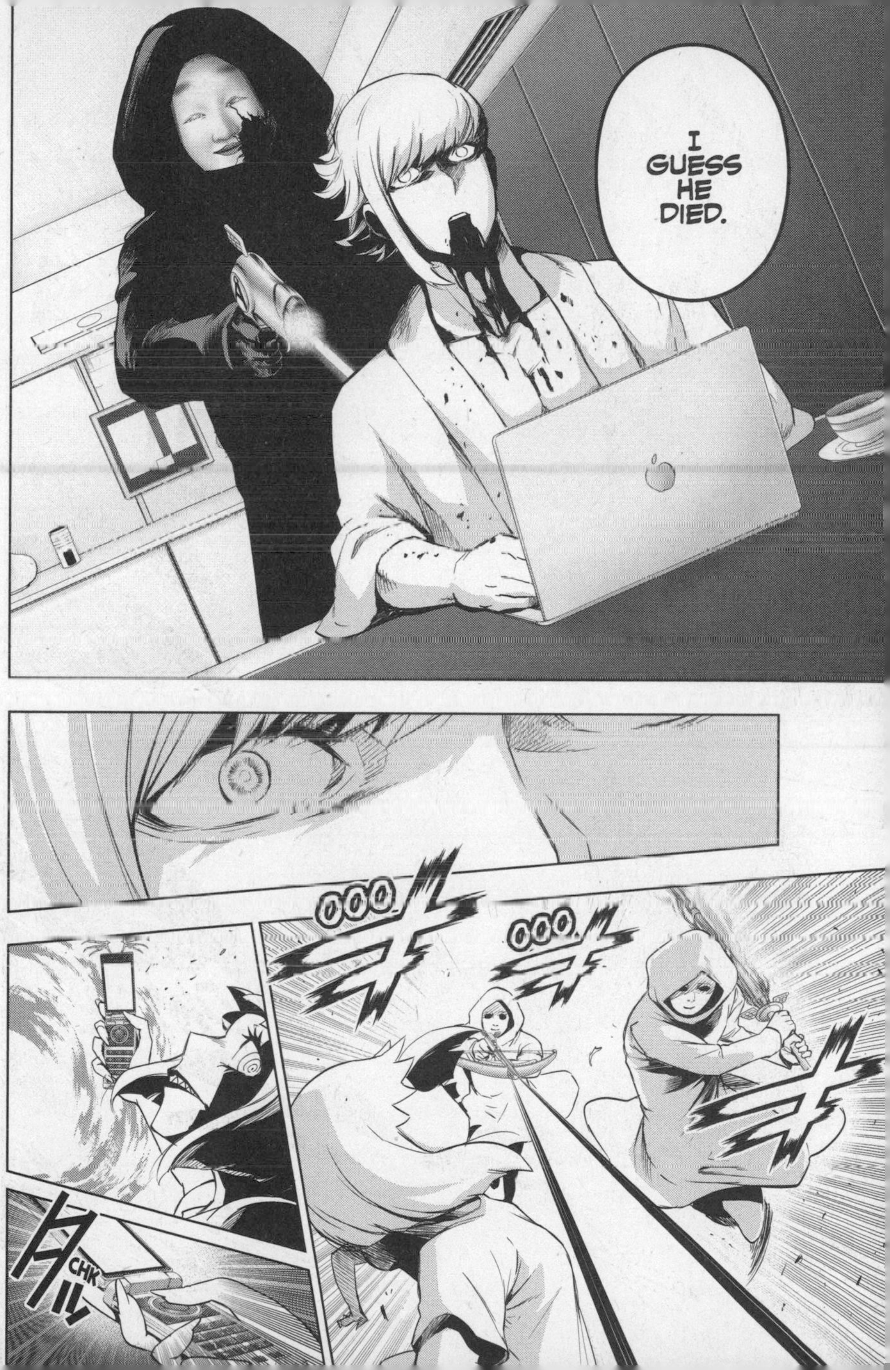
I GUESS HE DIED.
CHK

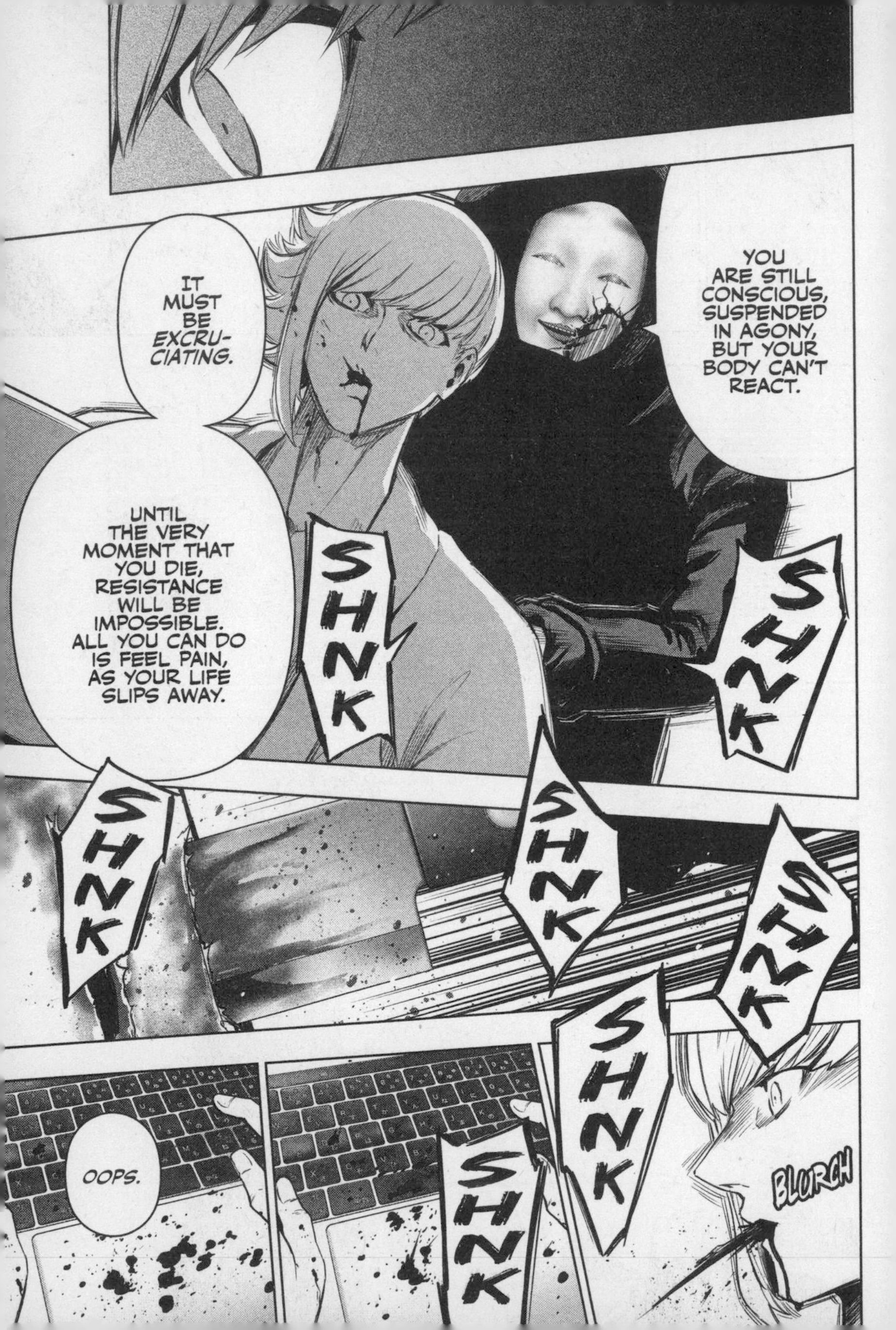
YOU ARE STILL CONSCIOUS, SUSPENDED IN AGONY, BUT YOUR BODY CAN'T REACT.
IT MUST BE EXCRUCIATING.
UNTIL THE VERY MOMENT THAT YOU DIE, RESISTANCE WILL BE IMPOSSIBLE. ALL YOU CAN DO IS FEEL PAIN, AS YOUR LIFE SLIPS AWAY.
SHNK
SHNK
SHNK
SHNK
SHNK
BLURCH
SHNK
SHNK
OOPS.

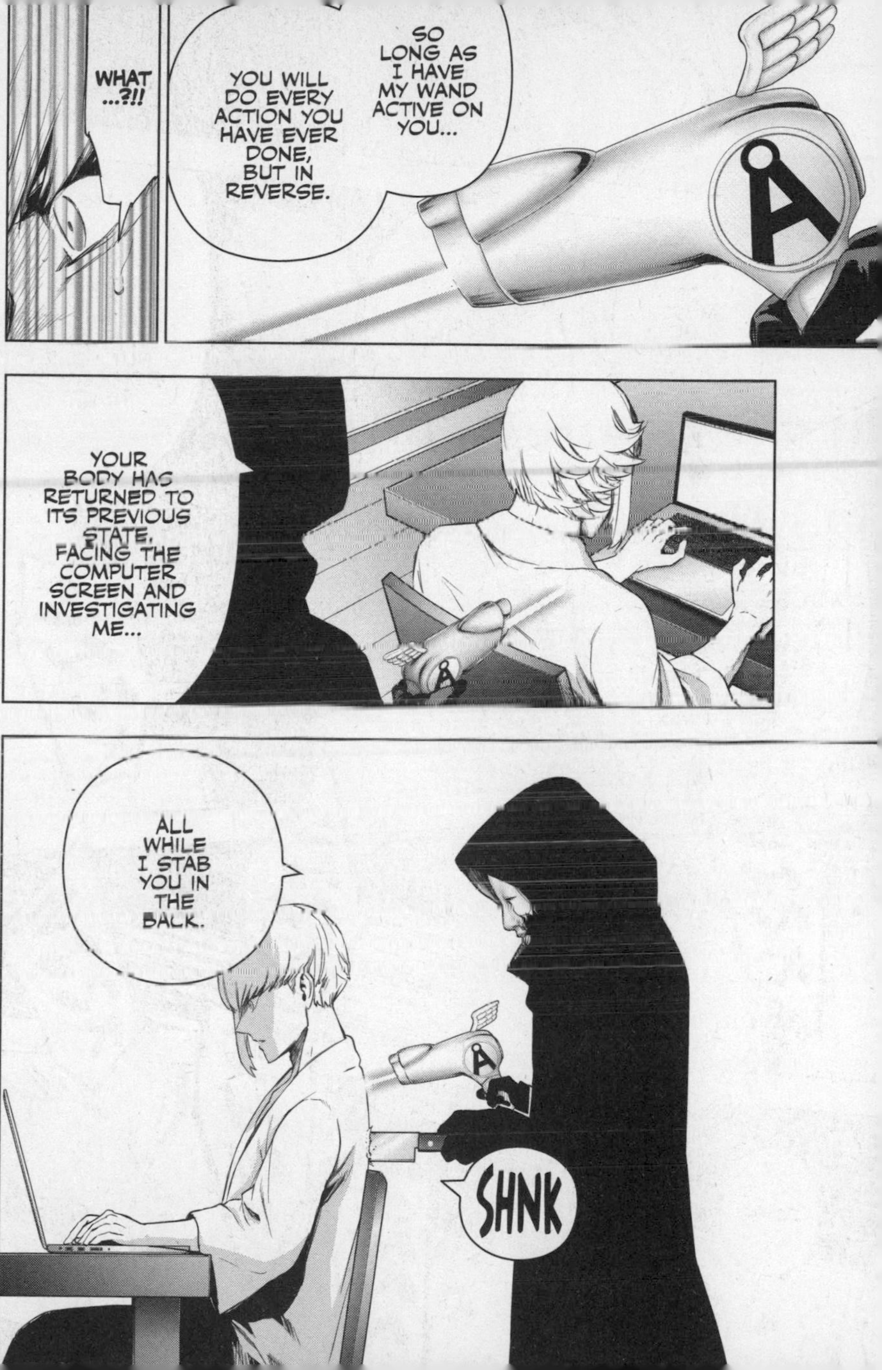
SO LONG AS I HAVE MY WAND ACTIVE ON YOU...
YOU WILL DO EVERY ACTION YOU HAVE EVER DONE, BUT IN REVERSE.
WHAT ...?!!
YOUR BODY HAS RETURNED TO ITS PREVIOUS STATE, FACING THE COMPUTER SCREEN AND INVESTIGATING ME...
ALL WHILE I STAB YOU IN THE BACK.
SHNK

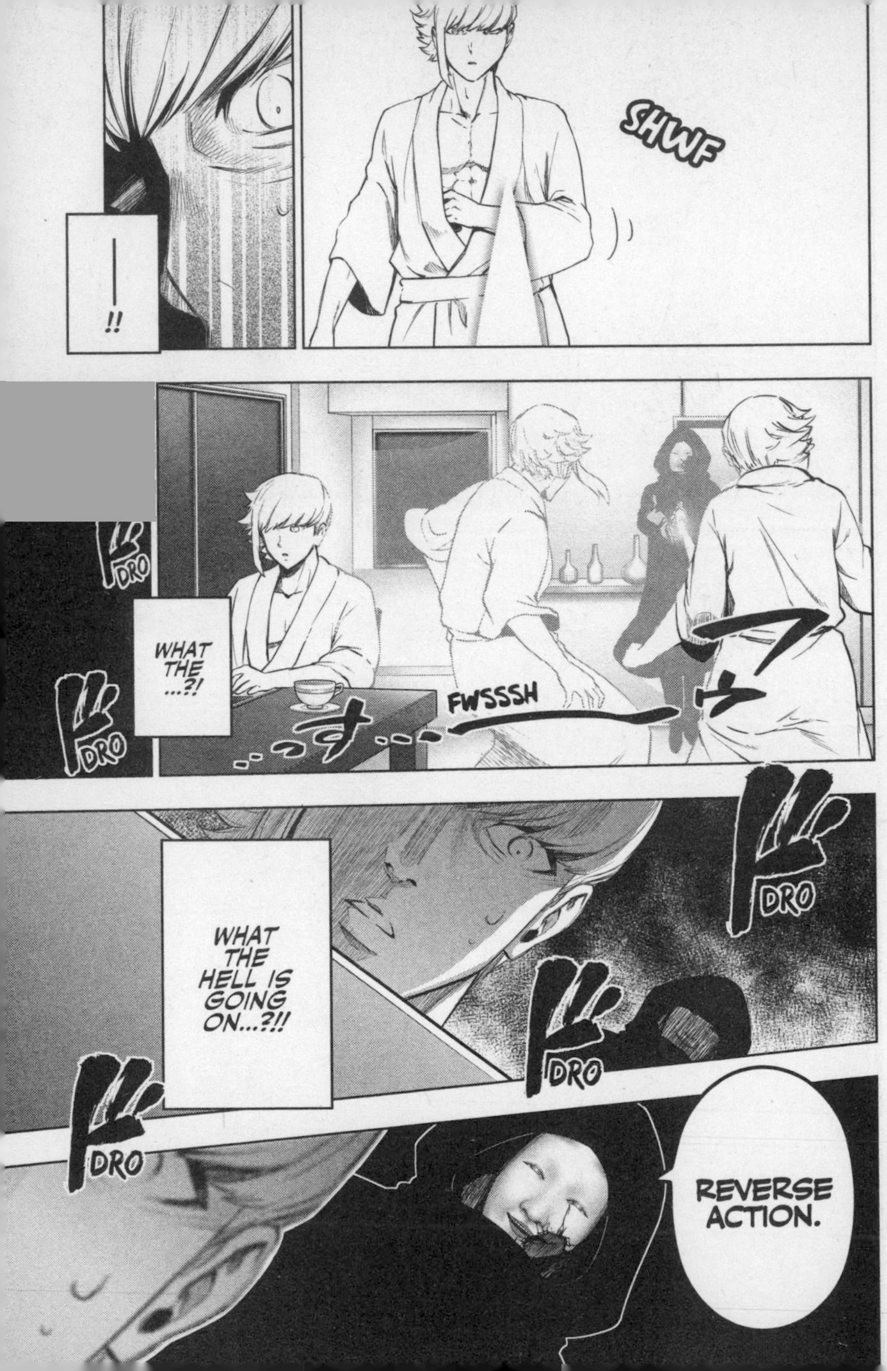
SHWF
—!!
DRO
DRO
WHAT THE ...?!
FWSSSH
DRO
WHAT THE HELL IS GOING ON...?!!
DRO
DRO
REVERSE ACTION.

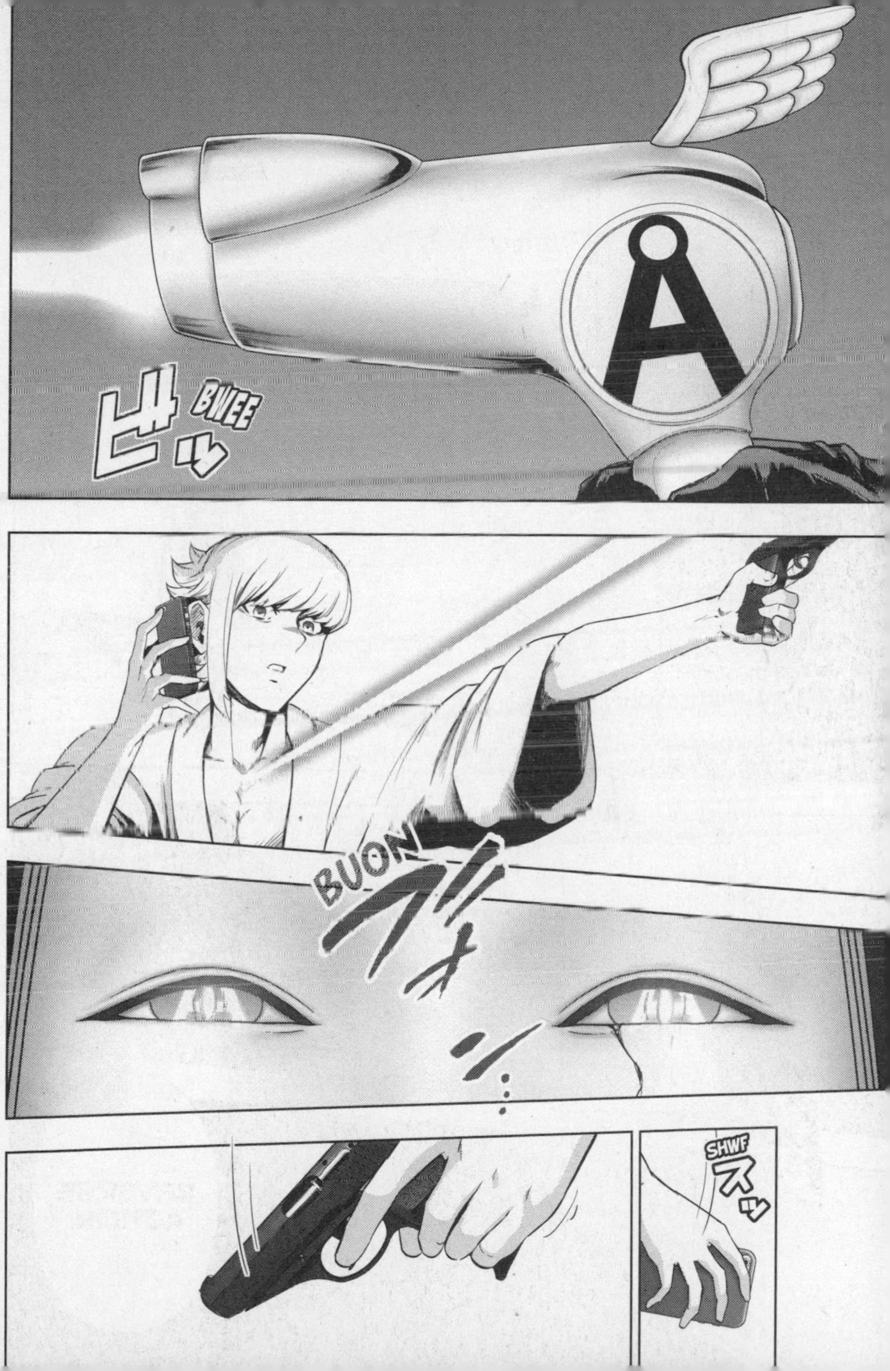
BWEE
ビッ
BUON
ブォン…
SHWF
スッ

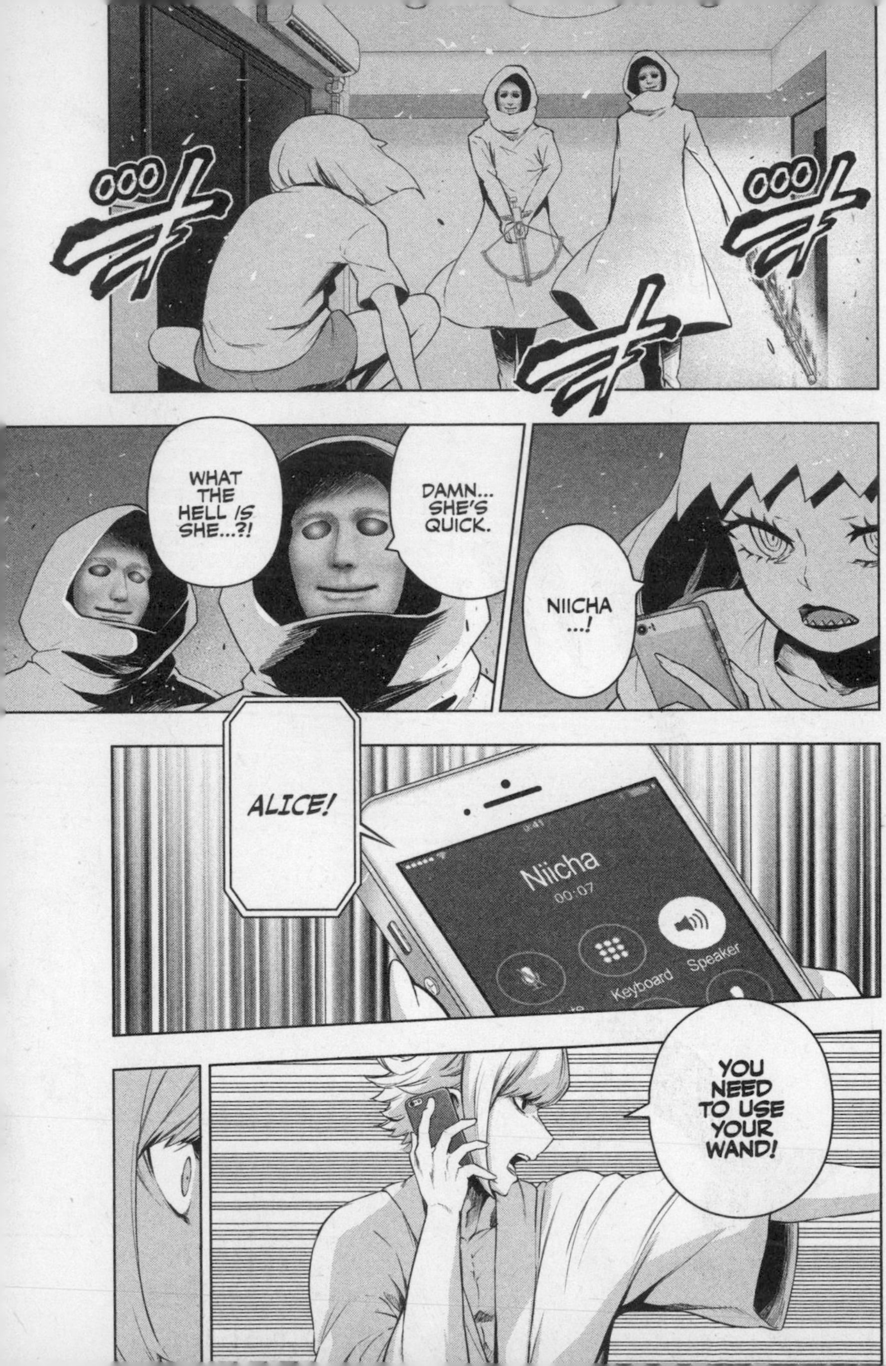
NIICHA ...!
DAMN... SHE'S QUICK.
WHAT THE HELL IS SHE...?!
ALICE!
Niicha
00:07
Speaker
Keyboard
YOU NEED TO USE YOUR WAND!

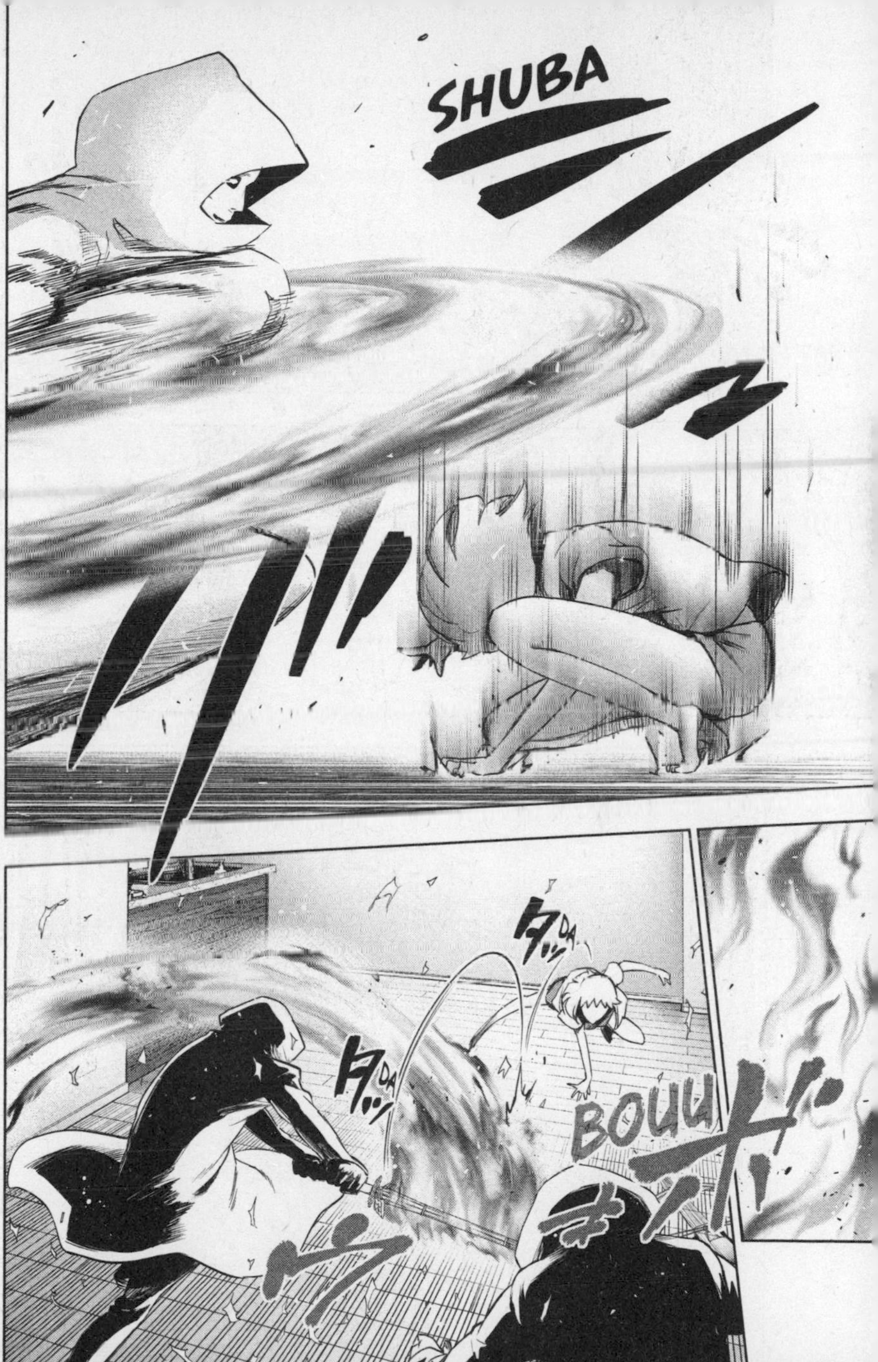
SHUBA
DA
BOUU
DA

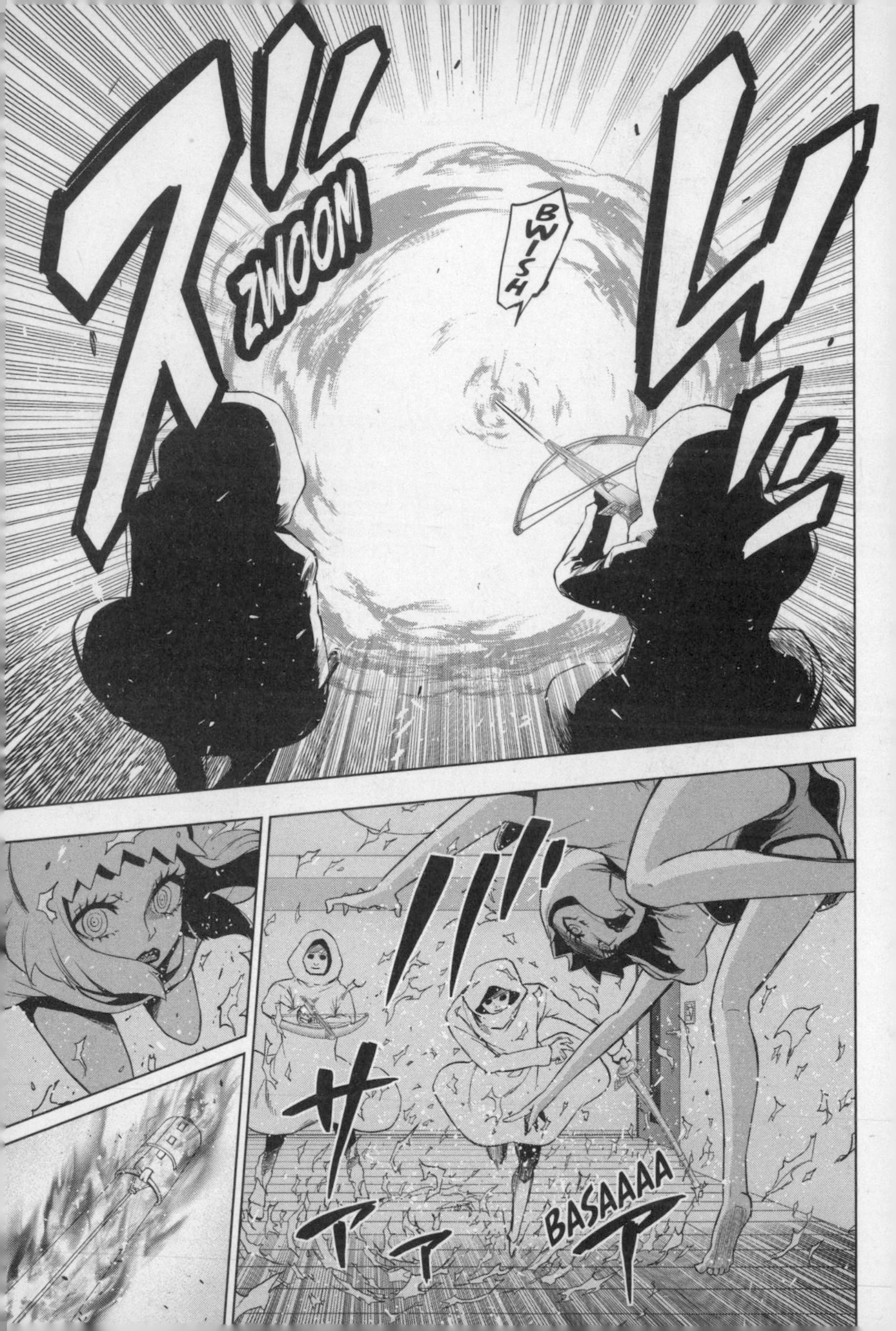
ZWOOM
BWISH
BASAAAA

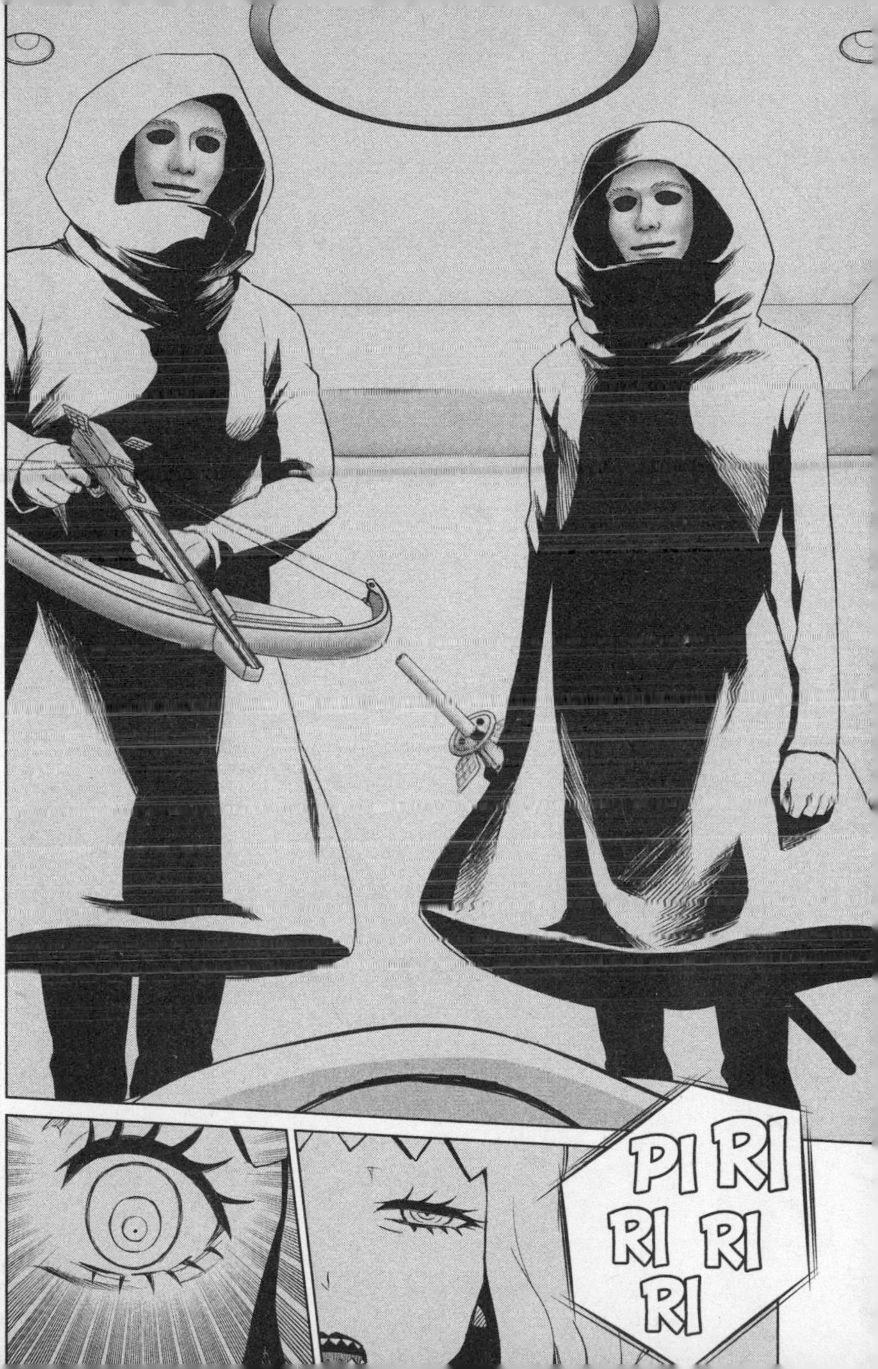
PI RI RI RI RI

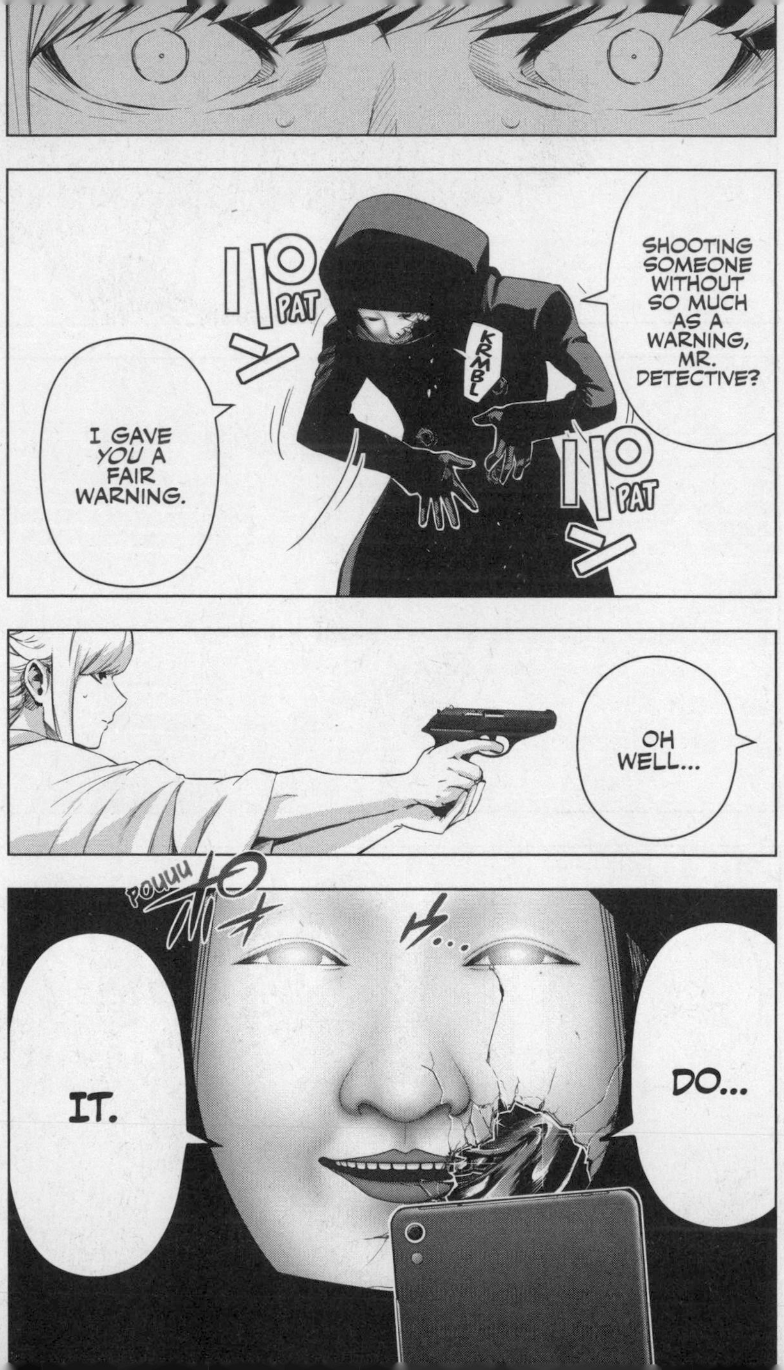

SHOOTING SOMEONE WITHOUT SO MUCH AS A WARNING, MR. DETECTIVE?
PAT
KRMBL
PAT
I GAVE *YOU* A FAIR WARNING.
OH WELL...
POUUU
DO...
IT.

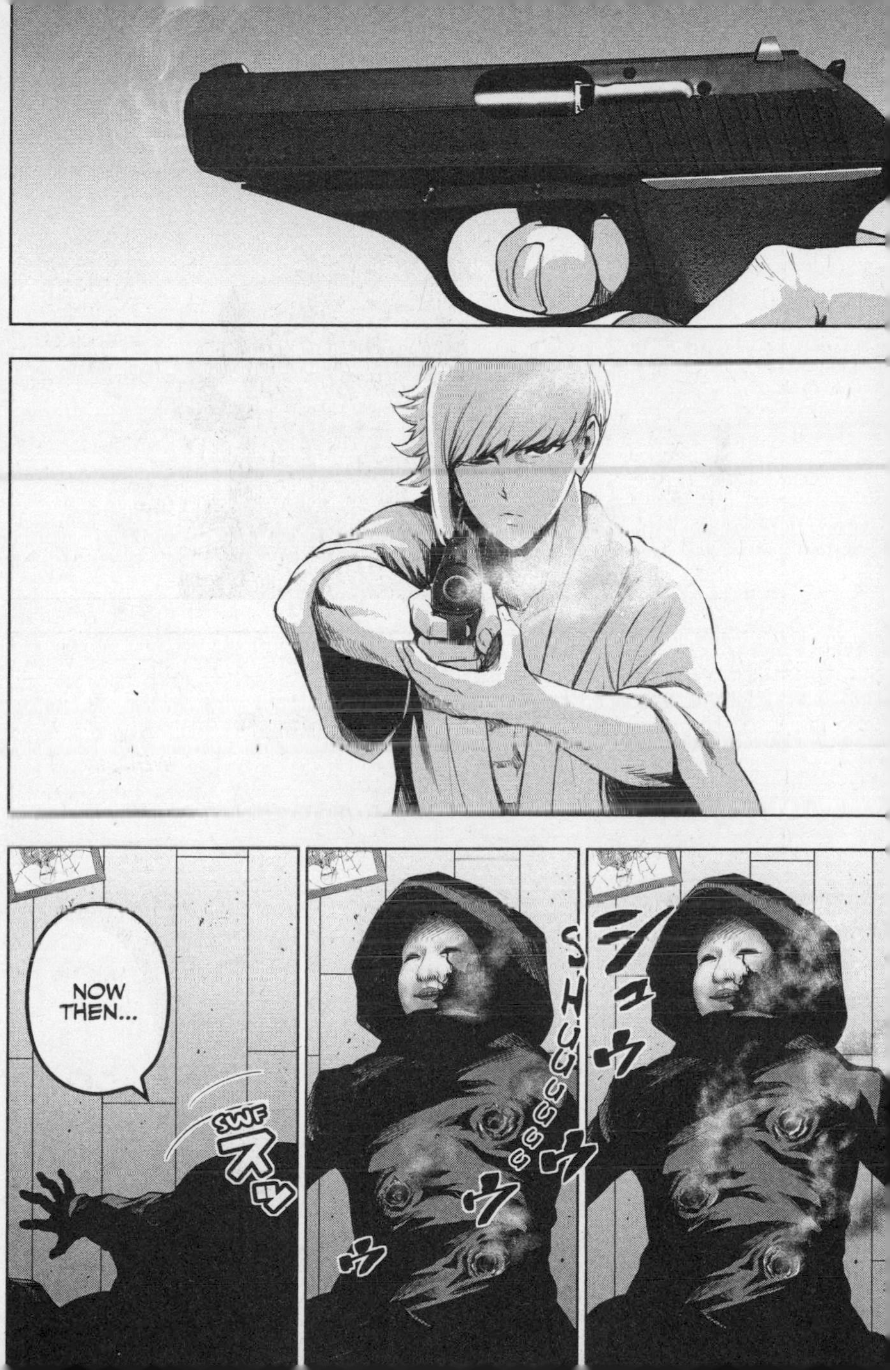
シュウウウウ
SHUUUUUU
NOW THEN...
SWF
スッ

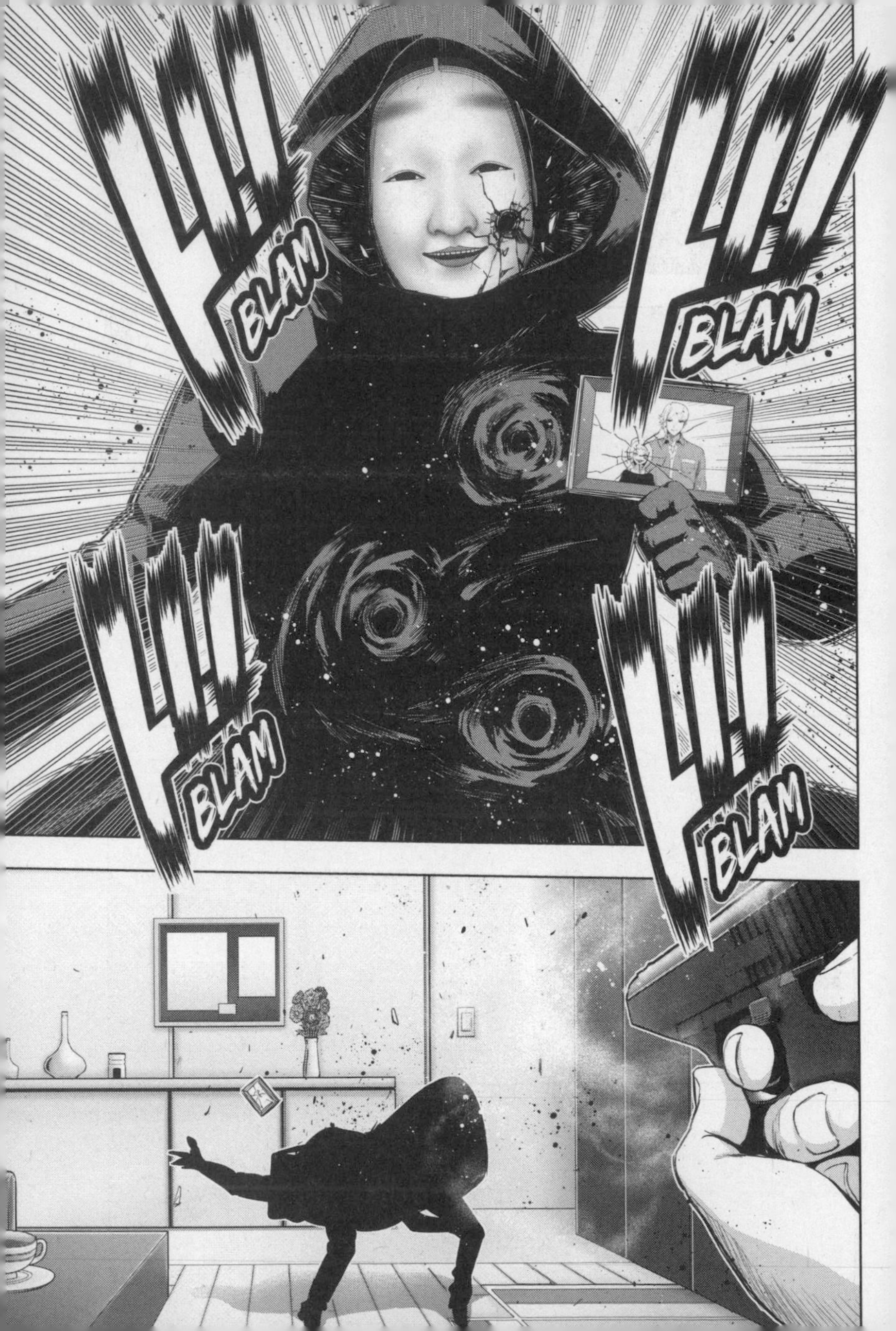
BLAM
BLAM
BLAM
BLAM

THIS IS NO IDLE THREAT.

SHE'S ALREADY IN THE PALM OF MY HAND.

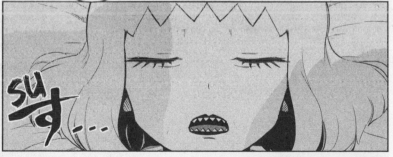

SU す...

ENTER.70
A'S IDENTITY, PART 2

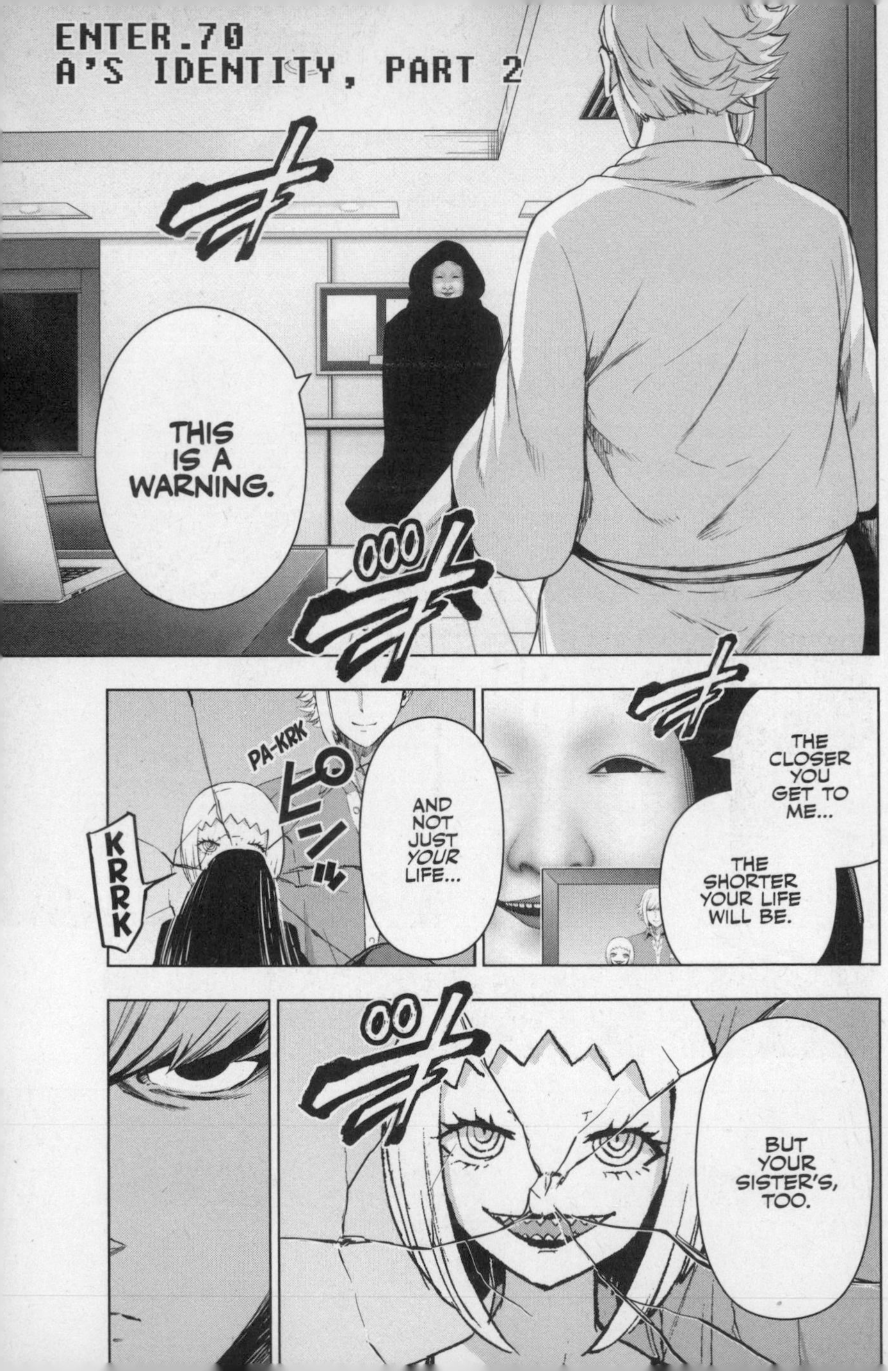

THIS IS A WARNING.
THE CLOSER YOU GET TO ME...
THE SHORTER YOUR LIFE WILL BE.
AND NOT JUST *YOUR* LIFE...
PA-KRK
KRRK
BUT YOUR SISTER'S, TOO.

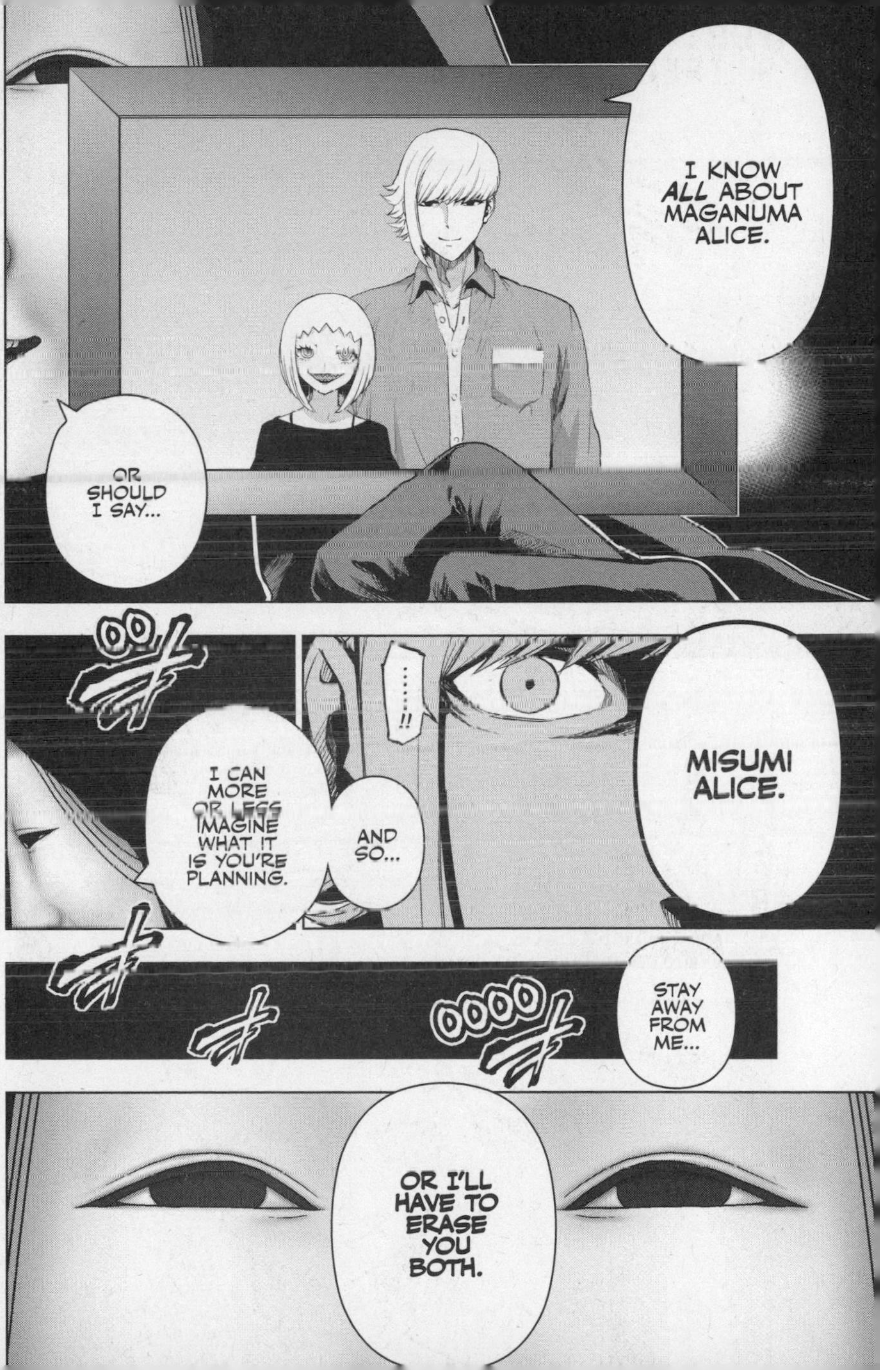
I KNOW ALL ABOUT MAGANUMA ALICE.
OR SHOULD I SAY...
MISUMI ALICE.
......!!
OO
AND SO...
I CAN MORE OR LESS IMAGINE WHAT IT IS YOU'RE PLANNING.
STAY AWAY FROM ME...
OOOO
OR I'LL HAVE TO ERASE YOU BOTH.

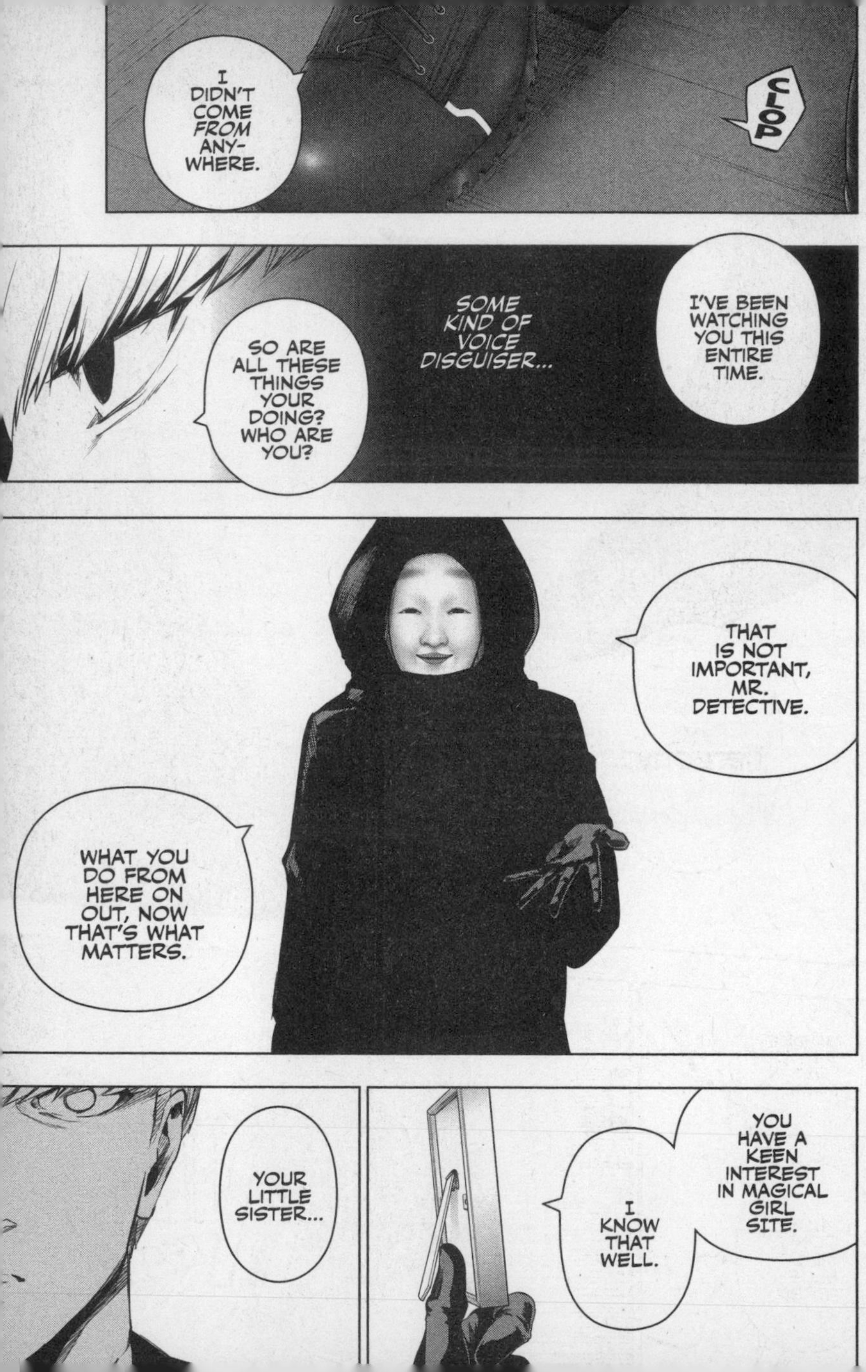
CLOP
I DIDN'T COME FROM ANYWHERE.
I'VE BEEN WATCHING YOU THIS ENTIRE TIME.
SOME KIND OF VOICE DISGUISER...
SO ARE ALL THESE THINGS YOUR DOING? WHO ARE YOU?
THAT IS NOT IMPORTANT, MR. DETECTIVE.
WHAT YOU DO FROM HERE ON OUT, NOW THAT'S WHAT MATTERS.
YOU HAVE A KEEN INTEREST IN MAGICAL GIRL SITE.
I KNOW THAT WELL.
YOUR LITTLE SISTER...

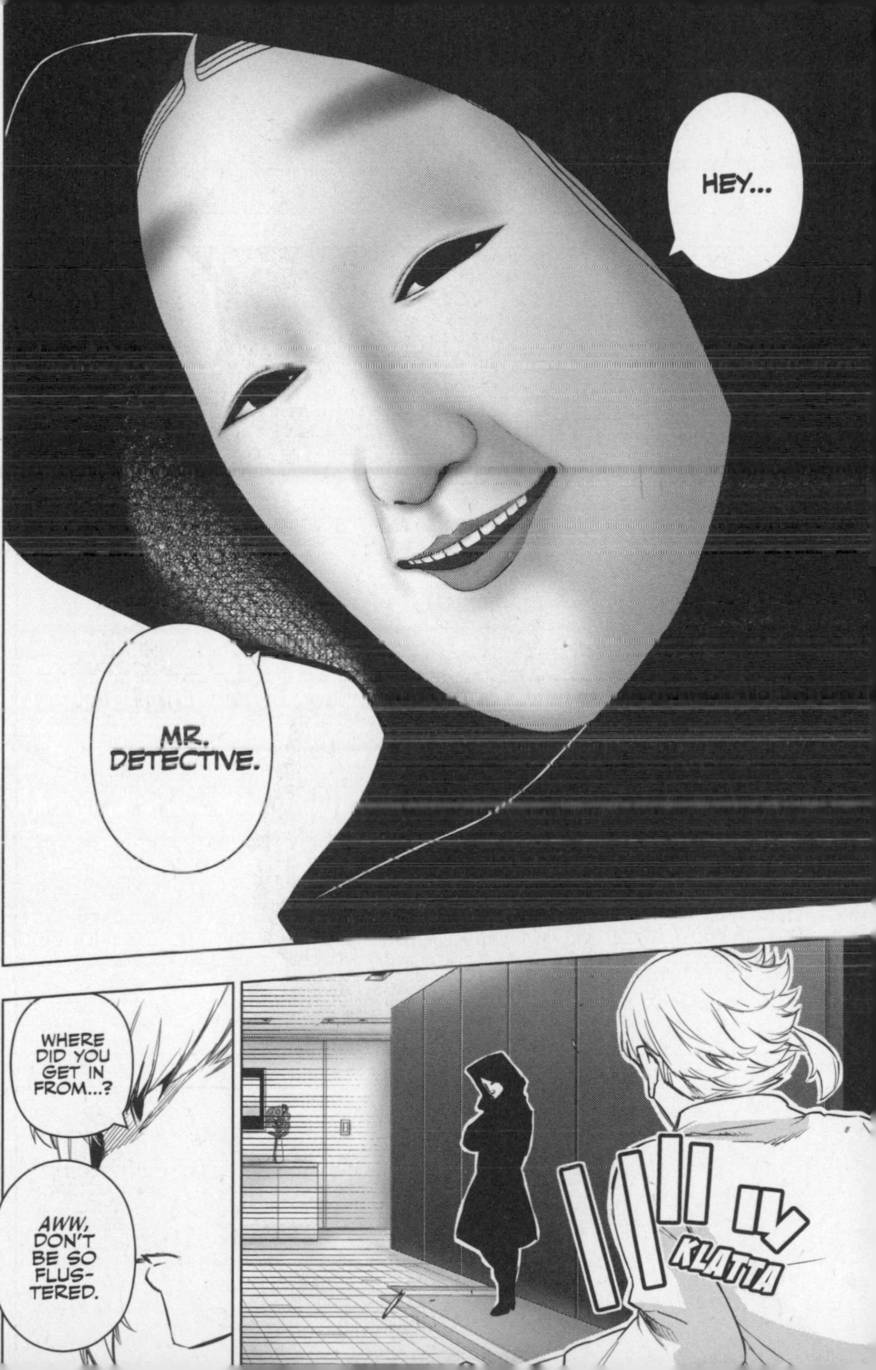
HEY...
MR. DETECTIVE.
KLATTA
WHERE DID YOU GET IN FROM...?
AWW, DON'T BE SO FLUS-TERED.

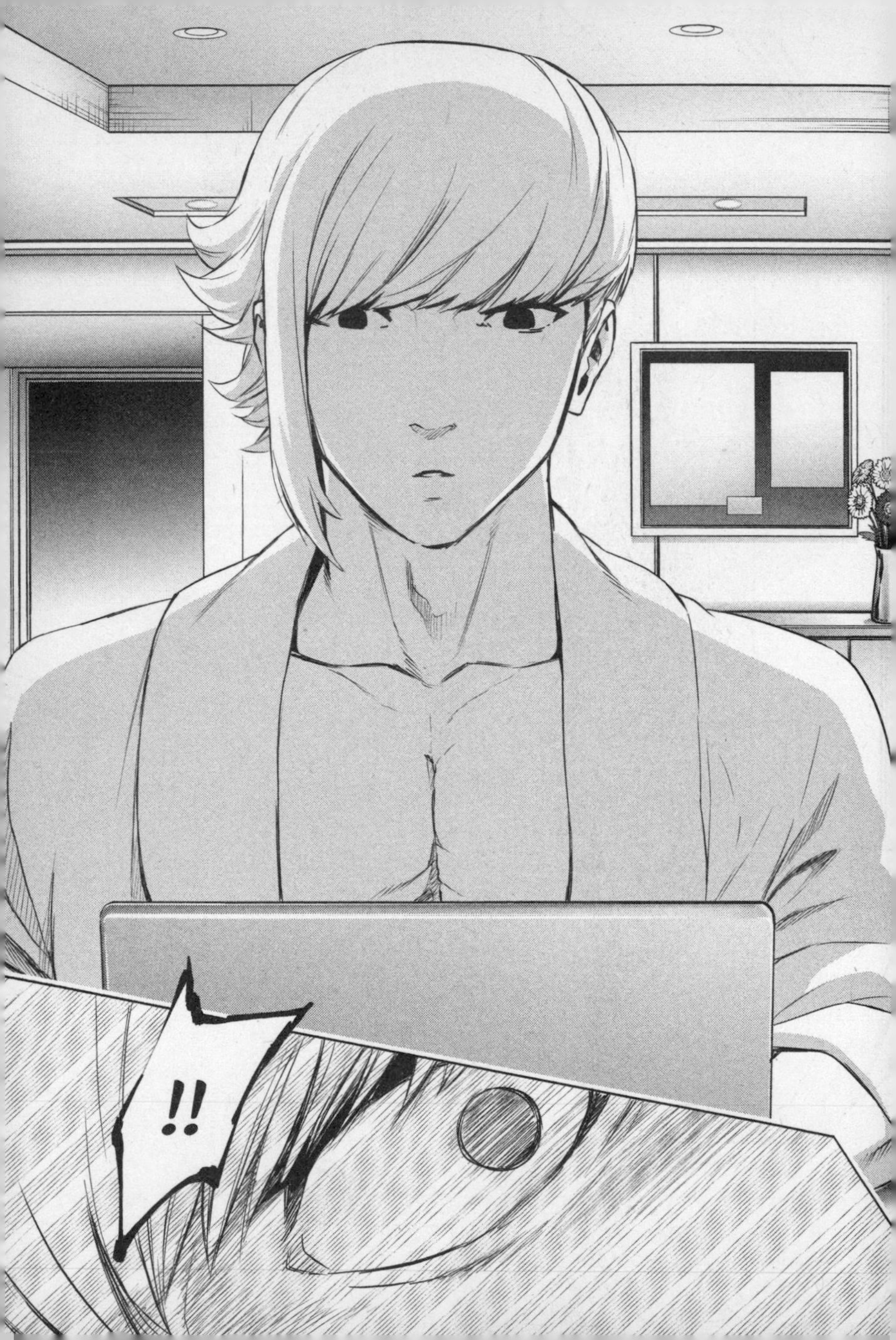
!!

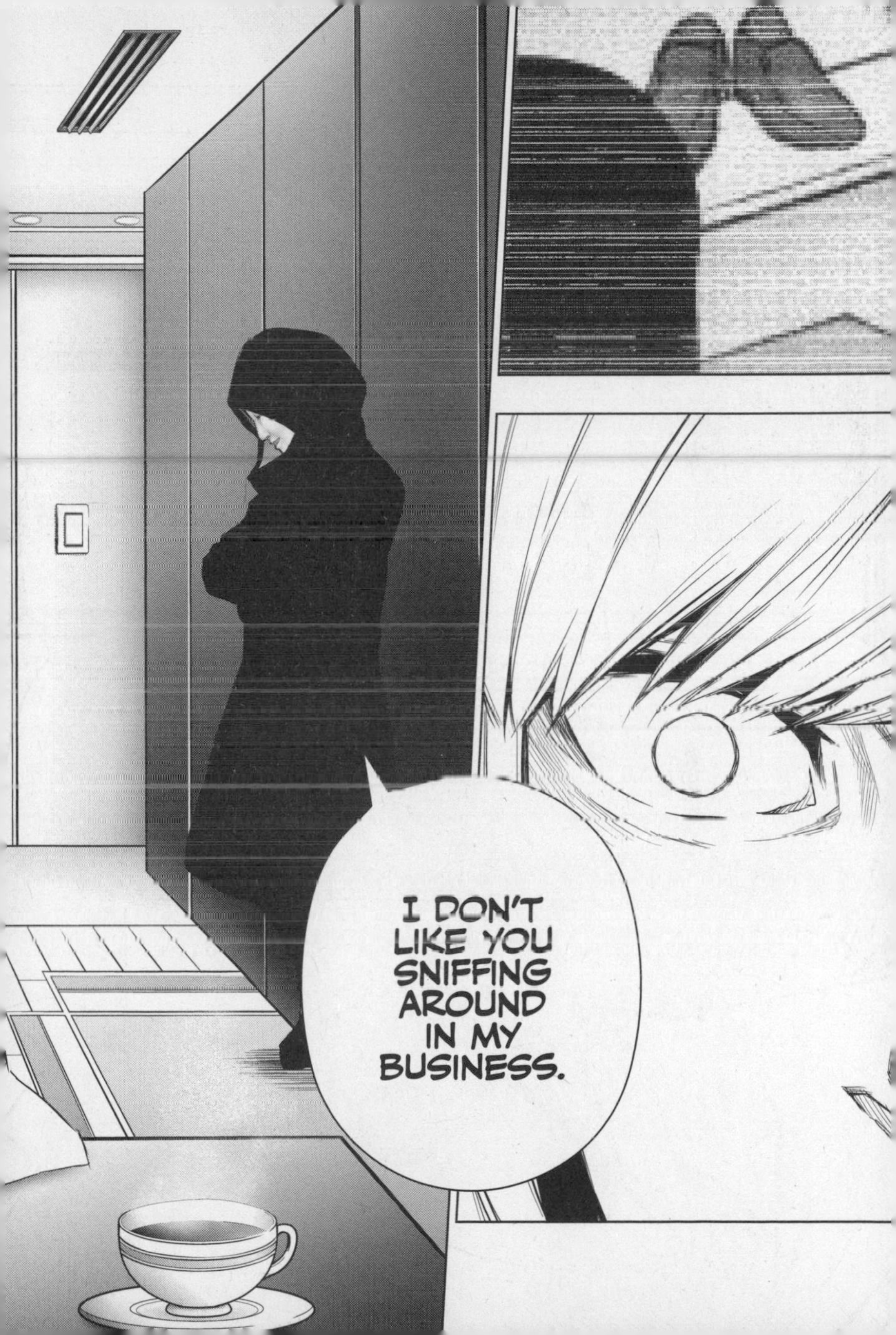
I DON'T LIKE YOU SNIFFING AROUND IN MY BUSINESS.

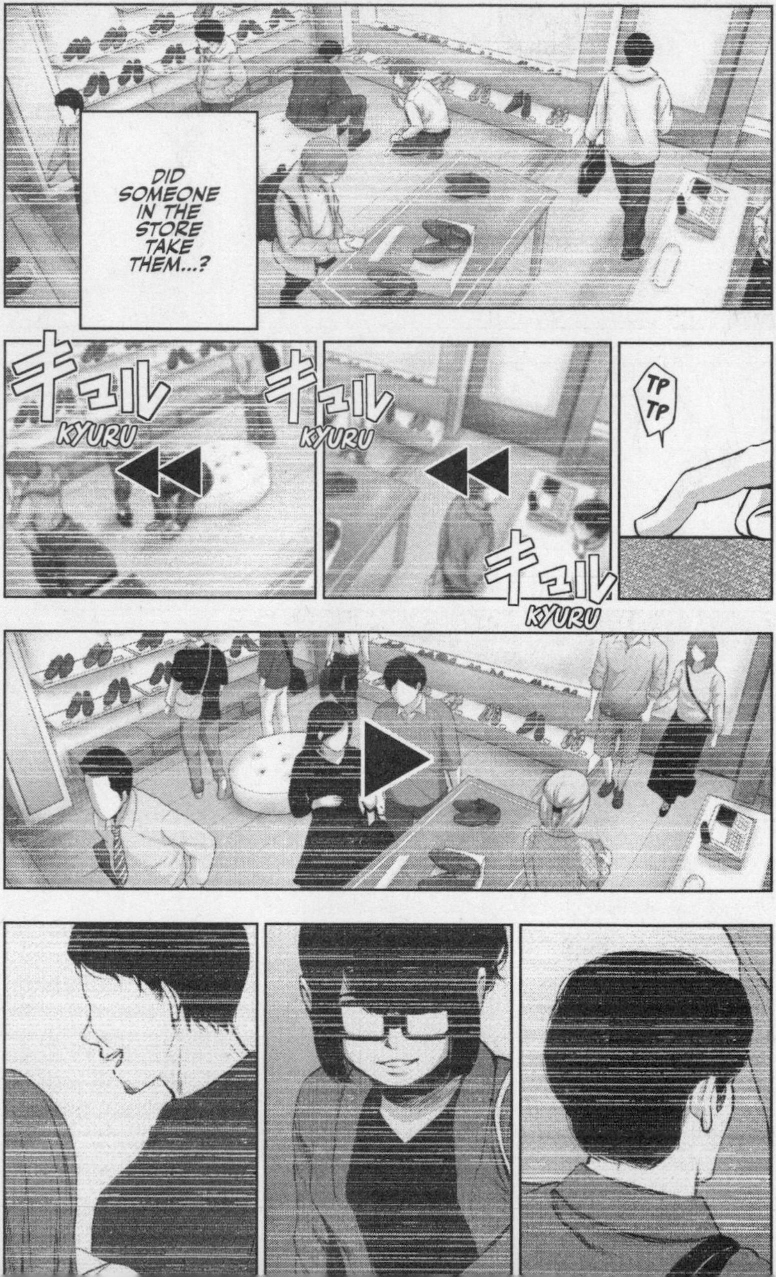
DID SOMEONE IN THE STORE TAKE THEM...?
TP TP
キュル
KYURU
キュル
KYURU
キュル
KYURU

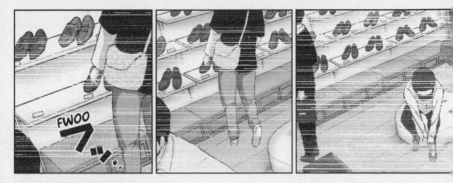

FWOO

7...

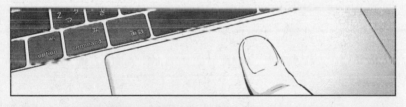

THEY DISAP-PEARED ...?

HOW COULD THAT HAPPEN?

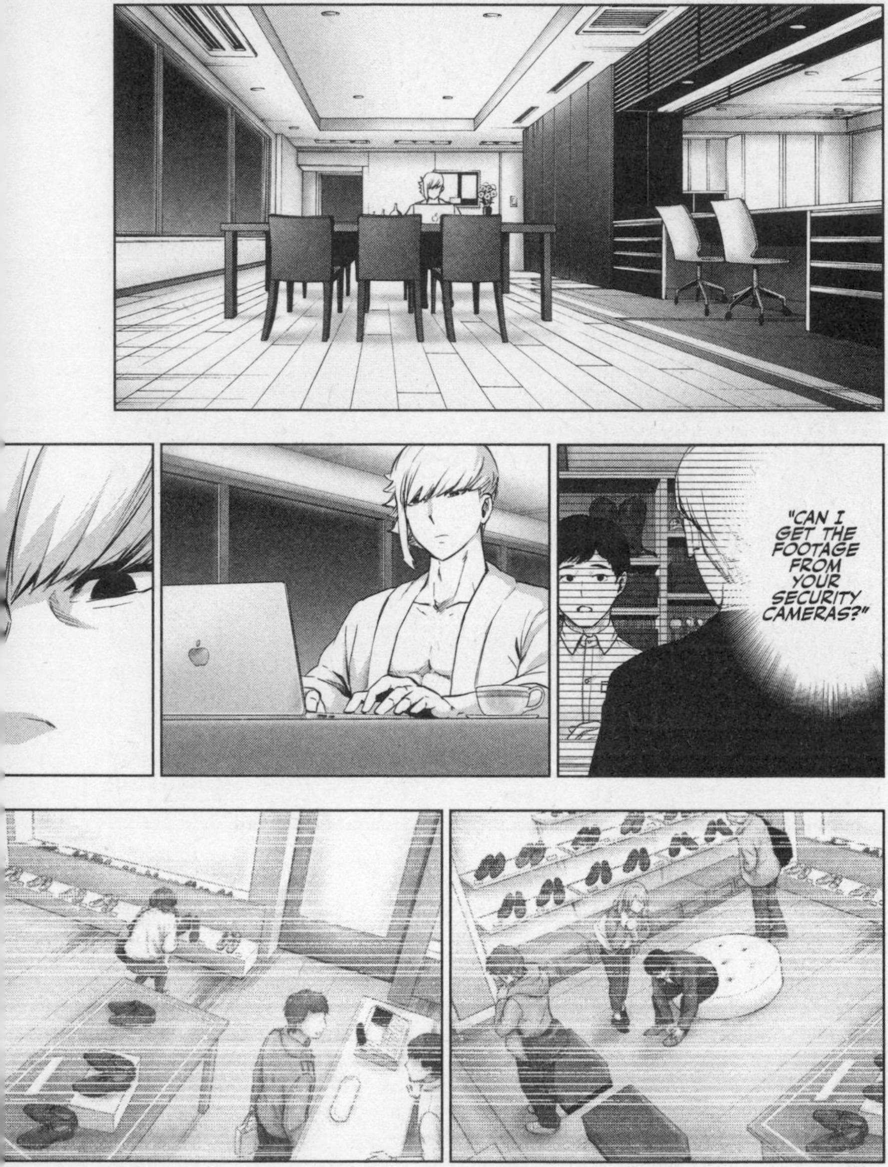
"CAN I GET THE FOOTAGE FROM YOUR SECURITY CAMERAS?"

ALL
RIGHT.

LATER
...

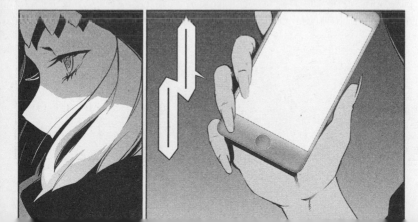

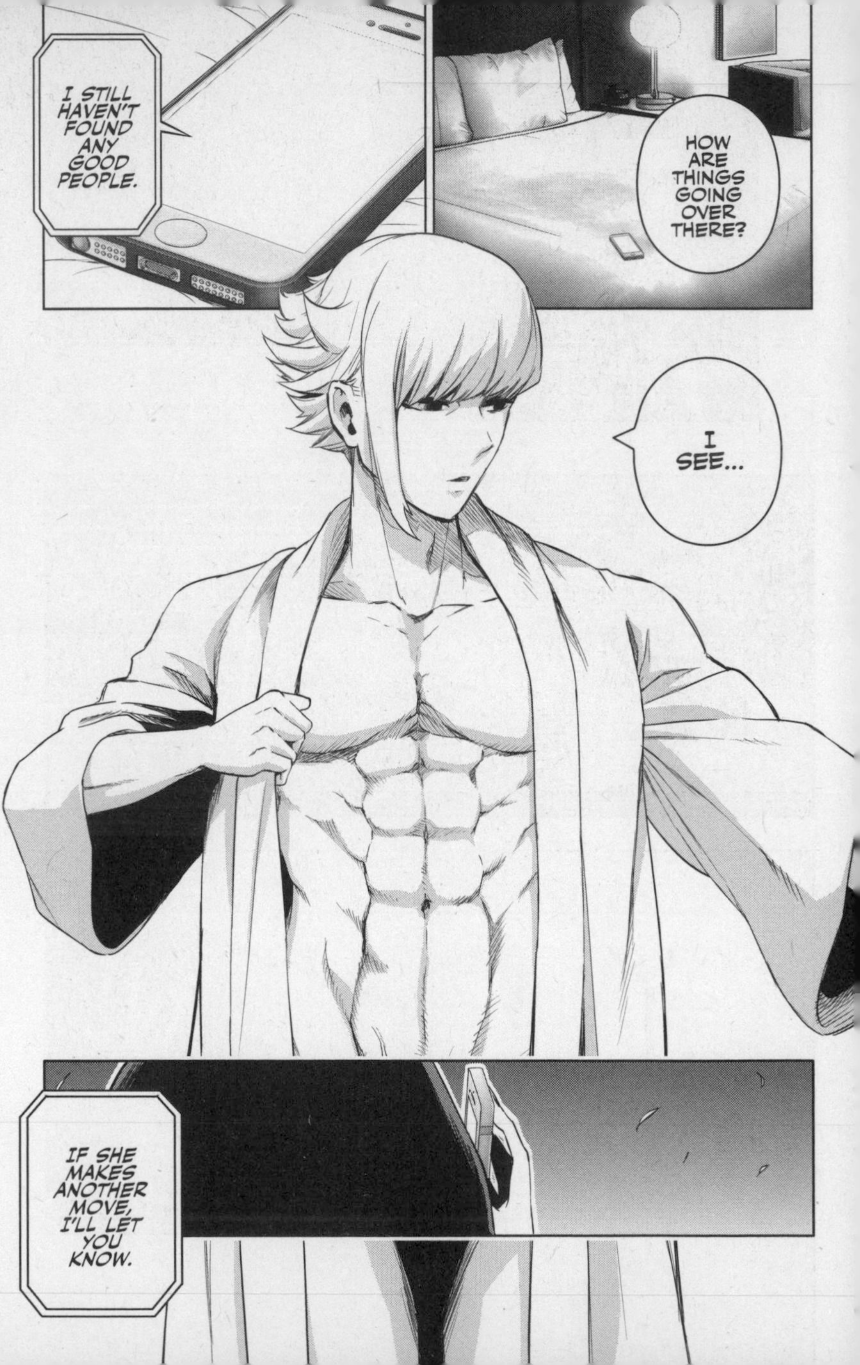
HOW ARE THINGS GOING OVER THERE?
I STILL HAVEN'T FOUND ANY GOOD PEOPLE.
I SEE...
IF SHE MAKES ANOTHER MOVE, I'LL LET YOU KNOW.

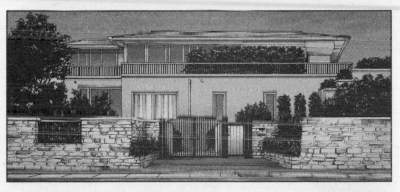

YEAH.

MISUMI

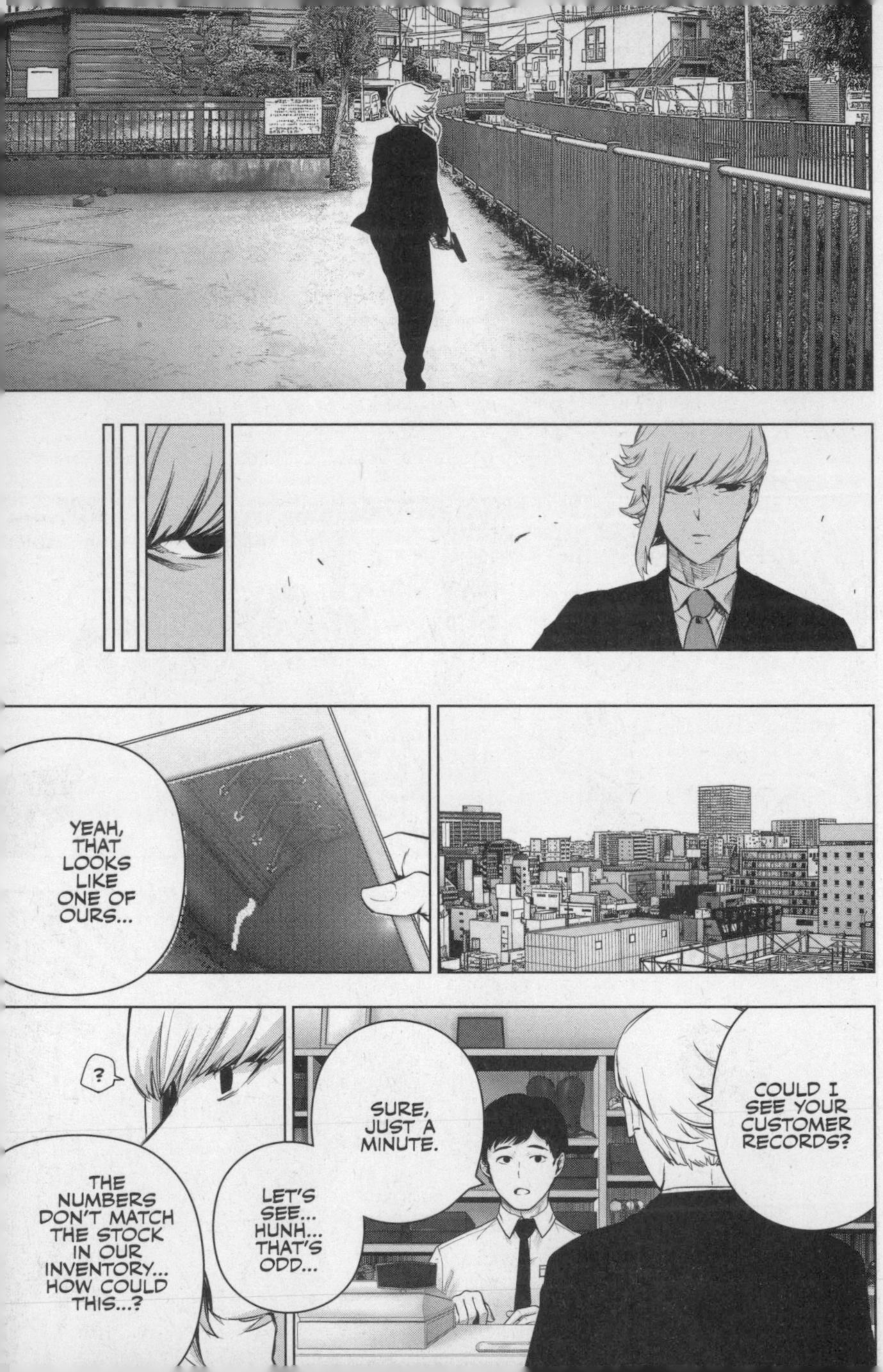
YEAH, THAT LOOKS LIKE ONE OF OURS...
COULD I SEE YOUR CUSTOMER RECORDS?
SURE, JUST A MINUTE.
LET'S SEE... HUNH... THAT'S ODD...
?
THE NUMBERS DON'T MATCH THE STOCK IN OUR INVENTORY... HOW COULD THIS...?

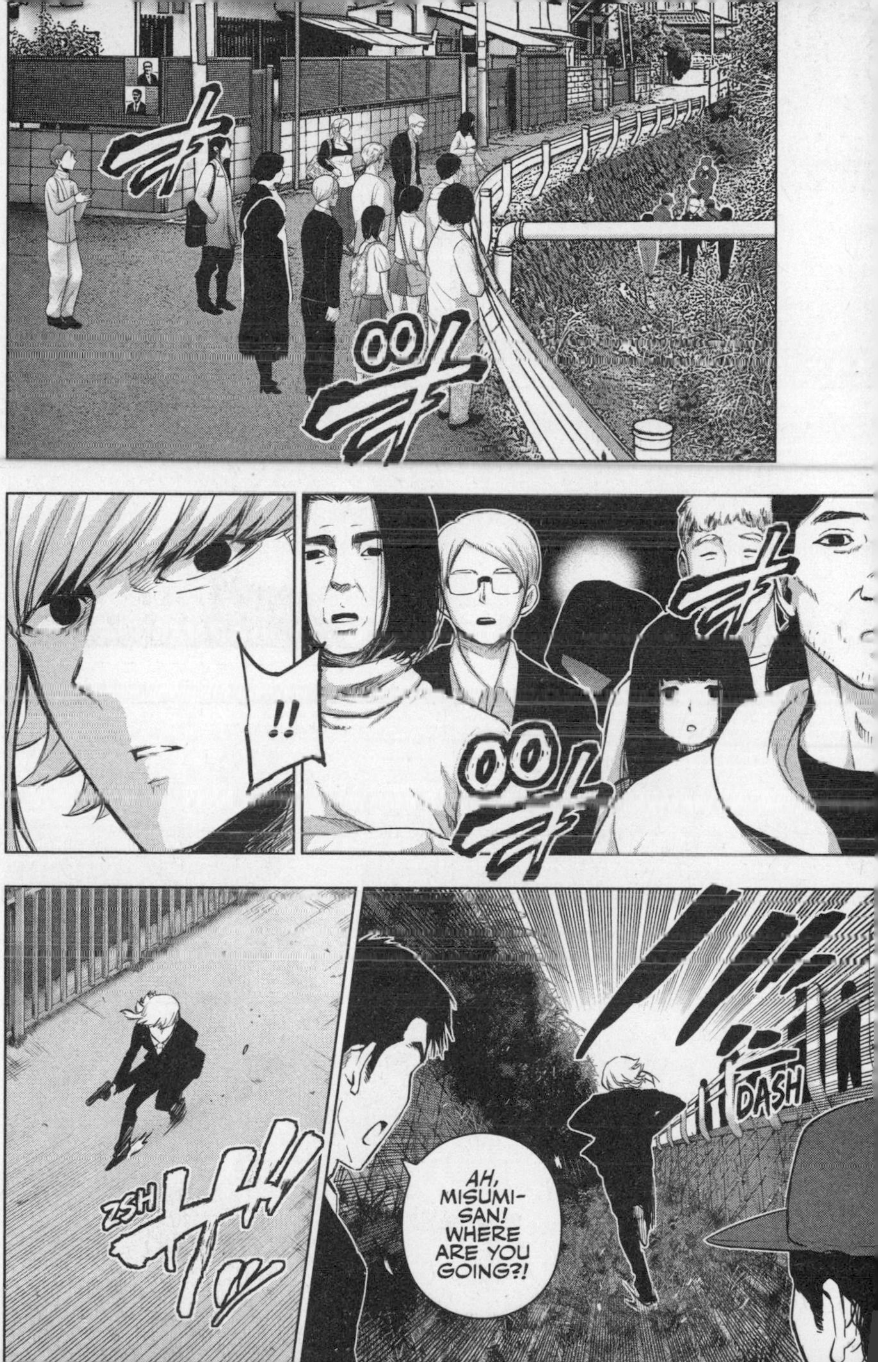
!!
DASH
AH, MISUMI-SAN! WHERE ARE YOU GOING?!
ZSH

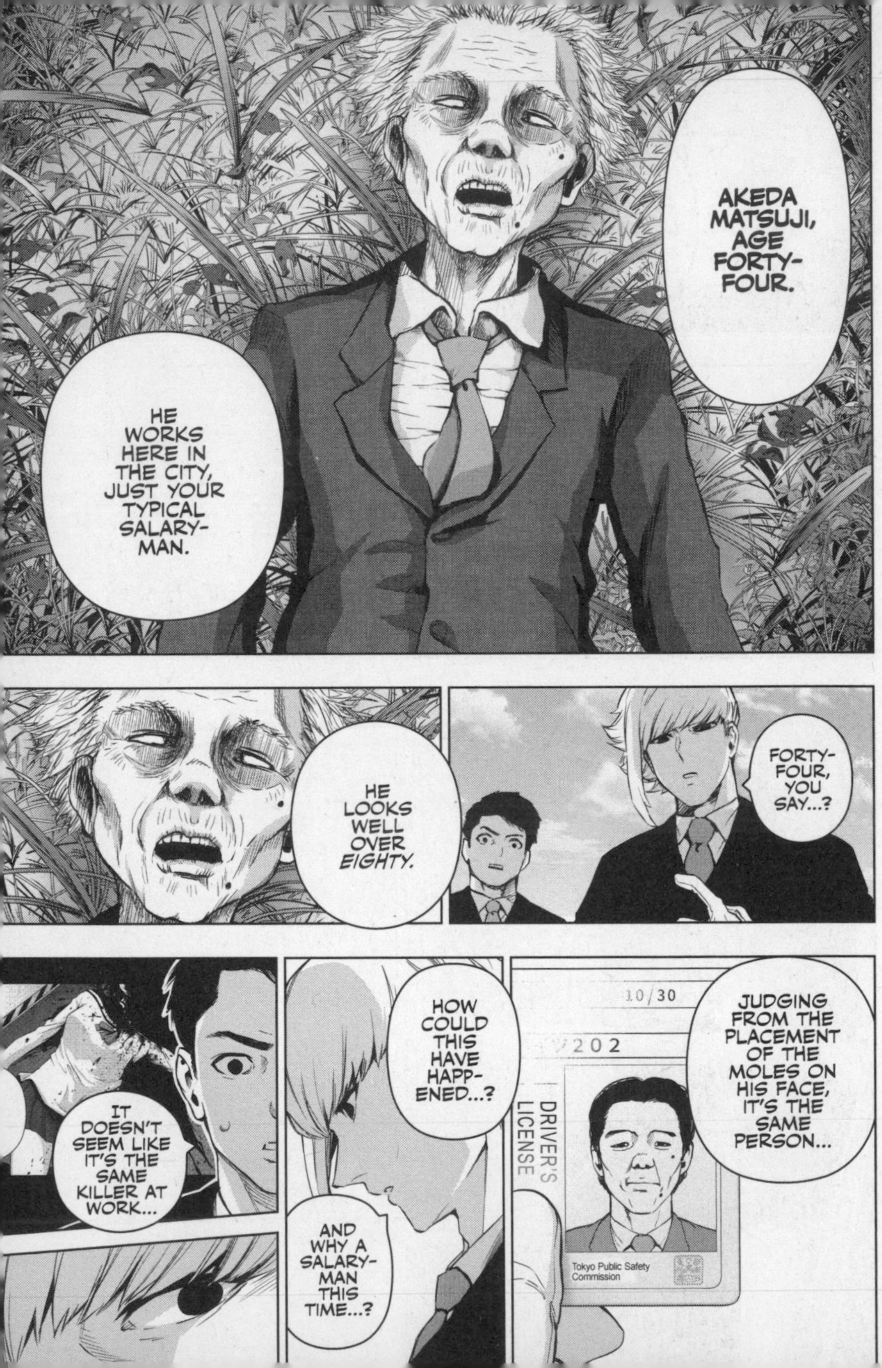
AKEDA MATSUJI, AGE FORTY-FOUR.
HE WORKS HERE IN THE CITY, JUST YOUR TYPICAL SALARYMAN.
FORTY-FOUR, YOU SAY...?
HE LOOKS WELL OVER *EIGHTY*.
10/30
202
DRIVER'S LICENSE
Tokyo Public Safety Commission
JUDGING FROM THE PLACEMENT OF THE MOLES ON HIS FACE, IT'S THE SAME PERSON...
HOW COULD THIS HAVE HAPPENED...?
AND WHY A SALARYMAN THIS TIME...?
IT DOESN'T SEEM LIKE IT'S THE SAME KILLER AT WORK...

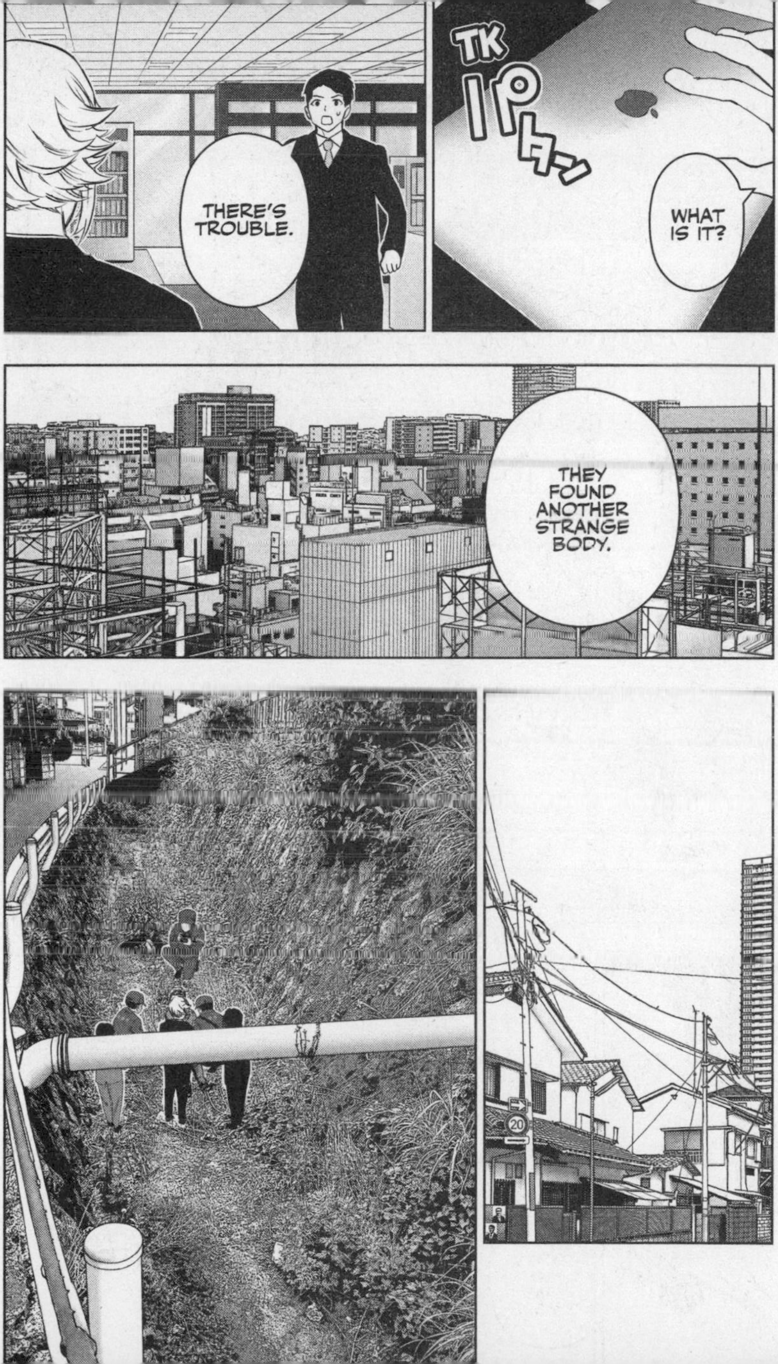
TK
WHAT IS IT?
THERE'S TROUBLE.
THEY FOUND ANOTHER STRANGE BODY.
20

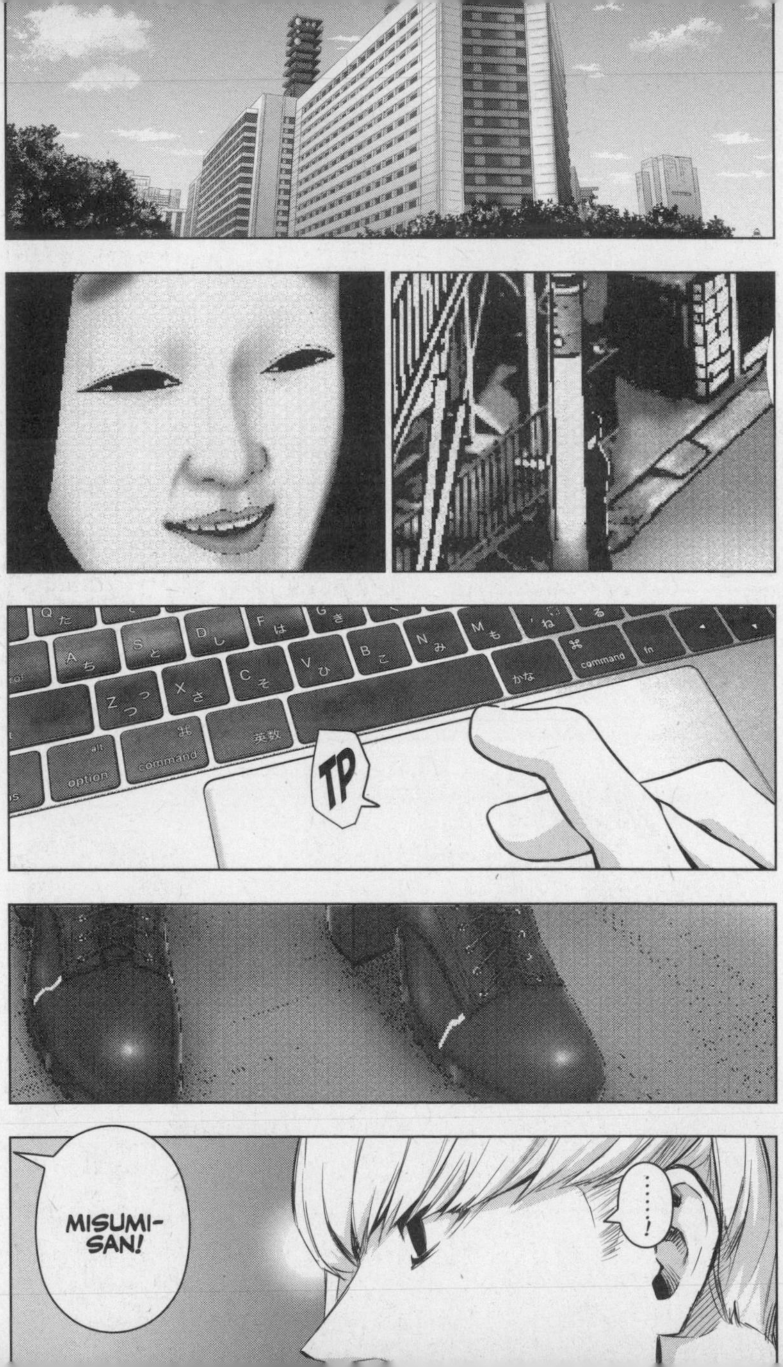
TP
......!
MISUMI-SAN!

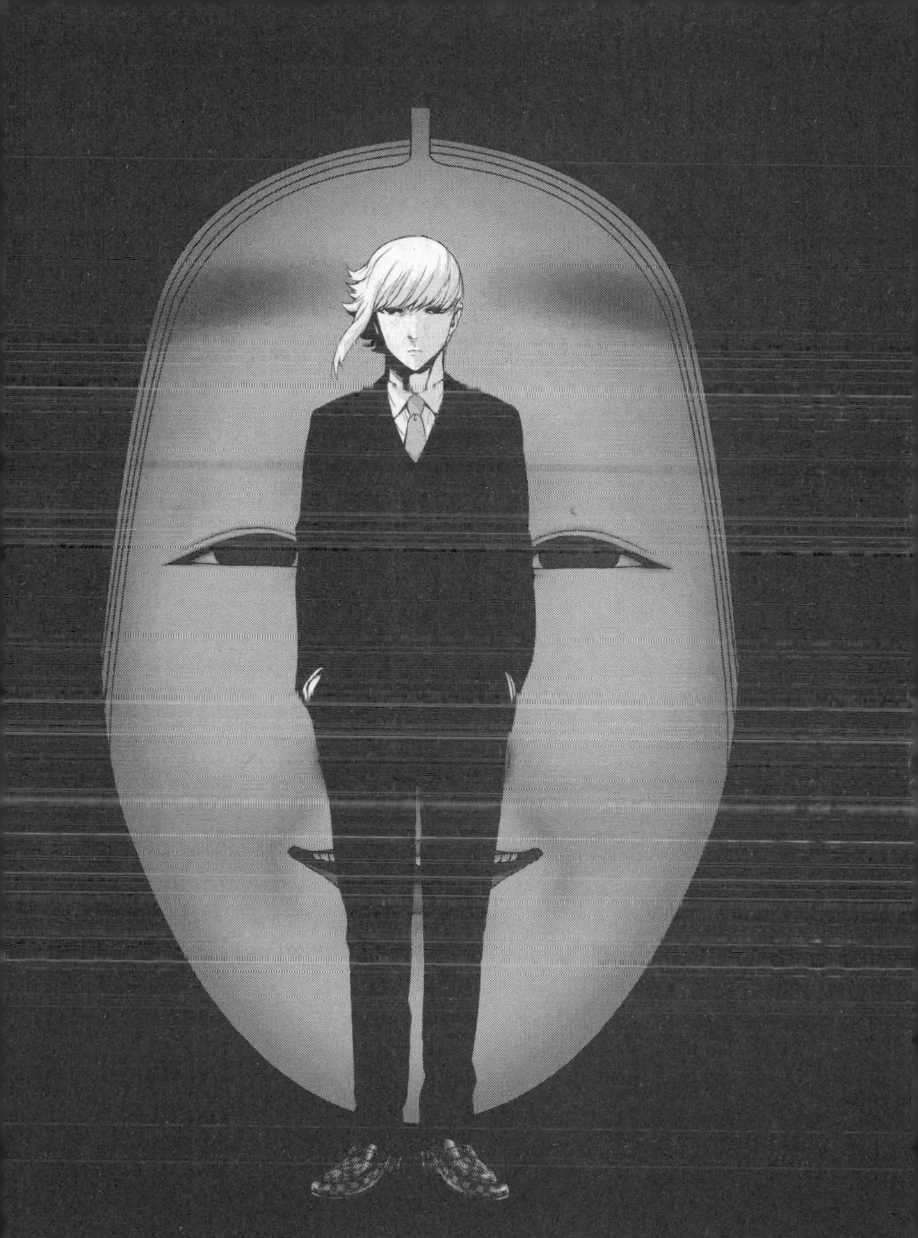

ENTER.69
A'S IDENTITY, PART 1

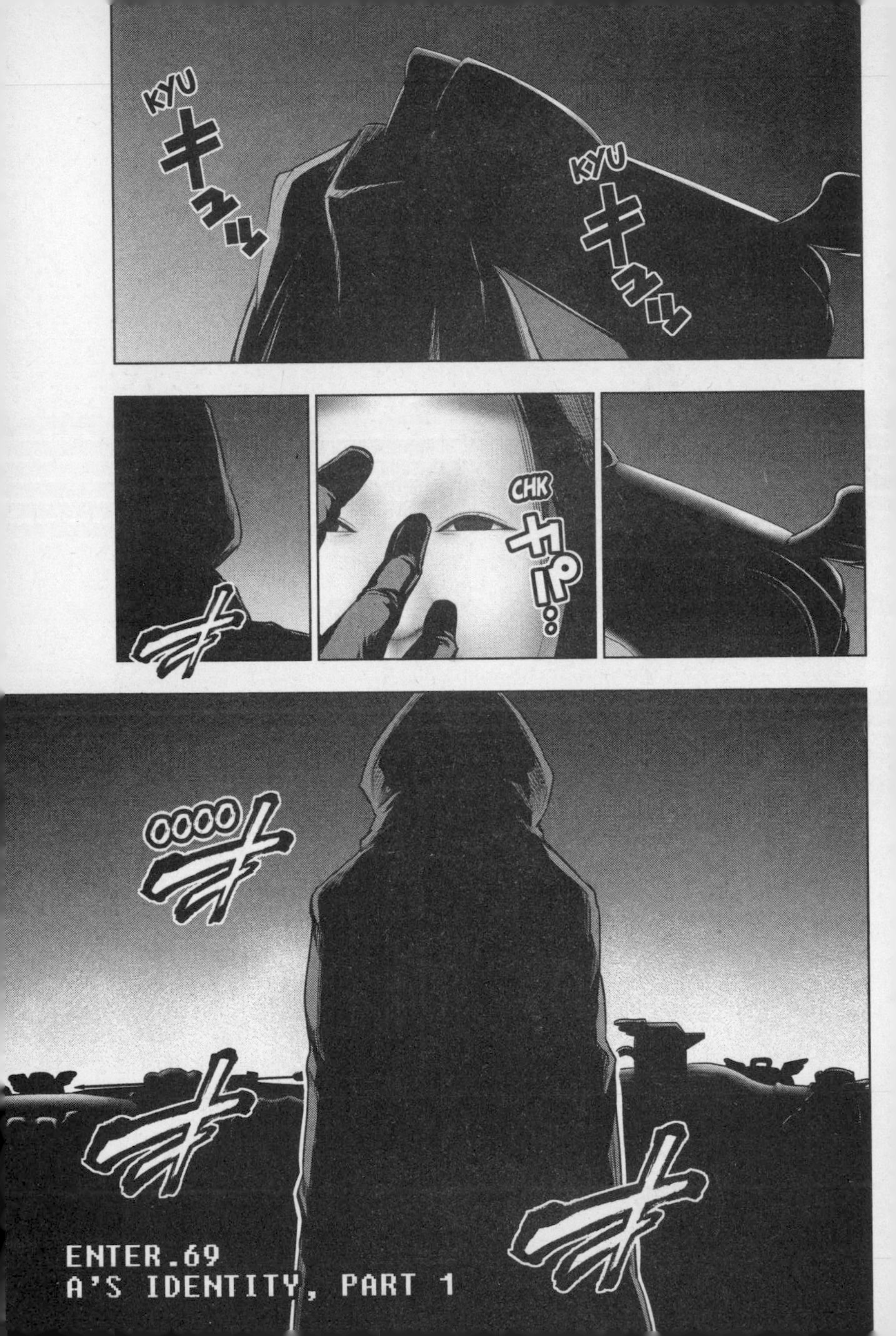
KYU
KYU
CHK
OOOO
ENTER.69
A'S IDENTITY, PART 1

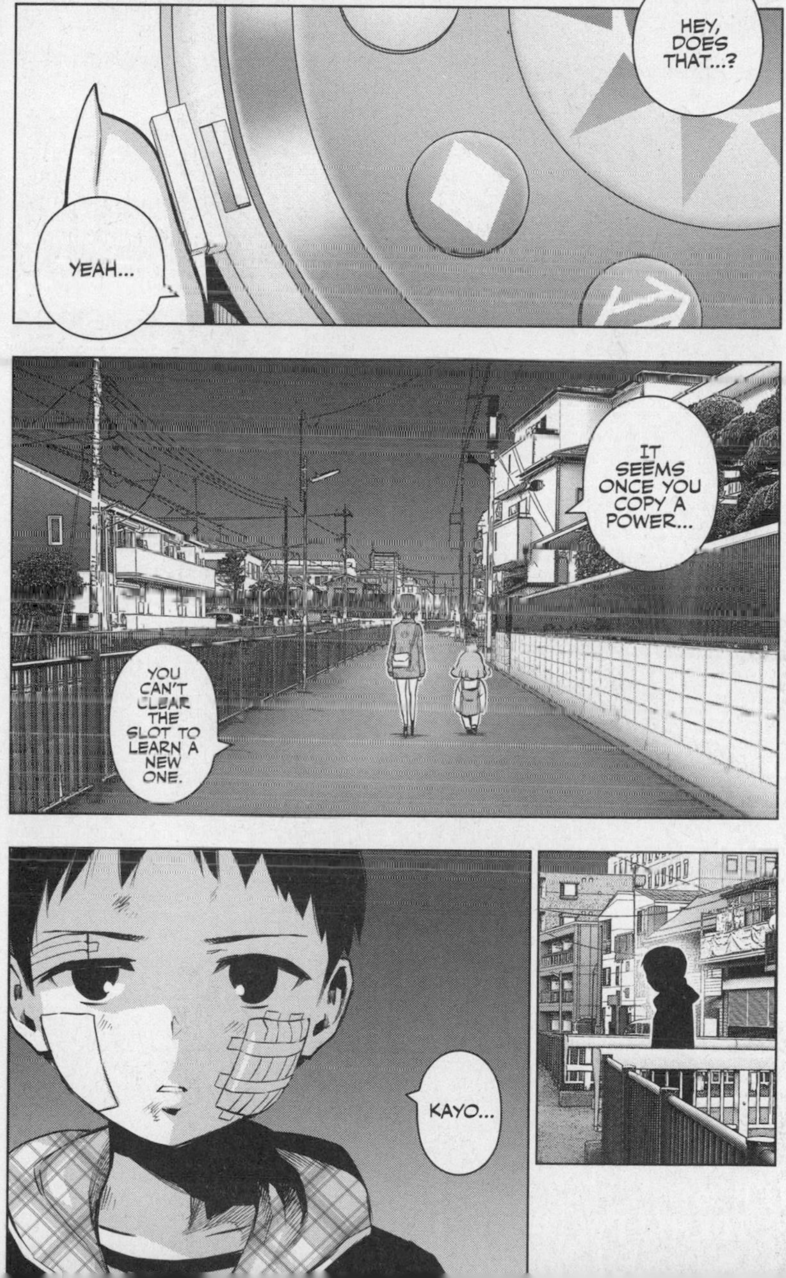
HEY, DOES THAT...?
YEAH...
IT SEEMS ONCE YOU COPY A POWER...
YOU CAN'T CLEAR THE SLOT TO LEARN A NEW ONE.
KAYO...

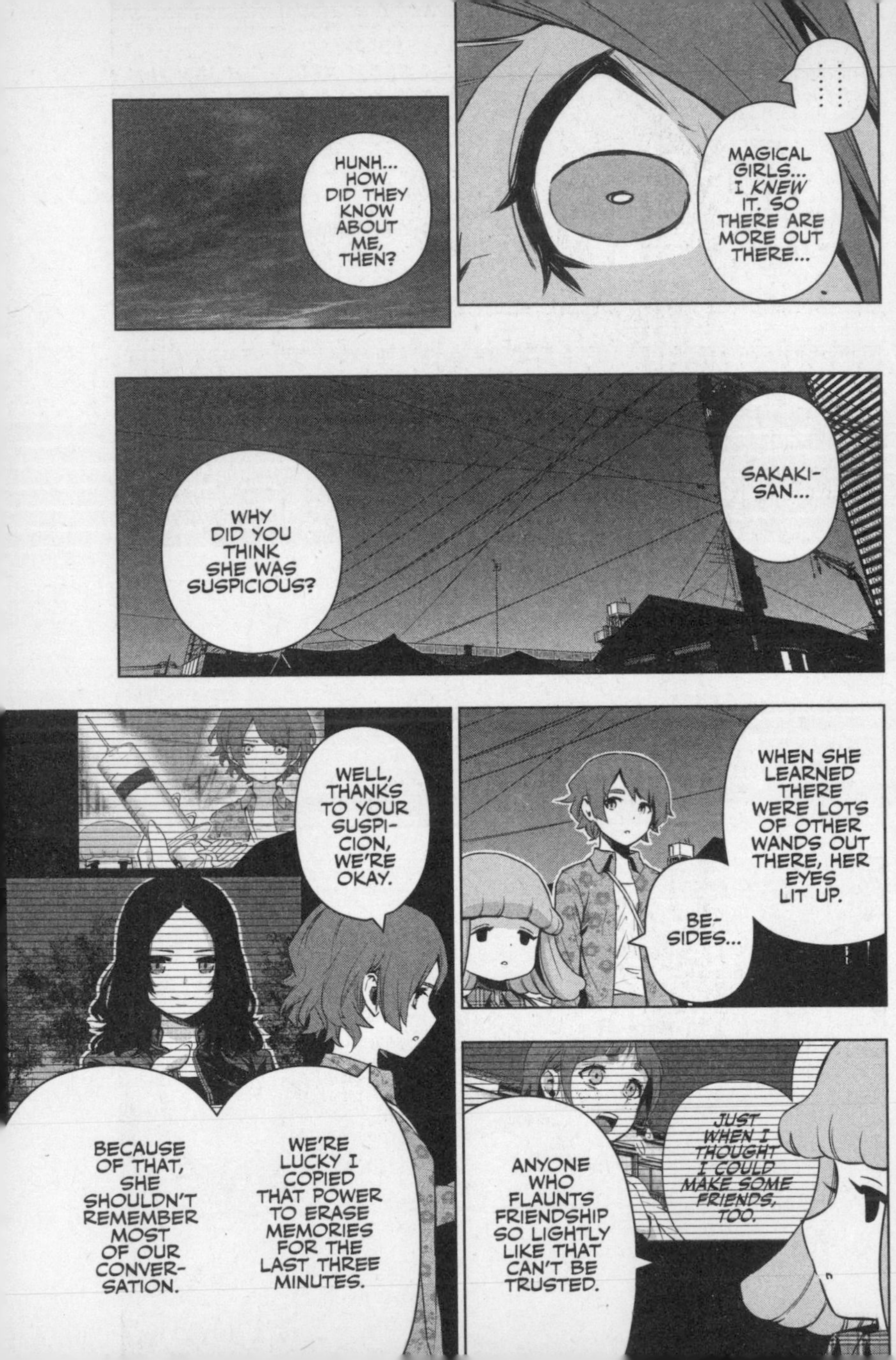
......
MAGICAL GIRLS... I *KNEW* IT. SO THERE ARE MORE OUT THERE...
HUNH... HOW DID THEY KNOW ABOUT ME, THEN?
SAKAKI-SAN...
WHY DID YOU THINK SHE WAS SUSPICIOUS?
WHEN SHE LEARNED THERE WERE LOTS OF OTHER WANDS OUT THERE, HER EYES LIT UP.
BESIDES...
JUST WHEN I THOUGHT I COULD MAKE SOME FRIENDS, TOO.
ANYONE WHO FLAUNTS FRIENDSHIP SO LIGHTLY LIKE THAT CAN'T BE TRUSTED.
WELL, THANKS TO YOUR SUSPICION, WE'RE OKAY.
WE'RE LUCKY I COPIED THAT POWER TO ERASE MEMORIES FOR THE LAST THREE MINUTES.
BECAUSE OF THAT, SHE SHOULDN'T REMEMBER MOST OF OUR CONVERSATION.

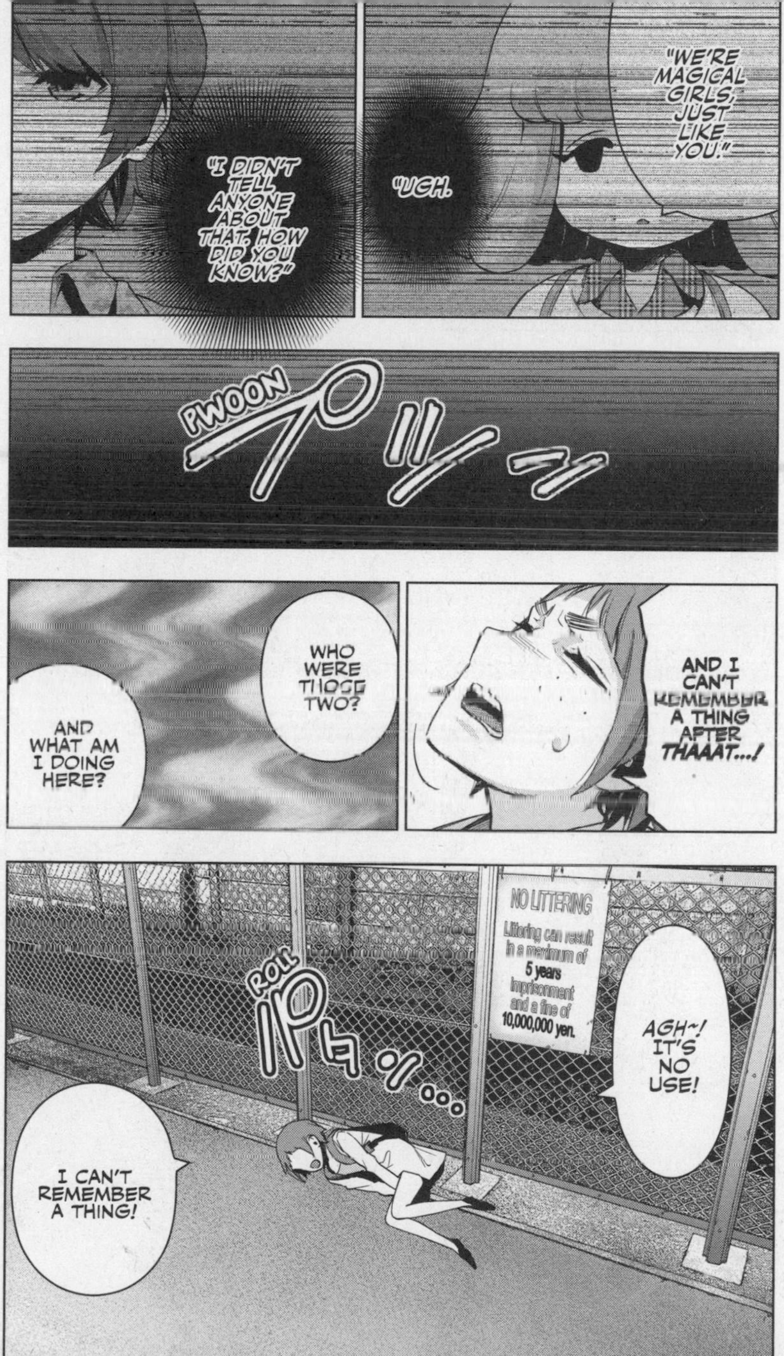
"WE'RE MAGICAL GIRLS, JUST LIKE YOU."
"UGH.
"I DIDN'T TELL ANYONE ABOUT THAT. HOW DID YOU KNOW?"
PWOON
AND I CAN'T REMEMBER A THING AFTER THAAAT...!
WHO WERE THOSE TWO?
AND WHAT AM I DOING HERE?
NO LITTERING
Littering can result in a maximum of 5 years imprisonment and a fine of 10,000,000 yen.
AGH~! IT'S NO USE!
ROLL
I CAN'T REMEMBER A THING!

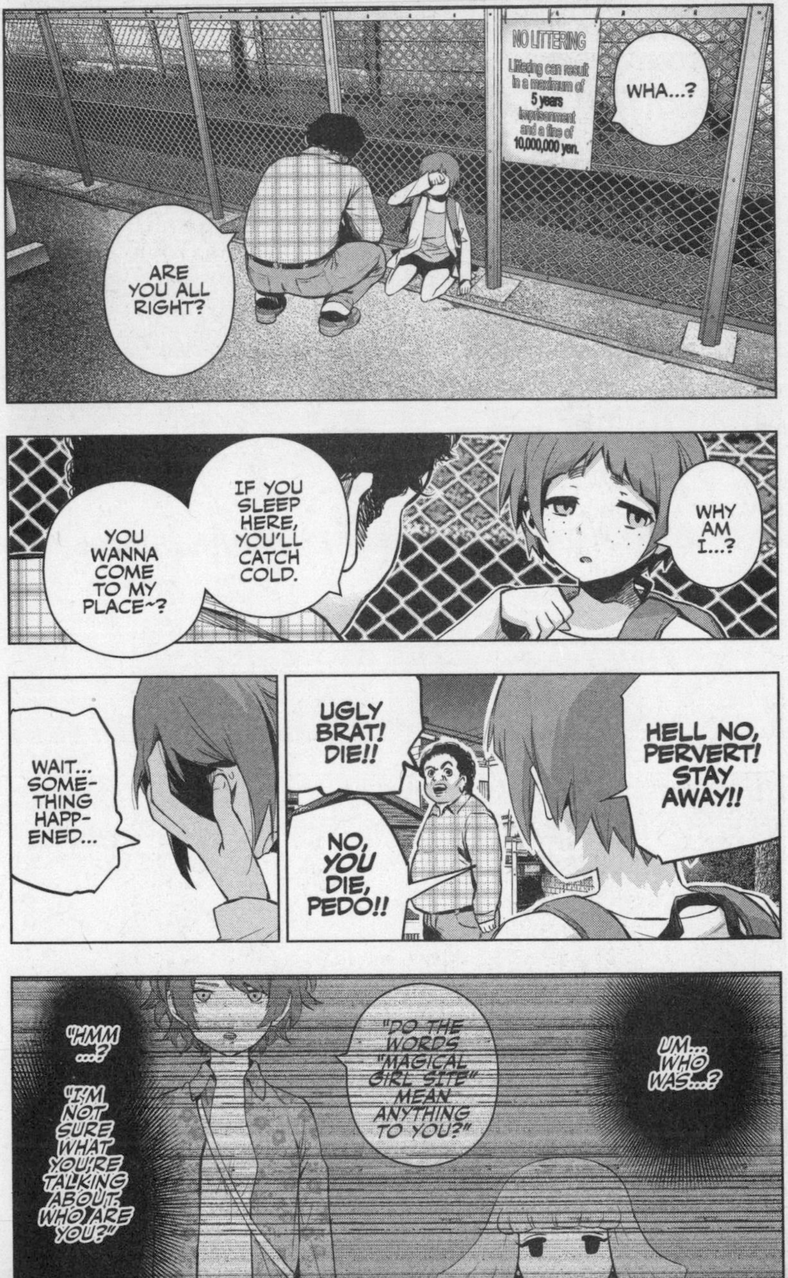
NO LITTERING
Littering can result in a maximum of 5 years imprisonment and a fine of 10,000,000 yen.
WHA...?
ARE YOU ALL RIGHT?
WHY AM I...?
IF YOU SLEEP HERE, YOU'LL CATCH COLD.
YOU WANNA COME TO MY PLACE~?
HELL NO, PERVERT! STAY AWAY!!
UGLY BRAT! DIE!!
NO, YOU DIE, PEDO!!
WAIT... SOMETHING HAPPENED...
UM... WHO WAS...?
"DO THE WORDS "MAGICAL GIRL SITE" MEAN ANYTHING TO YOU?"
"HMM...?
"I'M NOT SURE WHAT YOU'RE TALKING ABOUT. WHO ARE YOU?"

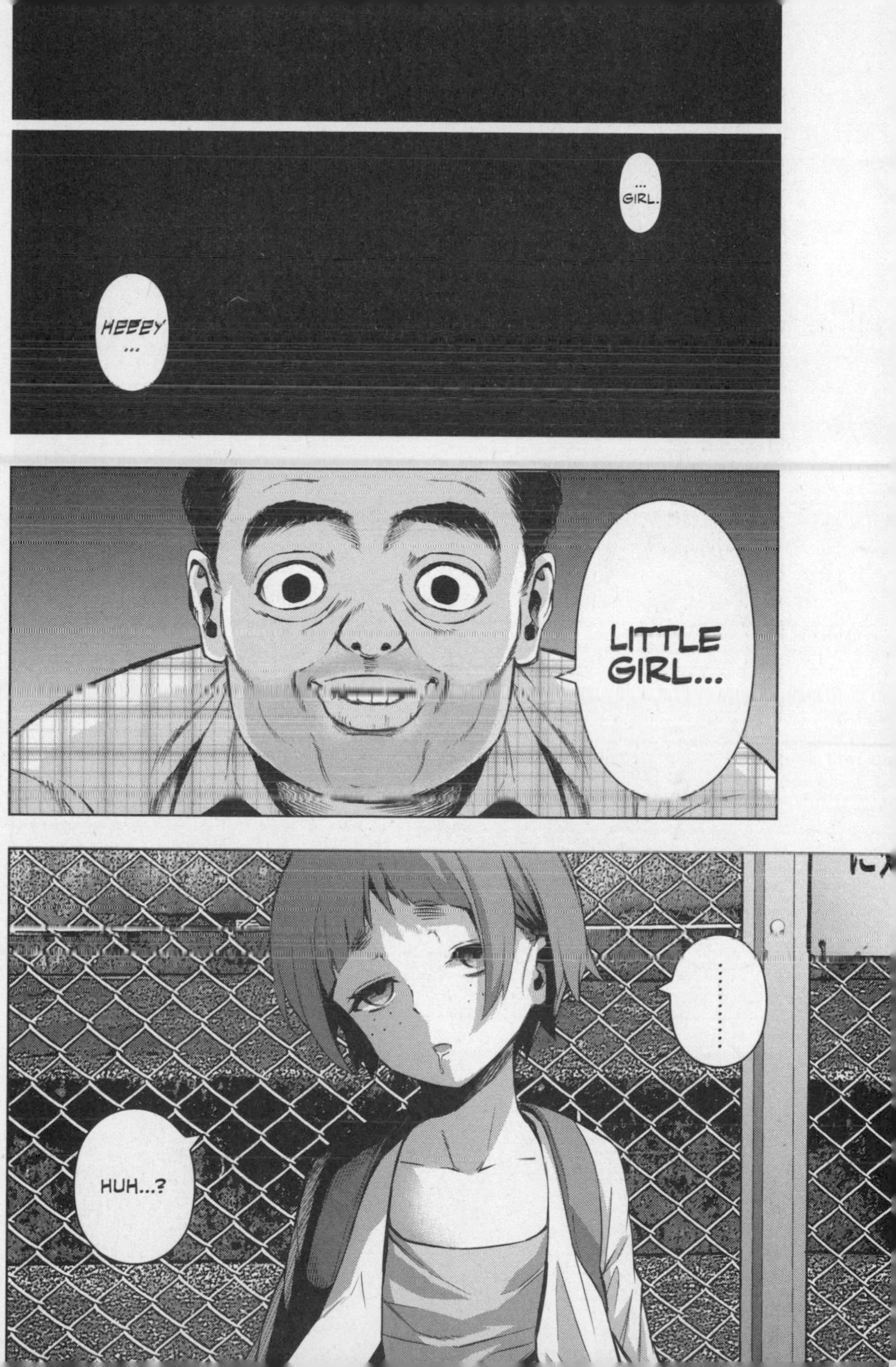

...GIRL.
HEEEY...
LITTLE GIRL...
......
HUH...?

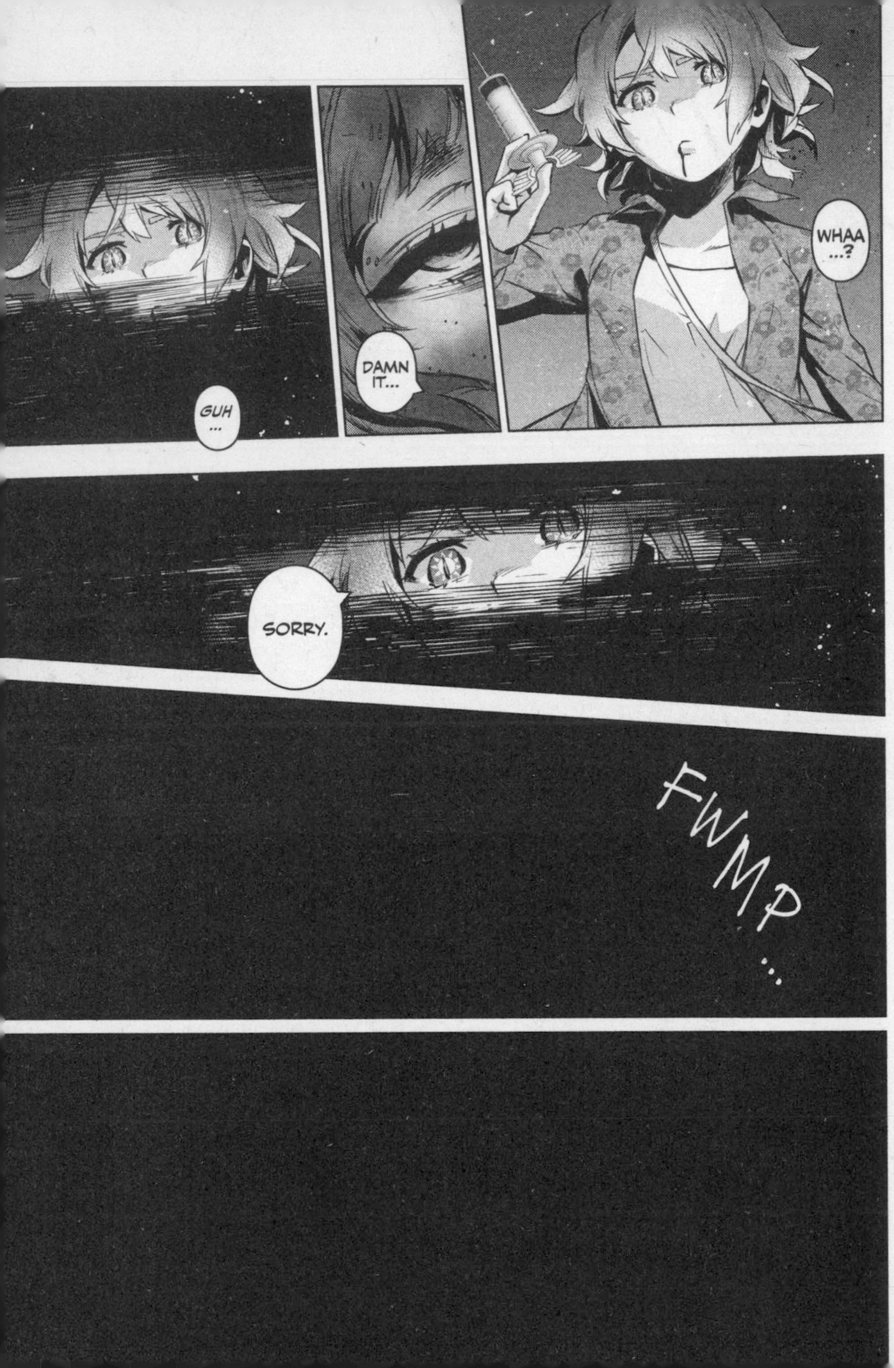
WHAA ...?
DAMN IT...
GUH ...
SORRY.
FWMP...

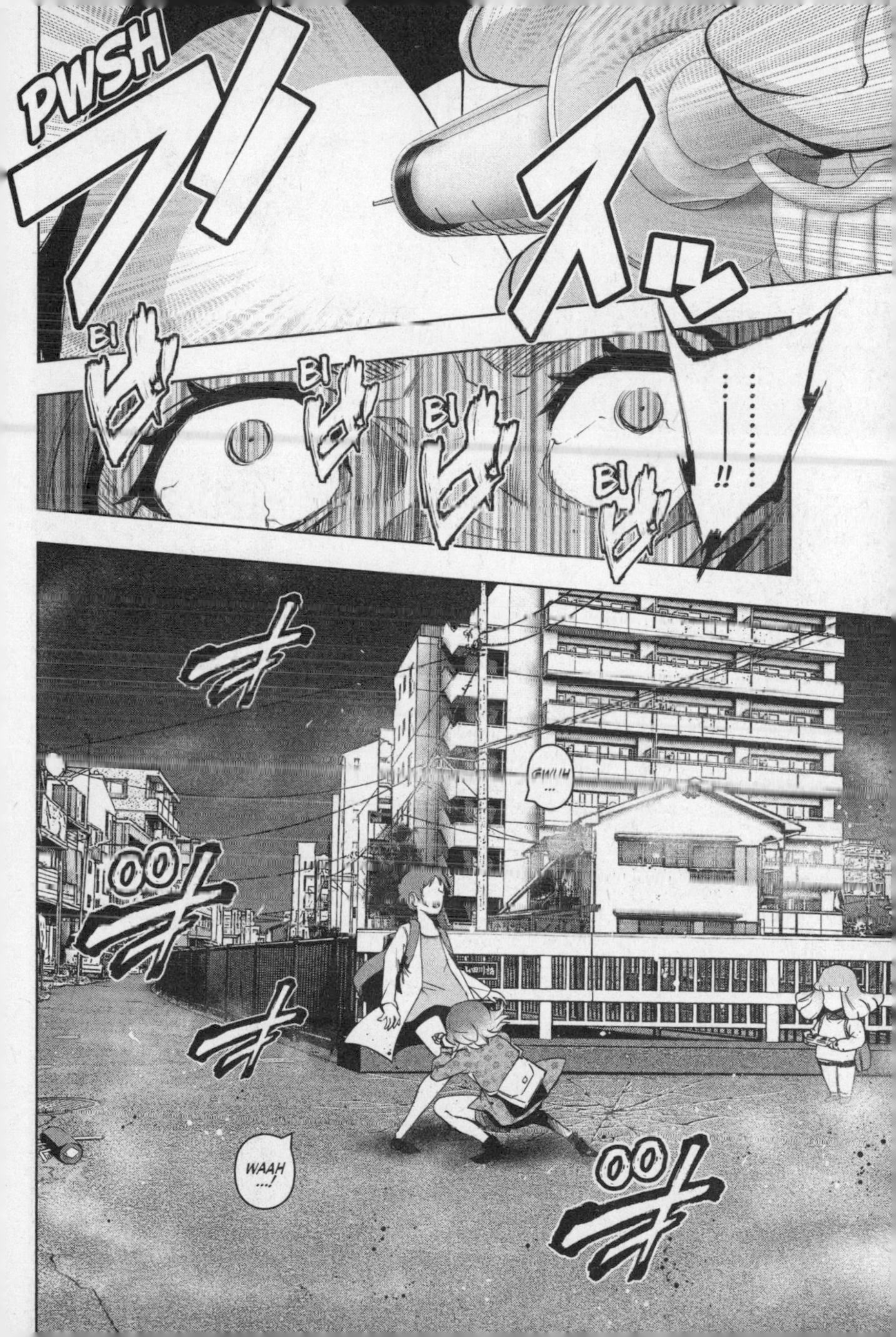
PWSH
......!!
BI
BI
BI
BI
GWUH ...
OO
WAAH ...!
OO

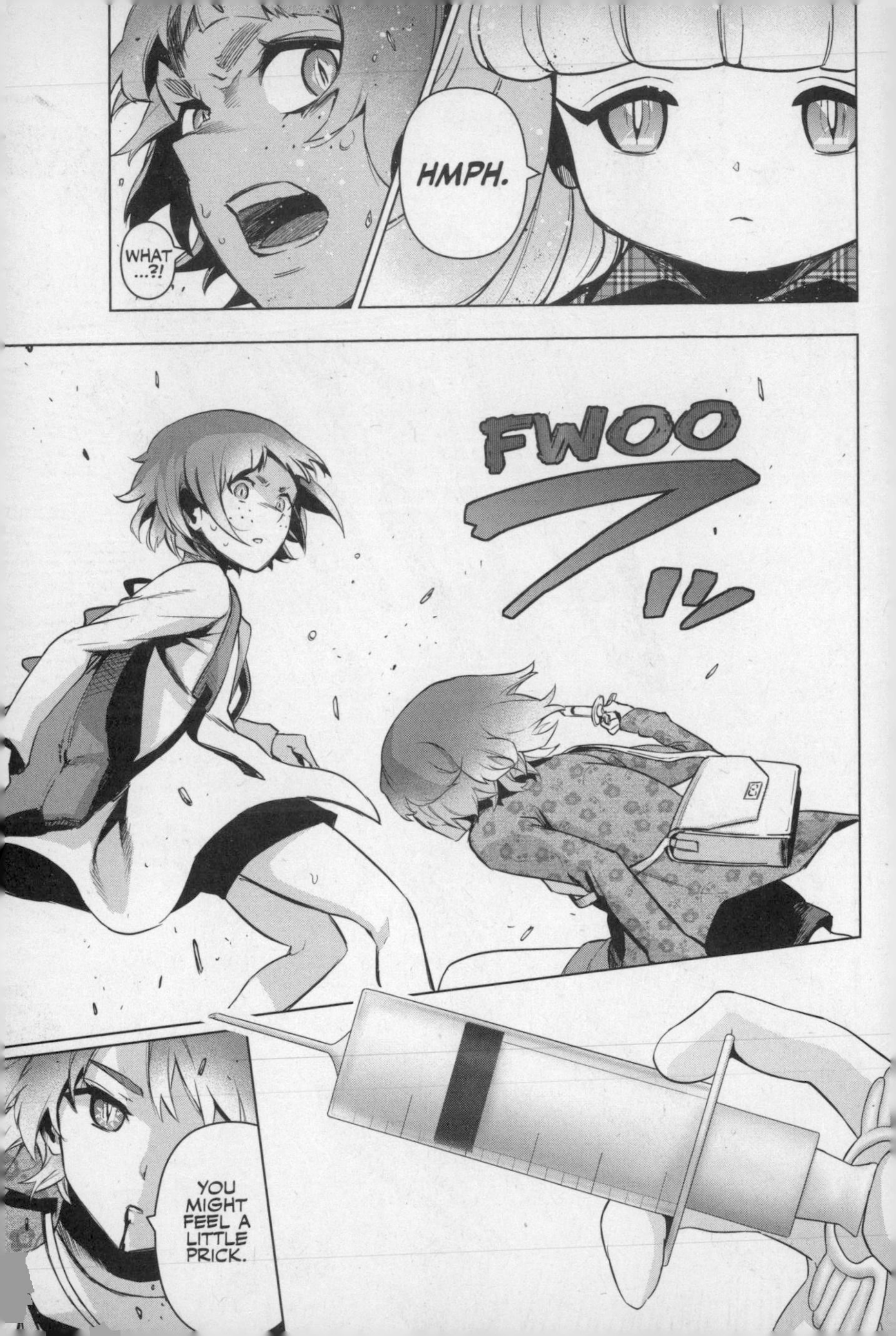
HMPH.
WHAT ...?!
FWOOSH
YOU MIGHT FEEL A LITTLE PRICK.

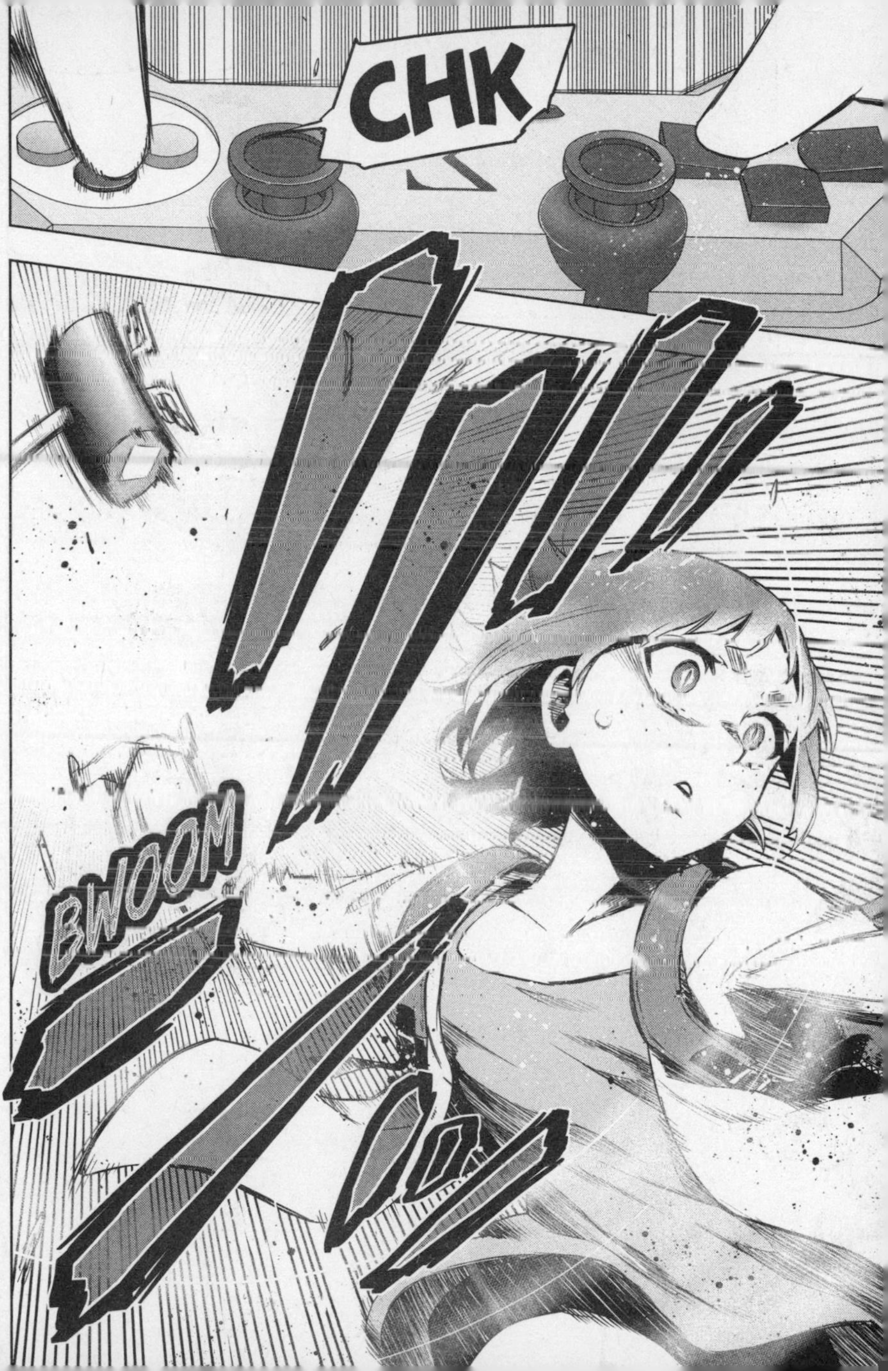
CHK
BWOOM

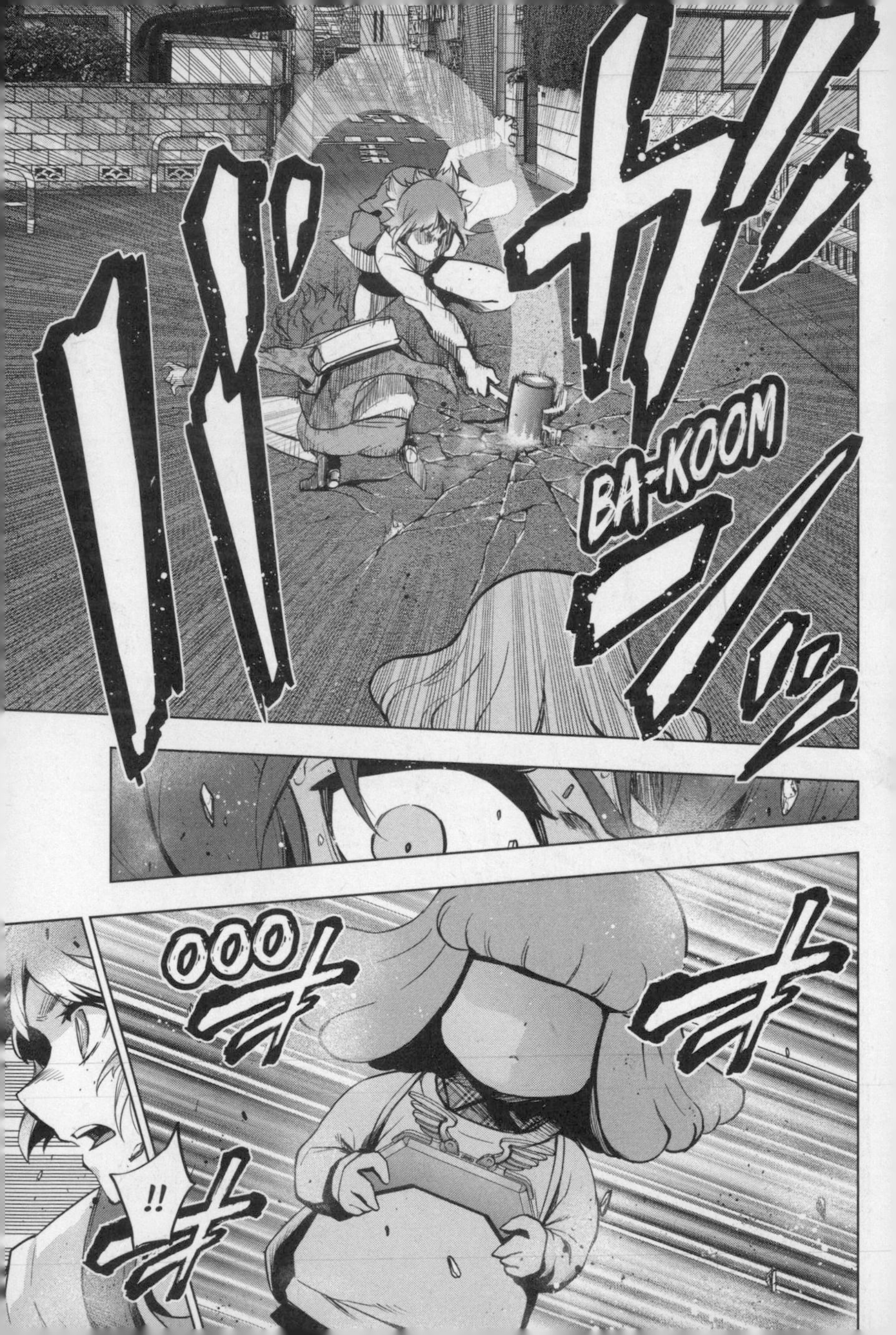
BA-KOOM
OOO
!!

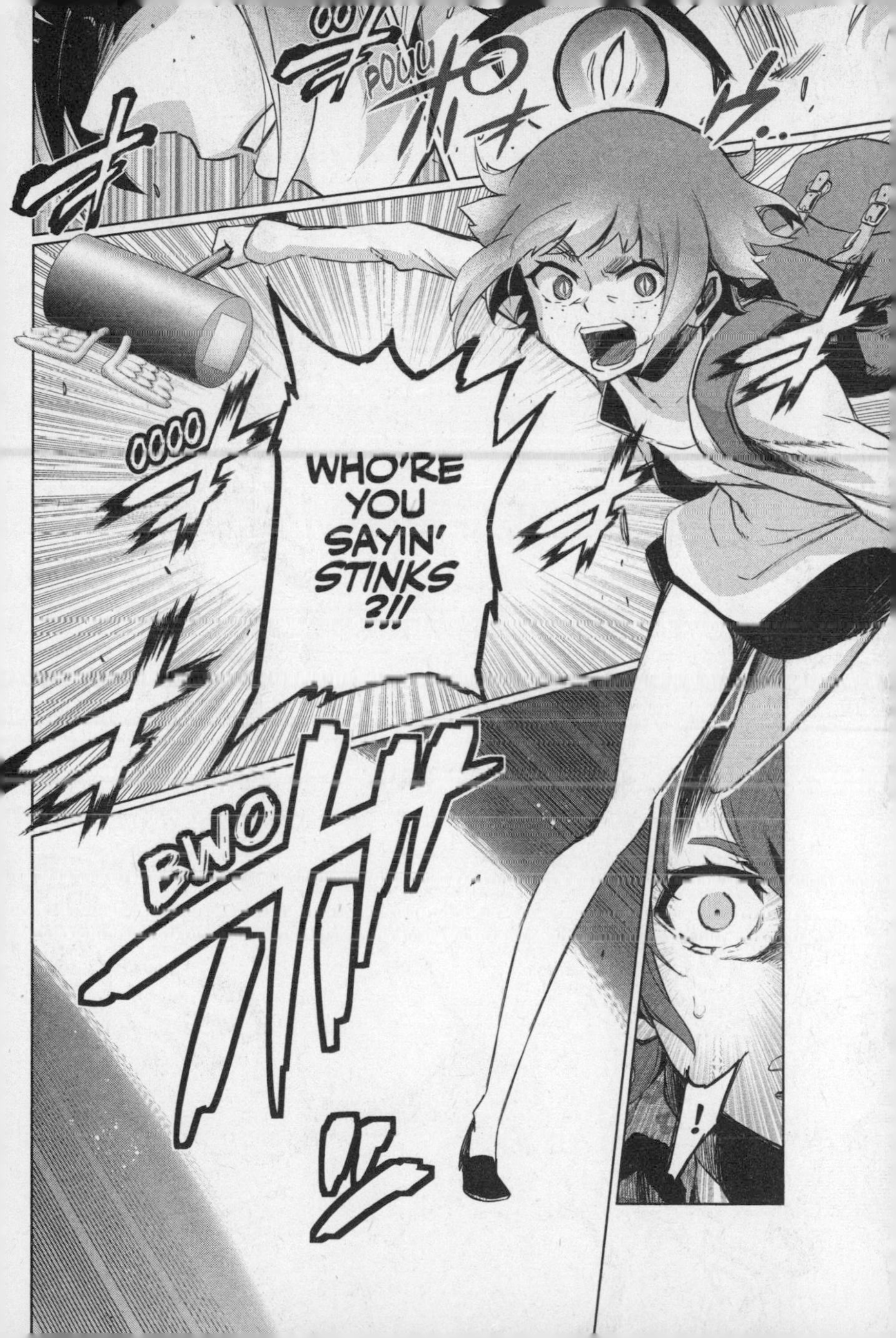
POUU
WHO'RE YOU SAYIN' STINKS ?!!
OOOO
BWO
!

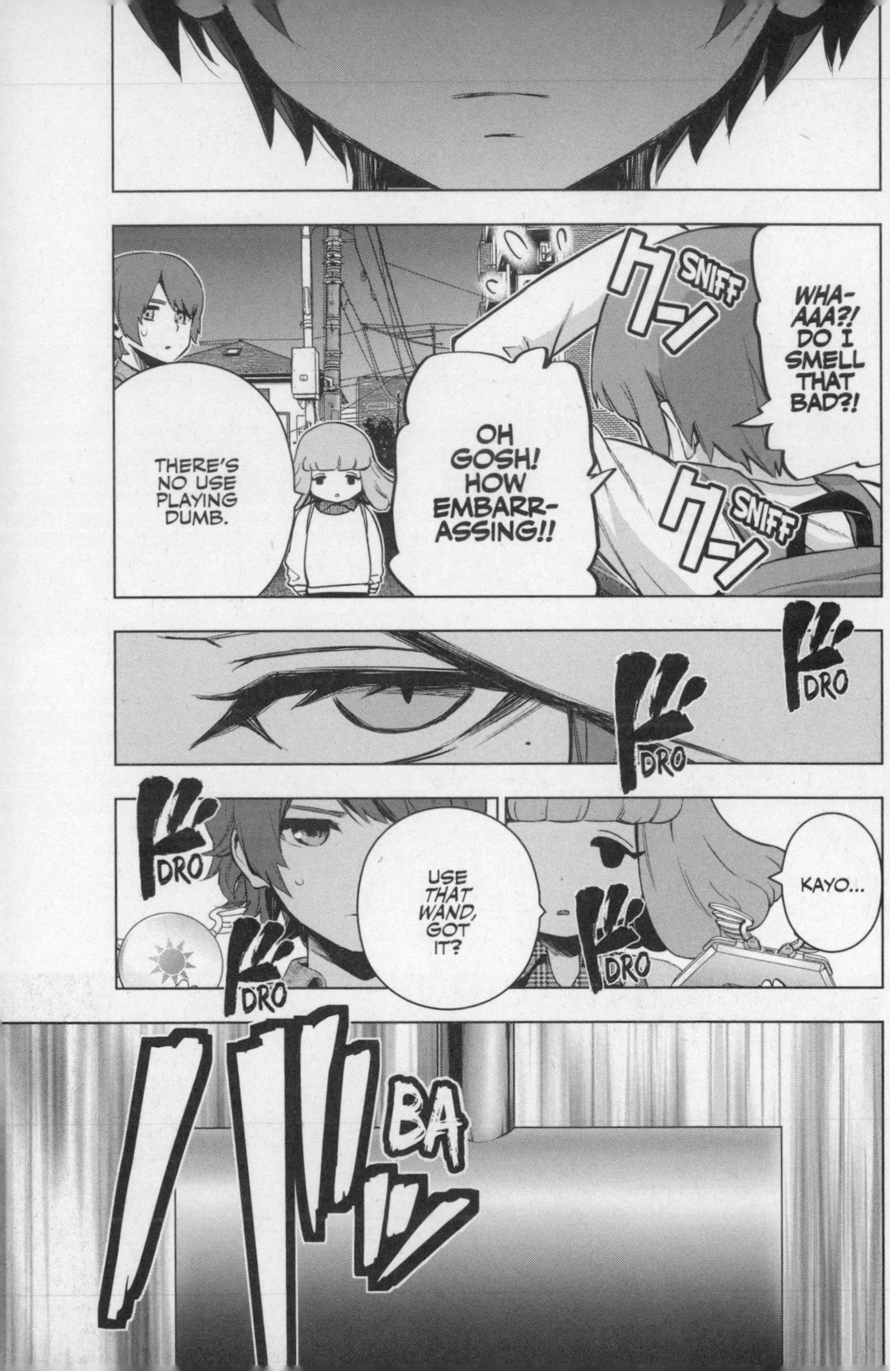
SNIFF
WHA-AAA?! DO I SMELL THAT BAD?!
SNIFF
OH GOSH! HOW EMBARR-ASSING!!
THERE'S NO USE PLAYING DUMB.
DRO
DRO
KAYO...
DRO
USE THAT WAND, GOT IT?
DRO
DRO
BA

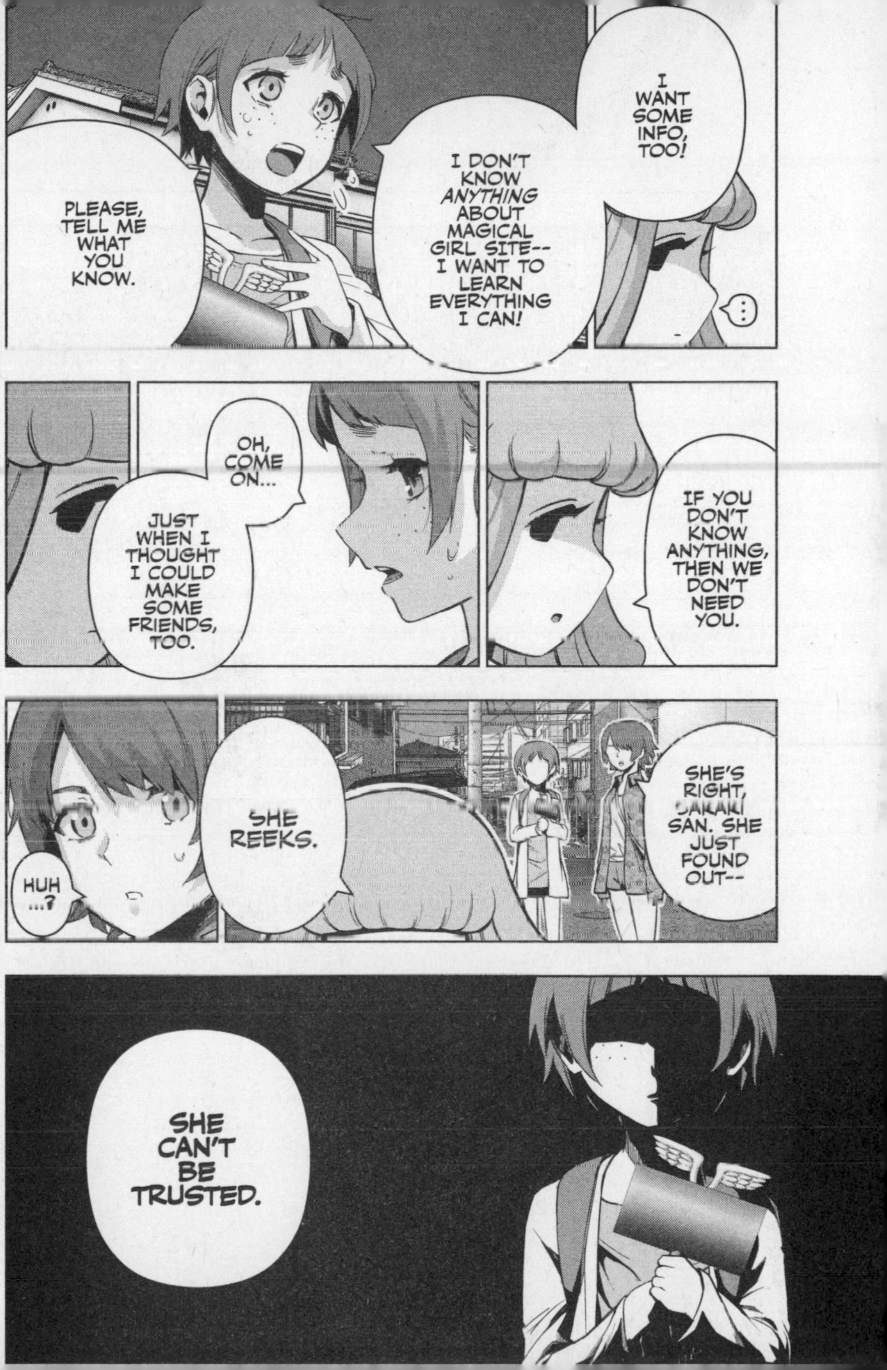
I WANT SOME INFO, TOO!
I DON'T KNOW *ANYTHING* ABOUT MAGICAL GIRL SITE-- I WANT TO LEARN EVERYTHING I CAN!
PLEASE, TELL ME WHAT YOU KNOW.
…
IF YOU DON'T KNOW ANYTHING, THEN WE DON'T NEED YOU.
OH, COME ON...
JUST WHEN I THOUGHT I COULD MAKE SOME FRIENDS, TOO.
SHE'S RIGHT, SAKAKI-SAN. SHE JUST FOUND OUT--
SHE REEKS.
HUH ...?
SHE CAN'T BE TRUSTED.

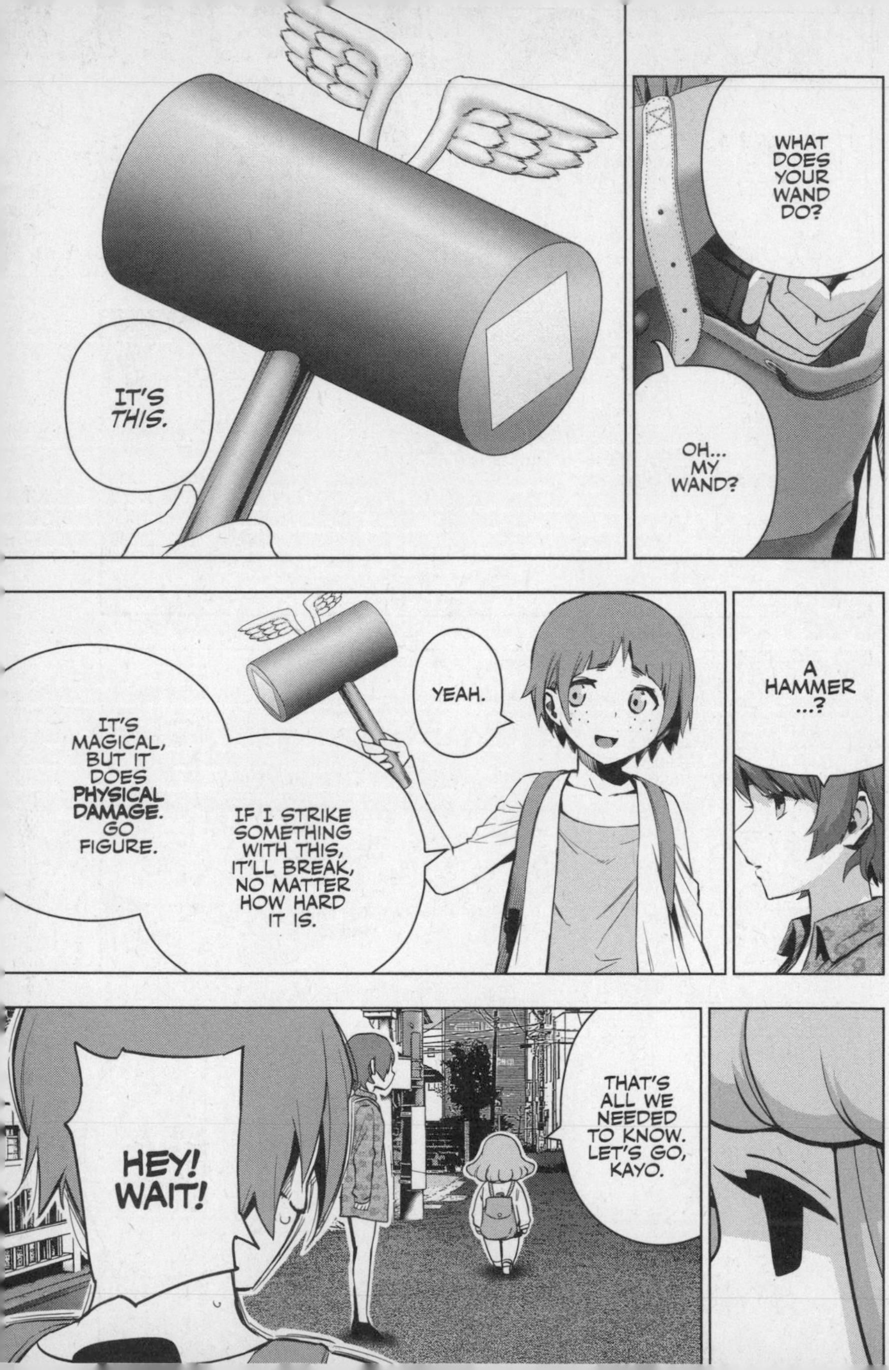
WHAT DOES YOUR WAND DO?
OH... MY WAND?
IT'S *THIS.*
A HAMMER ...?
YEAH.
IF I STRIKE SOMETHING WITH THIS, IT'LL BREAK, NO MATTER HOW HARD IT IS.
IT'S MAGICAL, BUT IT DOES **PHYSICAL DAMAGE.** GO FIGURE.
THAT'S ALL WE NEEDED TO KNOW. LET'S GO, KAYO.
HEY! WAIT!

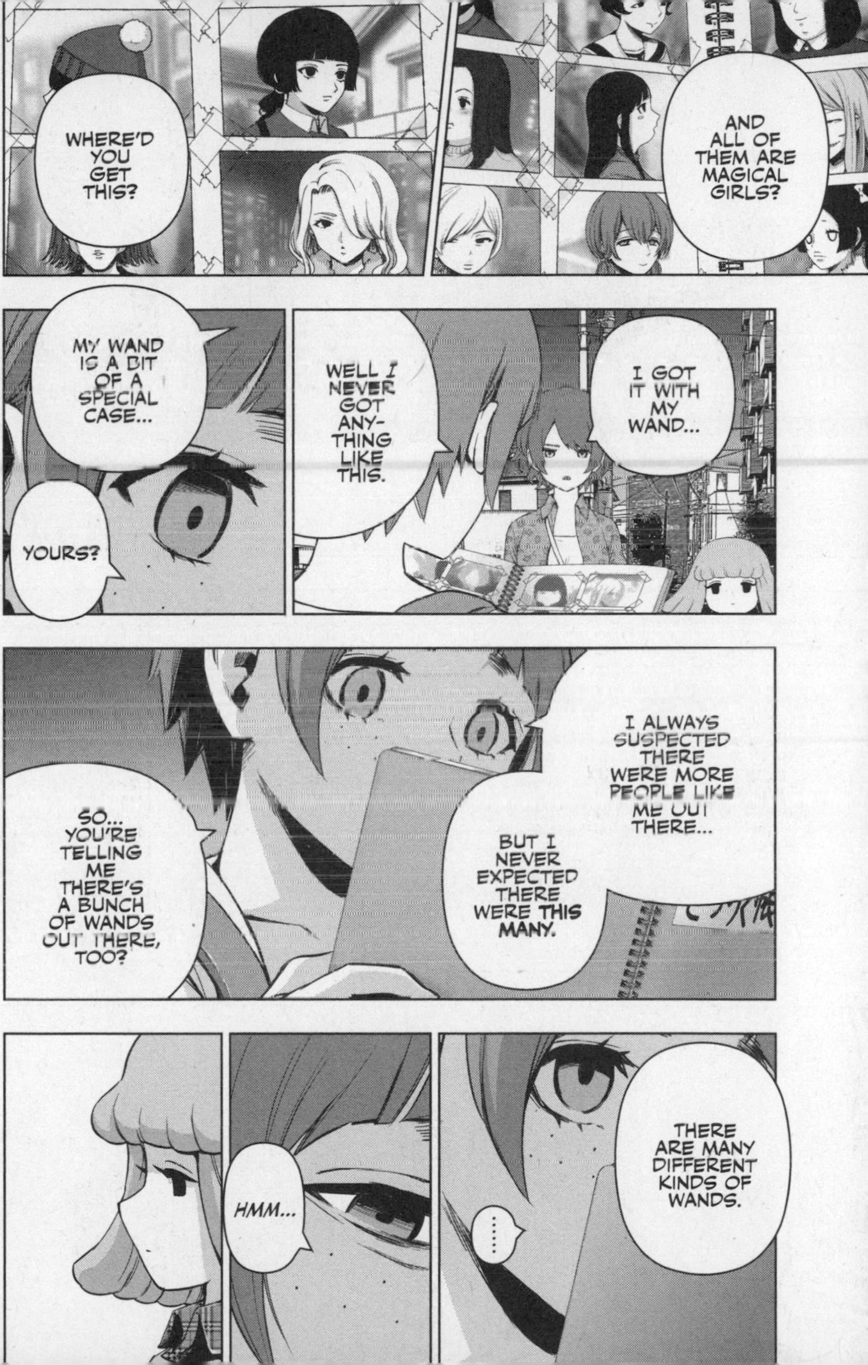
AND ALL OF THEM ARE MAGICAL GIRLS?
WHERE'D YOU GET THIS?
I GOT IT WITH MY WAND...
WELL I NEVER GOT ANYTHING LIKE THIS.
MY WAND IS A BIT OF A SPECIAL CASE...
YOURS?
I ALWAYS SUSPECTED THERE WERE MORE PEOPLE LIKE ME OUT THERE...
BUT I NEVER EXPECTED THERE WERE THIS MANY.
SO... YOU'RE TELLING ME THERE'S A BUNCH OF WANDS OUT THERE, TOO?
THERE ARE MANY DIFFERENT KINDS OF WANDS.
......
HMM...

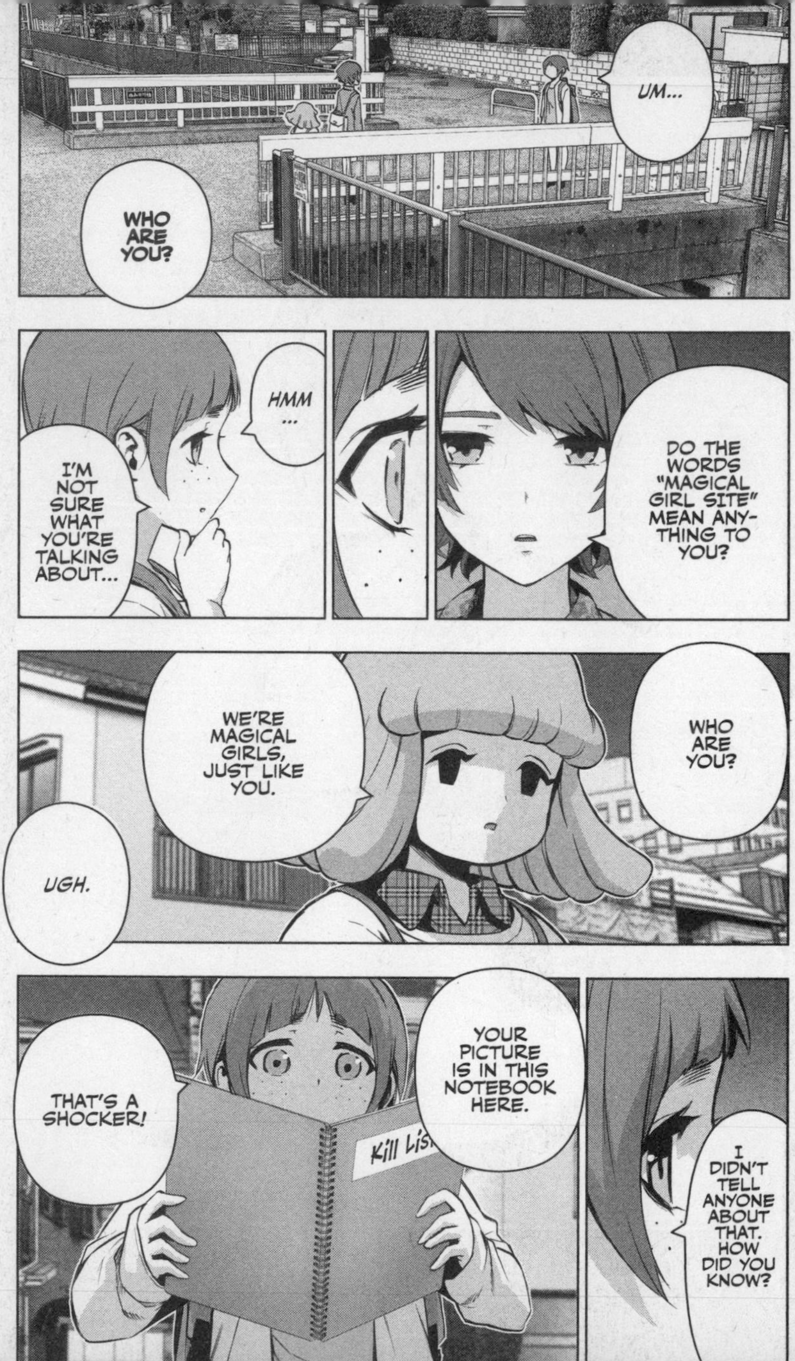
UM...
WHO ARE YOU?
DO THE WORDS "MAGICAL GIRL SITE" MEAN ANYTHING TO YOU?
HMM ...
I'M NOT SURE WHAT YOU'RE TALKING ABOUT...
WHO ARE YOU?
WE'RE MAGICAL GIRLS, JUST LIKE YOU.
UGH.
I DIDN'T TELL ANYONE ABOUT THAT. HOW DID YOU KNOW?
YOUR PICTURE IS IN THIS NOTEBOOK HERE.
Kill Lis
THAT'S A SHOCKER!

ENTER.68 SHIOI RINA

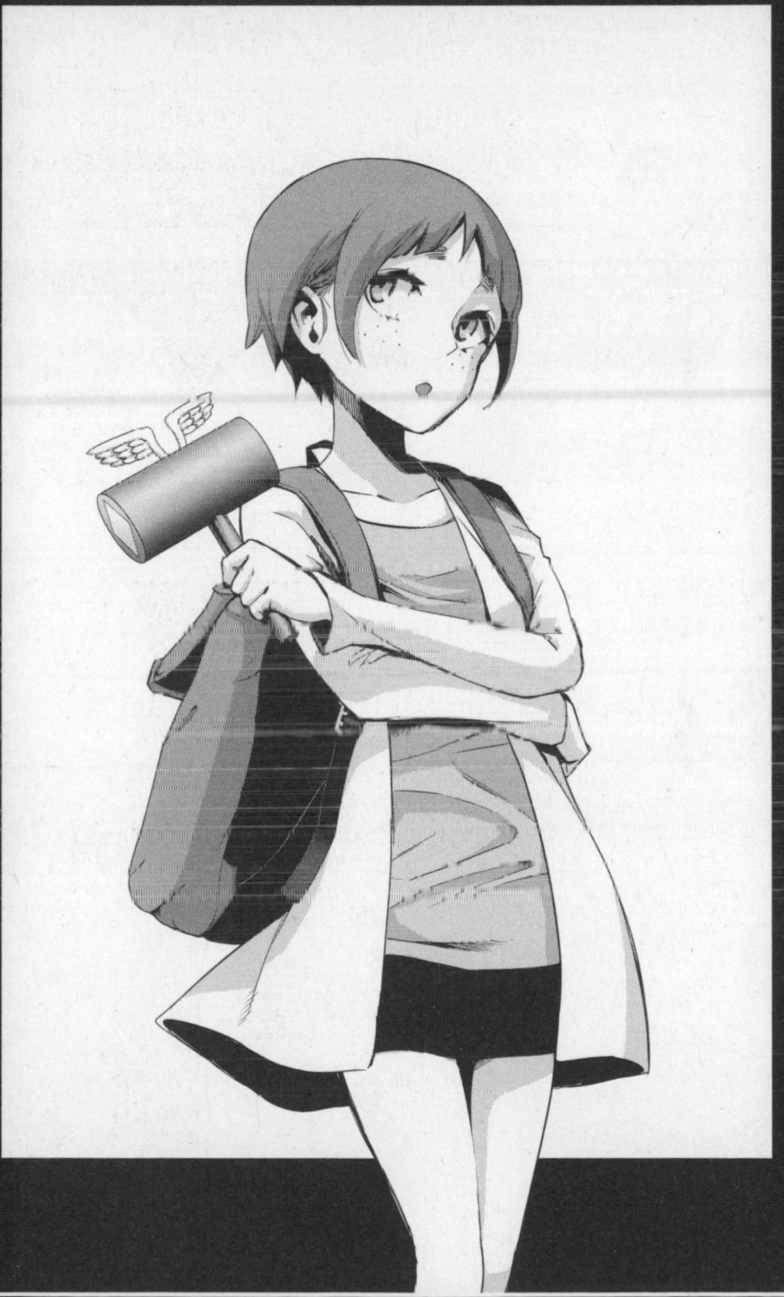

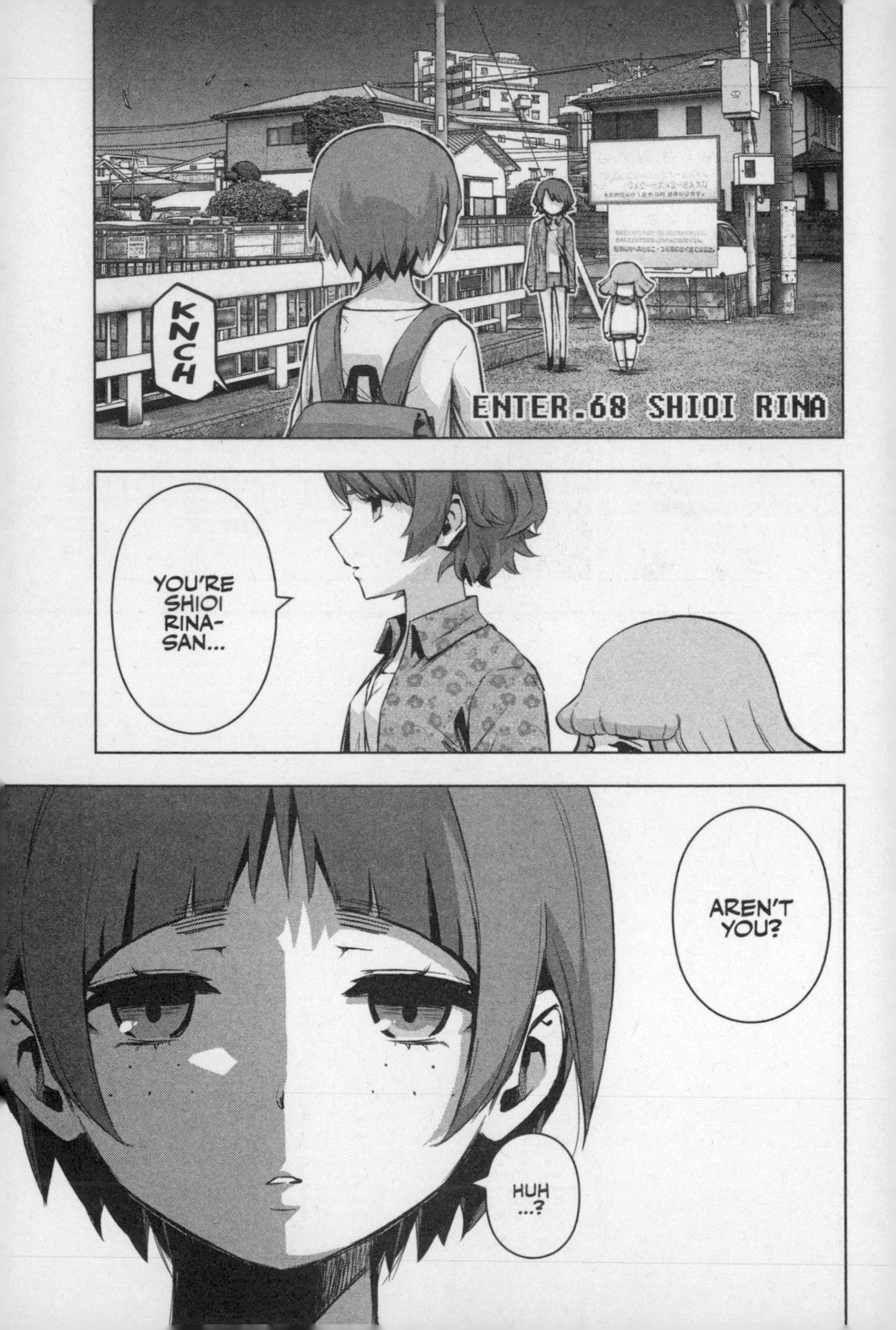
KNCH
ENTER.68 SHIOI RINA
YOU'RE SHIOI RINA-SAN...
AREN'T YOU?
HUH ...?

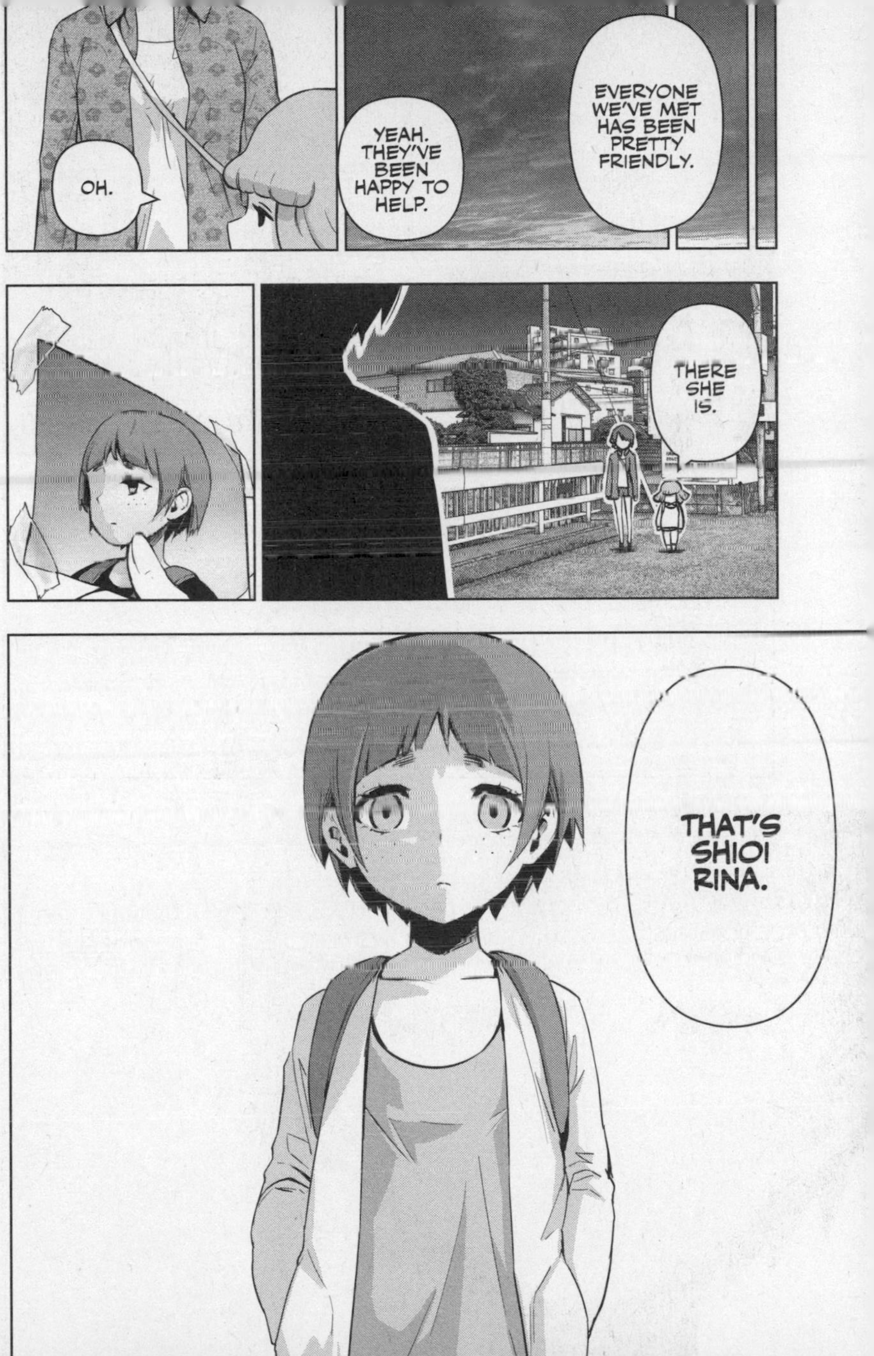
EVERYONE WE'VE MET HAS BEEN PRETTY FRIENDLY.
YEAH. THEY'VE BEEN HAPPY TO HELP.
OH.
THERE SHE IS.
THAT'S SHIOI RINA.

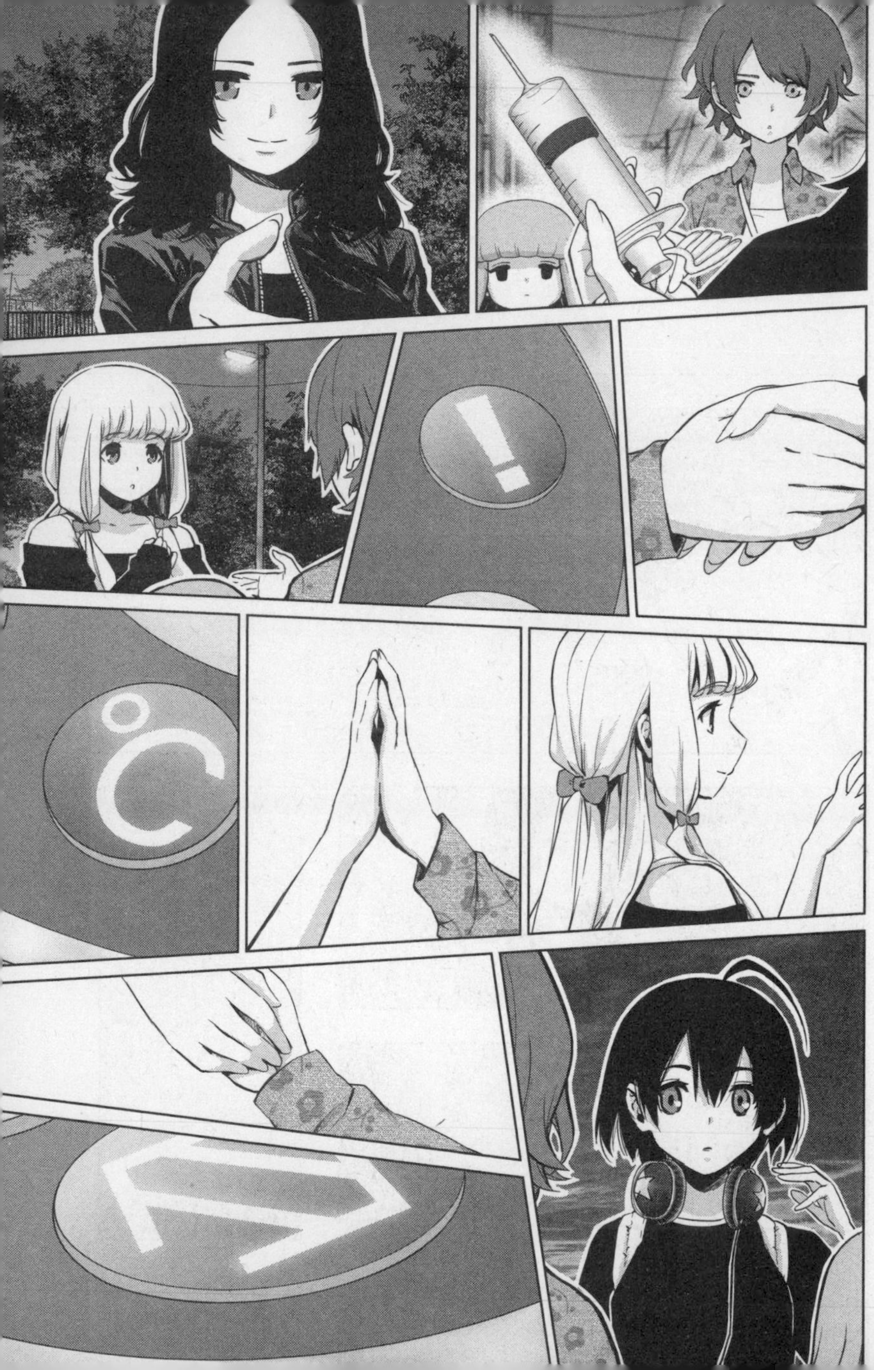

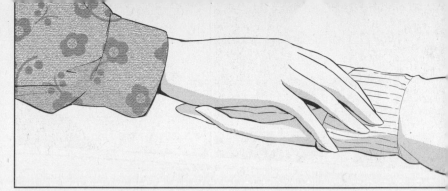

THANK YOU.

SEE YOU LATER! I'LL LINE YA!

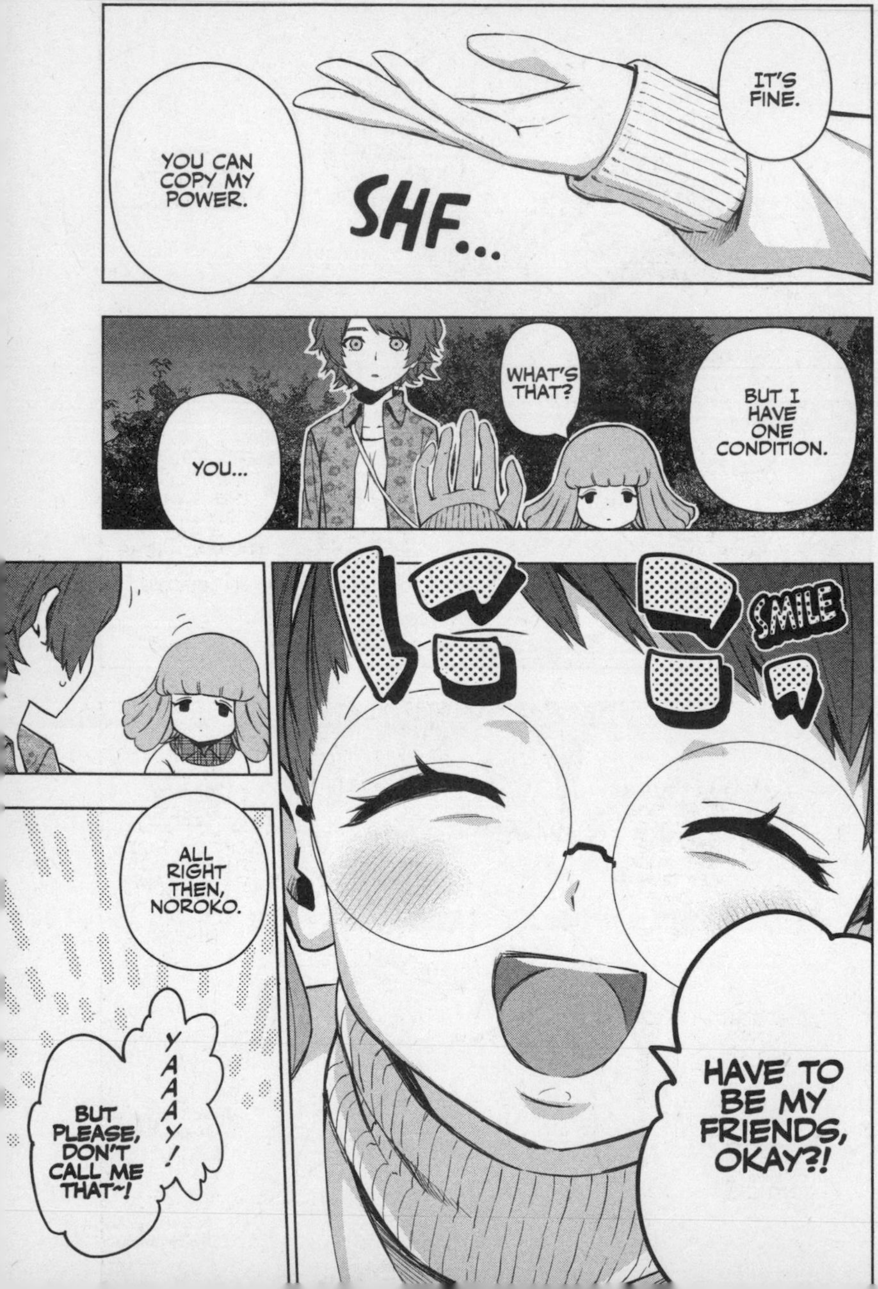
IT'S FINE.
SHF...
YOU CAN COPY MY POWER.
BUT I HAVE ONE CONDITION.
WHAT'S THAT?
YOU...
SMILE
HAVE TO BE MY FRIENDS, OKAY?!
ALL RIGHT THEN, NOROKO.
YAAAAY!
BUT PLEASE, DON'T CALL ME THAT~!

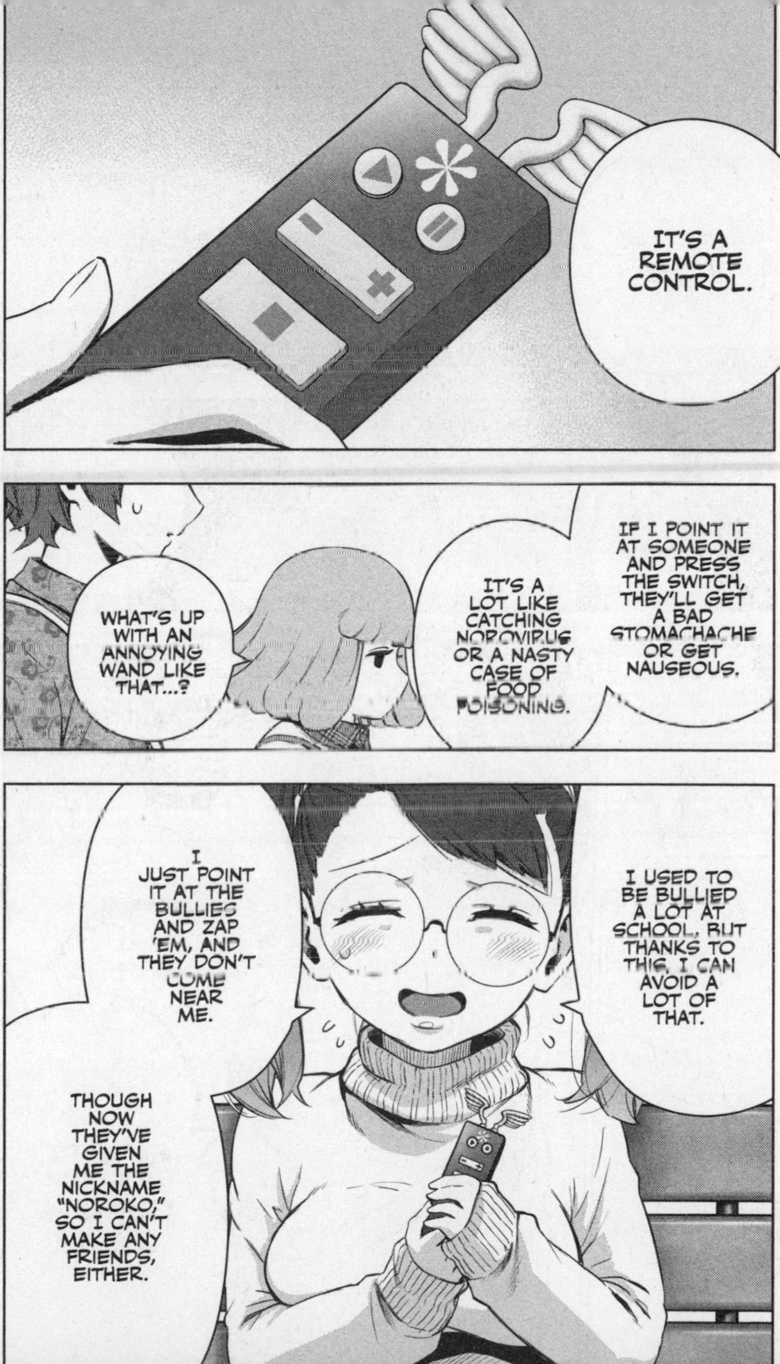
IT'S A REMOTE CONTROL.
IF I POINT IT AT SOMEONE AND PRESS THE SWITCH, THEY'LL GET A BAD STOMACHACHE OR GET NAUSEOUS.
IT'S A LOT LIKE CATCHING NOROVIRUS OR A NASTY CASE OF FOOD POISONING.
WHAT'S UP WITH AN ANNOYING WAND LIKE THAT...?
I USED TO BE BULLIED A LOT AT SCHOOL, BUT THANKS TO THIS, I CAN AVOID A LOT OF THAT.
I JUST POINT IT AT THE BULLIES AND ZAP 'EM, AND THEY DON'T COME NEAR ME.
THOUGH NOW THEY'VE GIVEN ME THE NICKNAME "NOROKO," SO I CAN'T MAKE ANY FRIENDS, EITHER.

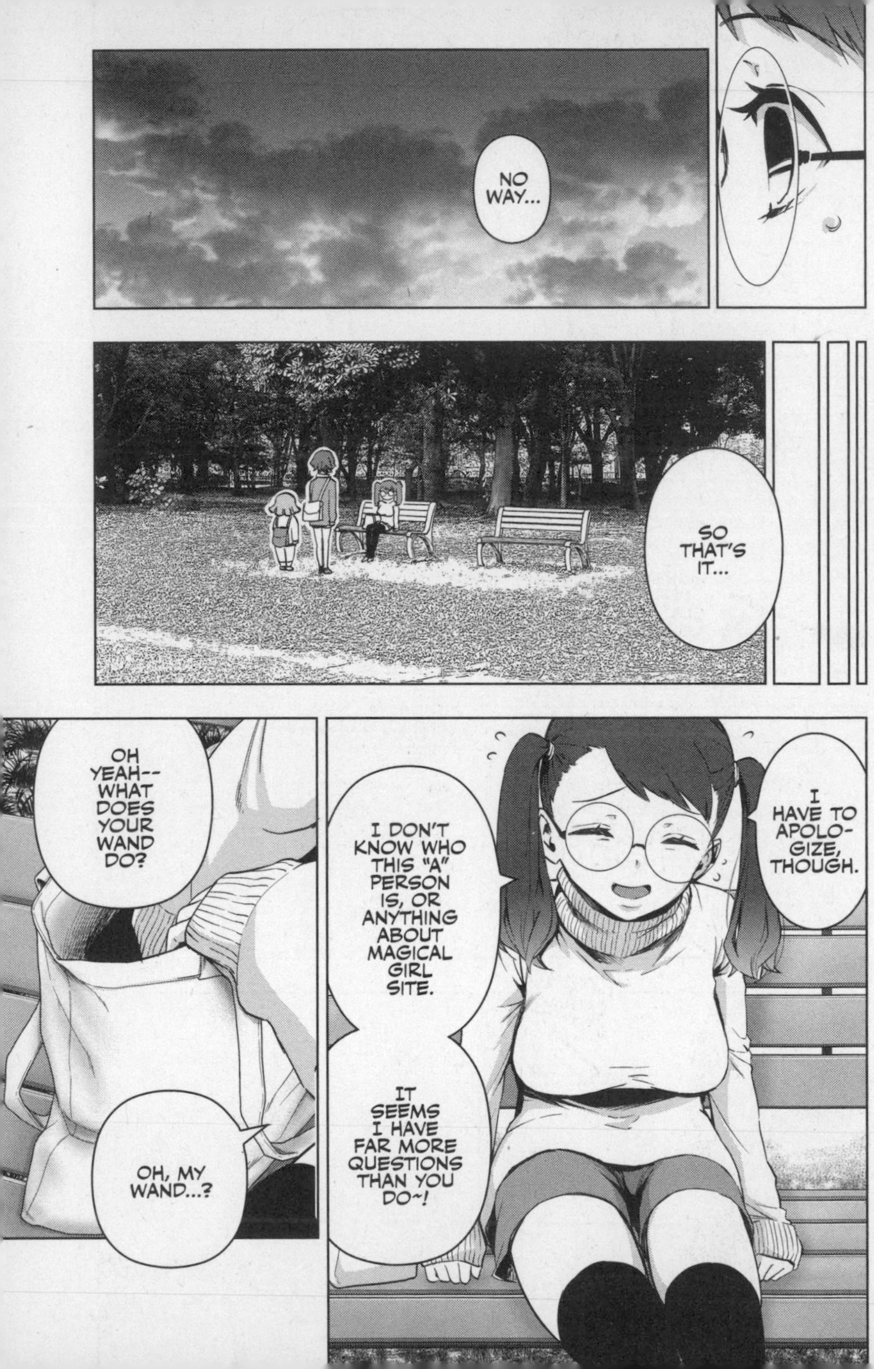
NO WAY...
SO THAT'S IT...
I HAVE TO APOLOGIZE, THOUGH.
I DON'T KNOW WHO THIS "A" PERSON IS, OR ANYTHING ABOUT MAGICAL GIRL SITE.
IT SEEMS I HAVE FAR MORE QUESTIONS THAN YOU DO~!
OH YEAH-- WHAT DOES YOUR WAND DO?
OH, MY WAND...?

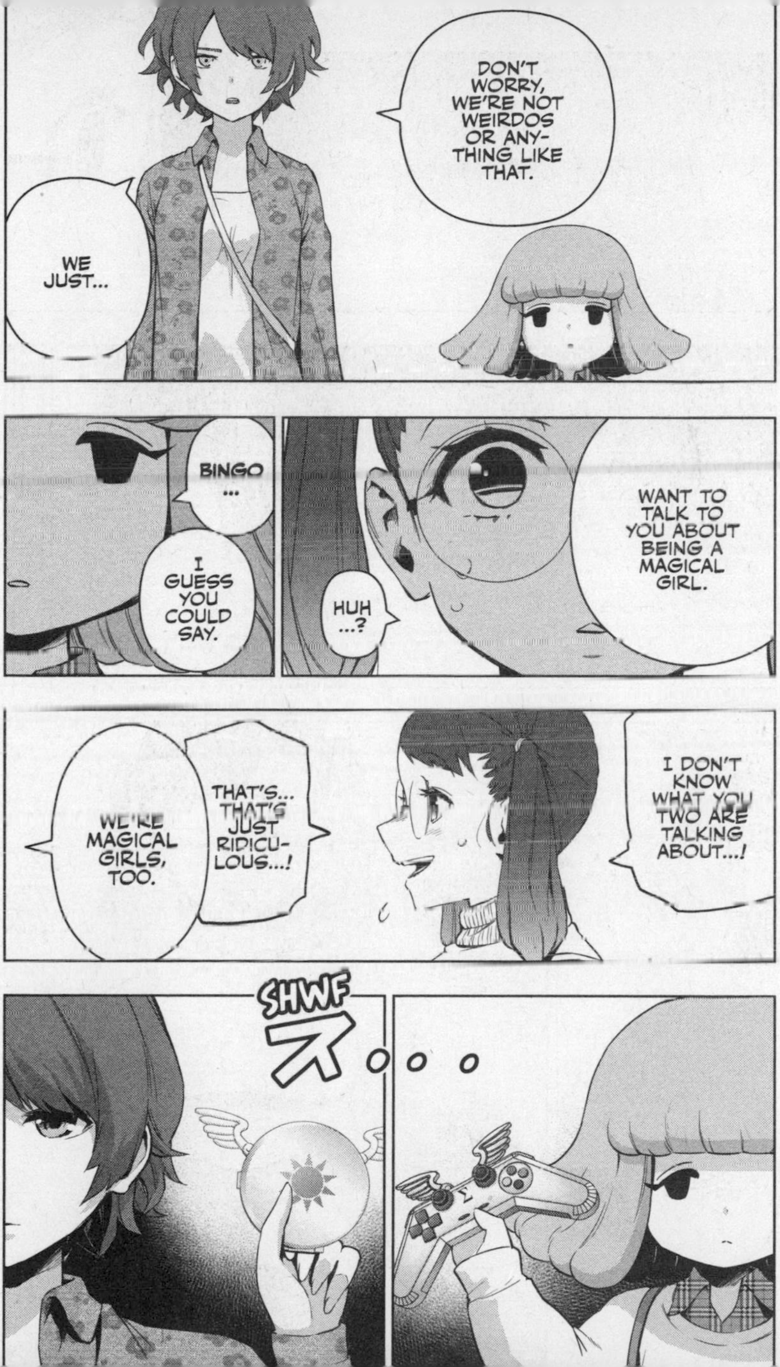
DON'T WORRY, WE'RE NOT WEIRDOS OR ANY-THING LIKE THAT.
WE JUST...
WANT TO TALK TO YOU ABOUT BEING A MAGICAL GIRL.
HUH ...?
BINGO ...
I GUESS YOU COULD SAY.
I DON'T KNOW WHAT YOU TWO ARE TALKING ABOUT...!
THAT'S... THAT'S JUST RIDICU-LOUS...!
WE'RE MAGICAL GIRLS, TOO.
SHWF
ス

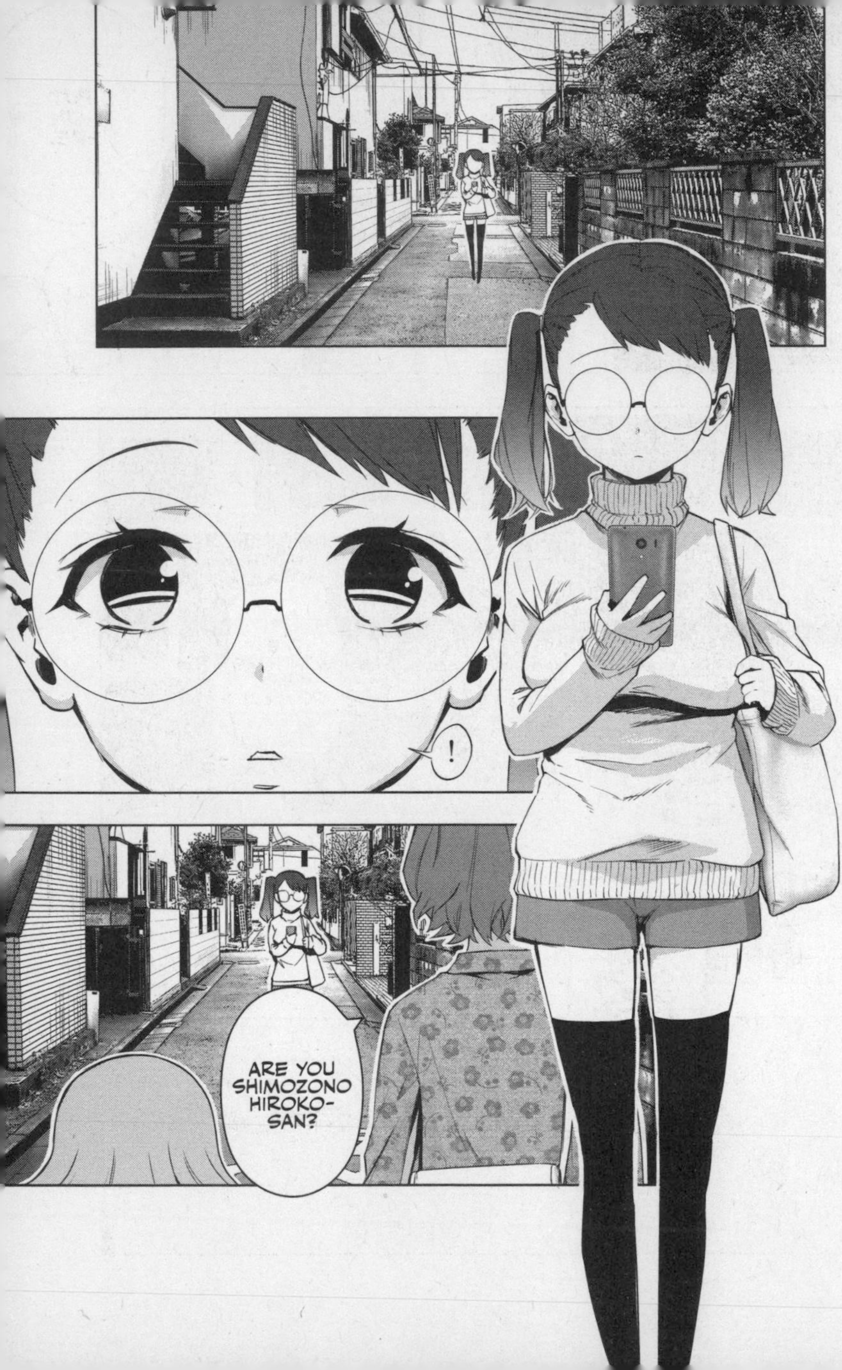
!
ARE YOU SHIMOZONO HIROKO-SAN?

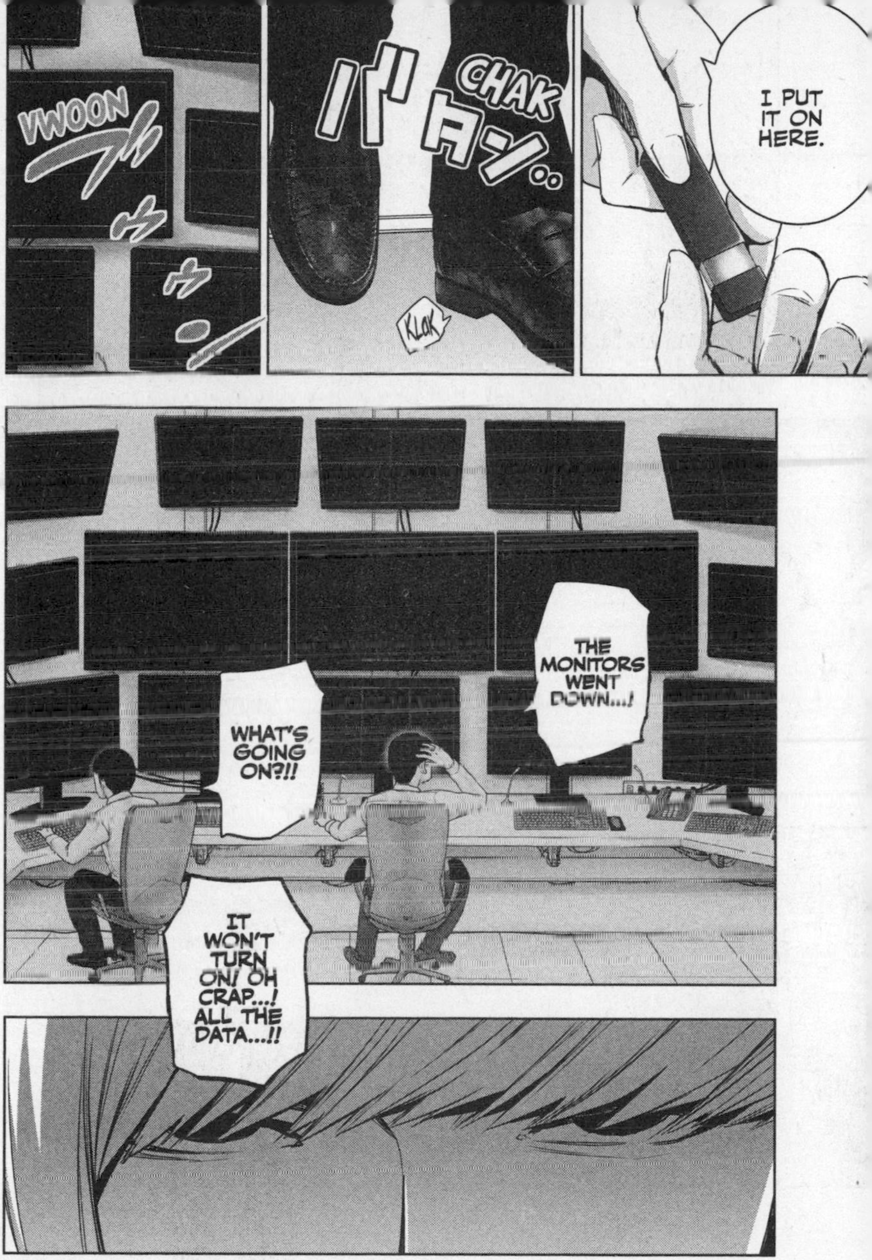
I PUT IT ON HERE.
CHAK
KLOK
VWOON
THE MONITORS WENT DOWN...!
WHAT'S GOING ON?!!
IT WON'T TURN ON! OH CRAP...! ALL THE DATA...!!

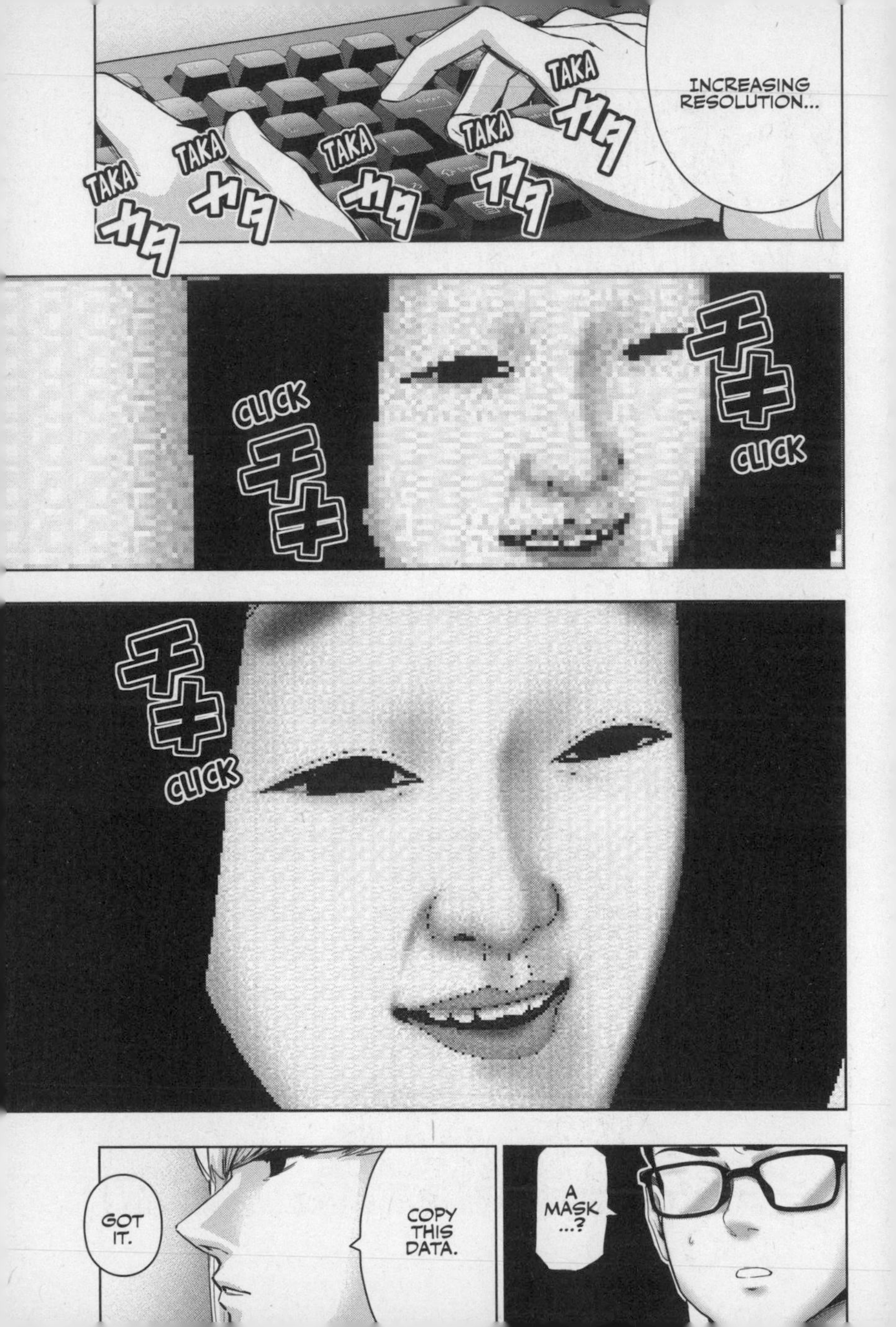
INCREASING RESOLUTION...
TAKA カタ
TAKA カタ
TAKA カタ
TAKA カタ
TAKA カタ
チキ CLICK
CLICK チキ
チキ CLICK
A MASK ...?
COPY THIS DATA.
GOT IT.

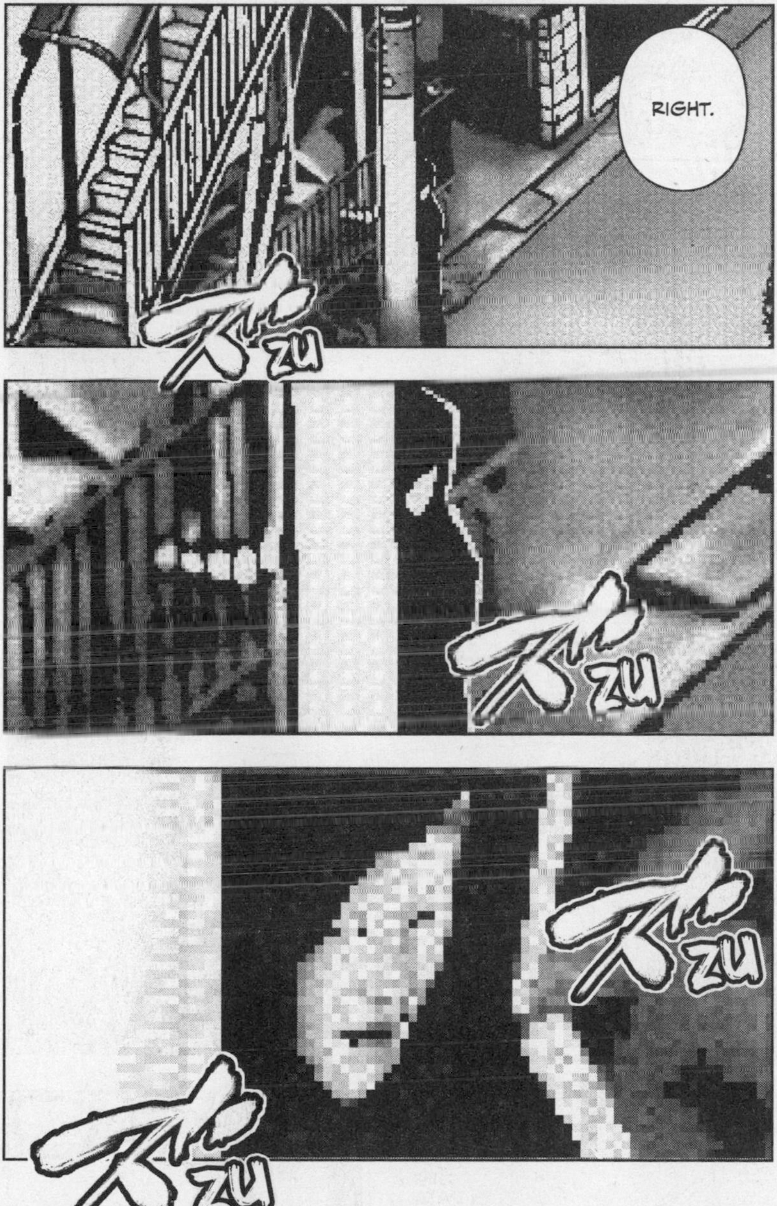
RIGHT.
ZU
ZU
ZU
ZU

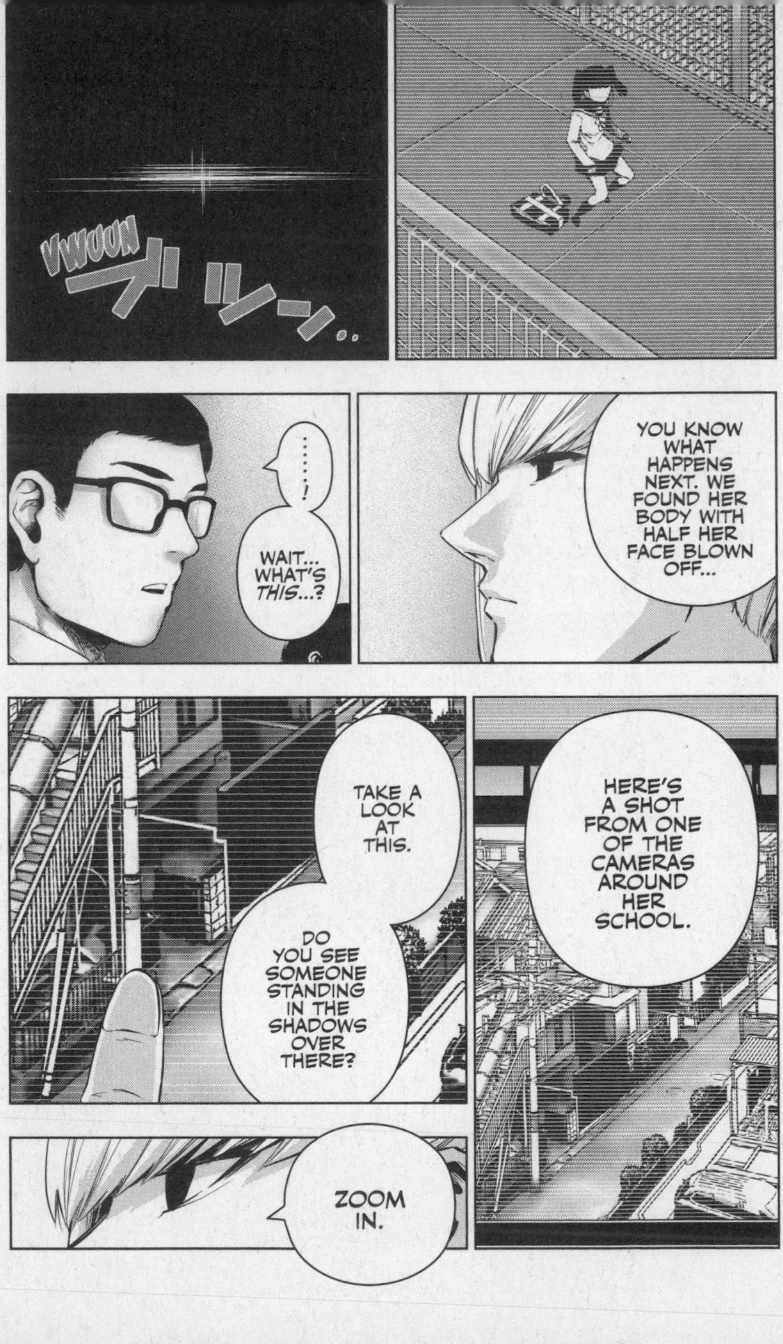
VWOON
YOU KNOW WHAT HAPPENS NEXT. WE FOUND HER BODY WITH HALF HER FACE BLOWN OFF...
......!
WAIT... WHAT'S *THIS*...?
HERE'S A SHOT FROM ONE OF THE CAMERAS AROUND HER SCHOOL.
TAKE A LOOK AT THIS.
DO YOU SEE SOMEONE STANDING IN THE SHADOWS OVER THERE?
ZOOM IN.

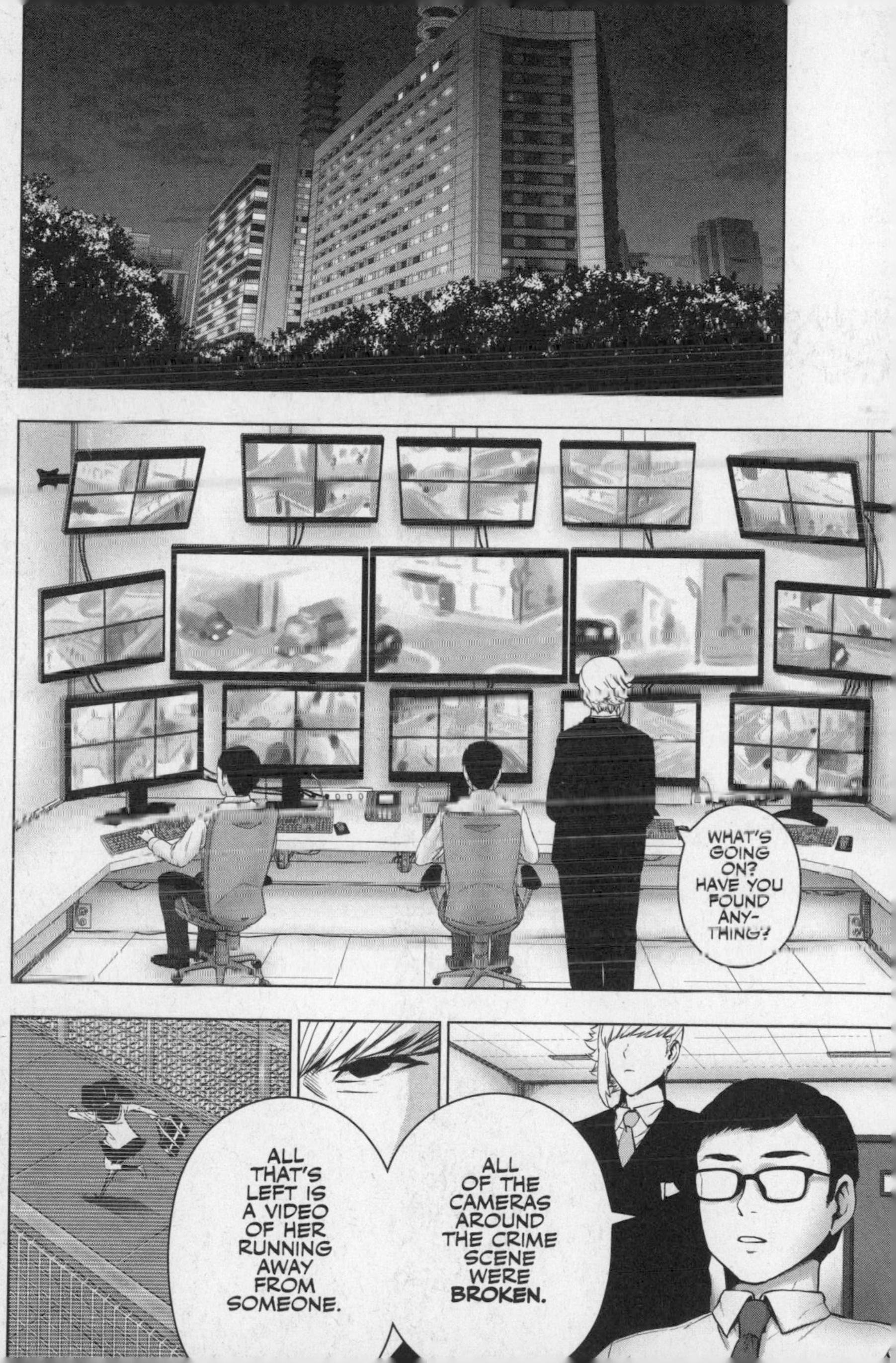
WHAT'S GOING ON? HAVE YOU FOUND ANYTHING?
ALL OF THE CAMERAS AROUND THE CRIME SCENE WERE BROKEN.
ALL THAT'S LEFT IS A VIDEO OF HER RUNNING AWAY FROM SOMEONE.

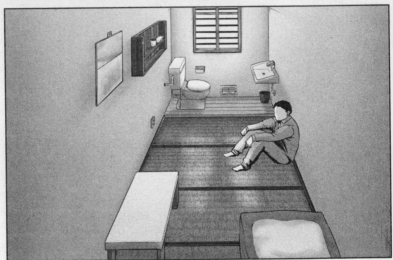

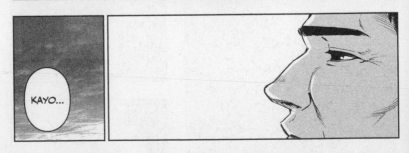

KAYO...

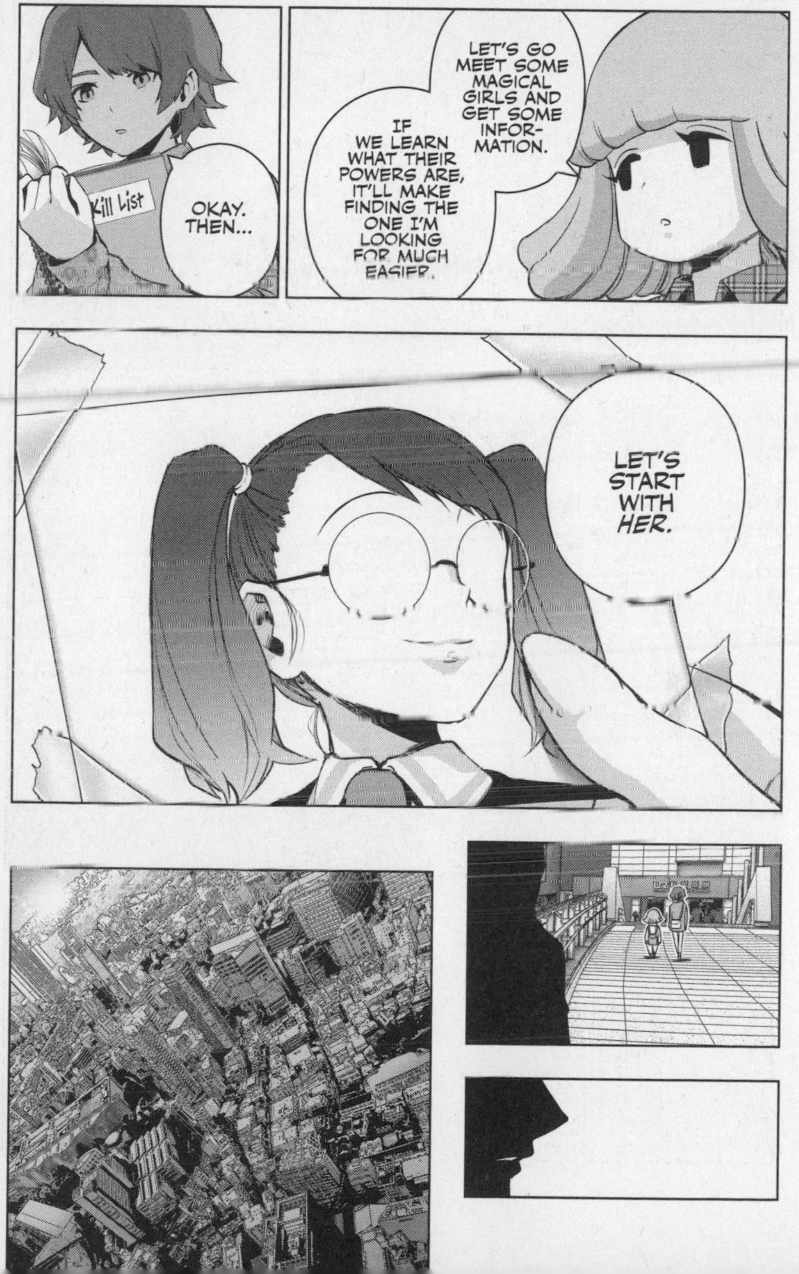
LET'S GO MEET SOME MAGICAL GIRLS AND GET SOME INFORMATION.
IF WE LEARN WHAT THEIR POWERS ARE, IT'LL MAKE FINDING THE ONE I'M LOOKING FOR MUCH EASIER.
OKAY. THEN...
Kill List
LET'S START WITH *HER.*

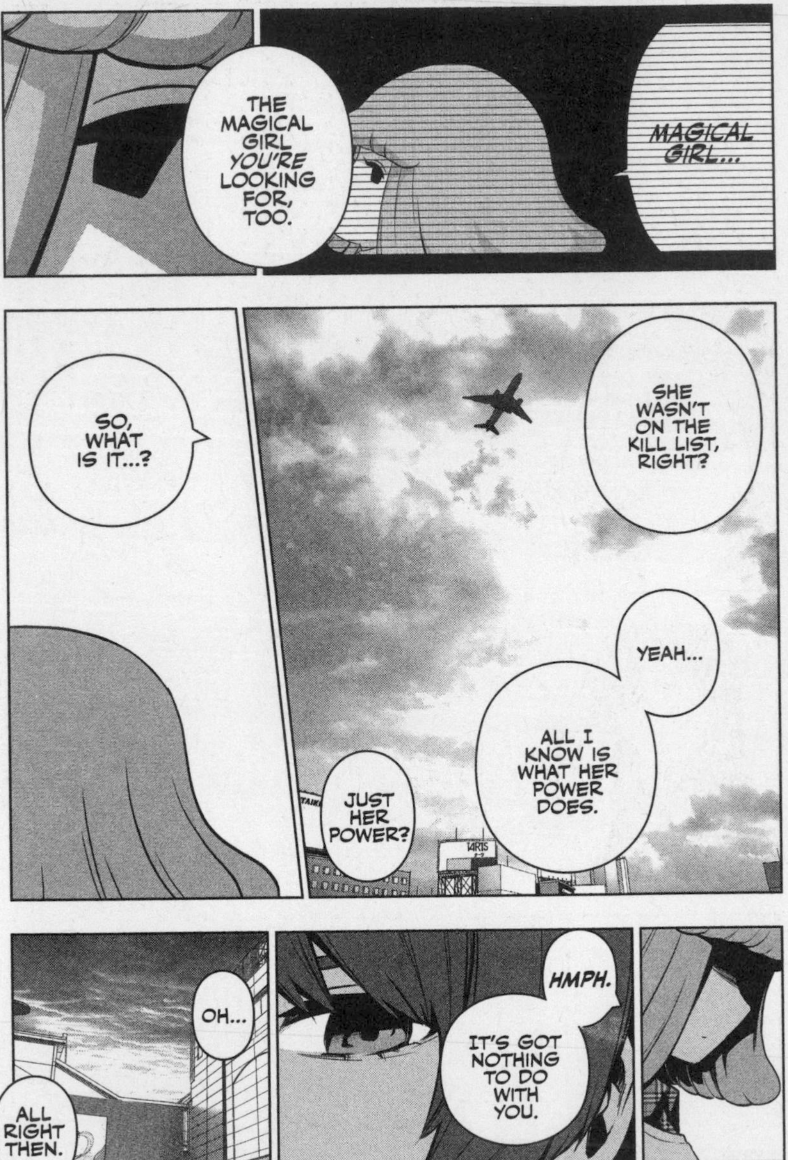
MAGICAL GIRL...
THE MAGICAL GIRL YOU'RE LOOKING FOR, TOO.
SHE WASN'T ON THE KILL LIST, RIGHT?
YEAH...
ALL I KNOW IS WHAT HER POWER DOES.
JUST HER POWER?
SO, WHAT IS IT...?
HMPH.
IT'S GOT NOTHING TO DO WITH YOU.
OH...
ALL RIGHT THEN.

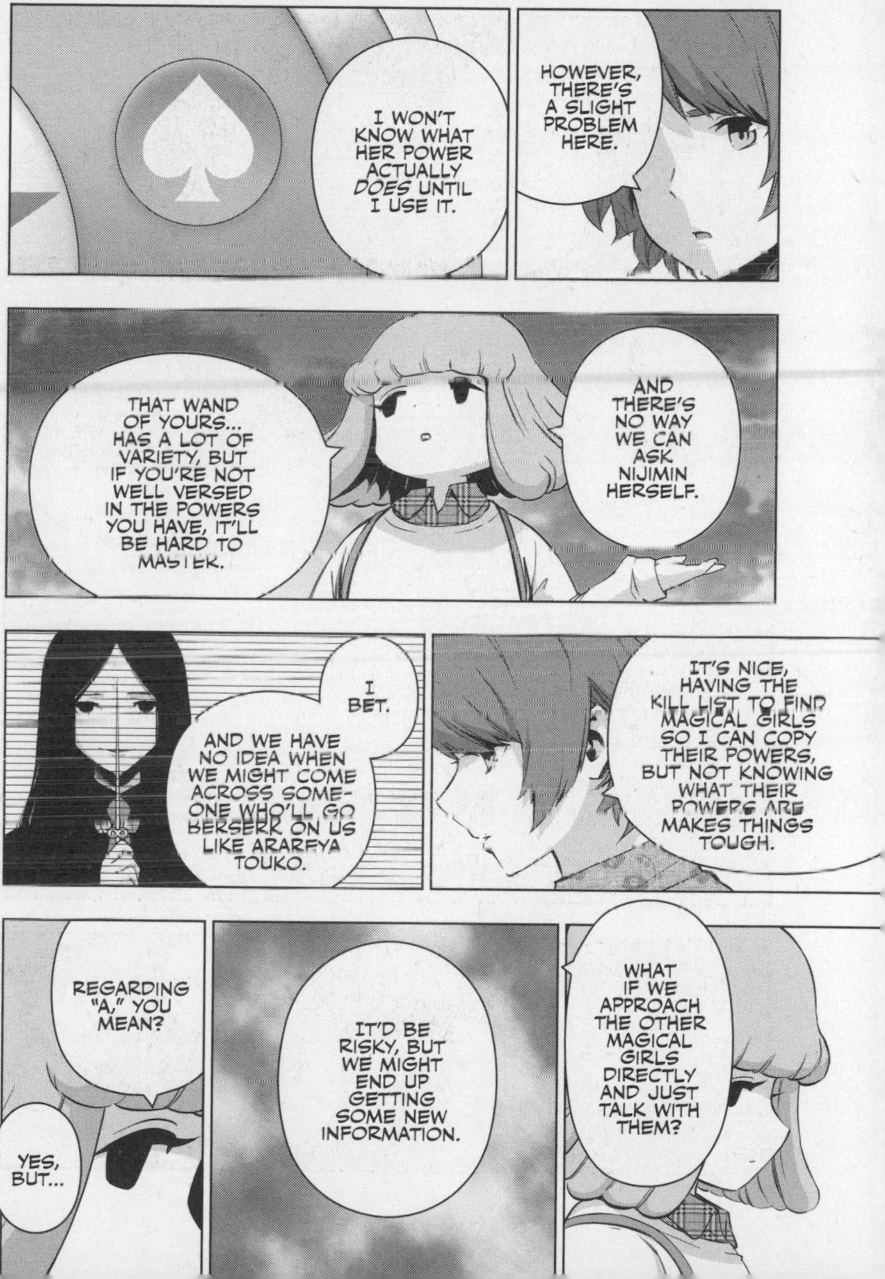
HOWEVER, THERE'S A SLIGHT PROBLEM HERE.
I WON'T KNOW WHAT HER POWER ACTUALLY *DOES* UNTIL I USE IT.
AND THERE'S NO WAY WE CAN ASK NIJIMIN HERSELF.
THAT WAND OF YOURS... HAS A LOT OF VARIETY, BUT IF YOU'RE NOT WELL VERSED IN THE POWERS YOU HAVE, IT'LL BE HARD TO MASTER.
IT'S NICE, HAVING THE KILL LIST TO FIND MAGICAL GIRLS SO I CAN COPY THEIR POWERS, BUT NOT KNOWING WHAT THEIR POWERS ARE MAKES THINGS TOUGH.
I BET.
AND WE HAVE NO IDEA WHEN WE MIGHT COME ACROSS SOME-ONE WHO'LL GO BERSERK ON US LIKE ARARFYA TOUKO.
WHAT IF WE APPROACH THE OTHER MAGICAL GIRLS DIRECTLY AND JUST TALK WITH THEM?
IT'D BE RISKY, BUT WE MIGHT END UP GETTING SOME NEW INFORMATION.
REGARDING "A," YOU MEAN?
YES, BUT...

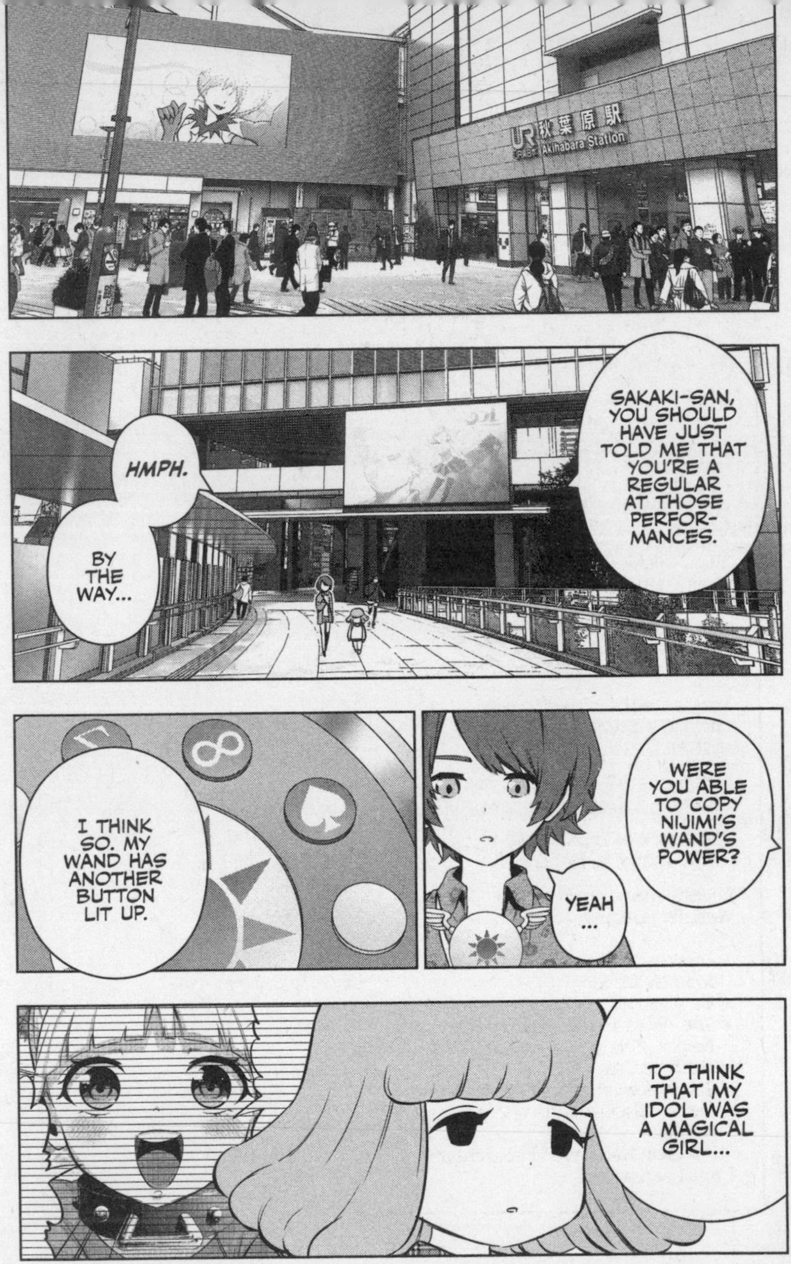
秋葉原駅
Akihabara Station
SAKAKI-SAN, YOU SHOULD HAVE JUST TOLD ME THAT YOU'RE A REGULAR AT THOSE PERFORMANCES.
HMPH.
BY THE WAY...
WERE YOU ABLE TO COPY NIJIMI'S WAND'S POWER?
YEAH...
I THINK SO. MY WAND HAS ANOTHER BUTTON LIT UP.
TO THINK THAT MY IDOL WAS A MAGICAL GIRL...

Sakaki
Sakura

Hmph.

Sex: Female
Age: 13
Date of Birth: July 14 (Cancer)
Height: 97cm
Blood Type: O
Birthplace: Tokyo

Interests/Hobbies: Drawing comics, staying at home as a recluse

Strengths: Good insight, strong sense of justice, quite powerful

Dislikes/Weakness: Waking up in the morning, dogs, milk

Likes: Anime and manga, sweets, watching people

- Dislikes anything that can't be done by force.
- Very mobile and active.
- She hates being teased about her height. She can only wear child-sized clothes.
- She has a lot of hair, so it always looks hideous when she gets out of bed.
- Her skin has never been chapped, not even once.

ENTER.67 SEARCH

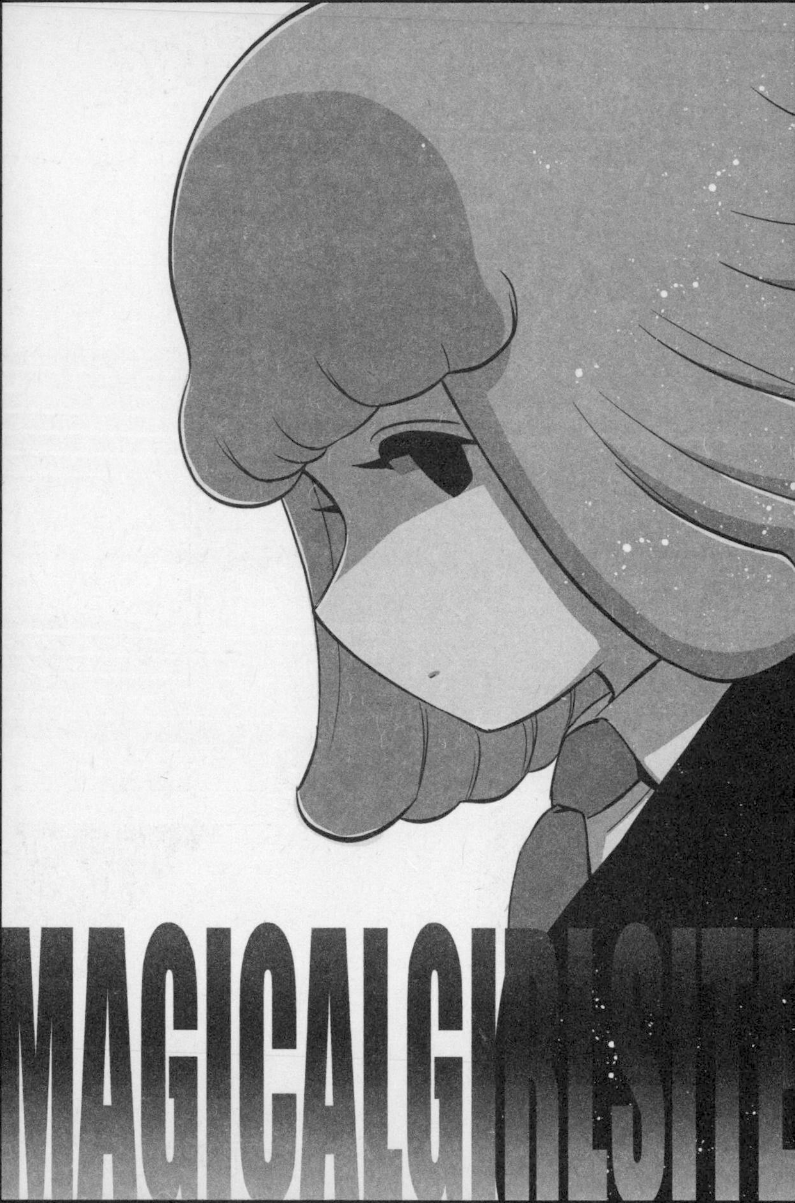
MAGICALGIRLSITE

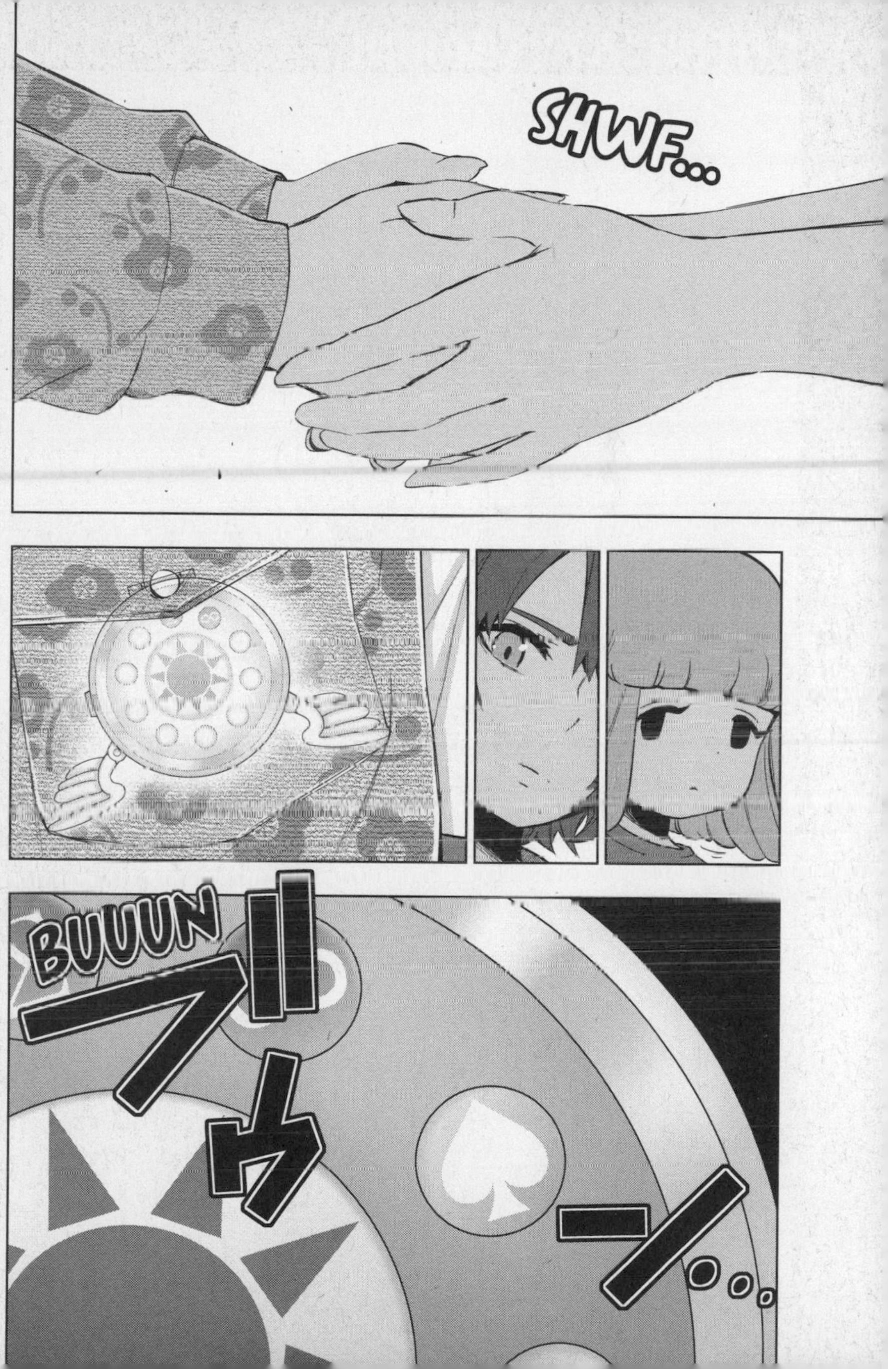
SHWF...
BUUUN

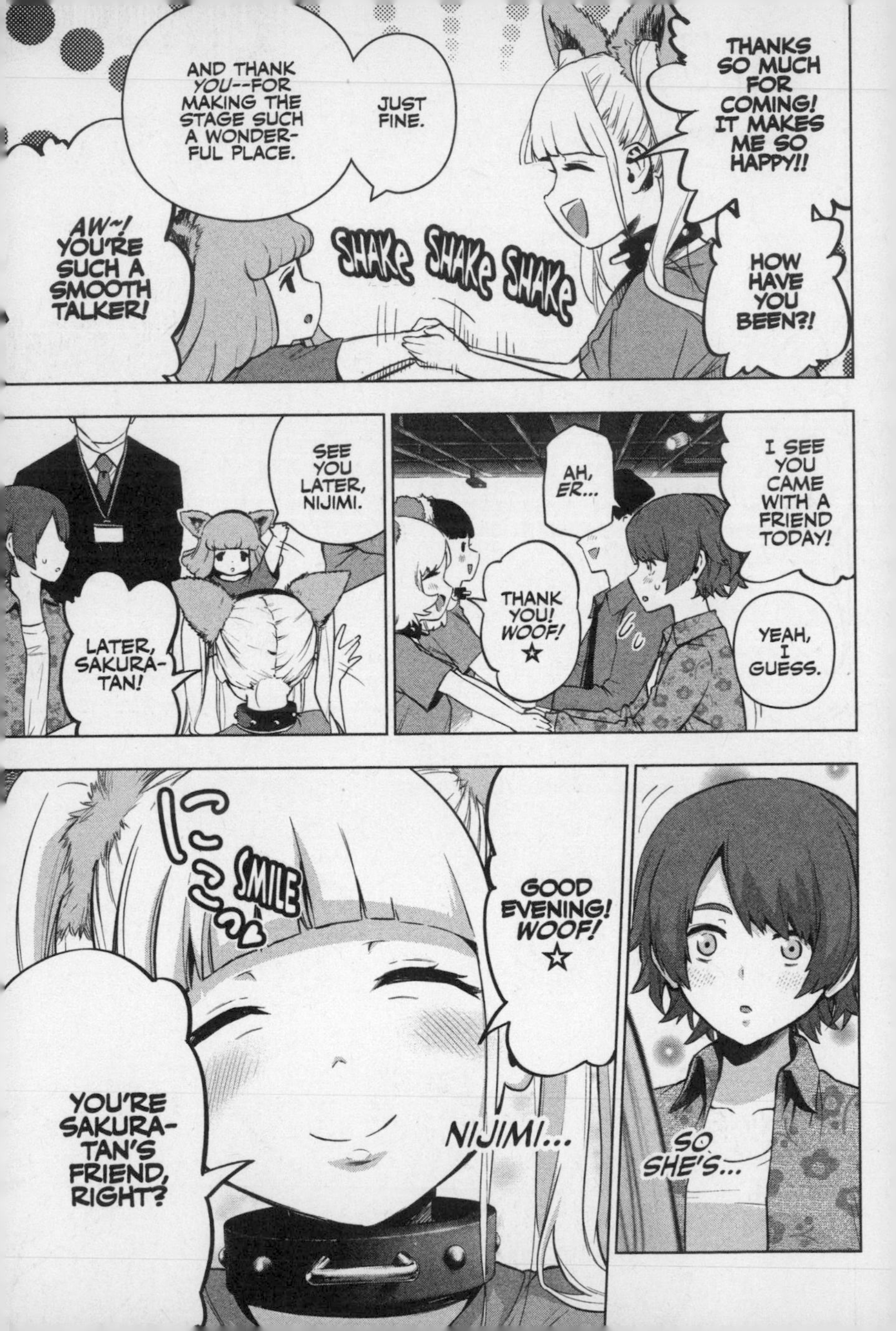
THANKS SO MUCH FOR COMING! IT MAKES ME SO HAPPY!!
HOW HAVE YOU BEEN?!
JUST FINE.
AND THANK *YOU*--FOR MAKING THE STAGE SUCH A WONDERFUL PLACE.
SHAKE SHAKE SHAKE
AW~! YOU'RE SUCH A SMOOTH TALKER!
I SEE YOU CAME WITH A FRIEND TODAY!
YEAH, I GUESS.
AH, ER...
THANK YOU! WOOF! ☆
SEE YOU LATER, NIJIMI.
LATER, SAKURA-TAN!
SO SHE'S...
GOOD EVENING! WOOF! ☆
SMILE
NIJIMI...
YOU'RE SAKURA-TAN'S FRIEND, RIGHT?

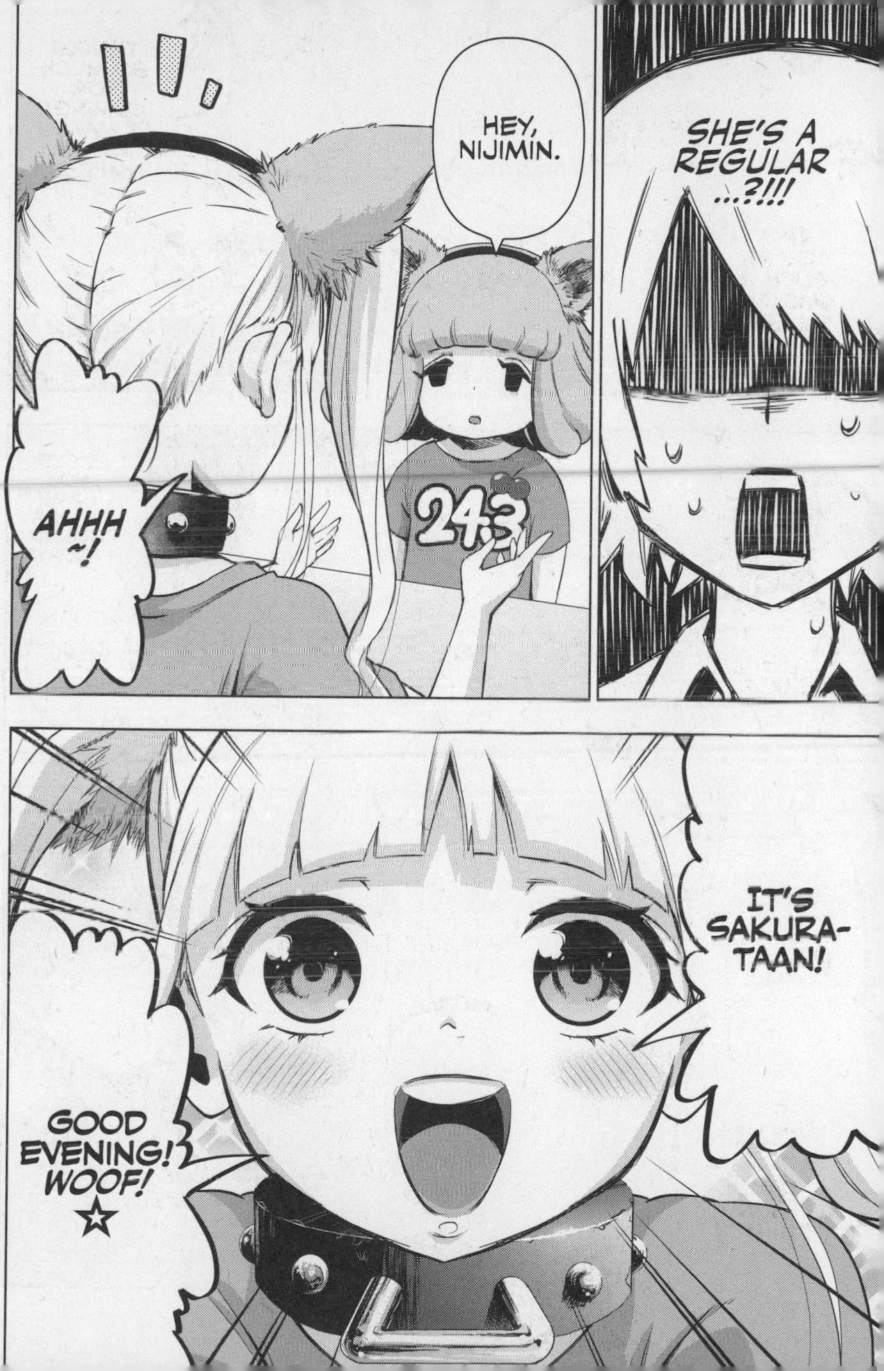
SHE'S A REGULAR ...?!!!
HEY, NIJIMIN.
AHHH ~!
IT'S SAKURA-TAAN!
GOOD EVENING! WOOF! ☆

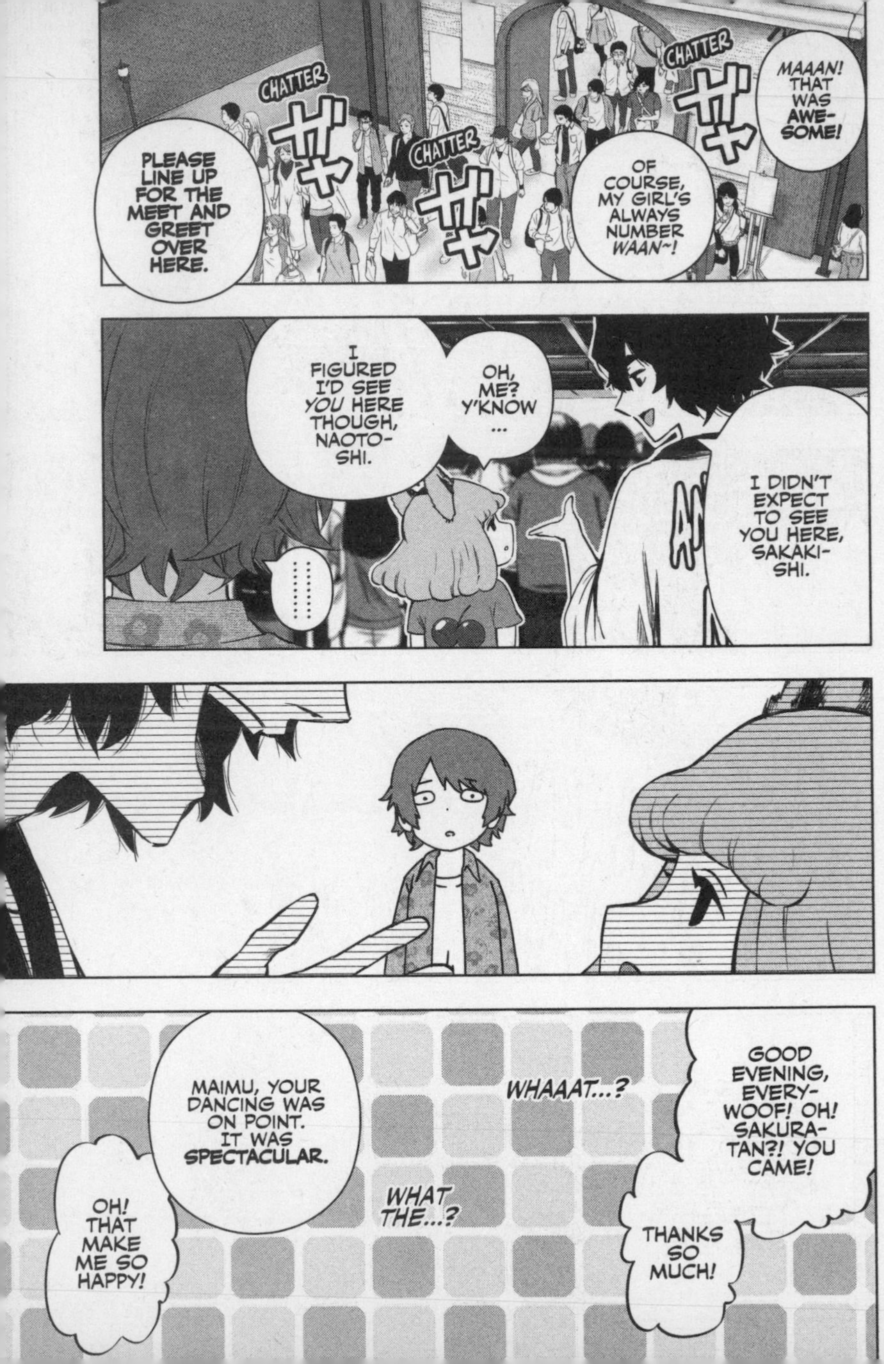
MAAAN! THAT WAS AWE-SOME!
CHATTER
OF COURSE, MY GIRL'S ALWAYS NUMBER *WAAN*~!
CHATTER
CHATTER
PLEASE LINE UP FOR THE MEET AND GREET OVER HERE.
I DIDN'T EXPECT TO SEE YOU HERE, SAKAKI-SHI.
OH, ME? Y'KNOW ...
I FIGURED I'D SEE *YOU* HERE THOUGH, NAOTO-SHI.
......
GOOD EVENING, EVERY-WOOF! OH! SAKURA-TAN?! YOU CAME!
THANKS SO MUCH!
WHAAAT...?
WHAT THE...?
MAIMU, YOUR DANCING WAS ON POINT. IT WAS **SPECTACULAR.**
OH! THAT MAKE ME SO HAPPY!

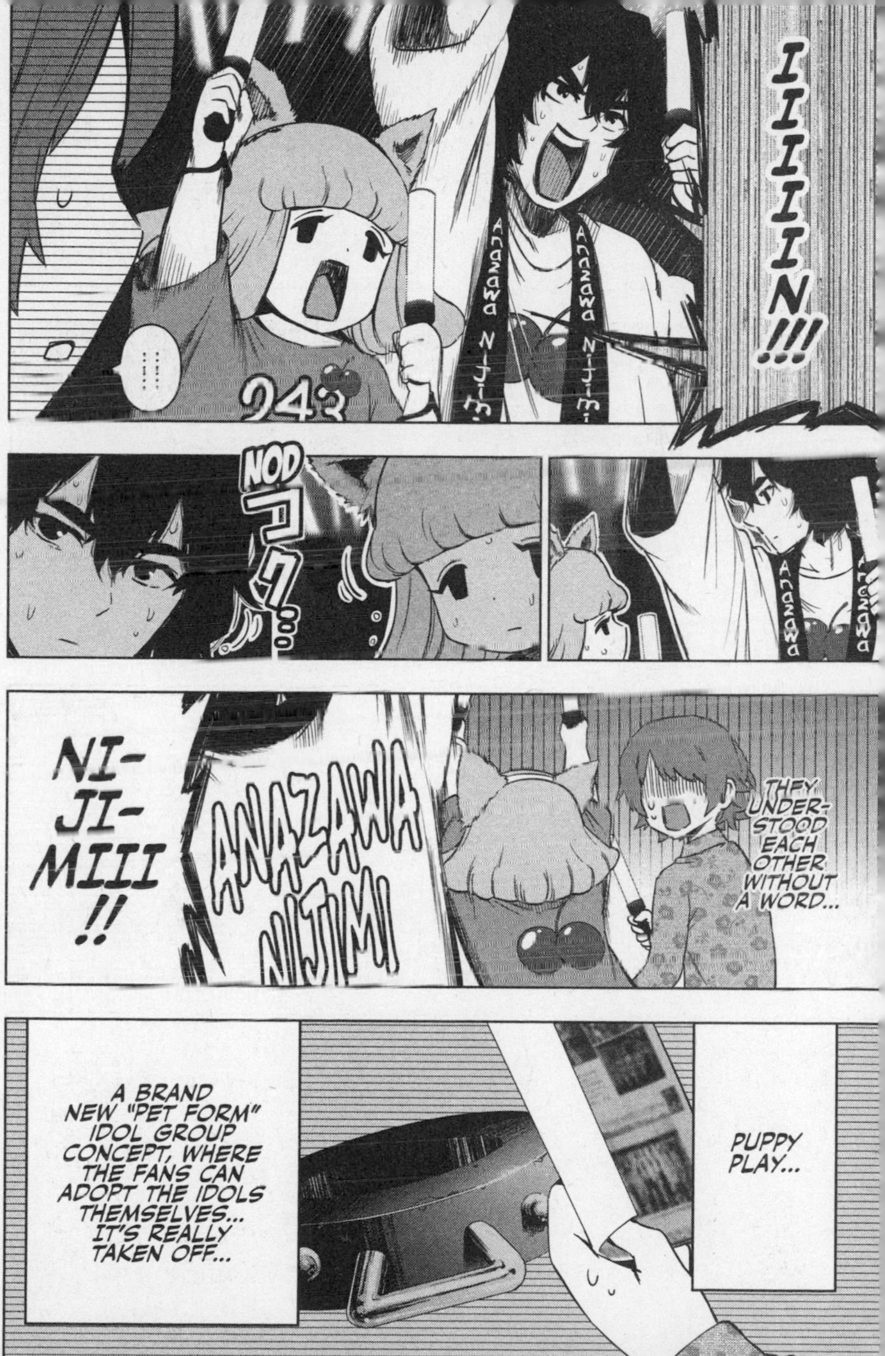
IIIIIIN!!!
...
Anazawa Nijimi
Anazawa Nijimi
943
NOD
Anazawa
Anazawa
THEY UNDERSTOOD EACH OTHER WITHOUT A WORD...
ANAZAWA NIJIMI
NI-JI-MIII!!
PUPPY PLAY...
A BRAND NEW "PET FORM" IDOL GROUP CONCEPT, WHERE THE FANS CAN ADOPT THE IDOLS THEMSELVES... IT'S REALLY TAKEN OFF...

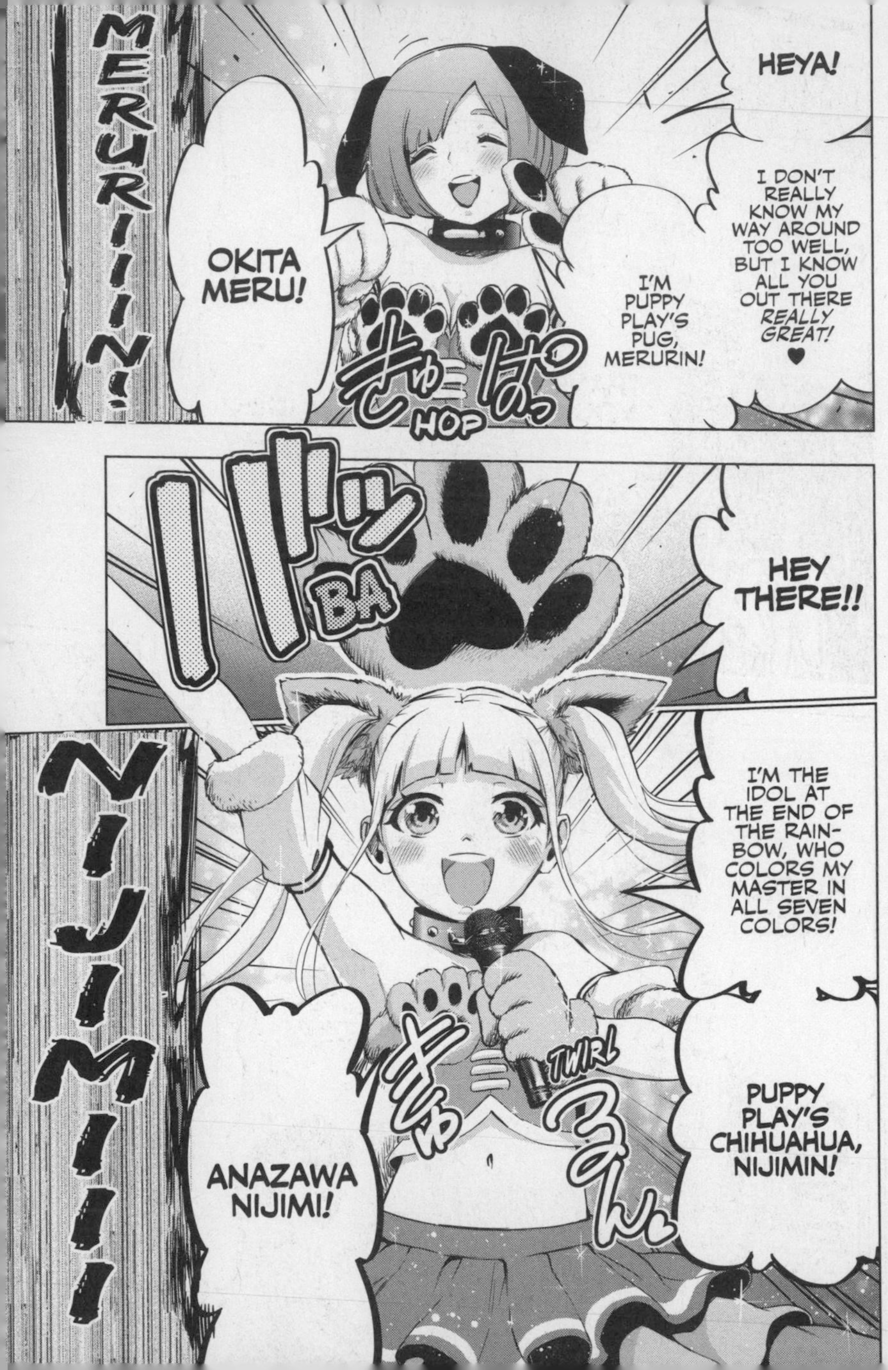
HEYA!
I DON'T REALLY KNOW MY WAY AROUND TOO WELL, BUT I KNOW ALL YOU OUT THERE *REALLY GREAT!* ♥
I'M PUPPY PLAY'S PUG, MERURIN!
きゅぱっ
HOP
OKITA MERU!
MERURIIIN!
HEY THERE!!
バッ
BA
I'M THE IDOL AT THE END OF THE RAIN-BOW, WHO COLORS MY MASTER IN ALL SEVEN COLORS!
PUPPY PLAY'S CHIHUAHUA, NIJIMIN!
きゅるん♥
TWIRL
ANAZAWA NIJIMI!
NIJIMIII!

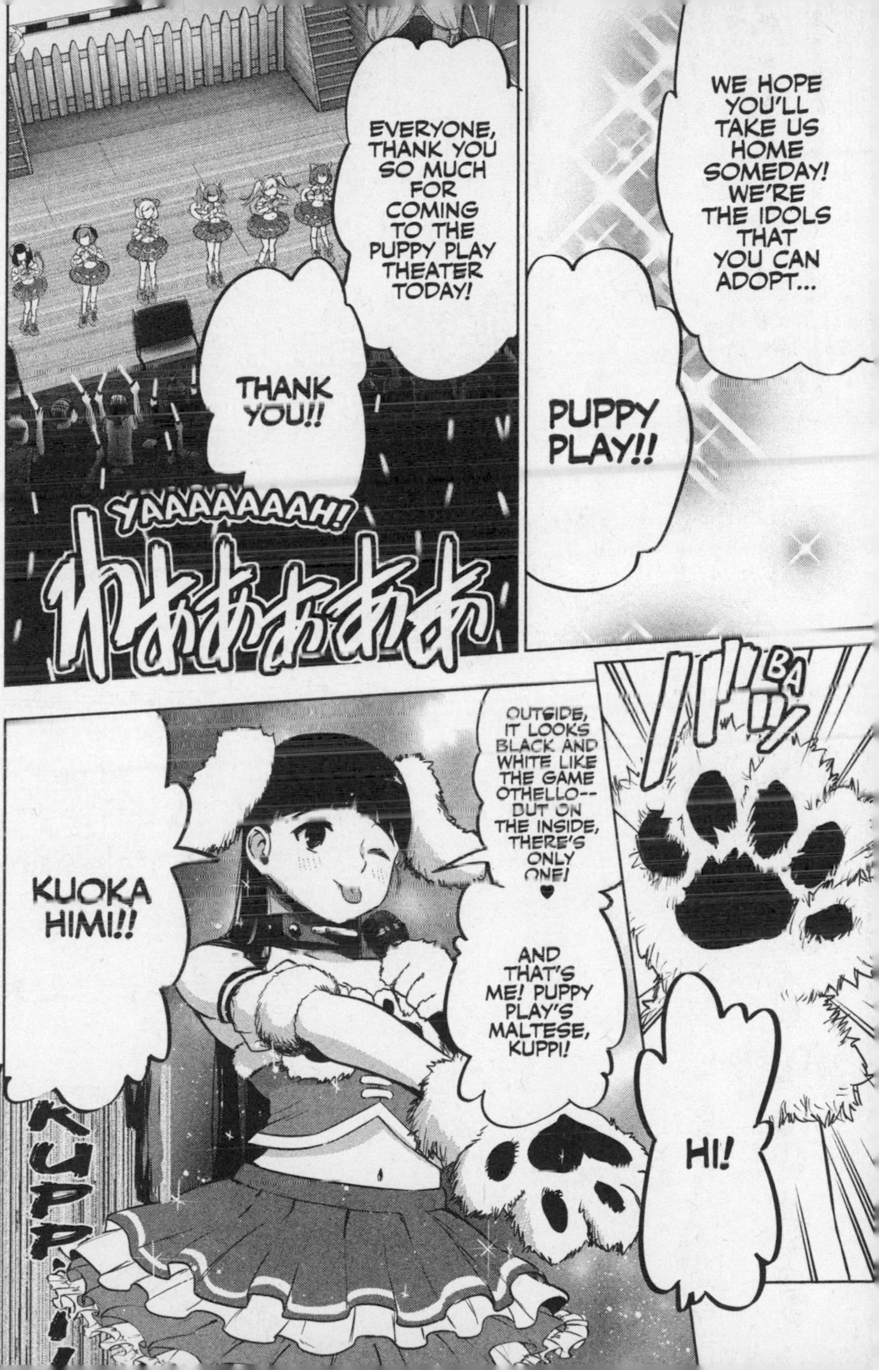
WE HOPE YOU'LL TAKE US HOME SOMEDAY! WE'RE THE IDOLS THAT YOU CAN ADOPT...
PUPPY PLAY!!
EVERYONE, THANK YOU SO MUCH FOR COMING TO THE PUPPY PLAY THEATER TODAY!
THANK YOU!!
YAAAAAAAAH!
わあああああ
BA
OUTSIDE, IT LOOKS BLACK AND WHITE LIKE THE GAME OTHELLO--BUT ON THE INSIDE, THERE'S ONLY ONE! ♥
HI!
AND THAT'S ME! PUPPY PLAY'S MALTESE, KUPPI!
KUOKA HIMI!!
KUPP...

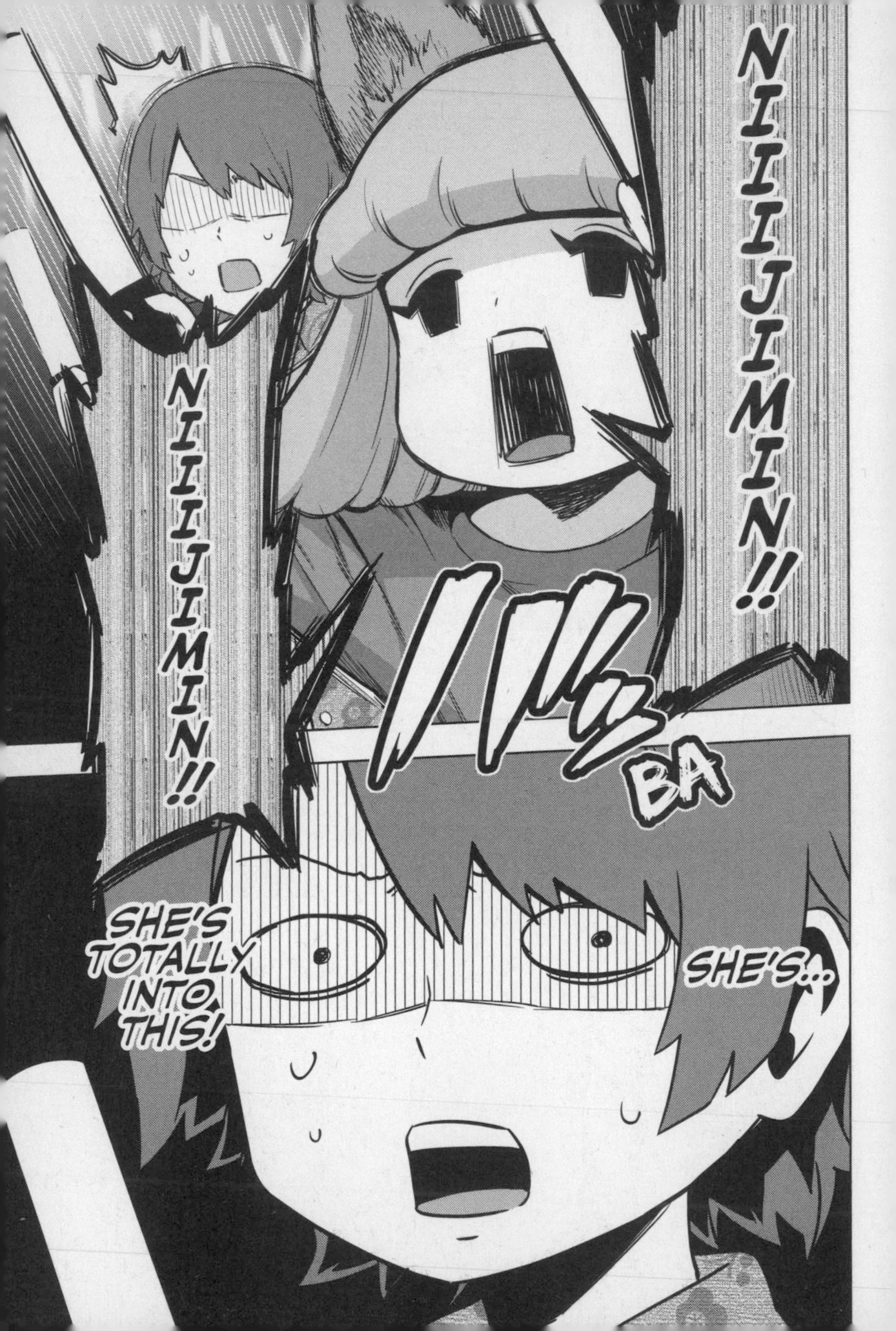
NIIIJIMIN!!
NIIIJIMIN!!
BA
SHE'S...
SHE'S TOTALLY INTO THIS!

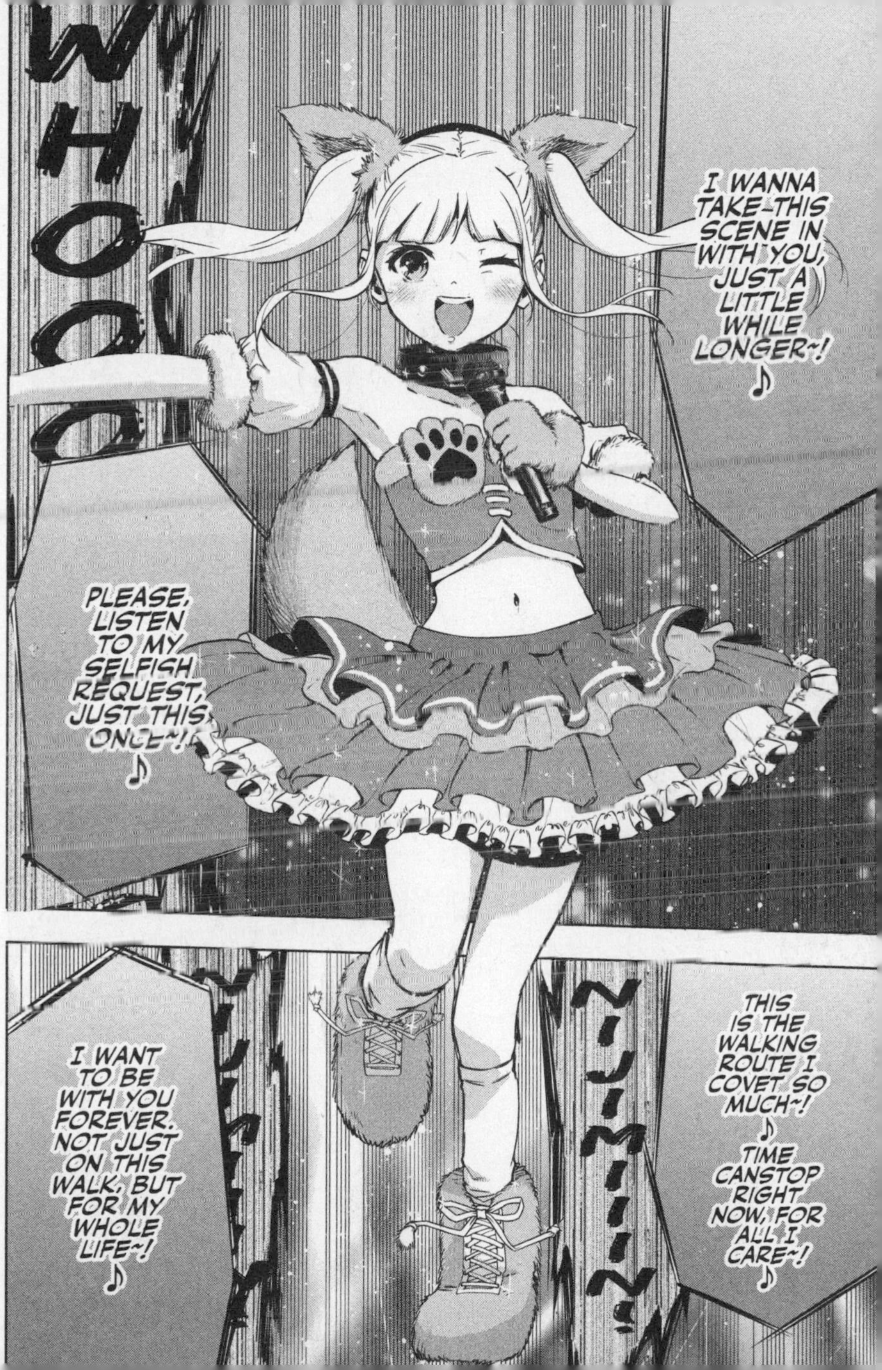
WHOOO
I WANNA TAKE THIS SCENE IN WITH YOU, JUST A LITTLE WHILE LONGER~! ♪
PLEASE, LISTEN TO MY SELFISH REQUEST, JUST THIS ONCE~! ♪
THIS IS THE WALKING ROUTE I COVET SO MUCH~! ♪
TIME CANSTOP RIGHT NOW, FOR ALL I CARE~! ♪
NIJIMIIIN~!
I WANT TO BE WITH YOU FOREVER. NOT JUST ON THIS WALK, BUT FOR MY WHOLE LIFE~! ♪

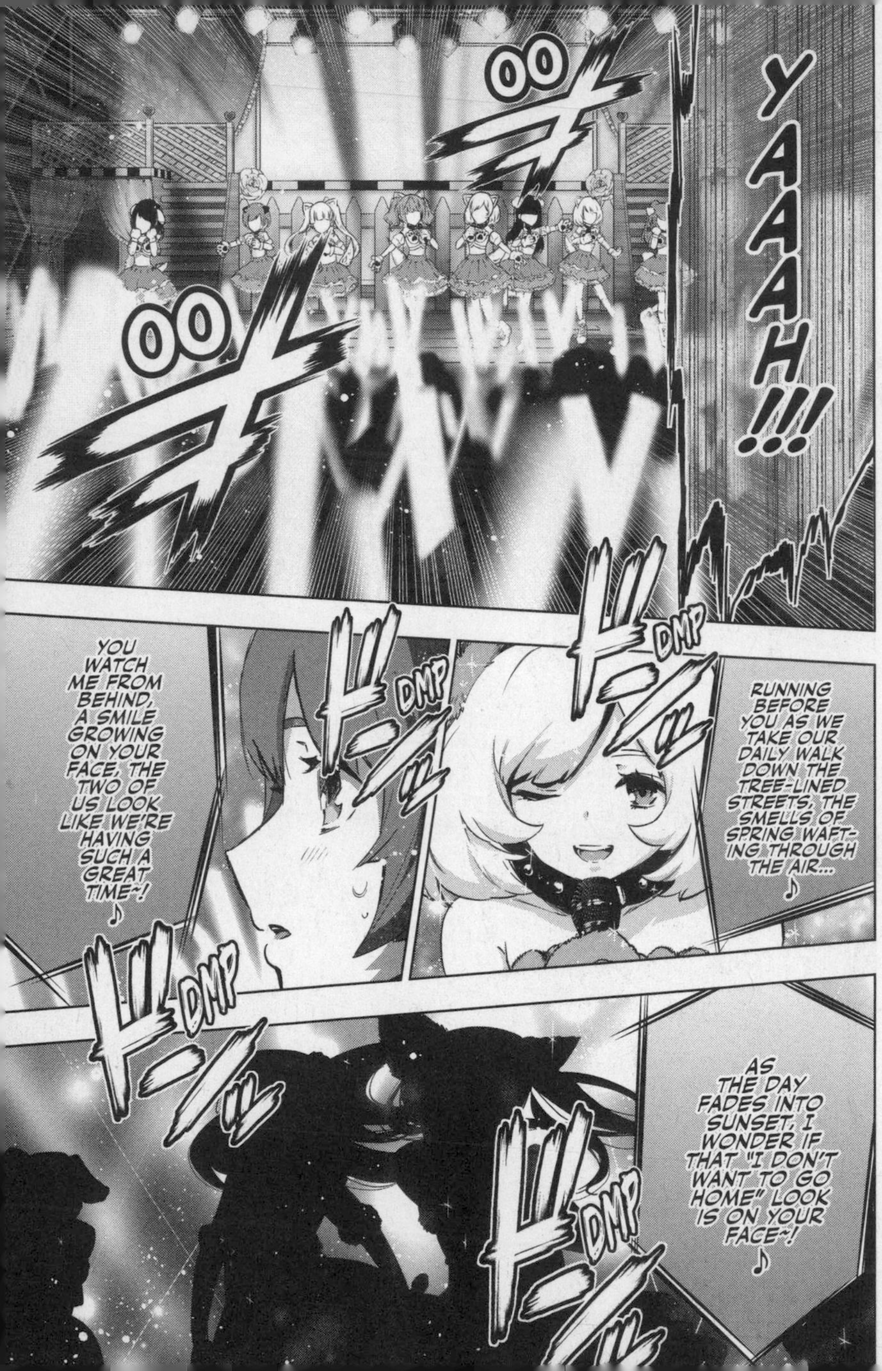
YAAAAH!!!
OO
OO
RUNNING BEFORE YOU AS WE TAKE OUR DAILY WALK DOWN THE TREE-LINED STREETS, THE SMELLS OF SPRING WAFT-ING THROUGH THE AIR... ♪
DMP
DMP
YOU WATCH ME FROM BEHIND, A SMILE GROWING ON YOUR FACE, THE TWO OF US LOOK LIKE WE'RE HAVING SUCH A GREAT TIME~! ♪
DMP
AS THE DAY FADES INTO SUNSET, I WONDER IF THAT "I DON'T WANT TO GO HOME" LOOK IS ON YOUR FACE~! ♪
DMP

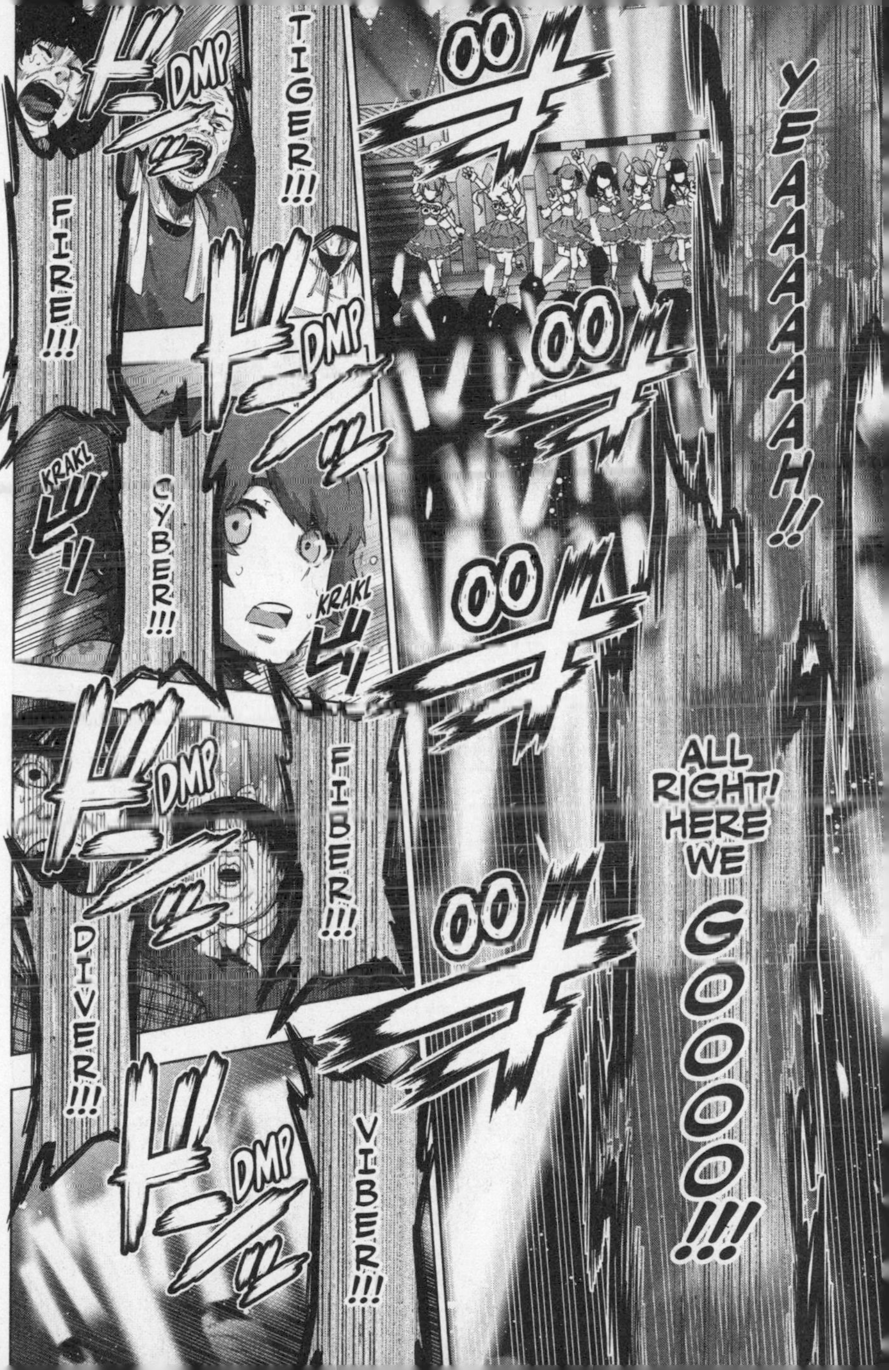
YEAAAAAAAH!!
ALL RIGHT! HERE WE GOOOOO!!!
OO
OO
OO
OO
TIGER!!!
DMP
DMP
FIRE!!!
KRAKL
CYBER!!!
KRAKL
FIBER!!!
DMP
DIVER!!!
VIBER!!!
DMP

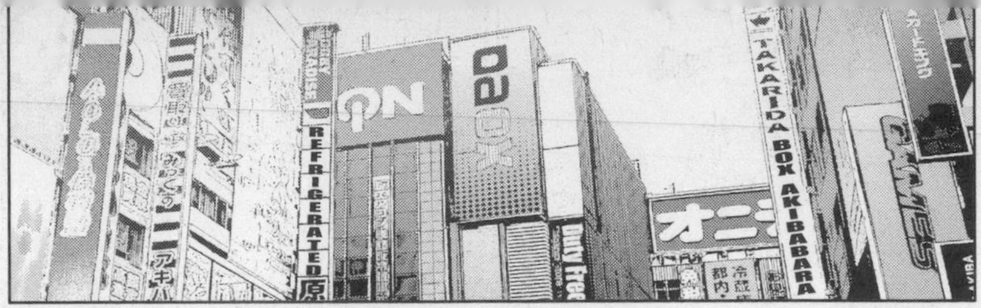
REFRIGERATED
TAKARIDA BOX AKIBABARA
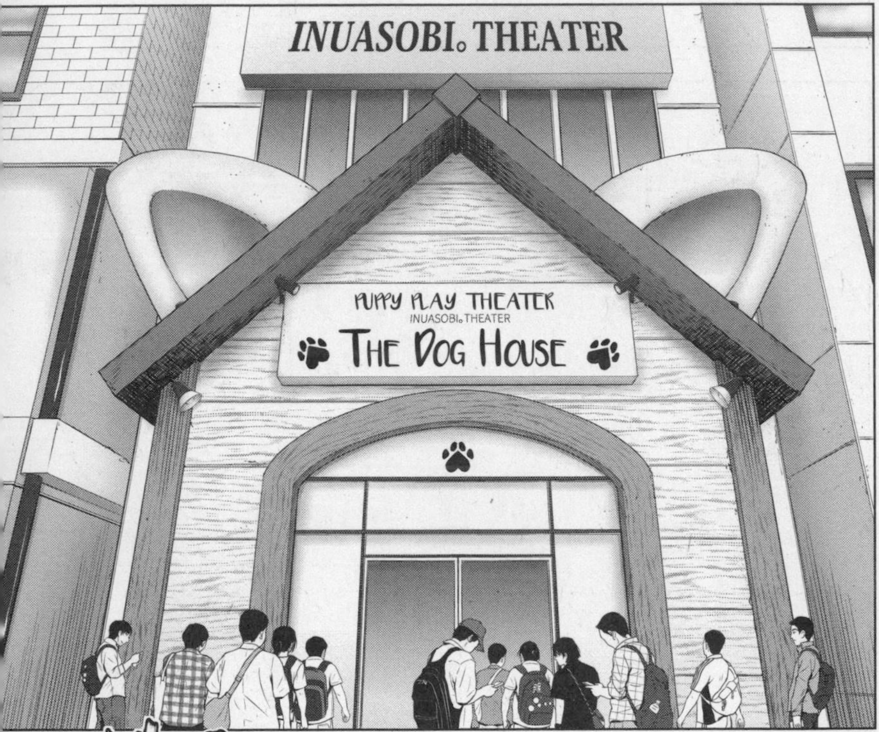
INUASOBI。THEATER
PUPPY PLAY THEATER
INUASOBI。THEATER
THE DOG HOUSE
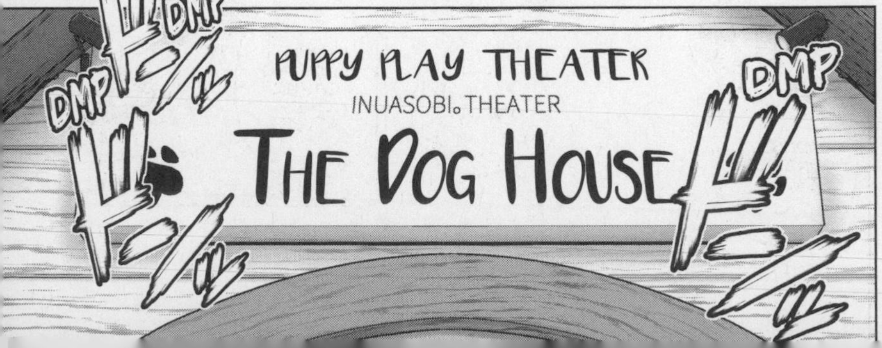
DMP
DMP
DMP
PUPPY PLAY THEATER
INUASOBI。THEATER
THE DOG HOUSE

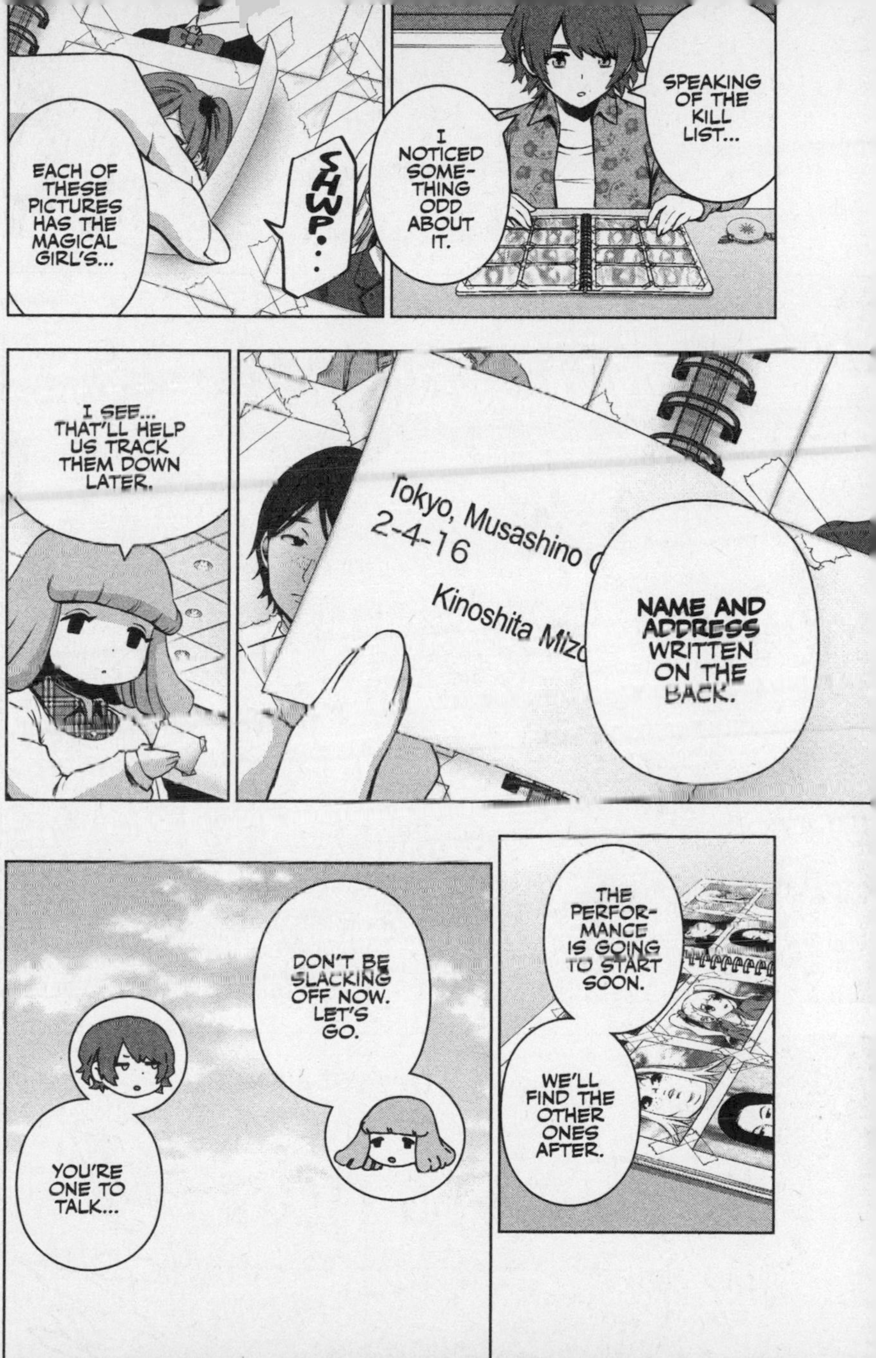
SPEAKING OF THE KILL LIST...
I NOTICED SOMETHING ODD ABOUT IT.
SHWP...
EACH OF THESE PICTURES HAS THE MAGICAL GIRL'S...
Tokyo, Musashino
2-4-16
Kinoshita Mizo
NAME AND ADDRESS WRITTEN ON THE BACK.
I SEE... THAT'LL HELP US TRACK THEM DOWN LATER.
THE PERFORMANCE IS GOING TO START SOON.
WE'LL FIND THE OTHER ONES AFTER.
DON'T BE SLACKING OFF NOW. LET'S GO.
YOU'RE ONE TO TALK...

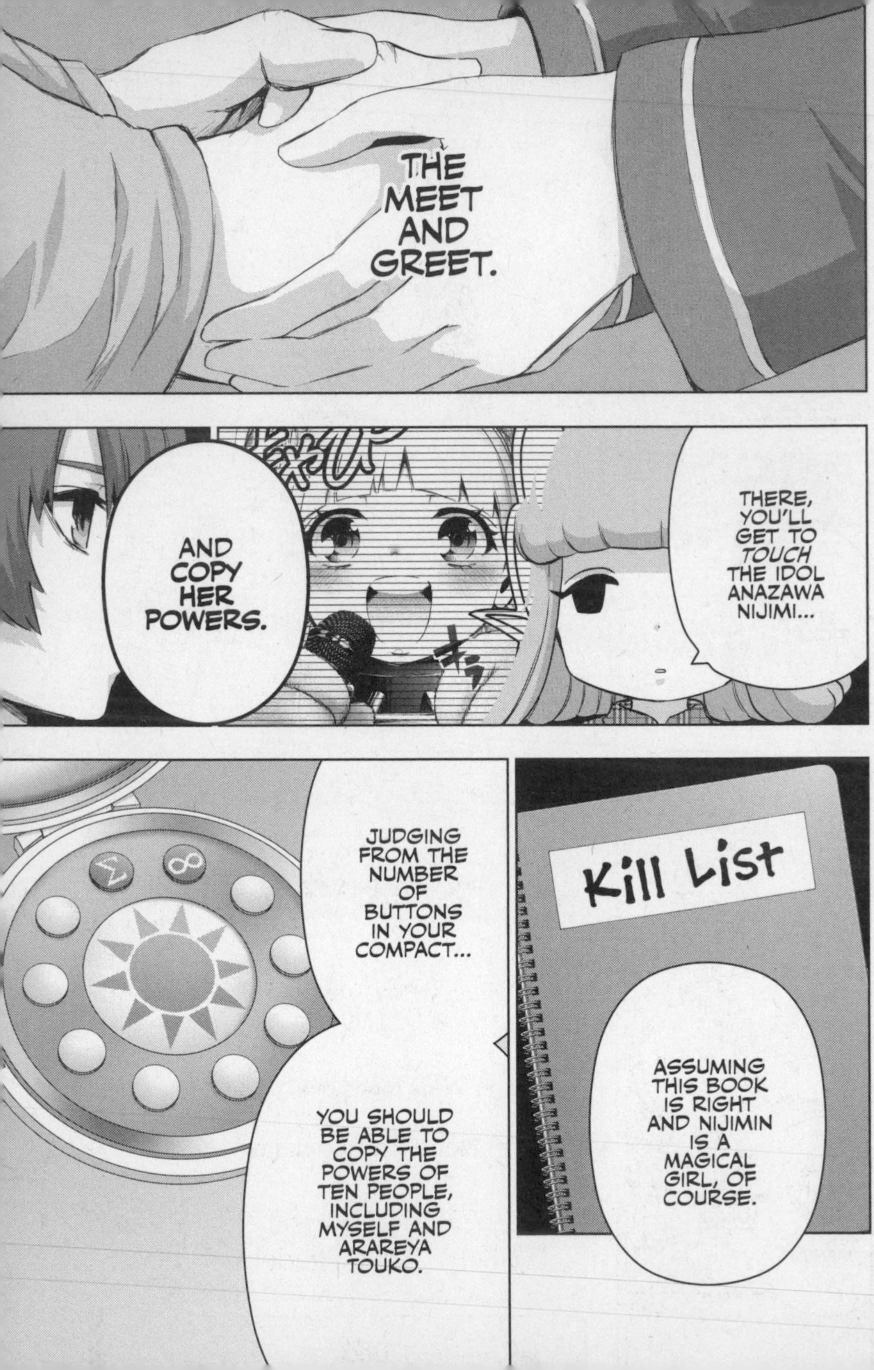
THE MEET AND GREET.
THERE, YOU'LL GET TO *TOUCH* THE IDOL ANAZAWA NIJIMI...
AND COPY HER POWERS.
Kill List
ASSUMING THIS BOOK IS RIGHT AND NIJIMIN IS A MAGICAL GIRL, OF COURSE.
JUDGING FROM THE NUMBER OF BUTTONS IN YOUR COMPACT...
YOU SHOULD BE ABLE TO COPY THE POWERS OF TEN PEOPLE, INCLUDING MYSELF AND ARAREYA TOUKO.

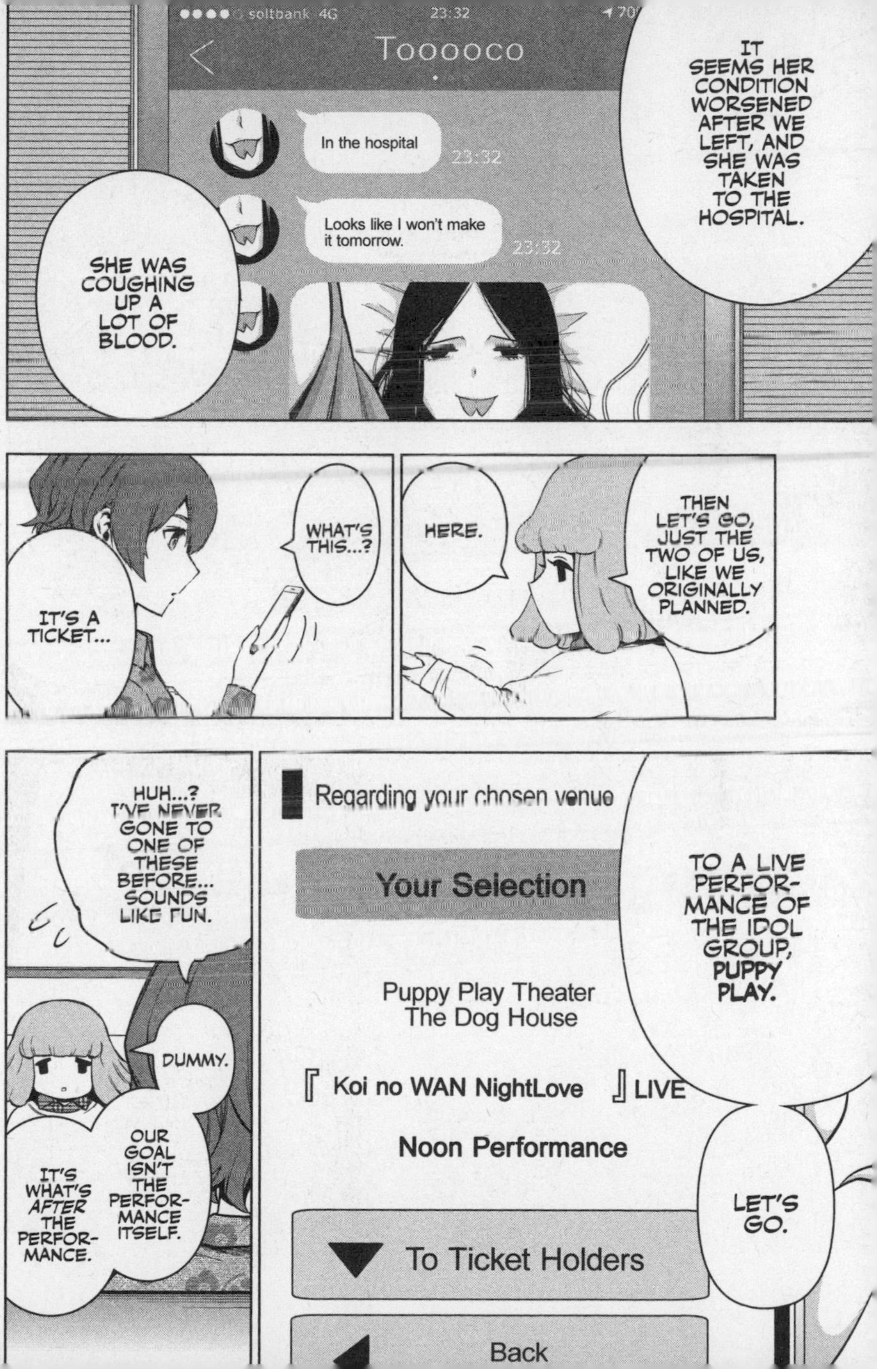
IT SEEMS HER CONDITION WORSENED AFTER WE LEFT, AND SHE WAS TAKEN TO THE HOSPITAL.
soltbank 4G 23:32
Tooooco
In the hospital 23:32
Looks like I won't make it tomorrow. 23:32
SHE WAS COUGHING UP A LOT OF BLOOD.
THEN LET'S GO, JUST THE TWO OF US, LIKE WE ORIGINALLY PLANNED.
HERE.
WHAT'S THIS...?
IT'S A TICKET...
TO A LIVE PERFORMANCE OF THE IDOL GROUP, PUPPY PLAY.
Regarding your chosen venue
Your Selection
Puppy Play Theater The Dog House
『Koi no WAN NightLove』LIVE
Noon Performance
LET'S GO.
To Ticket Holders
Back
HUH...? I'VE NEVER GONE TO ONE OF THESE BEFORE... SOUNDS LIKE FUN.
DUMMY.
OUR GOAL ISN'T THE PERFORMANCE ITSELF.
IT'S WHAT'S *AFTER* THE PERFORMANCE.

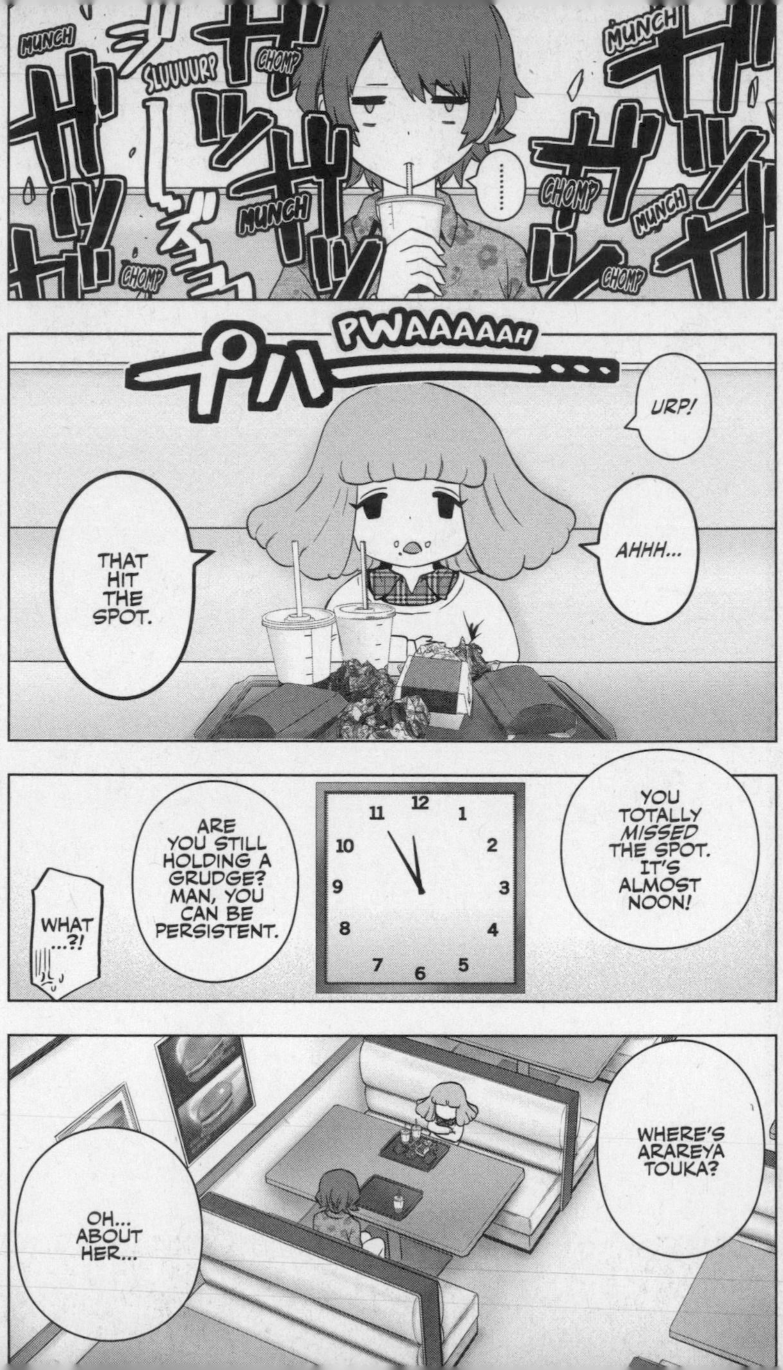
MUNCH
MUNCH
CHOMP
CHOMP
......
CHOMP
SLUUUURP
MUNCH
MUNCH
CHOMP
PWAAAAAH
URP!
AHHH...
THAT HIT THE SPOT.
YOU TOTALLY *MISSED* THE SPOT. IT'S ALMOST NOON!
ARE YOU STILL HOLDING A GRUDGE? MAN, YOU CAN BE PERSISTENT.
WHAT...?!
WHERE'S ARAREYA TOUKA?
OH... ABOUT HER...

Manga Covers: Mage of Love ☆ Exile | Yagiwa-san

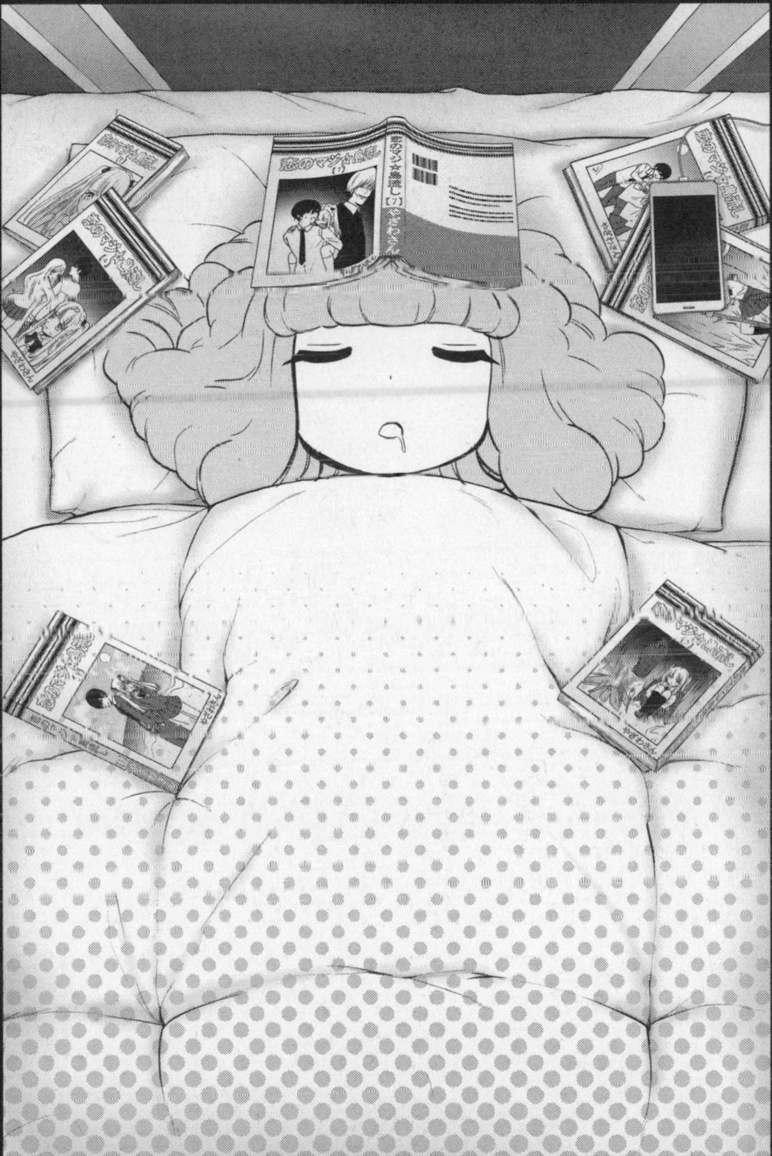
恋のマジ☆島流し【7】
やぎわさん

ENTER.66 PUPPY PLAY

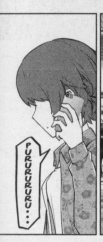

ENTER.66 PUPPY PLAY

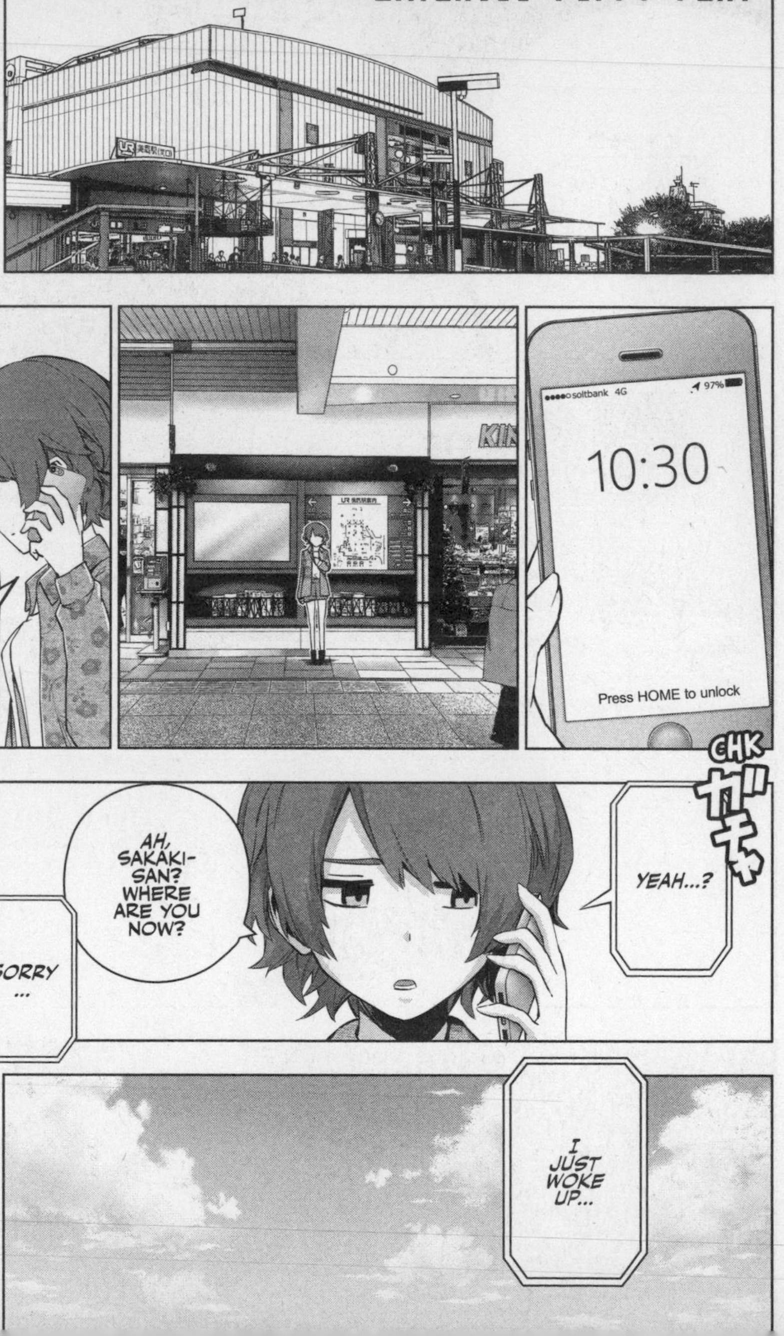
●●●●○ soltbank 4G 97%
10:30
Press HOME to unlock
PURURURURU...
CHK
ガチャ
YEAH...?
AH, SAKAKI-SAN? WHERE ARE YOU NOW?
SORRY ...
I JUST WOKE UP...

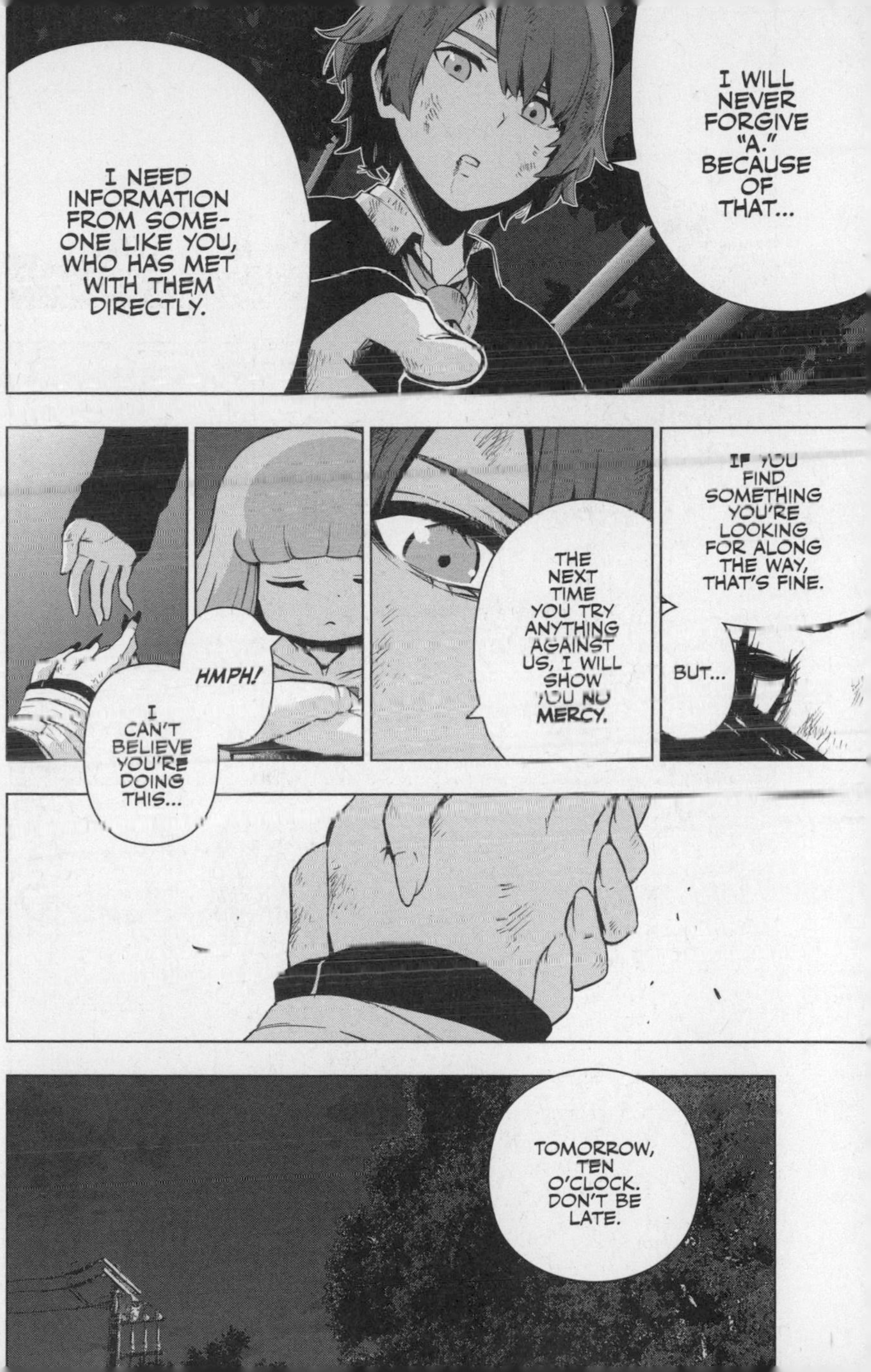
I WILL NEVER FORGIVE "A." BECAUSE OF THAT...
I NEED INFORMATION FROM SOME-ONE LIKE YOU, WHO HAS MET WITH THEM DIRECTLY.
IF YOU FIND SOMETHING YOU'RE LOOKING FOR ALONG THE WAY, THAT'S FINE.
BUT...
THE NEXT TIME YOU TRY ANYTHING AGAINST US, I WILL SHOW YOU NO MERCY.
HMPH!
I CAN'T BELIEVE YOU'RE DOING THIS...
TOMORROW, TEN O'CLOCK. DON'T BE LATE.

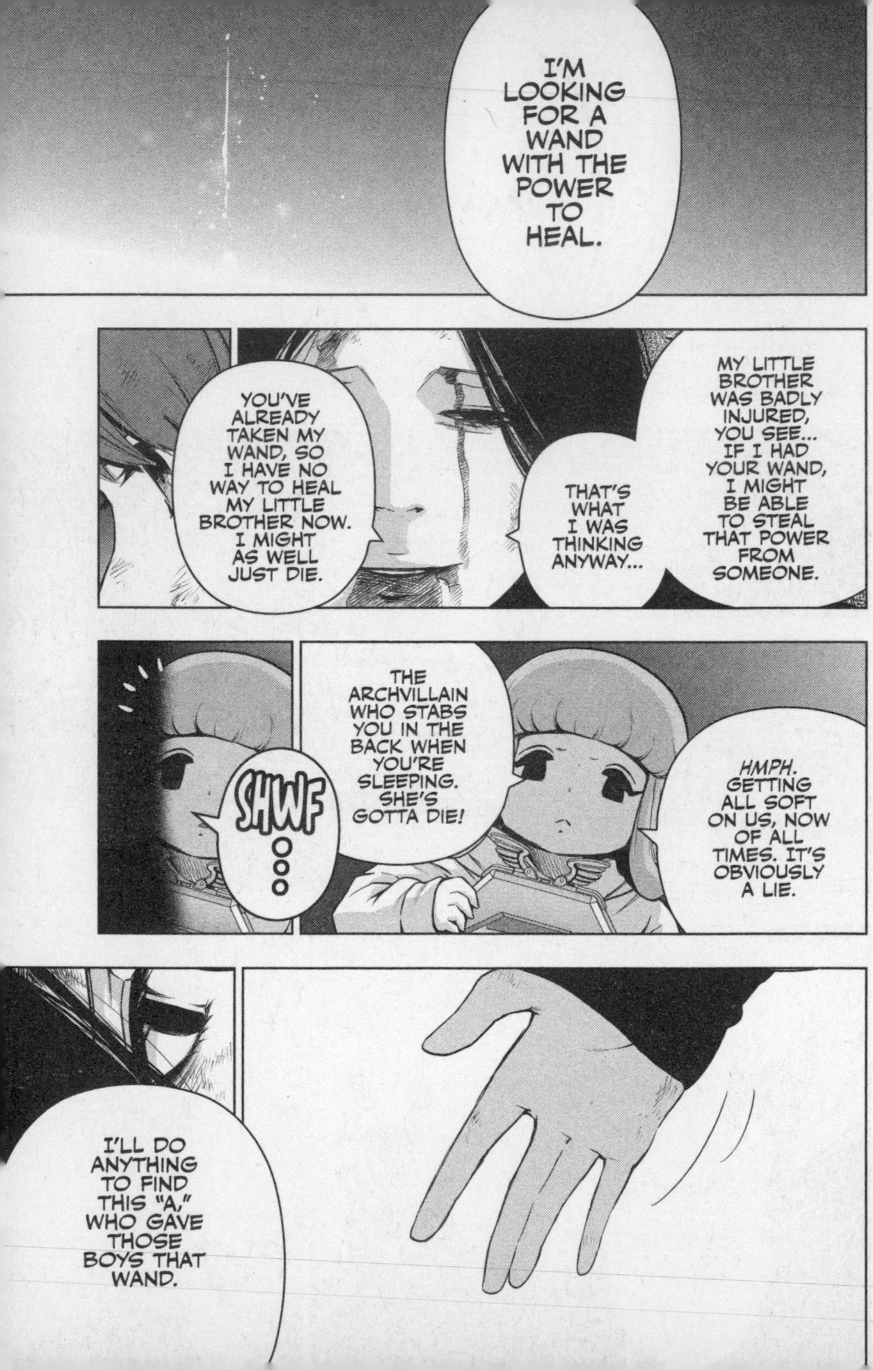
I'M LOOKING FOR A WAND WITH THE POWER TO HEAL.
MY LITTLE BROTHER WAS BADLY INJURED, YOU SEE... IF I HAD YOUR WAND, I MIGHT BE ABLE TO STEAL THAT POWER FROM SOMEONE.
THAT'S WHAT I WAS THINKING ANYWAY...
YOU'VE ALREADY TAKEN MY WAND, SO I HAVE NO WAY TO HEAL MY LITTLE BROTHER NOW. I MIGHT AS WELL JUST DIE.
HMPH. GETTING ALL SOFT ON US, NOW OF ALL TIMES. IT'S OBVIOUSLY A LIE.
THE ARCHVILLAIN WHO STABS YOU IN THE BACK WHEN YOU'RE SLEEPING. SHE'S GOTTA DIE!
SHWF
OOO
I'LL DO ANYTHING TO FIND THIS "A," WHO GAVE THOSE BOYS THAT WAND.

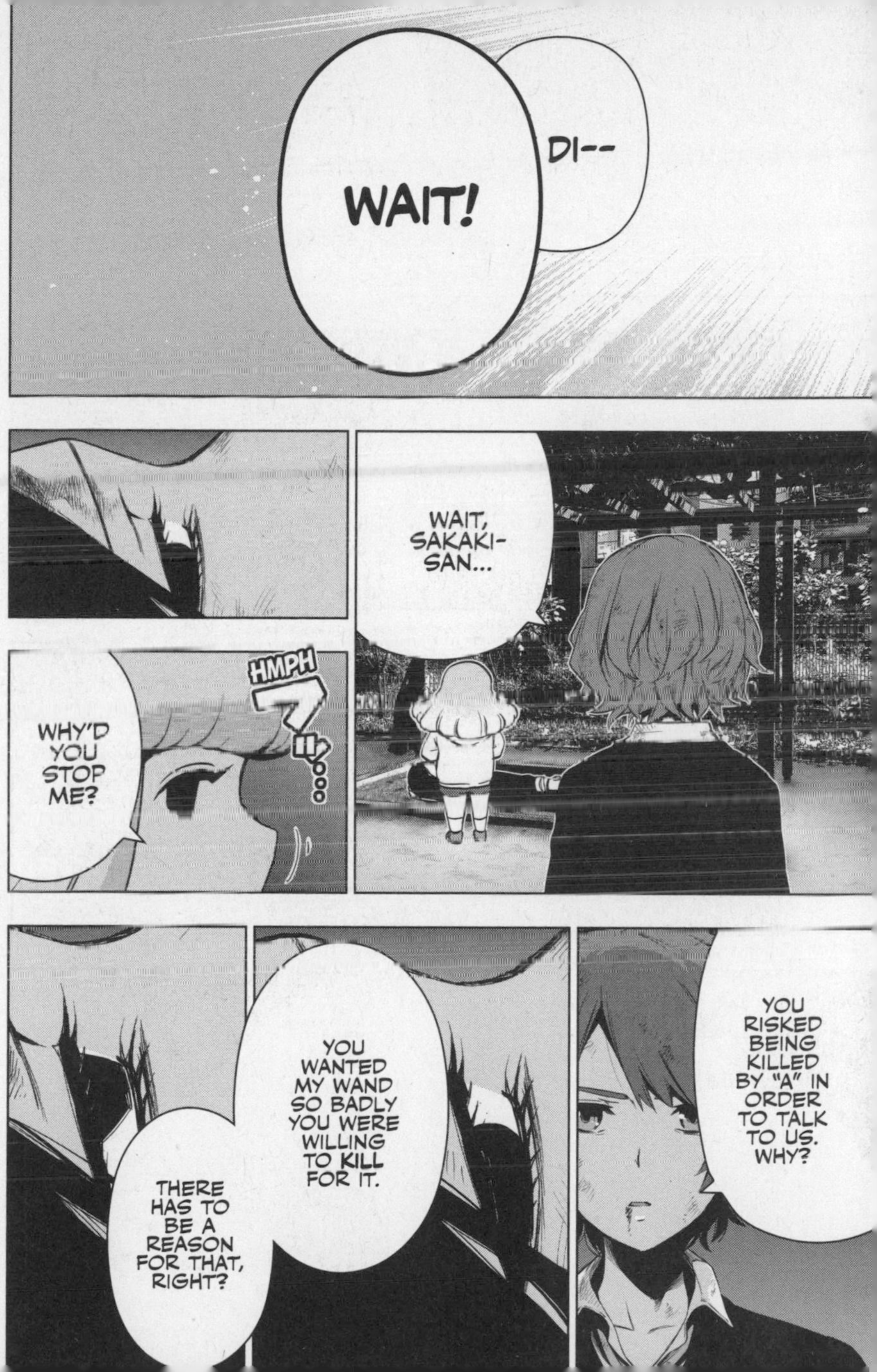
DI--
WAIT!
WAIT, SAKAKI-SAN...
HMPH
WHY'D YOU STOP ME?
YOU RISKED BEING KILLED BY "A" IN ORDER TO TALK TO US. WHY?
YOU WANTED MY WAND SO BADLY YOU WERE WILLING TO KILL FOR IT.
THERE HAS TO BE A REASON FOR THAT, RIGHT?

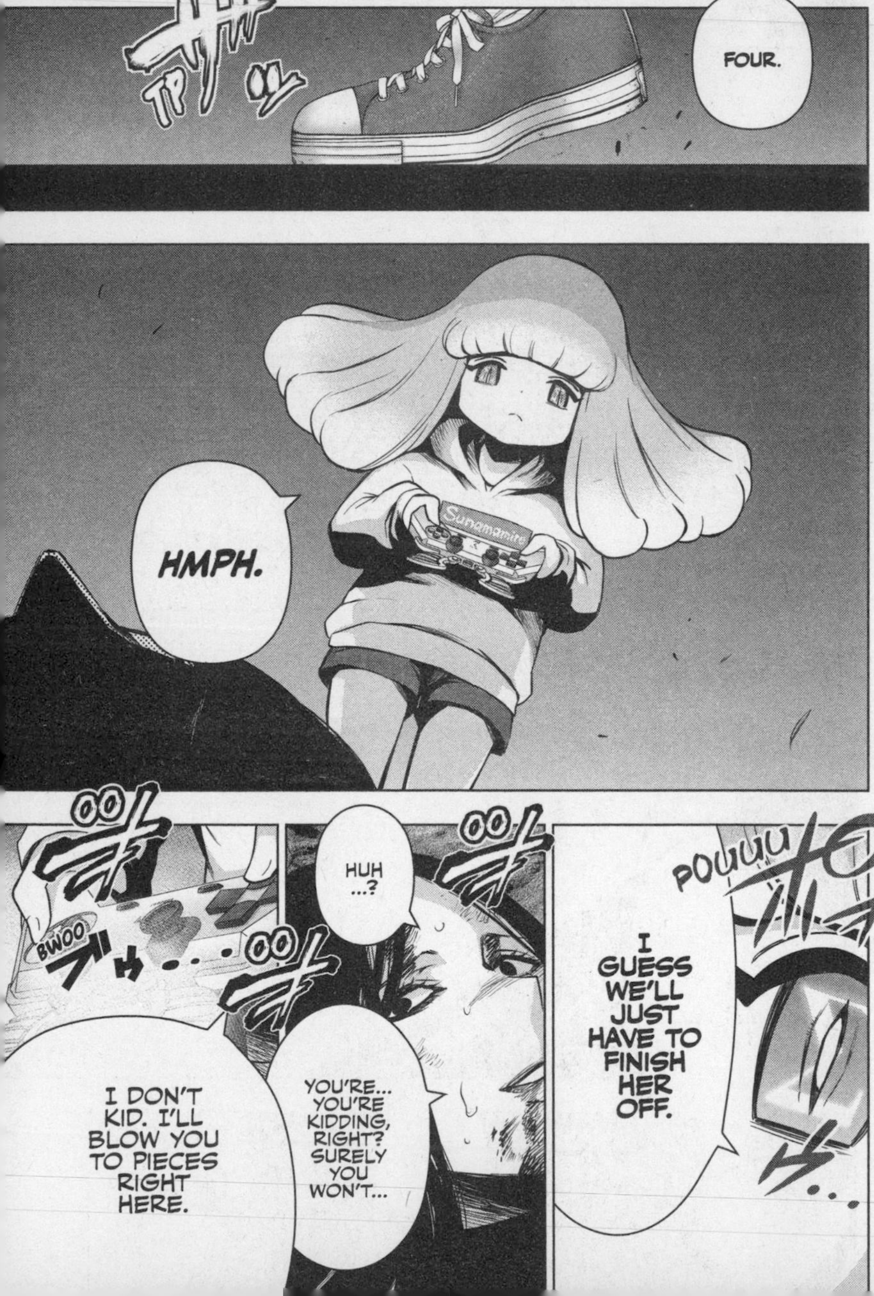
FOUR.
TP
HMPH.
POUUU
I GUESS WE'LL JUST HAVE TO FINISH HER OFF.
HUH ...?
YOU'RE... YOU'RE KIDDING, RIGHT? SURELY YOU WON'T...
BWOO
I DON'T KID. I'LL BLOW YOU TO PIECES RIGHT HERE.

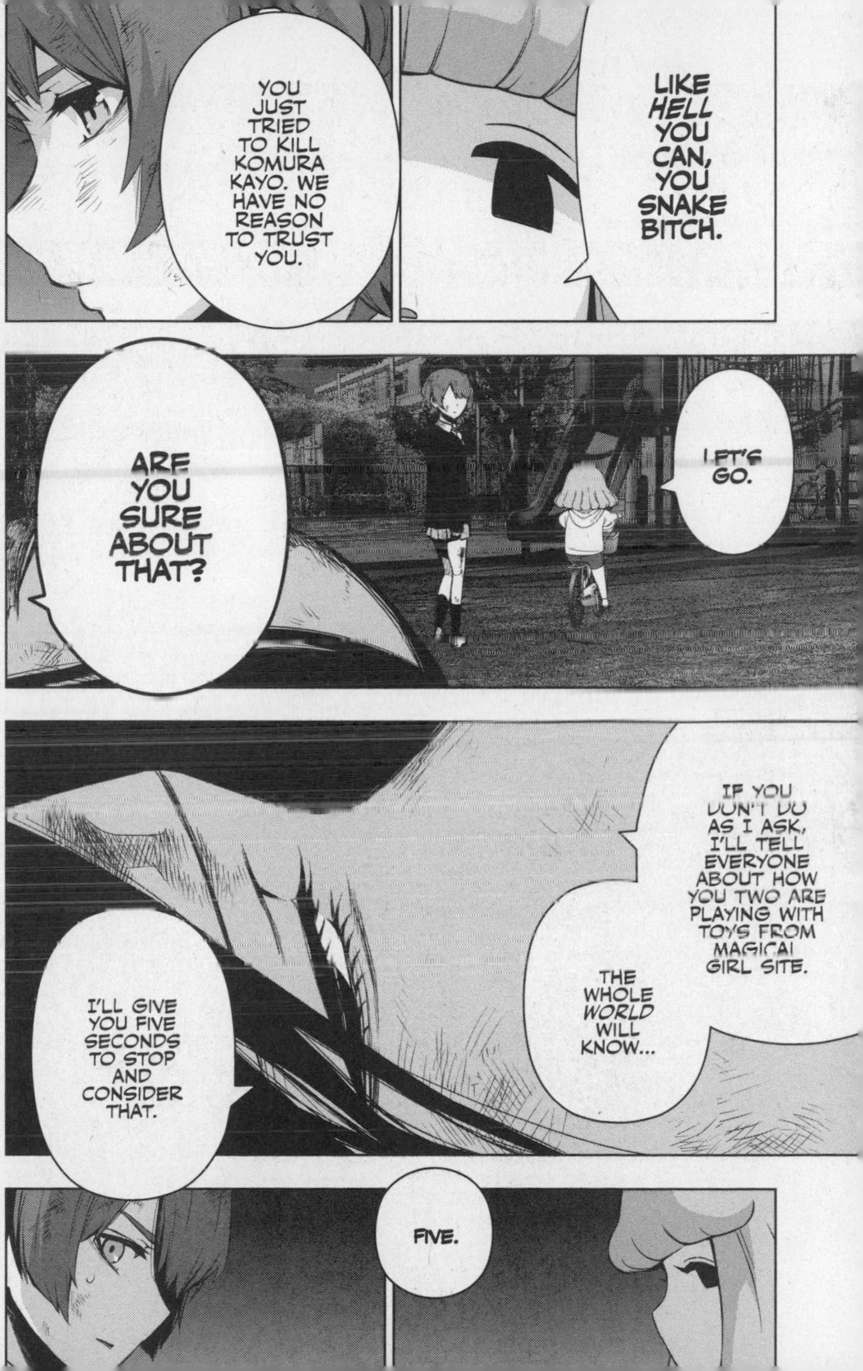
LIKE *HELL* YOU CAN, YOU SNAKE BITCH.
YOU JUST TRIED TO KILL KOMURA KAYO. WE HAVE NO REASON TO TRUST YOU.
LET'S GO.
ARE YOU SURE ABOUT THAT?
IF YOU DON'T DO AS I ASK, I'LL TELL EVERYONE ABOUT HOW YOU TWO ARE PLAYING WITH TOYS FROM MAGICAL GIRL SITE.
THE WHOLE *WORLD* WILL KNOW...
I'LL GIVE YOU FIVE SECONDS TO STOP AND CONSIDER THAT.
FIVE.

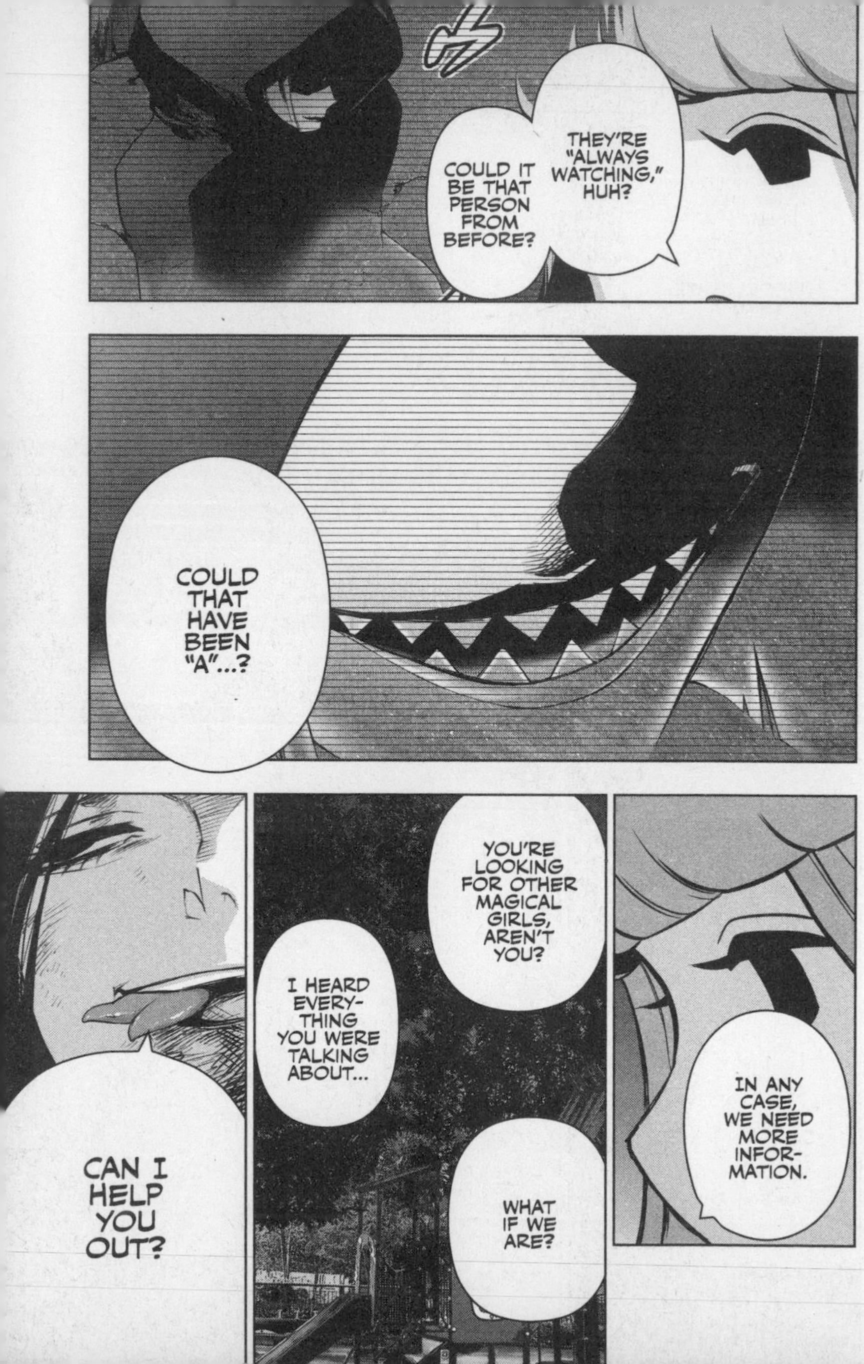
THEY'RE "ALWAYS WATCHING," HUH?
COULD IT BE THAT PERSON FROM BEFORE?
COULD THAT HAVE BEEN "A"...?
IN ANY CASE, WE NEED MORE INFOR-MATION.
YOU'RE LOOKING FOR OTHER MAGICAL GIRLS, AREN'T YOU?
I HEARD EVERY-THING YOU WERE TALKING ABOUT...
WHAT IF WE ARE?
CAN I HELP YOU OUT?

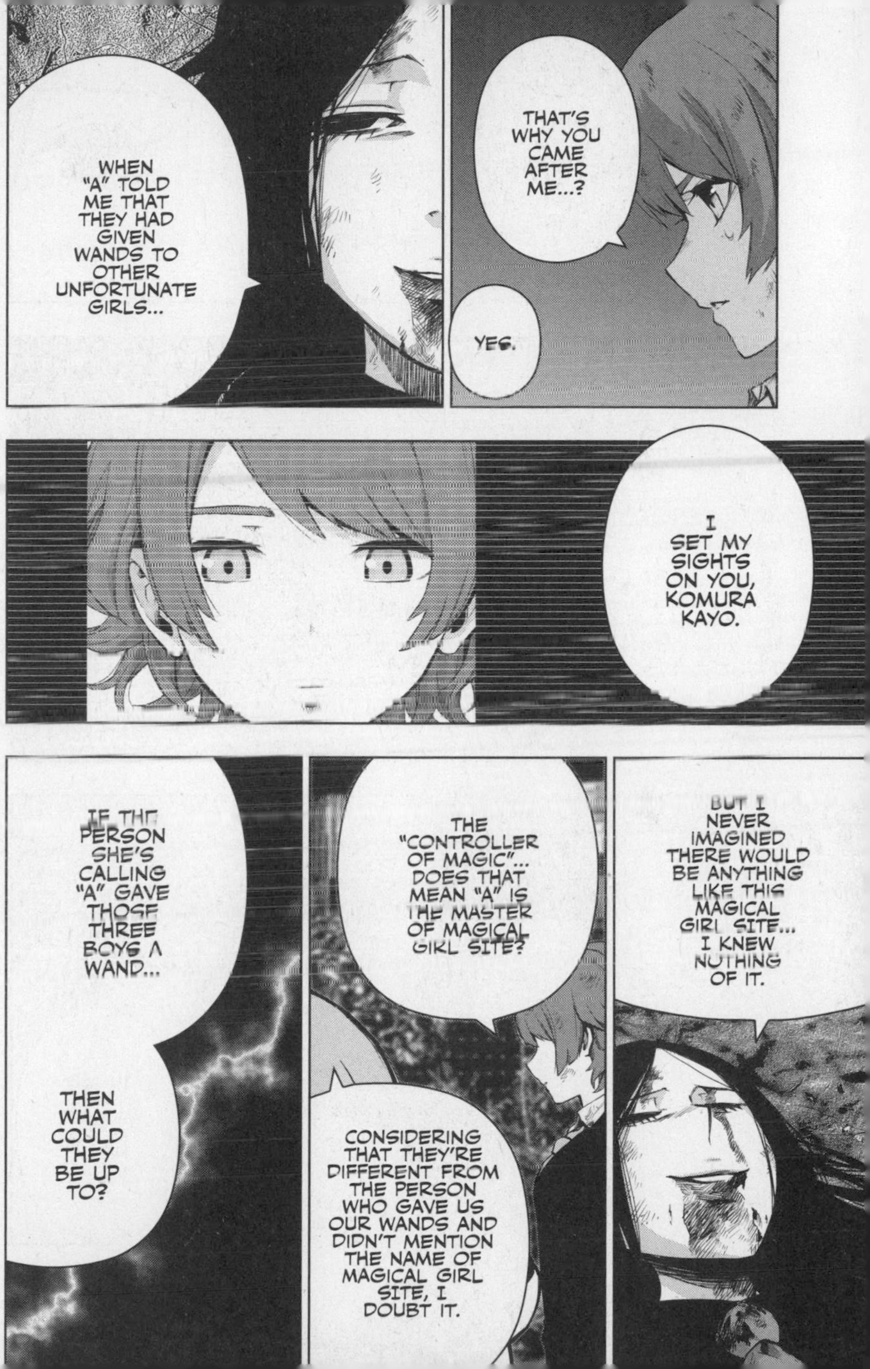
THAT'S WHY YOU CAME AFTER ME...?
YES.
WHEN "A" TOLD ME THAT THEY HAD GIVEN WANDS TO OTHER UNFORTUNATE GIRLS...
I SET MY SIGHTS ON YOU, KOMURA KAYO.
BUT I NEVER IMAGINED THERE WOULD BE ANYTHING LIKE THIS MAGICAL GIRL SITE... I KNEW NOTHING OF IT.
THE "CONTROLLER OF MAGIC"... DOES THAT MEAN "A" IS THE MASTER OF MAGICAL GIRL SITE?
CONSIDERING THAT THEY'RE DIFFERENT FROM THE PERSON WHO GAVE US OUR WANDS AND DIDN'T MENTION THE NAME OF MAGICAL GIRL SITE, I DOUBT IT.
IF THE PERSON SHE'S CALLING "A" GAVE THOSE THREE BOYS A WAND...
THEN WHAT COULD THEY BE UP TO?

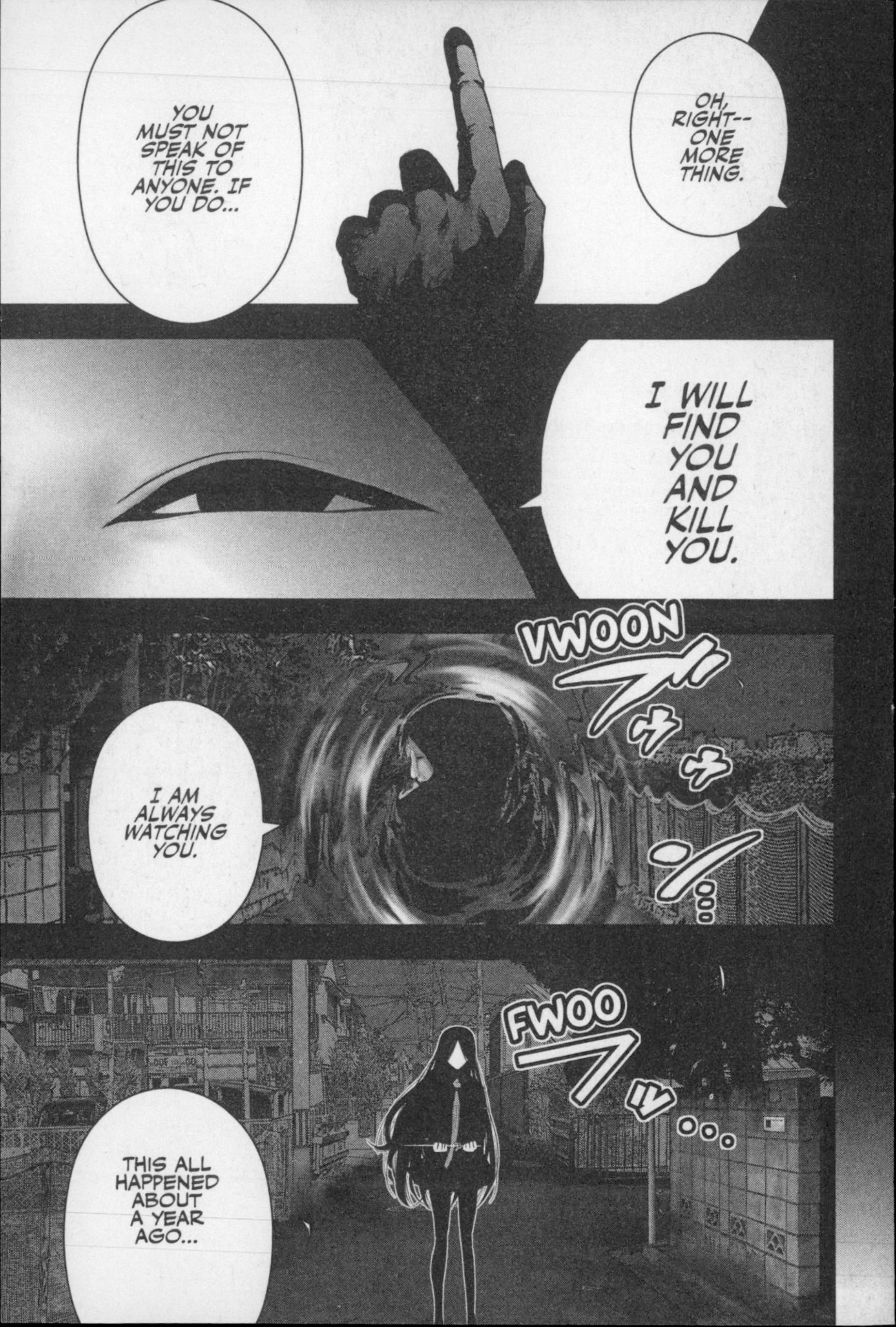
OH, RIGHT-- ONE MORE THING.
YOU MUST NOT SPEAK OF THIS TO ANYONE. IF YOU DO...
I WILL FIND YOU AND KILL YOU.
VWOON
I AM ALWAYS WATCHING YOU.
FWOO
THIS ALL HAPPENED ABOUT A YEAR AGO...

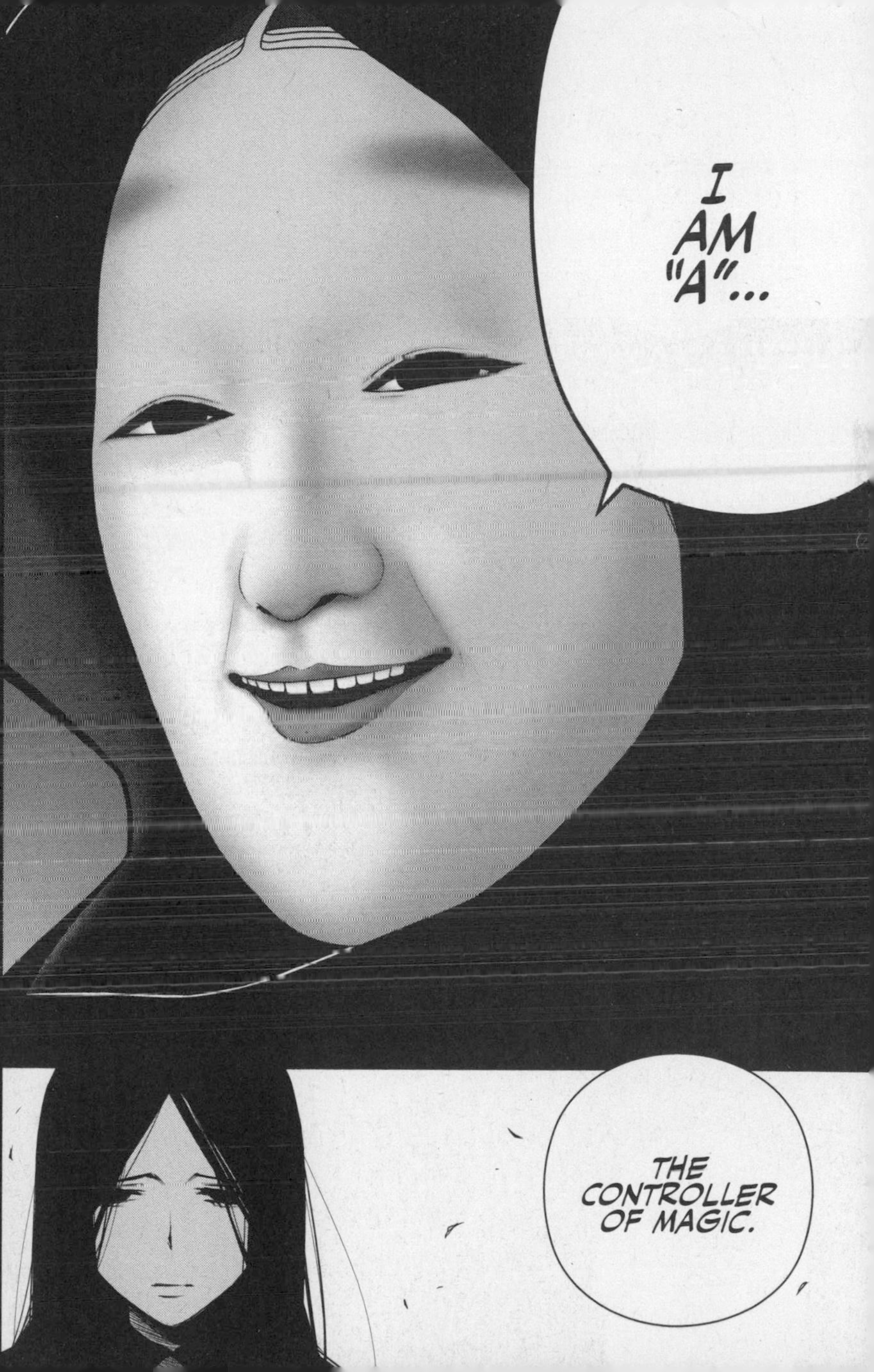
I AM "A"...
THE CONTROLLER OF MAGIC.

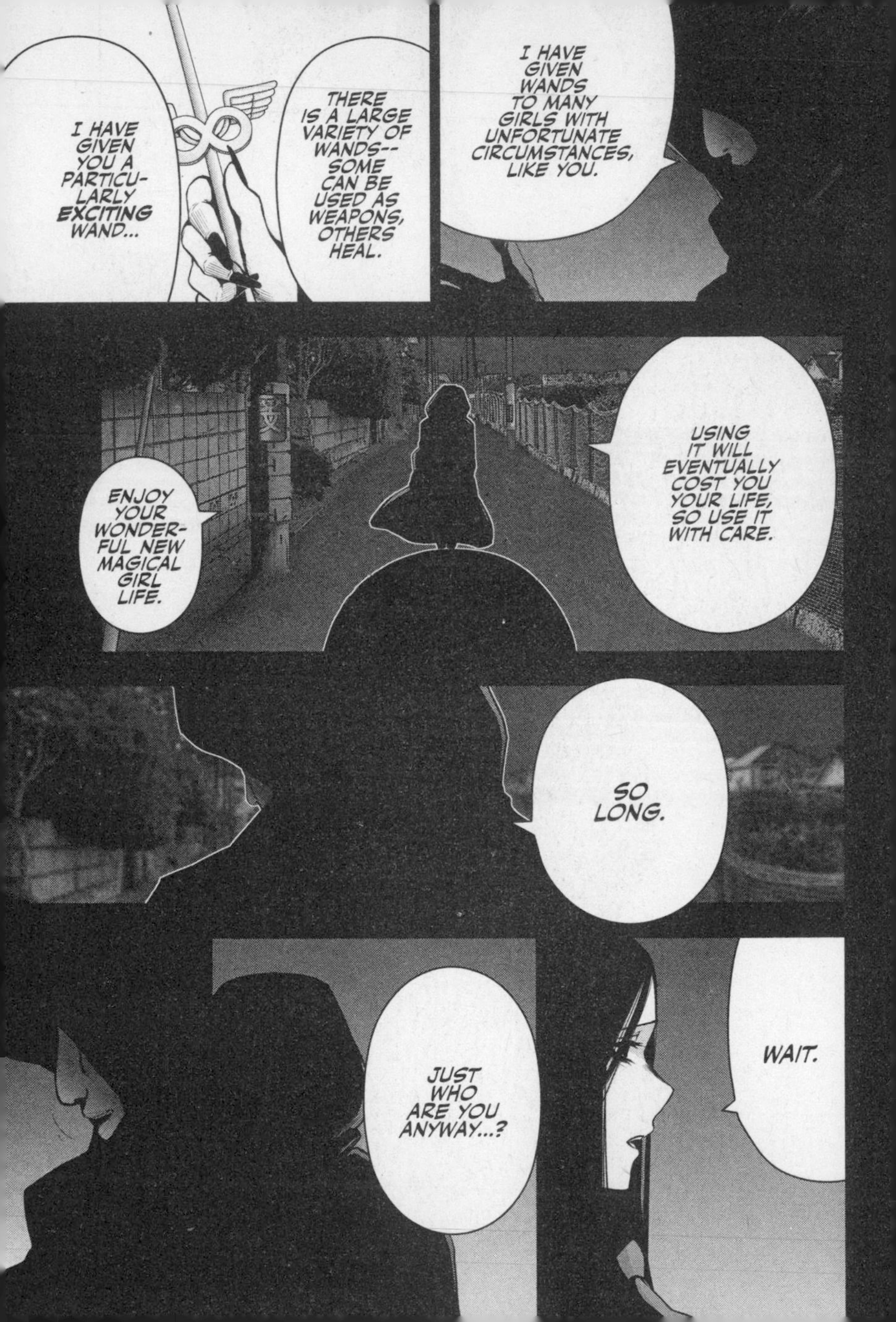
I HAVE GIVEN WANDS TO MANY GIRLS WITH UNFORTUNATE CIRCUMSTANCES, LIKE YOU.
THERE IS A LARGE VARIETY OF WANDS-- SOME CAN BE USED AS WEAPONS, OTHERS HEAL.
I HAVE GIVEN YOU A PARTICU-LARLY EXCITING WAND...
USING IT WILL EVENTUALLY COST YOU YOUR LIFE, SO USE IT WITH CARE.
ENJOY YOUR WONDER-FUL NEW MAGICAL GIRL LIFE.
SO LONG.
WAIT.
JUST WHO ARE YOU ANYWAY...?

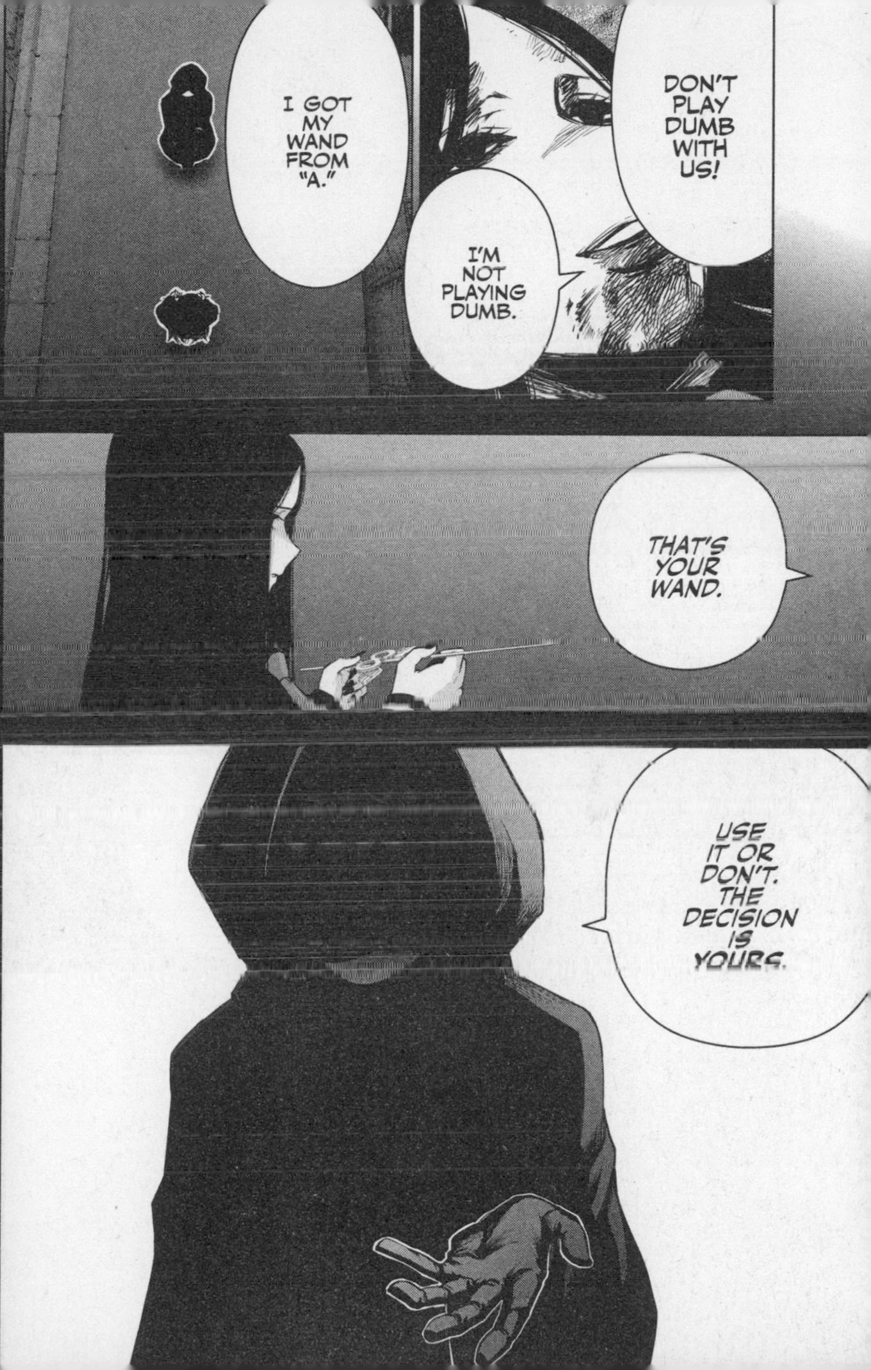
DON'T PLAY DUMB WITH US!
I'M NOT PLAYING DUMB.
I GOT MY WAND FROM "A."
THAT'S YOUR WAND.
USE IT OR DON'T. THE DECISION IS YOURS.

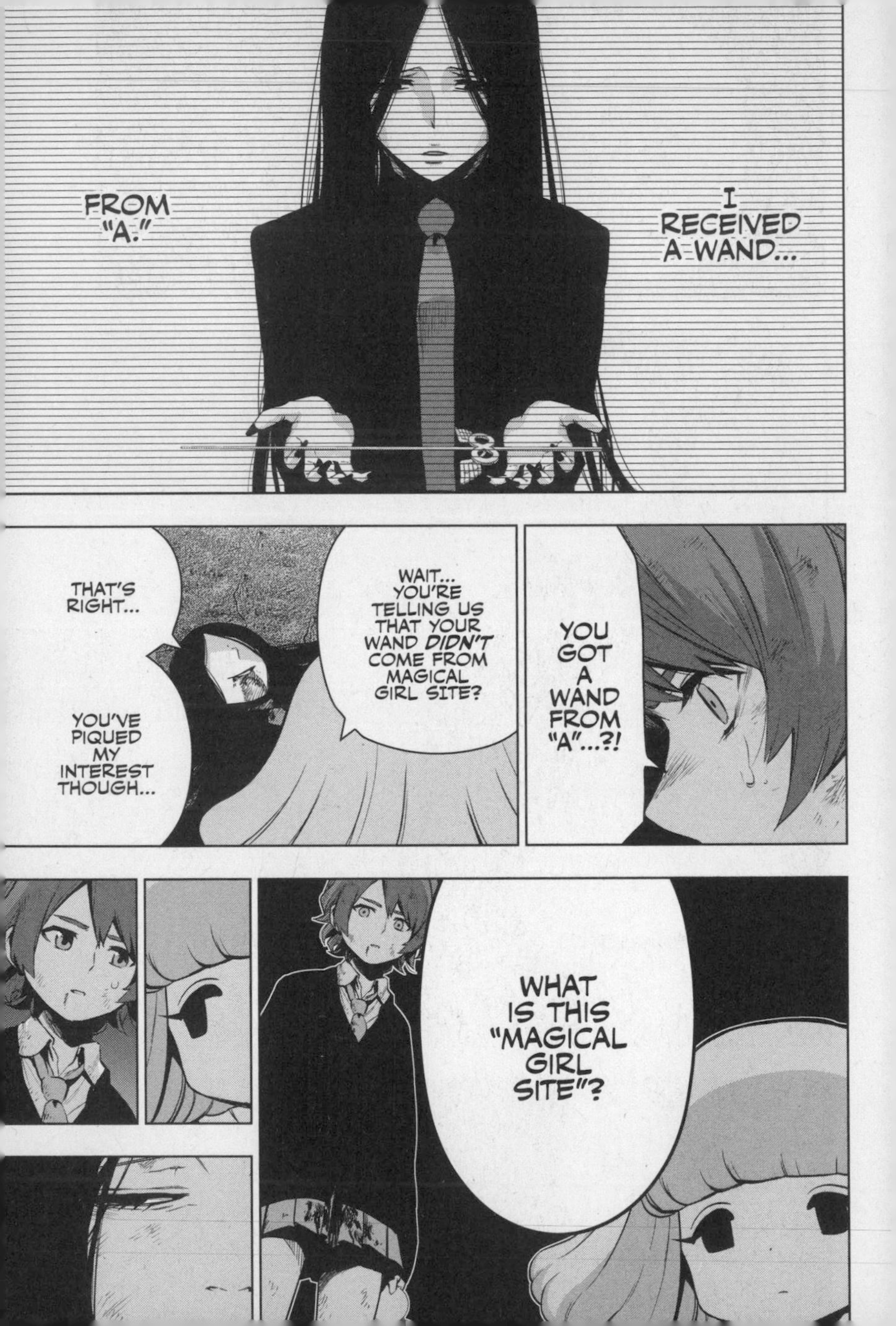
I RECEIVED A WAND...
FROM "A."
YOU GOT A WAND FROM "A"...?!
WAIT... YOU'RE TELLING US THAT YOUR WAND *DIDN'T* COME FROM MAGICAL GIRL SITE?
THAT'S RIGHT...
YOU'VE PIQUED MY INTEREST THOUGH...
WHAT IS THIS "MAGICAL GIRL SITE"?

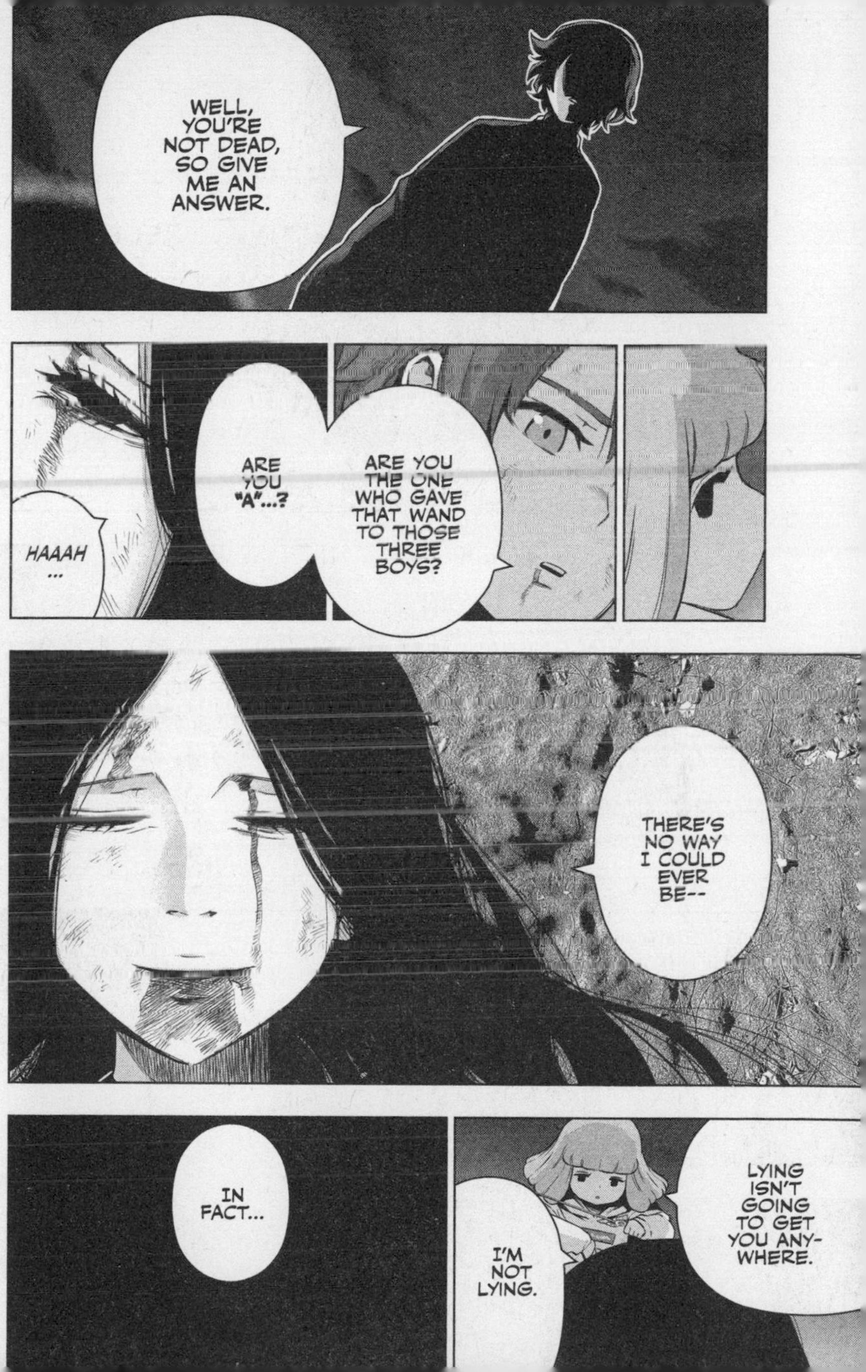
WELL, YOU'RE NOT DEAD, SO GIVE ME AN ANSWER.
ARE YOU THE ONE WHO GAVE THAT WAND TO THOSE THREE BOYS?
ARE YOU "A"...?
HAAAH...
THERE'S NO WAY I COULD EVER BE--
LYING ISN'T GOING TO GET YOU ANY-WHERE.
I'M NOT LYING.
IN FACT...

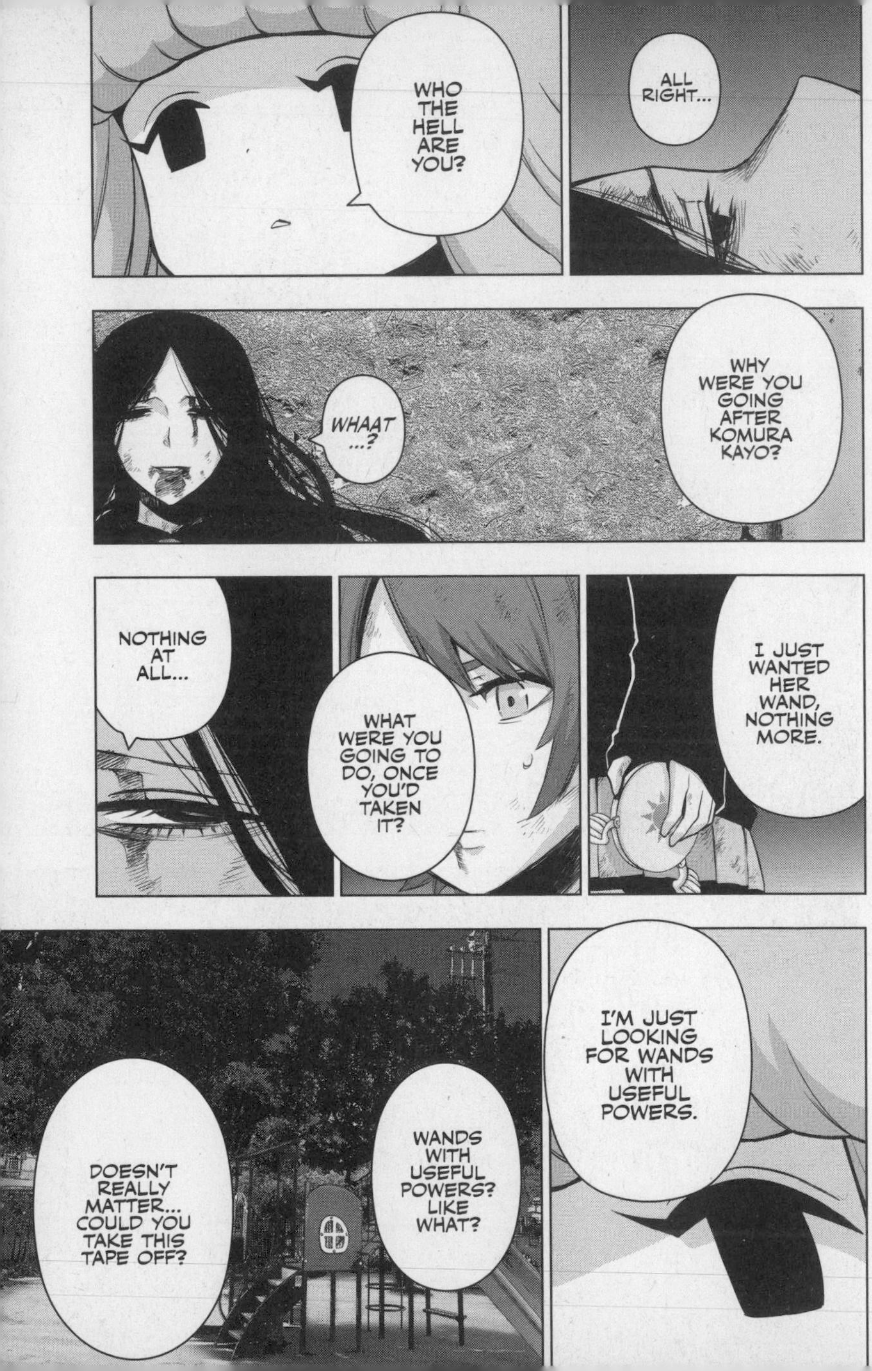
ALL RIGHT...
WHO THE HELL ARE YOU?
WHY WERE YOU GOING AFTER KOMURA KAYO?
WHAAT ...?
I JUST WANTED HER WAND, NOTHING MORE.
WHAT WERE YOU GOING TO DO, ONCE YOU'D TAKEN IT?
NOTHING AT ALL...
I'M JUST LOOKING FOR WANDS WITH USEFUL POWERS.
WANDS WITH USEFUL POWERS? LIKE WHAT?
DOESN'T REALLY MATTER... COULD YOU TAKE THIS TAPE OFF?

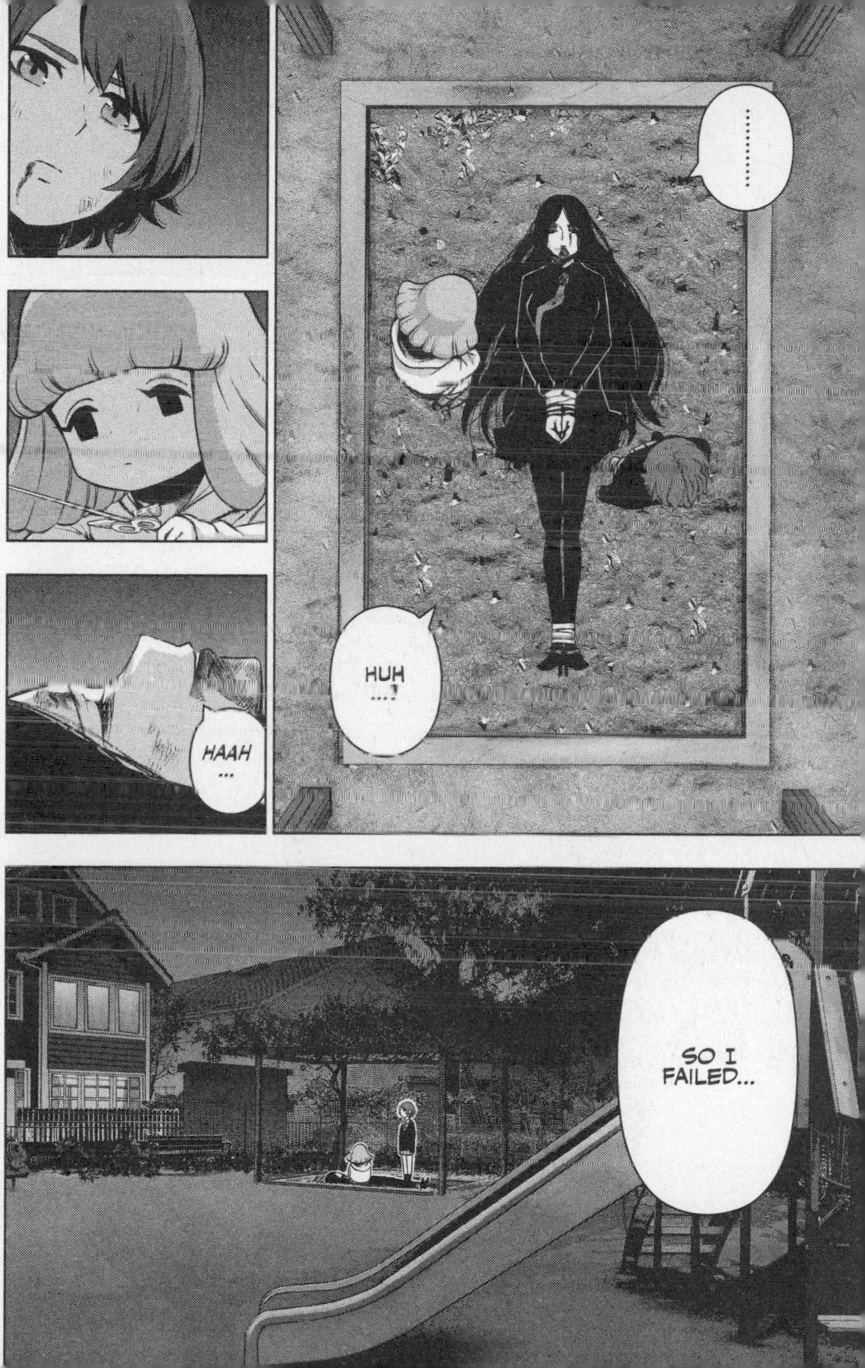
......
HUH...?
HAAH...
SO I FAILED...

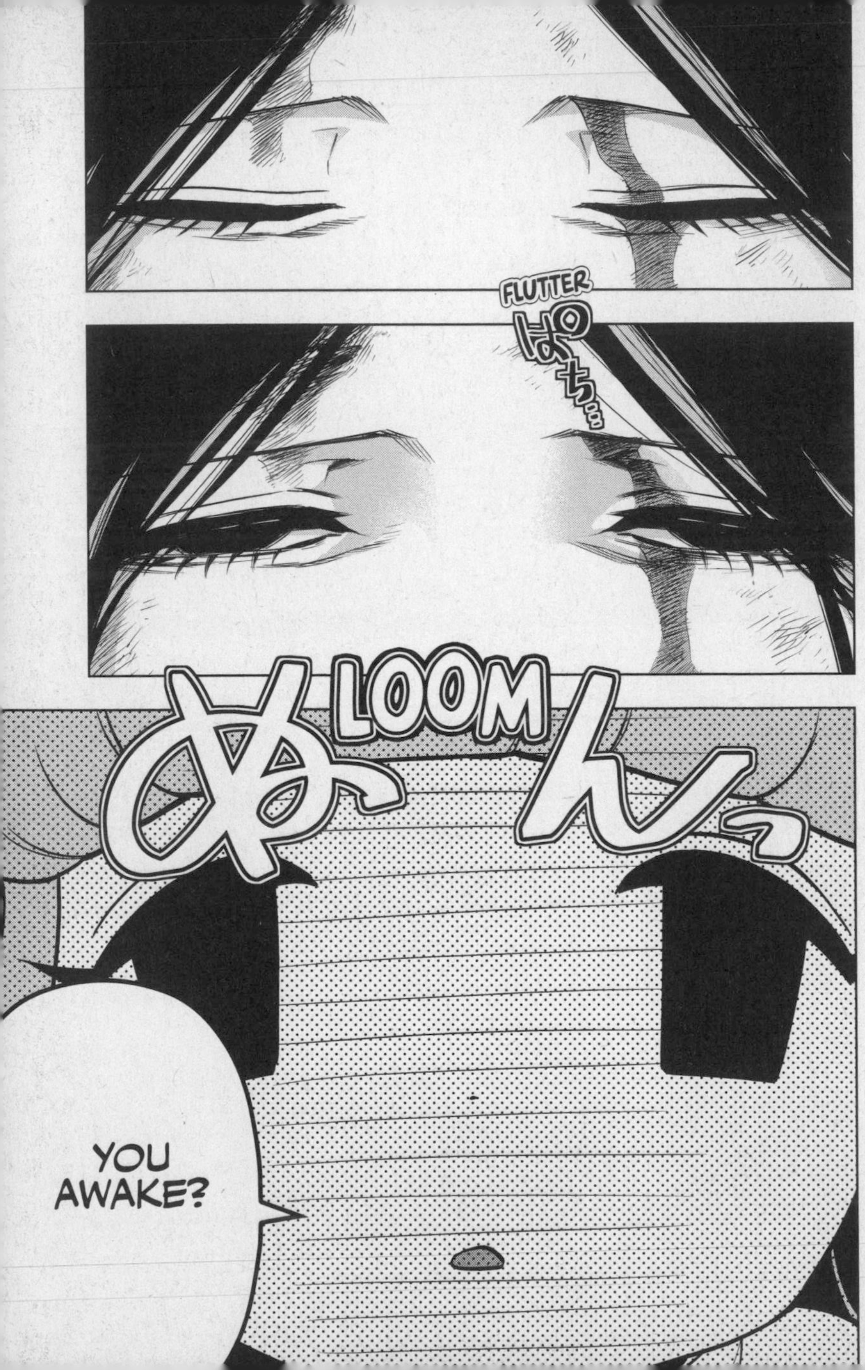
FLUTTER
ぱち…
LOOM
ぬんっ
YOU AWAKE?

ENTER.65
CONTROLLERS
OF MAGIC

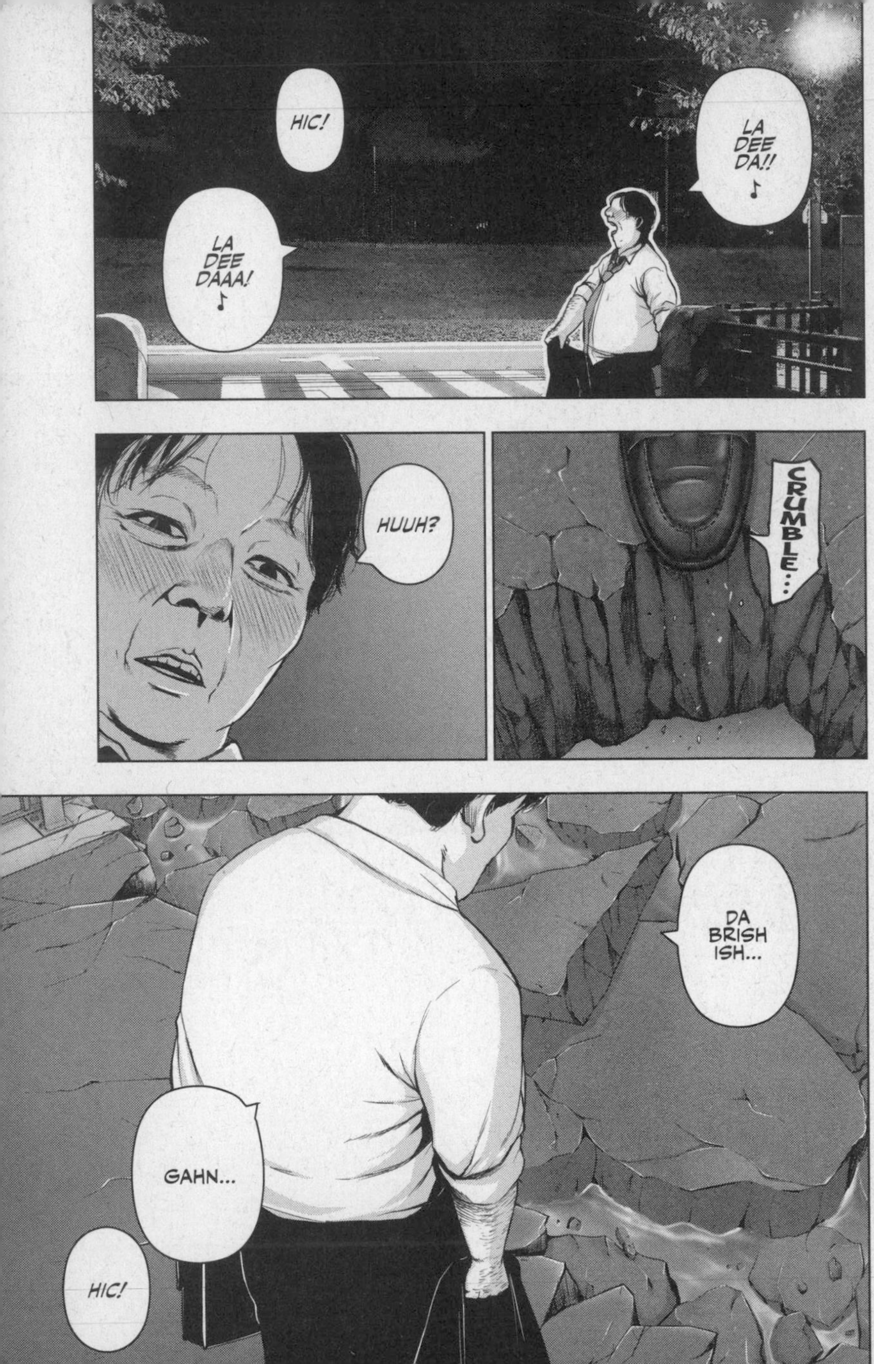
LA DEE DA!! ♪
HIC!
LA DEE DAAA! ♪
CRUMBLE...
HUUH?
DA BRISH ISH...
GAHN...
HIC!

●●●●● soltbank 4G 0:00

MEMO END

Kozumi Kayo's everyday life was turned upside-down when her father was arrested for the brutal murder of three boys, who were responsible for killing her little sister in a lynching incident some time ago. Called the "daughter of a murderer" at school, Kayo is constantly bullied and abused by her classmates, all while having to go home and take care of her bedridden mother. It is during this time that she is approached by Magical Girl SITE and given a wand and a "Kill List." Through this Kill List, she learns that another girl in her class, Sakaki Sakura, is also a Magical Girl. Having barely been acquaintances prior to this, the two of them form a relationship on the basis of gathering more information. It is then that Sakura tells Kayo about the theory that her sister was killed by a wand from Magical Girl SITE.

The case involving the death of her sister certainly had its holes and loose ends. There was no doubt that the three boys accused were at the murder scene. Furthermore, though her sister's body showed evidence of their brutality, the murder weapon was never found. Sakura proposed a theory that the boys had somehow obtained a wand from someone not affiliated with Magical Girl SITE. Following up on this theory, Kayo learned from her father that the boys had mentioned obtaining a wand from someone called "A." Soon afterwards, Kayo is attacked by a girl named Arareya Touko who actually knows "A," thus increasing the credibility of the boys' claims.

Who is this mysterious "A" figure? And what is the identity of the hooded figure that appeared (and then disappeared just as quickly) after the battle with Arareya Touko ended?!

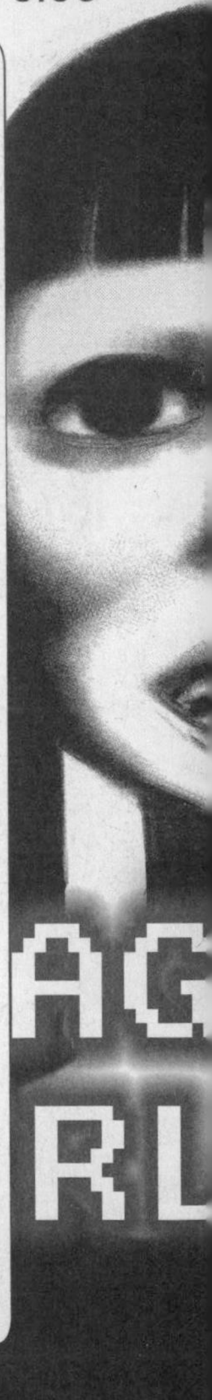

SUMMARY

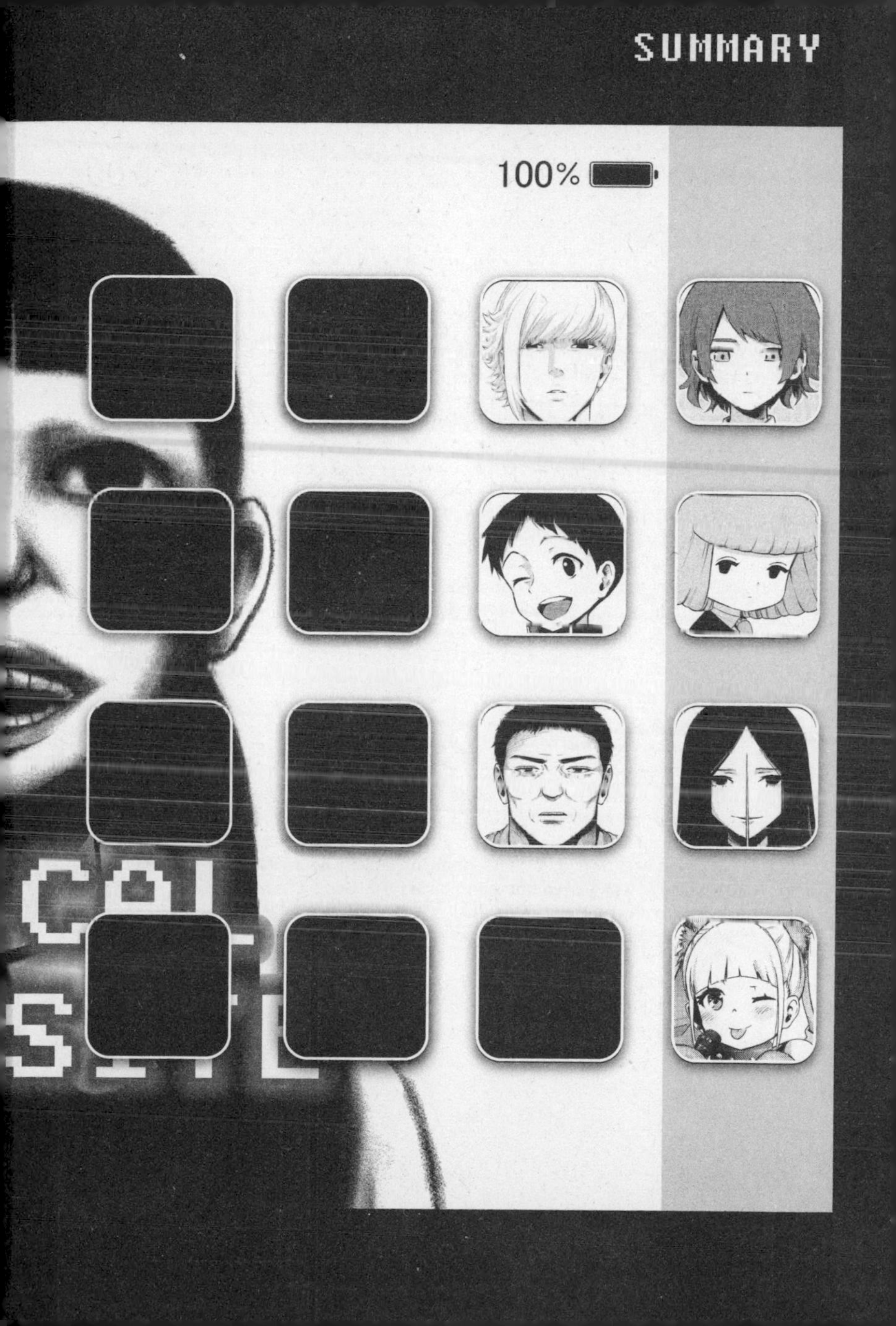
100%

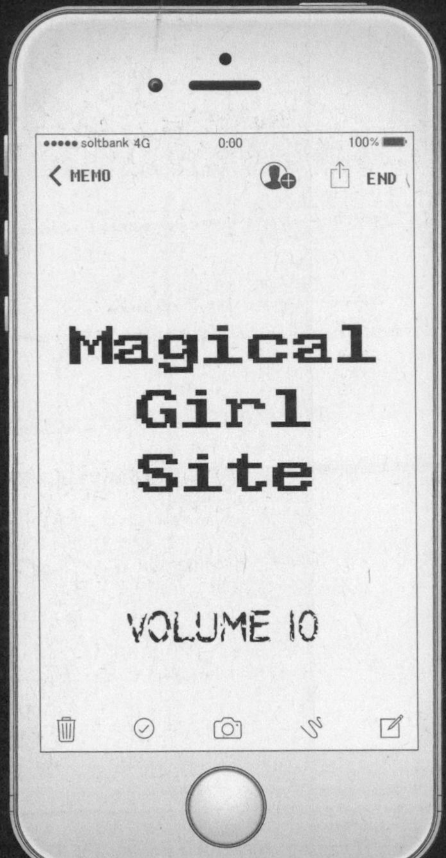

soltbank 4G
0:00
100%
MEMO
END
Magical
Girl
Site
VOLUME 10

AUTHOR
KENTARO SATO